13th International Joint Conference on Natural Language Processing and the 3rd Conference of the Asia-Pacific Chapter of the Association for Computational Linguistics (IJCNLP-AACL 2023)

Short Papers

Nusa Dua, Indonesia
1-4 November 2023

ISBN: 978-1-7138-8999-1

Printed from e-media with permission by:

Curran Associates, Inc.
57 Morehouse Lane
Red Hook, NY 12571

Some format issues inherent in the e-media version may also appear in this print version.

Printed with permission by Curran Associates, Inc. (2024)

Association for Computational Linguistics
209 N. Eighth Street
Stroudsburg, Pennsylvania 18360

Phone: 1-570-476-8006
Fax: 1-570-476-0860

acl@aclweb.org

Additional copies of this publication are available from:

Curran Associates, Inc.
57 Morehouse Lane
Red Hook, NY 12571 USA
Phone: 845-758-0400
Fax: 845-758-2633
Email: curran@proceedings.com
Web: www.proceedings.com

IJCNLP-AACL 2023

The 13th International Joint Conference on Natural Language Processing and the 3rd Conference of the Asia-Pacific Chapter of the Association for Computational Linguistics

Proceedings of the Conference (Volume 2: Short Papers)

November 1 – 4, 2023

The IJCNLP-AACL organizers gratefully acknowledge the support from the following sponsors.

Platinum

vivo

Gold

面壁智能 ModelBest

Silver

translated.

ZHIPU·AI

小牛翻译 NiuTrans.com

Message from the General Chair

Welcome to IJCNLP-AACL 2023, the 17th International Joint Conference on Natural Language Processsing (IJCNLP) and the 3rd Conference of the Asia-Pacific Chapter of the Association for Computational Linguistics (AACL). The conference will be held in Nusa Dua, Bali, Indonesia, during November 1-4, 2023.

The joint conferences of IJCNLP and AACL are organized by alternating leadership in the Asia-Pacific region, in odd years by Asian Federation of Natural Language Processing (AFNLP) and in even years by AACL, except when the annual meetings of ACL are offered in the region every three years, in which case the conferences will be offered and organized solely by ACL. This year, the conference is organized by AFNLP.

As President of AFNLP, I have formed the Conference Coordination Committee (CCC) last year with executive members of AFNLP: Sadao Kurohashi (Vice President), Min Zhang (Secretary), Liang-Chih Yu (Honorary Treasurer), and Minghui Dong (Web Master). Xuanjing Huang has participated in the meetings of the committee as AACL Representative. I am truly thankful for their dedication in the initial stages as CCC members, in particular during the selection of the Local Chairs together with the conference venue and the nomination and appointment of General Chair and Program Committee Chairs, and, after it is decided that I also serve as General Chair of the conference, for their service as respective chairs throughout the conference preparation stages. Their continued support has been of tremendous help and is much appreciated.

I would also like to thank deeply the entire organizing committee of the conference for their hardwork and superb handling of difficult situations, most of all due to the much limited time to address their respective tasks.

- Program Committe Chairs: Yuki Arase, Baotian Hu and Wei Lu have managed the most critical task of establishing the main program of the conference, which includes, among many others, forming and coordinating the Program Committee, constructing the call for papers with a timely theme track, overseeing the review process on both Softconf and ARR, making decisions on paper acceptance, selecting keynote speakers and putting together the program schedule, and most of all communicating with the reviewers, authors, and other committee members over numerous times during the entire process. This is a formidable task, and their efforts for leading to its successful completion are so much appreciated.

- Tutorial Chairs: Yun-Nung (Vivian) Chen and Sadao Kurohashi have gone through the tutorial proposals to select six tutorials that are well balanced both topically and geographically, actively fostering diversity and inclusion.

- Workshop Chairs: Kehai Chen and Lun-Wei Ku have gone over the workshop proposals to select eight strong workshops, NLPMC, WIESP, Eval4NLP, SocialNLP, SEA, FinNLP, NLInt, and ArtOfSafety.

- Demo Chairs: Sriparna Saha and Herry Sujaini have overseen the process of selecting papers among those submitted to the system demonstration session independently of the main program.

- Publication Chairs: Minghui Dong and Kotaro Funakoshi have put together all the documents and articles to construct the conference proceedings expertly, cordially and in a timely manner.

- Sponsorship Chairs: Min Zhang, Satoshi Sekine, Haofeng Wang, and Zhongqing Wang have worked hard to solicit funding to support the conference, and successfully, despite the short time to operate. We are all much grateful to the funding organizations for their generous help.

- Finance Chair: Liang-Chih Yu has always been the person to consult whenever any financial issues arise. Things are not yet fully over at the time of preparing for this message, but are believed to come to self-sustainment, with some room for financial aid as well, thanks to the valiant efforts of all the people involved.
- Website & App Chair: Juntao Li has worked single-handedly and dependably to reflect all the requests to post important news at our conference homepage.
- Publicity & Social Media Chairs: Koustava Goswami and JinYeong Bak have worked to disseminate information over social media as widely as possible whenever there are notable events for the conference.
- Handbook Chairs: Yasuhide Miura and Yunita Sari have worked very hard to meet the deadline for the conference handbook when there is really not much time left. The help of Sonoko Miura as Conference Handbook Designer is also gratefully acknowledged.
- Faculty Advisors to Student Research Workshop (SRW): Hyeju Jang, Yugo Murawaki, and Derek Fai Wong have worked to oversee the SRW, in particular communicating with its chairs, Dongfang Li, Rahmad Mahendra and Zilu Peter Tang. The efforts of the faculty advisors and SRW chairs are much appreciated.
- Diversity & Inclusion Chair: Hwanhee Lee has worked to resolve requests for financial aid, mostly in the form of registration waiver, and as amicably as possible, under a strict limit on granting such requests.
- Registration Chair: Dessi Puji Lestari has worked to oversee the process of registration, together with the kind help of Minghui Dong as the manager of the registration site.
- Local Chairs: Derry Wijaya, Ayu Purwarianti and Adila Alfa Krisnadhi have worked to resolve practically numerous issues, many times beyond the duties of local chairs, after successfully bidding to host the conference in Nusa Dua, Bali, Indonesia. It is with much gratitude and respect that I commend their efforts to the fullest.

In summary, I can only say that their sense of duty and responsibility has been critical to meeting and resolving so many difficulties that we faced along the way. Many, many thanks to all of them.

The mode of the conference has been determined early on to be hybrid, considering the fact that we are not fully over the coronavirus pandemic. However, it has not been quite clear until very recently whether we would need, and can afford, the top-notch professional service of an on-demand video platform such as Underline for a hybrid conference. I am very grateful to all the chairs for the remarkable patience and very happy with the concerted decision to go for the service of Underline, albeit in a limited scope. I wish to thank kindly Damira Mrsic and Sol Rosenberg, representatives of Underline, for the patience and expert help. I also thank Richard Gerber for the help with our use of Softconf.

The Local Chairs made a proposal to host the conference in Nusa Dua early on, but it took all of us a long time to finally come to a decision to choose Grand Hyatt Bali, Nusa Dua, Bali, Indonesia for its exceptional location in the region as the conference venue. Its daytime temperatures are expected to reach 31°C, with the nighttime temperatures of around 24°C. I wish a very pleasant time for all the off-line participants of the conference and an equally memorable time for all the on-line participants.

Welcome to the conference and Nusa Dua!

IJCNLP-AACL 2023 General Chair
Jong C. Park
Korea Advanced Institute of Science and Technology (KAIST)

Message from the Program Committee Co-Chairs

Welcome to IJCNLP-AACL 2023, the 13th International Joint Conference on Natural Language Processing and the 3rd Conference of the Asia-Pacific Chapter of the Association for Computational Linguistics. This year, we have organized the conference in a hybrid format to accommodate both in-person and virtual participation, making it accessible to everyone regardless of travel constraints. The physical conference takes place in Bali; we are looking forward to discussions on present and future research in NLP with all of you.

This conference has been made possible through the dedicated voluntary efforts of hundreds of individuals. We sincerely thank everyone involved, in particular:

- The incredible team of 30 SACs, 72 ACs, and 427 reviewers who carefully handled submissions.
- Our Best Paper Award Committee, Danushka Bollegala, Jing Jiang, Yang Liu (Tsinghua University), Nanyun (Violet) Peng, Xiaojun Wan, Taro Watanabe, and Koichiro Yoshino, who assessed the candidate papers under the tight schedule.
- Computational Linguistics Editor-in-Chief, Hwee Tou Ng, for exploring the presentation possibility of CL papers with us.
- The ARR technical team, Jonathan Kummerfeld, Nils Dycke, Yoshitomo Matsubara, Dhruv Naik, and Amanda Stent, for supporting IJCNLP-AACL 2023 to have submissions through ARR.
- Rich Gerber at Softconf, who always addressed our inquiries and issues quickly.
- The Program Chairs of conferences going on the same period of time, including Houda Bouamor, Juan Pino, Kalika Bali (EMNLP 2023), Maria Keet, Hung-Yi Lee, Sina Zarrieß (INLG 2023), Svetlana Stoyanchev, Shafiq Joty (SIGDIAL 2023), and Jennifer Dy, Sriraam Natarajan, Kristian Kersting, Sameer Singh, Prasad Tadepalli, Angela Yao (AAAI 2024), whom we cooperated with to preclude multiple submissions.
- The ACL Executive Committee, especially Yusuke Miyao (Conference Officer), for supporting IJCNLP-AACL 2023 with various advice on conference organization.
- The ACL Ethics Committee, Min-Yen Kan, for advising us to conduct ethics reviews.
- The past $*$ACL conference program chairs, in particular Jordan Boyd-Graber, Naoaki Okazaki, Anna Rogers (ACL 2023) for sharing their experiences that were crucial to avoid pitfalls and practically sharing tools to handle a large volume of submissions.
- ACL Anthology director, Matt Post, for supporting us to publish the proceedings.
- Underline team, Jernej Masnec, Luka Simic, Sol Rosenberg, Borna Bevanda, and Damira Mrsic (Underline Science, Inc.), for their professional services and supports to realize the online part of the conference.

The conference owes its existence to the collaborative efforts of multiple chairs of IJCNLP-AACL 2023. We are deeply grateful to:

- General Chair, Jong C. Park, who was responsible for and led the whole process.
- Publication Chairs, Minghui Dong and Kotaro Funakoshi, for compiling the proceedings and ensuring the correct formatting.

- Handbook Chairs, Yunita Sari and Yasuhide Miura, for creating the conference handbooks.
- Web Chair, Juntao Li, and Publicity & Social Media chairs, JinYeong Bak and Koustava Goswami, for distributing the important information on the web, which allowed efficient and timely communication.
- Local Chairs, Derry Wijaya, Ayu Purwarianti, and Adila Alfa Krisnadhi, who did everything for realizing the physical part of the conference.
- Our assistants, Jindi Yu, Senbao Shi, and Jiaxi Li for their help and support throughout the conference preparation period.

Last but not least, we extend our heartfelt gratitude to all the authors for their invaluable scientific contributions, which are at the very heart of IJCNLP-AACL 2023. We hope everyone will enjoy IJCNLP-AACL 2023 either on-site or online.

Submission and Acceptance

IJCNLP-AACL 2023 used two submission platforms: direct submission through SoftConf and submissions through ACL Rolling Review (ARR). We received 338 direct submissions (229 long and 109 short) and 25 commitments from ARR (19 long and 6 short), in total 363 valid papers went through the review process. The submissions came from 33 countries and regions of all over the world: 49.2% from Asia-Pacific, 26.7% from North America, 18.7% from Europe, 4.1% from Middle East, and 1.3% from Africa.

The direct submissions were thoroughly reviewed by 427 reviewers under 72 ACs and 30 SACs in 19 tracks. The ARR committed papers were handled by the SACs based on review and meta-review comments gained through ARR. Finally, we have accepted 94 submissions (72 long and 22 short) as the main conference papers accompanied by 37 Findings papers (23 long and 14 short), which results in the acceptance rates of 25.9% for the main conference (29.0% long and 19.1% short) and 36.1% when including the Findings papers (38.3% long and 31.3% short).

In adherence to the ACL code of ethics, we have conducted ethics reviews. Given the limited number of papers that raised ethical concerns, the program chairs assumed the responsibilities of ethics reviewers. Authors of papers that received ethics review comments were requested to address these concerns in their final versions.

The papers accepted to the main conference will be presented in the form of either oral and poster presentations. The presentation modes were determined solely based on the nature of the work, irrespective of review scores. There is no distinction in the proceedings regarding the presentation modes. The Findings papers will have optional lightning talks to introduce highlights of their work.

Design of Tracks

IJCNLP-AACL 2023 has incorporated 18 general areas reflecting the trends of the field. Most of these areas are consistent with the recent *ACL conferences. In addition, recognizing the conference centers on Asia-Pacific regions, which boast a variety of regional languages with limited language resources, we have introduced a special theme track this year: Large Language Models and Regional/Low-Resource Languages. The most popular areas were "NLP Applications," "Resources and Evaluation," and "Large Language Models and Regional/Low-Resource Languages."

- Dialogue and Interactive Systems
- Discourse and Pragmatics

- Generation and Summarization
- Information Extraction
- Information Retrieval and Text Mining
- Interpretability and Analysis of Models for NLP
- Language Modeling and Analysis
- Linguistic Theories, Cognitive Modeling, and Psycholinguistics
- Machine Learning for NLP
- Machine Translation and Multilingualism
- Multimodality: Speech, Vision, Robotics, and Beyond
- NLP Applications
- Question Answering
- Resources and Evaluation
- Semantics: Lexical, Sentence-level Semantics, Textual Inference, etc.
- Sentiment Analysis, Stylistic Analysis, and Argument Mining
- Society and NLP
- Syntax: Tagging, Chunking, Parsing, etc.
- Theme Track: Large Language Models and Regional/Low-Resource Languages

Limitations Section and Responsible NLP Checklist

Following ACL 2023, EMNLP 2022, and ARR, we made it mandatory to discuss limitations of a study and submit the responsible NLP checklist to foster the open and honest scientific discussions and promote consideration of responsibility in NLP research. We also encouraged authors to include Ethics Statements whenever there might be potential concerns. The Limitations Section and Ethics Statements did not count towards the page limit.

Best Paper Awards

Following the new ACL conference awards policy, we organized the Best Paper Award Committee to select the Best Paper Awards followed by Outstanding Paper Awards, together with two special awards, namely Social Impact Award and Resource Award. The committee assessed 15 papers nominated by reviewers. In addition, SACs of each track selected at most a paper for Area Chair's Awards. The award winners will be announced in a dedicated plenary session on November 4, 2023.

IJCNLP-AACL 2023 Program Comittee Co-Chairs
Yuki Arase (Osaka University)
Baotian Hu (Harbin Institute of Technology (Shenzhen))
Wei Lu (Singapore University of Technology and Design)

Message from the Local Co-Chairs

It is with immense excitement and a profound sense of achievement that we, the local co-chairs of IJCNLP-AACL 2023 - Ayu Purwarianti, Adila Krisnadhi, and myself - welcome you to the breathtaking island of Bali, Indonesia. The significance of this moment cannot be understated, as it marks the very first time that the IJCNLP or ACL conference has found its home in the enchanting Indonesian archipelago. This landmark occasion has doubled our excitement as local chairs, and we are thrilled to share this unique experience with all of you.

Since the moment when we were awarded the privilege of organizing IJCNLP-AACL 2023, we have been tirelessly working to ensure this conference exceeds all expectations. We embarked on an extensive quest to discover the perfect venue and event organizer, negotiated hybrid support, searched for sponsorships, all while meticulously managing the budget, and addressing an array of logistical details, all with the goal of enhancing your experience at the conference. While our commitment to delivering an exceptional event has remained steadfast, we did encounter some noteworthy challenges. The close proximity of EMNLP 2023, scheduled in nearby Singapore just one month after IJCNLP-AACL 2023 and whose submission deadline is also just a month after IJCNLP-AACL 2023's, might have created scheduling dilemmas for prospective authors and participants. We sincerely hope that, despite these challenges, our captivating Bali location will draw participants from around the globe, ensuring IJCNLP-AACL 2023 remains a highlight in the NLP conference calendar.

Another notable challenge has been attracting local participants to the conference. The absence of Scopus indexing for IJCNLP or AACL proceedings, a critical factor for researchers in Indonesia, has presented hurdles. We hope that in the future, as more NLP proceedings are indexed by Scopus, we can generate greater local interest and participation in the region.

On behalf of the local organizing team, I extend my heartfelt gratitude and appreciation to our General Chair, Jong Park; Publication Co-Chair, Minghui Dong; Finance Chair, Liang-Chih Yu; Tutorial Co-Chair, Sadao Kurohashi; Sponsorship Chair, Min Zhang; Registration Chair, Dessi Puji Lestari; and the PC co-chairs who have given so much help and support to the local co-chairs. I have learned a lot from you. Hosting the AACL-IJCNLP 2023 has been an invaluable learning experience for me, and it is an experience I will carry with me. I am also grateful for the contributions and hard work of the entire organizing committee and our kind sponsors, without whom none of this would have been possible.

We look forward to the exciting discussions, sharing of knowledge, and camaraderie that will define IJCNLP-AACL 2023. Welcome to Bali, and we sincerely hope you have one of the most wonderful conference experiences.

Warm regards,

IJCNLP-AACL 2023 Local Co-Chairs
Derry Tanti Wijaya (Monash University Indonesia)
Ayu Purwarianti (Institut Teknologi Bandung)
Adila Krisnadhi (Universitas Indonesia)

Organizing Committee

General Chair

Jong C. Park, Korea Advanced Institute of Science and Technology (KAIST)

Program Committee Chairs

Yuki Arase, Osaka University
Baotian Hu, Harbin Insitute of Technology (Shenzhen)
Wei Lu, Singapore University of Technology and Design

Tutorial Chairs

Yun-Nung (Vivian) Chen, National Taiwan University
Sadao Kurohashi, Kyoto University

Workshop Chairs

Kehai Chen, Harbin Institute of Technology (Shenzhen)
Lun-Wei Ku, Academia Sinica

Demo Chairs

Sriparna Saha, Indian Institute of Technology (Patna)
Herry Sujaini, University of Tanjunpura

Publication Chairs

Minghui Dong, Institute for Infocomm Research, A*Star
Kotaro Funakoshi, Tokyo Institute of Technology

Sponsorship Chairs

Min Zhang, Harbin Institute of Technology (Shenzhen)
Satoshi Sekine, RIKEN, AIP
Haofeng Wang, Tongji University (Shanghai)
Zhongqing Wang, Soochow University

Finance Chair

Liang-Chih Yu, Yuan Ze University

Website & App Chair

Juntao Li, Soochow University

Publicity & Social Media Chairs

Koustava Goswami, Adobe Research India
JinYeong Bak, SungKyunKwan University

Handbook Chairs

Yasuhide Miura, Fujifilm Corporation
Yunita Sari, Universitas Gadjah Mada
(Conference Handbook Designer: Sonoko Miura)

Faculty Advisors to Student Research Workshop

Hyeju Jang, Indiana University-Purdue University Indianapolis
Yugo Murawaki, Kyoto University
Derek Fai Wong, University of Macau

Diversity & Inclusion Chair

Hwanhee Lee, Chung Ang University

Registration Chair

Dessi Puji Lestari, Bandung Institute of Technology

Local Chairs

Derry Wijaya, Monash University Indonesia
Ayu Purwarianti, Bandung Institute of Technology
Adila Alfa Krisnadhi, University of Indonesia

AACL Representative

Xuanjing Huang, Fudan University

Program Comittee

Dialogue and Interactive Systems

Senior area chair: Michel Galley
Area chairs: Song Feng, Alexandros Papangelis, Lei Sha, Wei-Nan Zhang

Discourse and Pragmatics

Senior area chair: Bonnie Webber
Area chair: Yufang Hou

Generation and Summarization

Senior area chairs: Yue Dong, Dimitra Gkatzia
Area chairs: Meng Cao, Khyathi Raghavi Chandu, Bang Liu, Saad Mahamood, Lili Mou, Arabella Sinclair, Wen Xiao, Jiacheng Xu

Information Extraction

Senior area chairs: Ruihong Huang, Makoto Miwa
Area chairs: Jun Araki, Prafulla Kumar Choubey, Fenia Christopoulou, Wenlin Yao

Information Retrieval and Text Mining

Senior area chairs: Sophia Ananiadou, Muhao Chen
Area chairs: Yixin Cao, Fangyu Liu, Tulika Saha, Sheng Zhang, Hongming Zhang

Interpretability and Analysis of Models for NLP

Senior area chair: Kai-Wei Chang
Area chairs: Sunipa Dev, Yangfeng Ji, Xiaoqing Zheng

Language Modeling and Analysis

Senior area chairs: Naoya Inoue, Yang Liu (Microsoft)
Area chairs: Benjamin Heinzerling, Reid Pryzant, Keisuke Sakaguchi, Rui Zhang

Linguistic Theories, Cognitive Modeling, and Psycholinguistics

Senior area chairs: Ashutosh Modi, Yohei Oseki
Area chair: Pranava Madhyastha

Machine Learning for NLP

Senior area chairs: Lingpeng Kong, Sinno Jialin Pan
Area chairs: Jing Ma, Zhiyong Wu, Jingjing Xu, Shi Zong

Machine Translation and Multilingualism

Senior area chairs: Longyue Wang, Deyi Xiong
Area chairs: Liangyou Li, Xing Niu, Elena Voita, Baosong Yang, Biao Zhang

Multimodality: Speech, Vision, Robotics, and Beyond

Senior area chairs: Li Dong, Sakriani Sakti
Area chairs: Armen Aghajanyan, Zhe Gan, Florian Metze

NLP Applications

Senior area chairs: Jey Han Lau, Mingxuan Wang
Area chairs: Shanbo Cheng, Massimo Piccardi, Ehsan Shareghi, Yangqiu Song, Ekaterina Vylomova, Rong Ye, Zhirui Zhang

Question Answering

Senior area chair: Wenpeng Yin
Area chairs: Nitish Gupta, Hangfeng He, Zhiguo Wang

Resources and Evaluation

Senior area chairs: Eduardo Blanco, Joel Tetreault
Area chairs: Yvette Graham, Anne Lauscher, Junyi Jessy Li, Liling Tan, Alakananda Vempala

Semantics: Lexical, Sentence-level Semantics, Textual Inference, etc.

Senior area chair: Preslav Nakov
Area chairs: Atsushi Fujita, James Thorne, Marcos Zampieri

Sentiment Analysis, Stylistic Analysis, and Argument Mining

Senior area chair: Vincent Ng
Area chairs: Henning Wachsmuth, Jianfei Yu

Socicty and NLP

Senior area chair: Wei Gao
Area chairs: Firoj Alam, Shi Feng, Kokil Jaidka, Liang-Chih Yu

Syntax: Tagging, Chunking, Parsing etc.

Senior area chair: Kewei Tu
Area chair: Zhenghua Li

Theme Track: Large Language Models and Regional/Low-Resource Languages

Senior area chairs: Lei Li, Imed Zitouni
Area chairs: Boxing Chen, Zhiyu Chen, Stephan Peitz, Zhaopeng Tu, Lina Yao

Reviewers

Asad Abdi, Haithem Afli, Piush Aggarwal, Akiko Aizawa, Md. Shad Akhtar, Hend Al-Khalifa, Bharat Ram Ambati, Jie An, Anietie Andy, Eiji ARAMAKI, Arturo Argueta, Piyush Arora, Lukasz Augustyniak

Xuefeng Bai, Amir Bakarov, Mithun Balakrishna, Timothy Baldwin, Hritik Bansal, Christine Basta, Gábor Berend, Sabine Bergler, Dario Bertero, Arnab Bhattacharya, Pushpak Bhattacharyya, Anahita Bhiwandiwalla, Michael Bloodgood, Victoria Bobicev, Florian Boudin, Thomas Brovelli (Meyer), Wray Buntine, Miriam Butt

John Calvo Martinez, Ziqiang Cao, Spencer Caplan, Rémi Cardon, Dumitru-Clementin Cercel, Tuhin Chakrabarty, Tanmoy Chakraborty, Yllias Chali, Hou Pong Chan, Kehai Chen, Yubo Chen, Mei-Hua Chen, Xiaocong Chen, Yue Chen, Hsin-Hsi Chen, Fuxiang Chen, Hannah Chen, Sihao Chen, Xinchi Chen, Qian Chen, Qiang Chen, Kanzhi Cheng, Colin Cherry, Emmanuele Chersoni, KEY-SUN CHOI, Monojit Choudhury, Chenhui Chu, Abu Nowshed Chy

Aswarth Abhilash Dara, Avisha Das, Sarthak Dash, Gael de Chalendar, Mathieu Dehouck, Vera Demberg, Yue Deng, Yuntian Deng, Shumin Deng, Chris Develder, Maria Pia di Buono, Luigi Di Caro, Gaël Dias, Miguel Domingo, Shichao Dong, Mingwen Dong, Zi-Yi Dou, Aleksandr Drozd, Wanyu Du, Cunxiao Du, Junwen Duan, Kevin Duh, Jonathan Dunn

Hiroshi Echizen'ya, Steffen Eger, Ramy Eskander

Ming Fang, Hao Fei, Elisabetta Fersini, Alejandro Figueroa, Mauajama Firdaus, Margaret Fleck

Matteo Gabburo, Olivier Galibert, Abbas Ghaddar, Pranav Goel, Carlos Gómez-Rodríguez, Jesús González-Rubio, Isao Goto, Yulia Grishina, Yi Guan, Anupam Guha, Tunga Gungor

Udo Hahn, Na-Rae Han, Ting Han, Jie Hao, Maram Hasanain, Sabit Hassan, Yoshihiko Hayashi, Jie He, DELIA IRAZU HERNANDEZ FARIAS, Tsutomu Hirao, Tosho Hirasawa, Yi-Li Hsu, Po Hu, han hu, zhiyuan hu, Hang Hua, Shujian Huang, Zhongqiang Huang, Kaiyu Huang, Hen-Hsen Huang, Tenghao Huang, Jiangping Huang, Patrick Huber, Jena D. Hwang

Dmitry Ilvovsky, Kenji Imamura, Takashi Inui, Hitoshi Isahara, Etsuko Ishii, Hayate Iso

Palak Jain, Shoaib Jameel, Abhik Jana, Inigo Jauregi Unanue, Yangfeng Ji, Yuxiang Jia, Ridong Jiang, Jyun-Yu Jiang, Aditya Joshi, Prathyusha Jwalapuram

Besim Kabashi, Lis Kanashiro Pereira, Diptesh Kanojia, Sarvnaz Karimi, Börje Karlsson, Marzena Karpinska, Anisia Katinskaia, Daisuke Kawahara, Casey Kennington, Salam Khalifa, Joo-Kyung Kim, Hwichan Kim, David King, Tracy Holloway King, Julien Kloetzer, Philipp Koehn, Mamoru Komachi, Kanako Komiya, Myoung-Wan Koo, Yannis Korkontzelos, Fajri Koto, Canasai Kruengkrai, Lun-Wei Ku, Roland Kuhn, Shankar Kumar

Matthieu Labeau, Albert Y.S. Lam, Stefan Larson, Hung Le, Lung-Hao Lee, Gurpreet Lehal, Alessandro Lenci, Yves Lepage, Piji Li, Yun Li, Sheng Li, Junyi Li, Alexander Hanbo Li, Jiaqi Li, Bangzheng Li, Dongfang Li, Dingcheng Li, Yanran Li, Yuan-Fang Li, Tao Li, Zuchao Li, Weikang Li, Fangtao Li, Wei Li, Peifeng Li, Zekun Li, Lu Li, Baoli LI, Junhui Li, Si Li, Haoran LI, Chao-Chun Liang, Mark Liberman, Gilbert Lim, Marina Litvak, Fenglin Liu, Yongbin Liu, Qun Liu, Yiqun Liu, Yang Janet Liu, Yue Liu, Yao Liu, Zhe Liu, Han Liu, Sharid Loáiciga, Robert L Logan IV, Quanyu Long, Yunfei Long, Di Lu, Hanjia Lyu

Jianqiang Ma, Mounica Maddela, Tarek Mahmoud, Peter Makarov, Valentin Malykh, Muhammad Arslan Manzoor, Bruno Martins, Sahisnu Mazumder, John P. McCrae, Bridget McInnes, Fanchao Meng, Rui Meng, Tao Meng, Zaiqiao Meng, Mohsen Mesgar, Margot Mieskes, SeyedAbolghasem Mirroshandel,

Abhijit Mishra, Yusuke Miyao, Aditya Mogadala, Diego Molla, Sneha Mondal, Manuel Montes, Lori Moon, Hajime Morita, Larry Moss, Pramod Kaushik Mudrakarta, Emir Munoz, Dragos Munteanu

Masaaki Nagata, Tetsuji Nakagawa, Preksha Nema, Nam Nguyen, Nhung Nguyen, Truc-Vien T. Nguyen, Thien Nguyen, Eric Nichols, Garrett Nicolai, Massimo Nicosia, Jian-Yun Nie, Takashi Ninomiya, Masaaki Nishino, Sergiu Nisioi, Joakim Nivre, Pierre Nugues

Atul Kr. Ojha, Antoni Oliver

Santanu Pal, Chester Palen-Michel, Yi-Cheng Pan, Zhufeng Pan, Liang Pang, Nikos Papasarantopoulos, Jacob Parnell, Ioannis Partalas, Prasanna Parthasarathi, Marius Pasca, Sapan Patel, Pavel Pecina, Hengzhi Pei, Flammie Pirinen, Andrei Popescu-Belis, Fred Popowich, Animesh Prasad, Daniel Preotiuc-Pietro, Laurent Prévot, Emily Prud'hommeaux

Xinying Qiu

Alexandre Rademaker, Surangika Ranathunga, Yanghui Rao, Farzana Rashid, Hanumant Redkar, German Rigau, Anthony Rios, Bryan Routledge, Alla Rozovskaya

Fatiha Sadat, Saurav Sahay, Elizabeth Salesky, Avneesh Saluja, German Sanchis-Trilles, Bishal Santra, Anoop Sarkar, Ryohei Sasano, Asad Sayeed, Shigehiko Schamoni, Stephanie Schoch, William Schuler, Ethan Selfridge, Nasredine Semmar, Gregory Senay, Cory Shain, Raksha Sharma, Artem Shelmanov, Yangyang Shi, Tomohide Shibata, Kai Shu, Maryam Siahbani, Carina Silberer, Diego Silva, Michel Simard, Patrick Simianer, Sunayana Sitaram, Amy Siu, Hyun-Je Song, Xingyi Song, Marlo Souza, Balaji Vasan Srinivasan, Felix Stahlberg, Mark Steedman, Kristina Striegnitz, Yixuan Su, Katsuhito Sudoh, Yoshi Suhara, Derwin Suhartono, Alane Suhr, Kai Sun, Chengjie Sun, Marek Suppa

Zeerak Talat, George Tambouratzis, Akihiro Tamura, Bowen Tan, Zhiyang Teng, Camilo Thorne, Yufei Tian, Nasim Tohidi, Takenobu Tokunaga, Marc Tomlinson, Marwan Torki, Samia Touileb, Aashka Trivedi, Chen-Tse Tsai

Kiyotaka Uchimoto, Masao Utiyama

Rob van der Goot, David Vandyke, Natalia Vanetik, Clara Vania, Shikhar Vashishth, Rakesh Verma, Martin Villalba

Xintong Wang, Wei Wang, Di Wang, Hecong Wang, Zhaowei Wang, Guangtao Wang, Zijie Wang, Dexin Wang, Hai Wang, Wenya Wang, Jianzong Wang, Weiyue Wang, Zhongqing Wang, Hsin-Min Wang, Qingyun Wang, Derry Tanti Wijaya, Gijs Wijnholds, Kam-Fai Wong, Xianchao Wu, Stephen Wu, Fangzhao Wu, Zhiyong Wu

Tong Xiao, Jun Xie, Canwen Xu, Qiongkai Xu, Fangzhi Xu, Ruifeng Xu, Wenduan Xu, Hongfei Xu

Yadollah Yaghoobzadeh, Zhaohui Yan, Muqiao Yang, Eugene Yang, Haiqin Yang, Yaqin Yang, Wei Yang, Tae Yano, Kaisheng Yao, Seid Muhie Yimam, Qingyu Yin, Seunghyun Yoon, Masaharu Yoshioka, Heng Yu, Jianfei Yu, Xinchen Yu, Dong Yu, Frances Yung

Fadi Zaraket, Zenan Zhai, Yuqi Zhang, Zhuosheng Zhang, Tianyi Zhang, Wen Zhang, Dongyan Zhao, Xinran Zhao, Chao Zhao, Boyuan Zheng, Houquan Zhou, Yichao Zhou, Guangyou Zhou, Yi Zhu, Wanzheng Zhu, Su Zhu, Bowei Zou, Vilém Zouhar, Arkaitz Zubiaga

Outstanding Services

Outstanding ACs

We are indebt to these area chairs who offered a distinguished and professional meta-reviewing.

Jun Araki, Prafulla Kumar Choubey, Fenia Christopoulou, Shi Feng, Kokil Jaidka, Zhenghua Li, Massimo Piccardi, Lei Sha, Elena Voita, Henning Wachsmuth, Wenlin Yao, Rui Zhang

Outstanding Reviewers

The community has greatly benefited from these outstanding reviewers who delivered particularly insightful and constructive review comments.

Dario Bertero, Hsin-Hsi Chen, Colin Cherry, Sarthak Dash, Tunga Gungor, Hwichan Kim, Zuchao Li, Tao Li, Han Liu, Sergiu Nisioi, Zhufeng Pan, Anoop Sarkar, Akihiro Tamura, Stephen Wu, Frances Yung

Table of Contents

Self-Augmentation Improves Zero-Shot Cross-Lingual Transfer

Fei Wang[†]**, Kuan-Hao Huang**[‡]**, Kai-Wei Chang**[‡] **and Muhao Chen**[†]
[†]University of Southern California [‡]University of California, Los Angeles
{fwang598, muhaoche}@usc.edu {khhuang, kwchang}@cs.ucla.edu

Abstract

Zero-shot cross-lingual transfer is a central task in multilingual NLP, allowing models trained in languages with more sufficient training resources to generalize to other low-resource languages. Earlier efforts on this task use parallel corpora, bilingual dictionaries, or other annotated alignment data to improve cross-lingual transferability, which are typically expensive to obtain. In this paper, we propose a simple yet effective method, SALT, to improve the *zero-shot* cross-lingual transfer of the multilingual pretrained language models without the help of such external data. By incorporating code-switching and embedding mixup with self-augmentation, SALT effectively distills cross-lingual knowledge from the multilingual PLM and enhances its transferability on downstream tasks. Experimental results on XNLI and PAWS-X show that our method is able to improve zero-shot cross-lingual transferability without external data.[1]

1 Introduction

Zero-shot cross-lingual transfer is integral to many multilingual NLP tasks (Ma and Xia, 2014; Artetxe and Schwenk, 2019; Ahmad et al., 2019). For some NLP tasks, the task-specific training data are often not evenly provided in terms of quantity and quality for distinct languages, and may even be unavailable for particularly low-resource languages. Zero-shot cross-lingual transfer allows models trained in languages with sufficient training resources to generalize to other low-resource languages. Earlier efforts on this task use parallel corpora, bilingual dictionaries, or other annotated alignment data to improve cross-lingual transferability, which are typically expensive to obtain (Chi et al., 2021; Yang et al., 2022; Qin et al., 2020; Lee et al., 2021; Krishnan et al., 2021).

[1]Our code is available at `https://github.com/luka-group/SALT`.

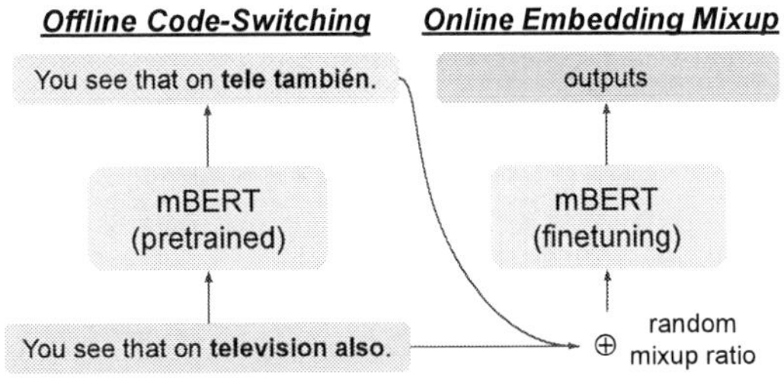

Figure 1: SALT distills the cross-lingual counterpart of each token from the multilingual PLM for code-switching and applies embedding mixup to improve the diversity of self-augmented features.

Recent analyses show that multilingual pretrained language models (PLMs) possess rich cross-lingual knowledge to facilitate the transfer (Pires et al., 2019; Conneau et al., 2020a; Huang et al., 2021). However, when being finetuned on a specific task in the source language, multilingual PLMs may catastrophically forget cross-lingual knowledge (Liu et al., 2021; Chalkidis et al., 2021). We argue that cross-lingual knowledge possessed by multilingual PLMs can be distilled and incorporated into task training data to preserve and improve models' cross-lingual transferability when fine-tuning on downstream tasks.

In this paper, we focus on the setting where no external cross-lingual alignment data are available and propose a simple yet effective Self-Augmented Language Transfer (SALT) method for multilingual PLMs. SALT introduces two self-augmentation techniques on monolingual task-specific training data as shown in Fig. 1. Before task training, an *offline* technique based on cross-lingual code-switching first uses the PLM to predict a cross-lingual counterpart of each token in the given training sample. Accordingly, this technique generates a cross-lingual augmentation of the training sample by substituting the tokens with their cross-lingual counterparts. During task training, an *on-*

Proceedings of the 13th International Joint Conference on Natural Language Processing and the 3rd Conference of the Asia-Pacific Chapter of the Association for Computational Linguistics (Volume 2: Short Papers), pages 1–9
November 1–4, 2023.

line self-augmentation technique based on embedding mixup (Zhang et al., 2018) randomly perturbs the representation of the training sample between the source and target languages. SALT allows the information about context-specific alignment of tokens to be distilled from the multilingual PLM, and to be further enhanced through perturbed training.

Experimental results on XNLI and PAWS-X benchmarks demonstrate that SALT achieves more improvements on zero-shot transferability than previous SOTA methods (Lewis et al., 2020; Huang et al., 2021). With self-augmentation on three target languages, SALT achieves 1.4% improvement on 15 languages of XNLI and 4.1% on 6 languages of PAWS-X in terms of average accuracy comparing with the base model.

2 Self-Augmentation

Our method distills cross-lingual token-level alignment from the multilingual PLM and incorporates the knowledge to task-specific data through code-switching. To further improve the diversity of augmentation for better generalization, we also apply a random embedding mixup. Following are the details of these two techniques.

2.1 Self-Augmentation with Code-Switching

SALT adopts a modified masked language modeling (MLM) method to distill cross-lingual token translation pairs. As multilingual PLMs, such as mBERT (Devlin et al., 2019) and XLM-R (Conneau et al., 2020a), are pre-trained with MLM, we can directly mask these models to predict cross-lingual tokens. Specifically, SALT makes two modifications to the original MLM learning objective. First, we let the model predict tokens only in a specific target language, and disregard all tokens not belonging to this language. Tokens in each target language are collected from a monolingual vocabulary list.[2] Second, to ensure that the semantics of predictions are similar to original tokens, we do not mask the original tokens when inputting the sentence to the multilingual PLM. This seeks to help the PLM better infer cross-lingual counterpart tokens given the references of original tokens in the input context.

Generated token-level cross-lingual substitutions with high enough predicted probabilities are used for code-switching. In this work, we adopt a fixed probability threshold for all target languages. We also predict synonyms in the source language with SALT. Since predicted probability in the source language and target languages are of different scales, we assign a different threshold for synonym prediction. This self-augmentation process is done offline before task training.

2.2 Self-Augmentation with Embedding Mixup

To further improve the diversity of self-augmented features and reduce the noise introduced by code-switching through smoothing, we propose an *online* self-augmentation technique based on cross-lingual embedding mixup (Guo et al., 2019). Specifically, for each token t_i in the generated sentence from code-switching, we interpolate its embedding with that of the original token s_i before code-switching. In detail, given the embedding of original token h_{s_i} and embedding of the substituted token h_{t_i}, the mixed up token embedding is generated as

$$h_i = r \cdot h_{s_i} + (1 - r) \cdot h_{t_i},$$

where $r = \{r_j\}, r_j \in [0, 1]$ is a random vector. In the embedding mixup, the interpolation coefficient of each embedding dimension j is independently generated from a uniform distribution to allow for more diverse combinations of embeddings in two languages. Applying this self-augmentation technique allows for randomly perturbing the training instance between the source and target language representation, leading to further improved transferability of the obtained task model.

2.3 Training

In this work, we use English as the source language and consider three target languages for code-switching, i.e. French, German and Spanish[3]. Before training the task model, on each original training sample in the source language, we generate an augmented sample in each target language *offline* with code-switching, where all predicted high-probability token substitutions are applied. Then during training, we further apply embedding mixup

[2] We adopt the top 10,000 words by frequency in target languages at `https://en.wiktionary.org/wiki/Wiktionary:Frequency_lists`.

[3] We compute the overlap between the model's vocabulary and the word list of each evaluation language, and select the top three languages with the highest overlap ratio. Note that Chinese, Japanese, and Korean are not selected because their words will be tokenized to characters by the model tokenizer used in this study.

Model	en	ar	bg	de	el	es	fr	hi	ru	sw	th	tr	ur	vi	zh	avg.	w/ en
without external data																	
mBERT	80.8	64.3	68.0	70.0	65.3	73.5	73.4	58.9	67.8	49.7	**54.1**	60.9	57.2	69.3	67.8	64.3	65.4
mBERT*	81.8	64.7	67.0	69.6	66.1	74.7	73.9	59.7	68.8	50.0	53.7	60.8	58.0	70.5	68.8	64.7	66.0
+RS-ADV	81.9	64.9	68.3	**71.7**	66.5	74.4	**74.5**	59.6	68.8	48.8	50.6	61.7	**59.2**	70.0	69.4	64.9	66.0
+RS-RP	**82.6**	65.4	68.7	70.5	67.2	**75.0**	74.1	59.8	69.5	48.4	50.5	59.7	57.9	70.5	69.7	64.8	66.0
+SALT	82.4	**65.9**	**69.6**	70.4	**67.8**	**75.0**	**74.5**	**61.1**	**69.6**	**50.6**	53.5	**62.0**	58.9	**70.9**	**69.8**	**65.7**	**66.8**
with external data (not directly comparable to our approach)																	
+RS-DA	81.0	66.4	69.9	71.8	68.0	74.7	74.2	62.7	70.6	51.1	55.7	62.9	60.9	71.8	71.4	66.6	67.6
+CoSDA-ML	82.9	68.0	72.7	74.1	70.9	76.9	76.7	65.5	73.2	51.0	59.8	63.9	62.3	73.6	73.8	68.7	69.7

Table 1: Average accuracy of zero-shot cross-lingual transfer on XNLI with 5 different random seeds. We provide detailed results of 15 languages and their average (w/ and w/o English). The highest scores are in bold. Significant improvements in comparison with mBERT baseline by t-test ($p \leq 0.05$) are underlined. We also provide results of methods with external data as the referenced upper bound. * We reproduce mBERT with our code base. Other baseline results are from previous papers.

to these augmented samples where the interpolation coefficient vector r is dynamically sampled in each step of training for each instance. While both self-augmentation techniques automatically switch and perturb the original training samples towards the target language(s), the labels on those training samples remain unchanged. Hence, the final task model is trained directly on the self-augmented training samples by optimizing the original learning objective of the task. This allows for robust zero-shot transfer of the task model by using only monolingual training data in the source language.

3 Experiment

In this section, we evaluate SALT to demonstrate that self-augmentation methods improve zero-shot cross-lingual transfer.

3.1 Setup

Following Huang et al. (2021), we consider two cross-lingual datasets. XNLI is a natural language inference (NLI) dataset, including premise-hypothesis pairs in 15 languages labeled as entailment/neutral/contradiction. PAWS-X is a paraphrase identification dataset, including sentence pairs in six languages with binary labels. On both datasets, we train and validate models with English data, and test them with data in all languages. We report the average accuracy of five-run experiment.

Baseline. We compare SALT with two SOTA zero-shot cross-lingual transfer methods without any external data. RS-ADV and RS-RP (Huang et al., 2021) enhance transferability by respectively adding adversarial and random embedding perturbation during task training on English data. We also provide results of three methods that use external data. RS-DA (Huang et al., 2021) augments training data by replacing words with predefined synonyms (Alzantot et al., 2018). CoSDA-ML (Qin et al., 2020) creates code-switching data with bilingual dictionaries. SCOPA (Lee et al., 2021) extends CoSDA-ML by mixing the hidden states of original and code-switched data with a fixed ratio.

Implementation Details. We evaluate the proposed method based on mBERT. For both sentence pair classification tasks, self-augmentation is conducted separately on each sentence. We augment one code-switched instance per language (including English, French, Spanish, and German) for each original instance. For other hyper-parameters, we follow the training scripts by Huang et al. (2021). More details are in Appx. §A.

3.2 Results

Tab. 1 shows the results on XNLI, where we observe that previous methods without external data have a positive influence on a few languages but have a negative influence on other languages. Their average improvement is however lesser in comparison to SALT which leads to an average improvement in accuracy by 1% as well as significant improvements in 9 out of 15 languages over mBERT. Our method also outperforms other baselines by at least 0.8% in terms of average accuracy (both w/ and w/o en). The results indicate that the model can benefit from cross-lingual knowledge distilled from itself. Moreover, augmenting the data to three target languages can bring improvements to all 14 target languages. For example, the

Model	en	de	es	fr	ja	ko	zh	avg.	w/ en
without external data									
mBERT	94.0	85.7	87.4	87.0	73.0	69.6	77.0	80.0	82.0
mBERT*	93.9	84.5	87.9	87.2	74.2	76.1	79.8	81.6	83.4
+RS-ADV	93.7	86.5	88.5	87.8	76.1	75.3	80.4	82.4	84.0
+RS-RP	**94.5**	87.4	**90.0**	**89.5**	77.9	**77.5**	**82.0**	**84.1**	**85.5**
+SALT	94.2	**87.9**	89.9	89.1	**78.6**	77.4	81.8	**84.1**	**85.5**
with external data (not directly comparable to our approach)									
+RS-DA	93.5	87.8	88.8	88.8	79.3	78.3	81.5	84.1	85.4
+CoSDA-ML	-	87.3	90.0	89.6	79.4	79.5	83.0	84.8	-
+SCOPA	-	88.6	90.3	89.7	81.5	80.1	84.1	85.7	-

Table 2: Average accuracy of zero-shot cross-lingual transfer on PAWS-X.

Model	avg.	avg. (incl. en)
SALT	**84.1**	**85.5**
- en-only	83.4	84.8
- w/o mixup	83.3	84.7
mBERT	81.6	83.4

Table 3: Ablation study on PAWS-X test set. *en-only* indicates only substitute original tokens to other English tokens. *w/o mixup* means embedding mixup is not used.

improvements on ar, bg, el, hi, tr and zh are 1.2%, 2.6%, 1.7%, 1.4%, 1.2% and 1.0%. Experiment on PAWS-X also shows that SALT can improve model performance in comparison with the vanilla setting (Tab. 2). However, RS-RP is also effective on this task and achieves comparable results. Considering that NLI requires inferring the logical consequence that can be dependent on various components of the two sentences, this complex reasoning process benefits more from the robust training of SALT. On the other hand, as a simpler task based on sentence similarity, paraphrase identification can be sufficiently improved based on random perturbation.

Generalized Setting. We further evaluate SALT in a generalized setting (Lewis et al., 2020; Huang et al., 2021) on XNLI. The new setting pairs up sentences from two different languages as the premise and the hypothesis, converting the original test data from 15 languages to 225 language pairs. SALT achieves 0.5% of improvement over the best baseline and 2.2% over the vanilla PLM in average. Full results on all language pairs are in Appx. §B. Despite the vocabulary gap between training and inference for baselines, SALT reduces this gap by code-switching and mixup.

Ablation Study. To further investigate the incorporated techniques in SALT, we conduct an ablation study on PAWS-X as shown in Tab. 3. Offline code-switching solely improves the average accuracy by 1.7%, while online embedding mixup further improves it by 0.8%. We also evaluate the influence of involved target languages in SALT. Code-switching with only English synonyms distilled from PLMs can bring an improvement of 1.8%, while involving three target languages further improves the performance by 0.7%.

4 Related Work

Zero-shot cross-lingual transfer has become an emerging research topic since it potentially reduces the effort of collecting labeled data for low-resource languages (Ahmad et al., 2019; Hu et al., 2020; Dufter and Schütze, 2020; Ruder et al., 2021; Chai et al., 2022; Huang et al., 2022). Earlier works directly apply multilingual PLMs, such as multilingual BERT (Devlin et al., 2019), XLM (Conneau and Lample, 2019), and XLM-R (Conneau et al., 2020a), and achieve surprisingly well performance on this setting. Recently, the performance is further improved with additional auxiliary data, such as parallel translation pairs (Chi et al., 2021; Wei et al., 2021; Yang et al., 2022; Feng et al., 2022), bilingual dictionaries (Cao et al., 2020; Qin et al., 2020; Liu et al., 2020b; Krishnan et al., 2021; Lee et al., 2021), and syntactic features (Subburathinam et al., 2019; Meng et al., 2019; Ahmad et al., 2021a,b).

Our work aligns more with another line of research that studies zero-shot cross-lingual transfer *without* using additional annotations. This includes unsupervised embedding alignment (Artetxe et al., 2020; Conneau et al., 2020b), robust training (Huang et al., 2021), and meta-learning (Nooralahzadeh et al., 2020). Our idea is motivated by the self-augmentation techniques (Feng et al., 2021; Xu et al., 2021) that are mostly explored for monolingual tasks, and the mixup techniques (Zhang et al., 2018; Lee et al., 2021; Yang et al., 2022) which seeks to smooth the embedding space.

5 Conclusion

In this paper, we propose SALT, a self-augmention method for zero-shot cross-lingual transfer of PLMs. SALT distills cross-lingual knowledge from PLMs and incorporates them into task training data through an offline code-switching technique, and an online embedding mixup technique to improve transferability with a smoothed representation space. Experiments and analyses based on XNLI and PAWS-X demonstrate promising improvement to SALT in terms of cross-lingual transfer without using external data.

Acknowledgement

We appreciate the reviewers for their insightful comments and suggestions. Fei Wang was supported by the Annenberg Fellowship at USC and the Amazon ML Fellowship. Muhao Chen was supported by the NSF Grants IIS 2105329 and ITE 2333736, by the Air Force Research Laboratory under agreement number FA8750-20-2-10002, by two Amazon Research Awards and a Cisco Research Award. Computing of this work was partly supported by a subaward of NSF Cloudbank 1925001 through UCSD.

Limitations

In this study, we adopt a fixed threshold to select tokens for code-switching. However, the optimal thresholds for different languages and instances can vary. Future research can develop efficient search algorithm to optimize the thresholds. While we have limited the proposed technique to discriminative natural language understanding tasks, future research can extend the proposed technique to generative multilingual PLMs, such as mT5 (Xue et al., 2021) and mBART (Liu et al., 2020a), on text generation tasks (Duan et al., 2019; Chen et al., 2021). Furthermore, we have opted for English as the source language. However, extending the application of SALT to other source languages could enhance the comprehensiveness of this study.

References

Wasi Ahmad, Zhisong Zhang, Xuezhe Ma, Eduard Hovy, Kai-Wei Chang, and Nanyun Peng. 2019. On difficulties of cross-lingual transfer with order differences: A case study on dependency parsing. In *Proceedings of the 2019 Conference of the North American Chapter of the Association for Computational Linguistics: Human Language Technologies, Volume 1 (Long and Short Papers)*, pages 2440–2452.

Wasi Uddin Ahmad, Haoran Li, Kai-Wei Chang, and Yashar Mehdad. 2021a. Syntax-augmented multilingual BERT for cross-lingual transfer. In *Proceedings of the 59th Annual Meeting of the Association for Computational Linguistics (ACL)*.

Wasi Uddin Ahmad, Nanyun Peng, and Kai-Wei Chang. 2021b. GATE: graph attention transformer encoder for cross-lingual relation and event extraction. In *Thirty-Fifth AAAI Conference on Artificial Intelligence (AAAI)*.

Moustafa Alzantot, Yash Sharma, Ahmed Elgohary, Bo-Jhang Ho, Mani Srivastava, and Kai-Wei Chang. 2018. Generating natural language adversarial examples. In *Proceedings of the 2018 Conference on Empirical Methods in Natural Language Processing*, pages 2890–2896, Brussels, Belgium. Association for Computational Linguistics.

Mikel Artetxe, Sebastian Ruder, and Dani Yogatama. 2020. On the cross-lingual transferability of monolingual representations. In *Proceedings of the 58th Annual Meeting of the Association for Computational Linguistics (ACL)*.

Mikel Artetxe and Holger Schwenk. 2019. Massively multilingual sentence embeddings for zero-shot cross-lingual transfer and beyond. *Transactions of the Association for Computational Linguistics*, 7:597–610.

Steven Cao, Nikita Kitaev, and Dan Klein. 2020. Multilingual alignment of contextual word representations. In *8th International Conference on Learning Representations (ICLR)*.

Yuan Chai, Yaobo Liang, and Nan Duan. 2022. Cross-lingual ability of multilingual masked language models: A study of language structure. In *Proceedings of the 60th Annual Meeting of the Association for Computational Linguistics (ACL)*.

Ilias Chalkidis, Manos Fergadiotis, and Ion Androutsopoulos. 2021. Multieurlex-a multi-lingual and multi-label legal document classification dataset for zero-shot cross-lingual transfer. In *Proceedings of the 2021 Conference on Empirical Methods in Natural Language Processing*, pages 6974–6996.

Guanhua Chen, Shuming Ma, Yun Chen, Li Dong, Dongdong Zhang, Jia Pan, Wenping Wang, and Furu Wei. 2021. Zero-shot cross-lingual transfer of neural machine translation with multilingual pretrained encoders. In *Proceedings of the 2021 Conference on*

Empirical Methods in Natural Language Processing, pages 15–26.

Zewen Chi, Li Dong, Furu Wei, Nan Yang, Saksham Singhal, Wenhui Wang, Xia Song, Xian-Ling Mao, Heyan Huang, and Ming Zhou. 2021. Infoxlm: An information-theoretic framework for cross-lingual language model pre-training. In *Proceedings of the 2021 Conference of the North American Chapter of the Association for Computational Linguistics: Human Language Technologies (NAACL-HLT)*.

Alexis Conneau, Kartikay Khandelwal, Naman Goyal, Vishrav Chaudhary, Guillaume Wenzek, Francisco Guzmán, Édouard Grave, Myle Ott, Luke Zettlemoyer, and Veselin Stoyanov. 2020a. Unsupervised cross-lingual representation learning at scale. In *Proceedings of the 58th Annual Meeting of the Association for Computational Linguistics*, pages 8440–8451.

Alexis Conneau and Guillaume Lample. 2019. Cross-lingual language model pretraining. In *Advances in Neural Information Processing Systems 32: Annual Conference on Neural Information Processing Systems 2019 (NeurIPS)*.

Alexis Conneau, Shijie Wu, Haoran Li, Luke Zettlemoyer, and Veselin Stoyanov. 2020b. Emerging cross-lingual structure in pretrained language models. In *Proceedings of the 58th Annual Meeting of the Association for Computational Linguistics (ACL)*.

Jacob Devlin, Ming-Wei Chang, Kenton Lee, and Kristina Toutanova. 2019. BERT: pre-training of deep bidirectional transformers for language understanding. In *Proceedings of the 2019 Conference of the North American Chapter of the Association for Computational Linguistics: Human Language Technologies (NAACL-HLT)*.

Xiangyu Duan, Mingming Yin, Min Zhang, Boxing Chen, and Weihua Luo. 2019. Zero-shot cross-lingual abstractive sentence summarization through teaching generation and attention. In *Proceedings of the 57th Annual Meeting of the Association for Computational Linguistics*, pages 3162–3172.

Philipp Dufter and Hinrich Schütze. 2020. Identifying necessary elements for bert's multilinguality. In *Proceedings of the 2020 Conference on Empirical Methods in Natural Language Processing (EMNLP)*.

Fangxiaoyu Feng, Yinfei Yang, Daniel Cer, Naveen Arivazhagan, and Wei Wang. 2022. Language-agnostic BERT sentence embedding. In *Proceedings of the 60th Annual Meeting of the Association for Computational Linguistics (ACL)*.

Steven Y. Feng, Varun Gangal, Jason Wei, Sarath Chandar, Soroush Vosoughi, Teruko Mitamura, and Eduard H. Hovy. 2021. A survey of data augmentation approaches for NLP. In *Findings of the Association for Computational Linguistics (ACL-Findings)*.

Hongyu Guo, Yongyi Mao, and Richong Zhang. 2019. Augmenting data with mixup for sentence classification: An empirical study. *arXiv preprint arXiv:1905.08941*.

Junjie Hu, Sebastian Ruder, Aditya Siddhant, Graham Neubig, Orhan Firat, and Melvin Johnson. 2020. XTREME: A massively multilingual multi-task benchmark for evaluating cross-lingual generalisation. In *Proceedings of the 37th International Conference on Machine Learning (ICML)*.

Kuan-Hao Huang, Wasi Ahmad, Nanyun Peng, and Kai-Wei Chang. 2021. Improving zero-shot cross-lingual transfer learning via robust training. In *Proceedings of the 2021 Conference on Empirical Methods in Natural Language Processing*, pages 1684–1697.

Kuan-Hao Huang, I-Hung Hsu, Prem Natarajan, Kai-Wei Chang, and Nanyun Peng. 2022. Multilingual generative language models for zero-shot cross-lingual event argument extraction. In *Proceedings of the 60th Annual Meeting of the Association for Computational Linguistics (ACL)*.

Jitin Krishnan, Antonios Anastasopoulos, Hemant Purohit, and Huzefa Rangwala. 2021. Multilingual code-switching for zero-shot cross-lingual intent prediction and slot filling. In *Proceedings of the 1st Workshop on Multilingual Representation Learning*, pages 211–223.

Dohyeon Lee, Jaeseong Lee, Gyewon Lee, Byung-gon Chun, and Seung-won Hwang. 2021. Scopa: Soft code-switching and pairwise alignment for zero-shot cross-lingual transfer. In *Proceedings of the 30th ACM International Conference on Information & Knowledge Management*, pages 3176–3180.

Patrick S. H. Lewis, Barlas Oguz, Ruty Rinott, Sebastian Riedel, and Holger Schwenk. 2020. MLQA: evaluating cross-lingual extractive question answering. In *Proceedings of the 58th Annual Meeting of the Association for Computational Linguistics (ACL)*.

Yinhan Liu, Jiatao Gu, Naman Goyal, Xian Li, Sergey Edunov, Marjan Ghazvininejad, Mike Lewis, and Luke Zettlemoyer. 2020a. Multilingual denoising pre-training for neural machine translation. *Transactions of the Association for Computational Linguistics*, 8:726–742.

Zihan Liu, Genta Indra Winata, Zhaojiang Lin, Peng Xu, and Pascale Fung. 2020b. Attention-informed mixed-language training for zero-shot cross-lingual task-oriented dialogue systems. In *The Thirty-Fourth AAAI Conference on Artificial Intelligence (AAAI)*.

Zihan Liu, Genta Indra Winata, Andrea Madotto, and Pascale Fung. 2021. Preserving cross-linguality of pre-trained models via continual learning. In *Proceedings of the 6th Workshop on Representation Learning for NLP (RepL4NLP-2021)*, pages 64–71.

Xuezhe Ma and Fei Xia. 2014. Unsupervised dependency parsing with transferring distribution via parallel guidance and entropy regularization. In *Proceedings of the 52nd Annual Meeting of the Association for Computational Linguistics (Volume 1: Long Papers)*, pages 1337–1348.

Tao Meng, Nanyun Peng, and Kai-Wei Chang. 2019. Target language-aware constrained inference for cross-lingual dependency parsing. In *Proceedings of the 2019 Conference on Empirical Methods in Natural Language Processing and the 9th International Joint Conference on Natural Language Processing, (EMNLP-IJCNLP)*.

Farhad Nooralahzadeh, Giannis Bekoulis, Johannes Bjerva, and Isabelle Augenstein. 2020. Zero-shot cross-lingual transfer with meta learning. In *Proceedings of the 2020 Conference on Empirical Methods in Natural Language Processing (EMNLP)*.

Telmo Pires, Eva Schlinger, and Dan Garrette. 2019. How multilingual is multilingual bert? In *Proceedings of the 57th Annual Meeting of the Association for Computational Linguistics*, pages 4996–5001.

Libo Qin, Minheng Ni, Yue Zhang, and Wanxiang Che. 2020. Cosda-ml: multi-lingual code-switching data augmentation for zero-shot cross-lingual nlp. In *Proceedings of the Twenty-Ninth International Conference on International Joint Conferences on Artificial Intelligence*, pages 3853–3860.

Sebastian Ruder, Noah Constant, Jan Botha, Aditya Siddhant, Orhan Firat, Jinlan Fu, Pengfei Liu, Junjie Hu, Dan Garrette, Graham Neubig, and Melvin Johnson. 2021. XTREME-R: towards more challenging and nuanced multilingual evaluation. In *Proceedings of the 2021 Conference on Empirical Methods in Natural Language Processing (EMNLP)*.

Ananya Subburathinam, Di Lu, Heng Ji, Jonathan May, Shih-Fu Chang, Avirup Sil, and Clare R. Voss. 2019. Cross-lingual structure transfer for relation and event extraction. In *Proceedings of the 2019 Conference on Empirical Methods in Natural Language Processing and the 9th International Joint Conference on Natural Language Processing (EMNLP-IJCNLP)*.

Xiangpeng Wei, Yue Hu, Rongxiang Weng, Luxi Xing, Heng Yu, and Weihua Luo. 2021. On learning universal representations across languages. In *9th International Conference on Learning Representations (ICLR)*.

Thomas Wolf, Lysandre Debut, Victor Sanh, Julien Chaumond, Clement Delangue, Anthony Moi, Pierric Cistac, Tim Rault, Rémi Louf, Morgan Funtowicz, et al. 2019. Huggingface's transformers: State-of-the-art natural language processing. *arXiv preprint arXiv:1910.03771*.

Yifei Xu, Jingqiao Zhang, Ru He, Liangzhu Ge, Chao Yang, Cheng Yang, and Ying Nian Wu. 2021. Sas: Self-augmented strategy for language model pretraining. *arXiv preprint arXiv:2106.07176*.

Linting Xue, Noah Constant, Adam Roberts, Mihir Kale, Rami Al-Rfou, Aditya Siddhant, Aditya Barua, and Colin Raffel. 2021. mt5: A massively multilingual pre-trained text-to-text transformer. In *Proceedings of the 2021 Conference of the North American Chapter of the Association for Computational Linguistics: Human Language Technologies*, pages 483–498.

Huiyun Yang, Huadong Chen, Hao Zhou, and Lei Li. 2022. Enhancing cross-lingual transfer by manifold mixup. In *10th International Conference on Learning Representations (ICLR)*.

Hongyi Zhang, Moustapha Cisse, Yann N Dauphin, and David Lopez-Paz. 2018. mixup: Beyond empirical risk minimization. In *International Conference on Learning Representations*.

A Implementation Details

We implement our model based on Huggingface Transformers (Wolf et al., 2019). We apply the uncased base version of mBERT model consisting of 110M parameters. We set the probability threshold for token substitution to 1e-3 for English synonym replacement and 1e-7 for code-switching in other languages. We run experiments with a NVIDIA GeForce RTX 2080 GPU. It takes about 1 hour for training on PAWS-X and 5 hours on XNLI.

B Results of Generalized Setting

Results for SALT, RS-RP and vanilla mBERT on XNLI under generalized setting are shown in Tab. 4, Tab. 5 and Tab. 6 respectively. Baseline results of RS-RP and vanilla mBERT are copied from Huang et al. (2021).

	en	es	de	fr	bg	ru	el	th	sw	vi	ar	zh	hi	ur	tr	avg.
en	82.9	73.2	67.5	72.3	66.5	67.4	60.7	46.6	40.4	67.4	62.1	68.7	56.9	53.6	55.2	62.8
es	74.9	75.4	64.6	70.7	64.4	66.1	61.1	44.9	39.7	64.6	61.0	63.8	55.0	50.2	54.3	60.7
de	72.9	68.9	70.0	68.0	63.9	66.3	59.4	45.1	40.3	63.5	60.5	62.7	56.8	54.2	55.1	60.5
fr	75.9	72.2	66.0	74.3	64.2	65.3	60.6	45.5	39.7	65.2	62.0	64.5	55.4	52.0	54.7	61.2
bg	69.8	66.0	61.6	64.2	69.6	66.5	59.3	45.5	38.9	60.2	60.2	60.4	54.8	50.6	53.0	58.7
ru	70.6	67.0	63.3	65.4	65.0	69.8	58.2	44.2	38.7	61.6	59.9	61.1	54.3	50.1	52.9	58.8
el	64.9	63.7	59.1	62.2	60.3	60.5	67.9	45.6	40.2	59.4	59.0	56.3	53.0	49.8	52.1	56.9
th	55.0	52.9	49.8	52.0	51.5	51.7	50.8	53.5	37.9	53.2	52.5	51.1	48.4	47.1	46.0	50.2
sw	54.2	52.6	48.9	50.5	49.9	49.5	49.2	42.6	50.3	49.9	50.8	49.7	47.5	47.1	47.2	49.3
vi	69.8	63.3	59.2	63.1	58.2	61.1	57.0	46.3	38.5	71.0	57.3	64.8	52.9	49.1	49.2	57.4
ar	65.7	62.6	57.6	61.4	59.2	59.9	57.1	45.5	39.2	59.3	66.3	58.0	54.1	51.5	51.9	56.6
zh	69.8	62.5	58.4	61.7	57.7	59.5	53.1	43.9	38.3	63.0	57.0	70.3	50.8	48.0	49.4	56.2
hi	62.2	57.8	56.4	57.4	56.5	57.5	54.9	45.4	38.7	56.5	56.3	56.4	61.9	55.6	52.0	55.0
ur	61.0	54.6	54.3	56.6	52.9	55.1	51.2	43.6	38.9	54.0	55.3	54.3	57.2	58.9	50.1	53.2
tr	62.2	57.8	56.0	56.8	56.3	55.5	54.2	43.7	39.9	55.4	55.4	55.7	54.0	51.4	62.2	54.4
avg.	67.5	63.4	59.5	62.4	59.7	60.8	57.0	45.5	40.0	60.3	58.4	59.8	54.2	51.3	52.3	56.8

Table 4: Results for SALT on XNLI.

	en	es	de	fr	bg	ru	el	th	sw	vi	ar	zh	hi	ur	tr	avg.
en	82.6	71.2	65.9	70.3	62.0	65.7	57.0	44.1	40.9	64.1	58.9	65.7	52.8	49.2	51.2	60.1
es	74.9	75.0	65.4	71.2	63.0	65.6	59.5	44.5	40.8	62.9	60.1	62.6	52.5	48.7	51.7	59.9
de	72.6	68.0	70.5	67.4	61.7	64.9	58.0	44.4	41.4	61.0	58.8	61.4	53.6	50.4	52.2	59.1
fr	74.7	71.6	65.2	74.1	62.1	64.8	58.4	44.4	40.8	62.7	59.5	62.4	52.7	48.9	51.7	59.6
bg	68.5	66.0	62.9	65.1	68.7	66.8	59.4	45.1	41.1	59.7	59.4	59.7	53.5	49.6	51.8	58.5
ru	69.9	67.1	63.5	65.9	65.0	69.5	58.2	44.7	40.9	60.8	59.2	60.6	53.1	49.5	51.5	58.6
el	63.9	63.3	59.3	62.0	59.8	61.0	67.2	44.7	41.3	57.3	57.7	55.7	51.4	48.2	50.7	56.2
th	56.4	54.1	51.7	53.3	51.9	52.9	51.0	50.5	40.1	52.5	51.8	51.3	48.2	46.3	46.8	50.6
sw	54.1	52.3	49.6	50.9	49.1	49.7	48.6	41.8	48.4	48.7	49.8	48.1	45.4	44.5	47.1	48.6
vi	69.9	65.0	60.5	64.1	58.6	61.8	56.0	45.1	40.4	70.5	57.4	63.4	51.5	48.0	49.1	57.4
ar	64.9	62.8	58.7	61.7	58.7	60.7	56.3	44.7	41.1	58.1	65.4	57.1	52.2	49.6	50.3	56.1
zh	71.1	64.8	60.8	64.1	59.0	61.6	53.9	43.5	40.8	63.0	56.8	69.7	50.9	47.8	49.7	57.2
hi	62.2	58.9	56.7	57.9	56.5	58.3	54.3	44.5	40.8	55.3	55.8	55.3	59.8	54.2	50.4	54.7
ur	61.2	56.7	56.1	57.3	54.4	57.0	53.2	43.7	40.8	54.1	56.3	54.6	56.9	57.9	49.9	54.0
tr	62.4	59.2	57.0	58.6	56.7	57.9	54.2	43.7	40.9	54.8	55.1	54.9	52.2	48.8	59.7	54.4
avg.	67.3	63.7	60.3	62.9	59.1	61.2	56.4	44.6	41.4	59.0	57.5	58.8	52.4	49.4	50.9	56.3

Table 5: Results for RS-RP on XNLI.

	en	es	de	fr	bg	ru	el	th	sw	vi	ar	zh	hi	ur	tr	avg.
en	82.3	70.3	65.8	69.7	60.5	63.1	55.3	44.6	41.1	63.9	57.7	64.6	52.0	49.5	52.3	59.5
es	73.5	74.3	62.9	69.0	60.5	63.7	57.3	44.6	40.6	61.4	57.9	60.8	50.4	47.1	51.6	58.4
de	71.8	65.5	70.8	65.6	59.5	63.3	55.8	44.3	41.0	60.2	56.5	60.1	52.5	49.4	52.0	57.9
fr	73.6	69.0	64.0	73.8	59.5	63.1	55.7	44.1	40.5	62.2	57.3	61.6	51.1	48.5	51.8	58.4
bg	67.8	63.7	60.8	62.5	68.2	64.2	56.0	44.2	39.9	57.4	56.3	57.8	51.2	47.2	50.3	56.5
ru	69.1	65.2	62.6	64.4	62.7	68.7	55.0	44.2	39.9	59.0	56.7	58.6	50.6	46.8	50.0	56.9
el	62.7	61.4	58.0	60.2	57.1	57.7	66.4	44.4	40.5	56.4	55.6	54.0	49.6	46.8	50.7	54.8
th	54.8	52.0	49.9	51.3	49.1	50.4	49.0	53.0	39.4	51.1	49.9	49.3	45.9	44.8	45.4	49.0
sw	54.2	51.2	48.7	50.5	47.2	47.9	47.9	41.8	50.0	48.5	49.1	48.5	45.4	44.4	45.8	48.1
vi	67.4	60.3	57.4	61.2	52.9	57.1	52.9	44.2	39.8	70.3	53.3	62.0	49.2	45.9	47.5	54.8
ar	63.9	60.4	57.0	59.5	54.5	57.1	53.3	43.9	40.4	55.4	64.8	55.2	50.3	48.4	49.9	54.3
zh	67.9	59.9	57.2	59.9	53.4	56.5	50.4	42.7	39.6	60.8	53.5	69.2	48.0	45.7	48.0	54.2
hi	61.4	55.5	55.0	55.3	52.6	54.4	51.9	43.8	40.3	53.8	53.1	53.7	59.7	52.7	49.9	52.9
ur	60.1	54.0	53.9	55.1	48.8	51.5	49.6	41.9	39.7	50.0	52.1	52.3	54.4	57.7	48.2	51.3
tr	61.0	55.1	53.6	55.1	52.0	52.6	50.9	42.4	40.7	52.3	52.0	53.2	49.7	47.3	60.9	51.9
avg.	66.1	61.2	58.5	60.9	55.9	58.1	53.8	44.3	40.9	57.5	55.1	57.4	50.7	48.1	50.3	54.6

Table 6: Results for mBERT on XNLI.

Learning to Predict Concept Ordering for Common Sense Generation

Tianhui Zhang **Danushka Bollegala** **Bei Peng**
University of Liverpool, Amazon
{tianhui.zhang, danushka, bei.peng}@liverpool.ac.uk

Abstract

Prior work has shown that the ordering in which concepts are shown to a commonsense generator plays an important role, affecting the quality of the generated sentence. However, it remains a challenge to determine the optimal ordering of a given set of concepts such that a natural sentence covering all the concepts could be generated from a pretrained generator. To understand the relationship between the ordering of the input concepts and the quality of the generated sentences, we conduct a systematic study considering multiple language models (LMs) and concept ordering strategies. We find that `BART-large` model consistently outperforms all other LMs considered in this study when fine-tuned using the ordering of concepts as they appear in CommonGen training data as measured using multiple evaluation metrics. Moreover, the larger GPT3-based large language models (LLMs) variants do not necessarily outperform much smaller LMs on this task, even when fine-tuned on task-specific training data. Interestingly, human annotators significantly reorder input concept sets when manually writing sentences covering those concepts, and this ordering provides the best sentence generations independently of the LM used for the generation, outperforming a probabilistic concept ordering baseline.[1]

1 Introduction

In Generative Commonsense Reasoning (GCR) (Lin et al., 2020), the goal is to generate a natural commonsense adhering sentence that covers all of the input concepts. GCR is a challenging natural language generation (NLG) task because it requires (a) relational reasoning using background commonsense knowledge associated with the input concepts, and (b) compositional generalisation ability to work on unseen concept combinations. CommonGen dataset (Lin et al., 2020) was specifically developed to evaluate the ability of a generative model to produce sentences covering a given set of concepts. For example, given the set of concepts {*ball*, *batter*, *pitcher*, *throw*}, a human annotator would come up with a sentence such as *The **pitcher throws** the **ball**, and the **batter** hits a home run!* The input concepts (shown in boldface fonts) are ordered in a specific manner in the produced sentence such as to create a commonsense bearing sentence.

Although neural generation systems produce fluent texts when compared to template-based methods, they fall short in fluency and faithfulness to the input and do not allow control over the output structure (Puzikov and Gurevych, 2018). Similar observations are made by prior work on GCR, where the input ordering of concepts has been reported to influence the quality of the generated sentences (Zhao et al., 2022; Yang et al., 2023). However, the relationship between (a) the ordering of the concepts given as the input to a neural text generation model and (b) the architecture of the underlying LM used in the generator remains unexplored, which is the focus of our study in this paper. Although we consider the concept ordering problem in the context of GCR, we note that it has broader relevance to other tasks in NLP such as multi-document summarisation (Bollegala et al., 2005, 2006, 2012) and textual coherence modelling (Barzilay and Lapata, 2005)

We evaluate the quality of the sentences generated by five commonsense generation LMs: `BERT-gen` (Bao et al., 2020), `BART-base` (Lewis et al., 2019), `T5-base` (Raffel et al., 2019), `BART-large` (Lewis et al., 2019) and `T5-large` (Raffel et al., 2019), where the input concepts are ordered following three different strategies as described in § 3.2. We use seven evaluation metrics to compare the generated sentences against human-written sentences in CommonGen. Specifically, we fine-tune each LM on the train

[1]Code: https://github.com/TianhuiZhang/concept_ordering

Proceedings of the 13th International Joint Conference on Natural Language Processing and the 3rd Conference of the Asia-Pacific Chapter of the Association for Computational Linguistics (Volume 2: Short Papers), pages 10–19
November 1–4, 2023.

sentences in CommonGen dataset using next token prediction as the training objective.

We find `BART-large` to consistently outperform the other LMs across several evaluation metrics when fine-tuned using the ordering of concepts as they appear in CommonGen training data. To further compare the concept ordering in the model-generated sentence against the human-generated sentence for the same set of concepts, we use the Kendall rank correlation coefficient (i.e., Kendall's τ) as an evaluation metric. We find that there exists only a weak correlation ($\tau = 0.328$) between the ordering of concepts shown to the human annotators and the ordering in which those concepts appear in the sentences written by those annotators. This indicates that human annotators significantly reorder the input concepts when writing sentences that convey commonsense relationships among given concepts. Interestingly, all the generator models we compare in this paper are able to produce better quality sentences when they are presented with the input concepts in the same ordering as ordered in the sentences.

2 Related Work

Concept Ordering. Concept Ordering aims to reorder the given concepts in a sequence according to their importance and inner relevance. Recent work by Ou et al. (2022) highlighted the effectiveness of pre-trained language models, such as BART (Lewis et al., 2019), in tasks related to concept ordering. Huang et al. (2023) fine-tune the LM to find the most complementary concepts to the given one. Hoyle et al. (2021) and (Zhao et al., 2022) show that suitable concept ordering could increase the quality of the generated sentences. In this work, we aim to explore the relation between the concept ordering and different LMs, assessing their performance in the GCR task.

Generative Commonsense Reasoning. Recently, a series of works have been proposed to evaluate the commonsense reasoning quality of the model's generation. One strand of research leverages these generations as the external commonsense explanation (Chen et al., 2023) or chain-of-thought (Zhang et al., 2023), aiding models in various tasks, including question answering. Another approach compares the generation with the references, examining if the model could write as natural as human, such as CommonGen (Lin et al., 2020) and ROCStories (Mostafazadeh et al., 2016). Liu et al. (2021) and Liu et al. (2022) incorporate external knowledge into pre-trained LMs to enrich the generation information.

Text Generation. Prior work on text generation from structured data such as RDF has shown that the ordering in which a set of entities shown to neural text generation models significantly influences the quality of the generated text (Moryossef et al., 2019; Zhao et al., 2020). Unlike template-based generation methods (Reiter and Dale, 2000; Gatt and Krahmer, 2018), neural text generation methods such as Seq2Seq (Sutskever et al., 2014) models perform *text planning* (how to order the inputs) as well as *plan realisation* (how to verbalise the plan) as a single end-to-end task (Gardent et al., 2017).

3 Methods

3.1 Task definition

Given a set $\mathcal{X} = \{x_1, x_2, \ldots, x_m\}$ of lemmatised tokens representing concepts x_i, the goal of the GCR task is to generate a natural and grammatically correct sentence $\boldsymbol{y} = y_1, y_2, \ldots, y_n$, with tokens (or sub-tokens) y_j. Note that $\mathcal{X}$ is an *unordered* set of concepts, while the tokens in $\boldsymbol{y}$ are ordered. We must use *all* concepts in $\mathcal{X}$ when generating $\boldsymbol{y}$. However, we are allowed to use different morphological forms (inflections) of the concepts for this purpose. Typically in CommonGen dataset ca. $m = 5$, whereas n is determined by the generator model used to produce $\boldsymbol{y}$. Given a set of concepts $\mathcal{X}$, there exists $m!$ number of possible ordering of concepts.

Let us denote one such ordering by $\boldsymbol{x} = x_1, x_2, \ldots, x_m$. Given $\boldsymbol{x}$, a generator parameterised by $\boldsymbol{\theta}$ produces the output sequence $\boldsymbol{y} = y_1, y_2, \ldots y_n$ according to the generation probabilities given by (1).

$$p(\boldsymbol{y}|\boldsymbol{x};\boldsymbol{\theta}) = \prod_{i=2}^{n} p(y_i|y_{1:i-1}, \boldsymbol{x};\boldsymbol{\theta}) \quad (1)$$

We generate sentences $\boldsymbol{y}$ using different pre-trained generators for the same set of concepts $\mathcal{X}$, ordered using different strategies as described in § 3.2.

3.2 Concept Ordering Strategies

We name the ordering of input concepts in a train/test instance in CommonGen as the **Original** ordering. We propose three different strategies to re-order the Original ordering for the purpose of fine-tuning LMs using the CommonGen training instances. In **Random** ordering, the concepts in the input set are randomly ordered. The **Example** ordering considers the ordering of concepts as they appear in a human-written example sentence in the CommonGen train dataset.[2] However, this concept ordering information is not available at test time, we thus use Random Ordering of input concept sets at test time even for the LMs fine-tuned using the Example Ordering.

We induce a **Probabilistic** ordering among the concepts in a given set using transition probabilities $p(x_j|x_i)$ for ordering the concept x_j after x_i because we want to find a method that could be used both at training and test times and do not extract the concept ordering from pre-trained models' outputs. Therefore, inspired by Glove word embeddings (Pennington et al., 2014), which use the co-occurrence information between words, we use the co-occurrence frequency of each concept pair inside the paths of the ConceptNet to determine the ordering in a given concept set. Specifically, we first perform random walks over the ConceptNet graph starting from vertices that appear in the CommonGen train sentences, limiting to a maximum path length of five concepts. Next, we count the number of paths, $\#(x_i \rightarrow x_j)$, where x_i appears before x_j. The transition probabilities are estimated from the path counts as in (2).

$$p(x_j|x_i) = \frac{\#(x_i \rightarrow x_j)}{\#(x_i \rightarrow x_j) + \#(x_j \rightarrow x_i)} \quad (2)$$

Finally, the probability of generating an ordering $\boldsymbol{x} = x_1, x_2, \ldots, x_m$ is computed assuming a first-order Markov chain such that $p(\boldsymbol{x}) = \prod_{i=2}^{m} p(x_i|x_{i-1})$. The **Probabilistic** ordering strategy enables us to incorporate external knowledge from ConceptNet for the purpose of determining the ordering of input concepts. Moreover, unlike the **Example** ordering, **Probabilistic** ordering can be used both at training and test times.

4 Experiments

4.1 Experiments setting

Dataset: Our experiments are conducted on the CommonGen dataset (Lin et al., 2020), which contains 3.5K distinct concept sets (32651/993/1497) with 67389/4018/6042 human written sentences in the training/development/test splits. Each instance contains ca. 3-5 input concepts with multiple human-written reference sentences.

Evaluation Metrics: We conduct two types of evaluations. First, to evaluate the quality of the generated sentences, we employ the following generation evaluation metrics: BLEU (Papineni et al., 2002), , ROUGE (Lin, 2004), METEOR (Banerjee and Lavie, 2005), CIDEr (Vedantam et al., 2015) and SPICE (Anderson et al., 2016). We report the Coverage of concepts (Lin et al., 2020), which is defined as the average percentage of input concepts that are present in the generated sentences. Second, we evaluate the ordering of the concepts produced by different LMs (in the order that they appear in the generated sentences) by comparing that to the ordering in human-written test example sentences using the Kendall rank correlation coefficient ($\tau \in [-1, 1]$). A higher τ indicates a closer correlation between a concept ordering and their order observed in reference sentences. If there are multiple human-written sentences with different orderings for the same input concept set, we take the highest τ over all of the orderings.

4.2 Results

Main Results: We use each concept ordering method to fine-tune five LMs: BERT-Gen (Bao et al., 2020), T5-base/large (Raffel et al., 2019), and BART-base/large (Lewis et al., 2019). Implementation details and hyperparameters can be found in Appendix C. To assess the effectiveness of the concept set ordering strategies, we compare their performance against two types of prior methods. The first uses the **Original** ordering specified in CommonGen (Lin et al., 2020) to fine-tune LMs. The second set includes models that incorporate external knowledge, such as KG-BART (Liu et al., 2021) and EKI-BARTD_{out} (Fan et al., 2020), as well as models that improve performance through pre-training tasks, such as CALM (Zhou et al., 2021), NeuroLogic (Lu et al., 2021), and the [MASK] (Yang et al., 2023).

As shown in Table 1, both **Probabilistic** and **Example** ordering outperform the **Original** Ordering presented in CommonGen (Lin et al., 2020). This shows that refining the ordering strategy for input concepts could enhance an LM's performance in commonsense generation. Moreover, **Example**

[2] As detailed in Appendix A, in our preliminary experiments, we evaluated three different input formats for a concept ordering: (a) space delimited, (b) comma delimited, and (c) space delimited with a special end-of-ordering token (i.e., [ORDERING]). We found the input format method (c) to perform slightly better than the other two, albeit no significant improvements were observed.

	Model	BLEU3	BLEU4	ROUGE-2	ROUGE-L	METEOR	CIDEr	SPICE	Coverage
Original Ordering (Lin et al., 2020)	BERT-Gen	30.4	21.1	18.1	40.5	27.3	12.5	27.3	86.1
	T5-base	26.0	16.4	14.6	34.6	23.0	9.2	22.0	76.7
	BART-large	36.3	26.3	*22.2*	42.0	*30.9*	13.9	30.6	*97.4*
	T5-large	*39.0*	*28.6*	22.0	*43.0*	30.1	*15.0*	*31.6*	95.3
Random ordering	BERT-Gen	30.5	21.1	18.0	40.1	27.4	12.6	27.4	86.5
	BART-base	36.0	26.6	22.0	43.3	28.8	13.9	28.5	92.0
	T5-base	37.7	26.9	20.9	43.2	30.2	15.1	31.2	94.2
	BART-large	*42.4*	*31.8*	*23.8*	44.7	*32.8*	*16.6*	*32.3*	*98.8*
	T5-large	40.6	30.0	23.1	*44.9*	31.5	15.9	32.1	97.6
Probabilistic ordering	BERT-Gen	29.1	19.9	16.9	38.6	26.7	12.2	26.7	85.7
	BART-base	33.5	23.8	20.4	41.2	28.0	13.4	27.8	92.6
	T5-base	37.6	26.8	20.5	42.4	30.6	15.1	31.1	96.4
	BART-large	38.5	28.0	21.8	42.4	*31.7*	15.4	32.2	*98.8*
	T5-large	*40.8*	*29.8*	*22.2*	*43.9*	31.6	*16.2*	*32.4*	95.7
Example ordering	BERT-Gen	33.0	23.6	19.3	41.8	28.9	13.7	28.8	93.3
	BART-base	36.0	26.8	22.7	44.4	29.3	14.7	29.1	97.5
	T5-base	40.0	30.0	22.7	45.0	31.3	16.0	32.3	97.6
	BART-large	***44.3***	***33.8***	***24.5***	***45.6***	***32.8***	***17.2***	33.1	***99.1***
	T5-large	43.4	32.7	23.8	45.6	32.3	16.9	***33.5***	98.0
Other Prior Methods	KG-BART	42.1	30.9	23.4	44.5	32.9	17.5	32.7	98.7
	EKI-BARTD_{out}	42.9	26.3	24.4	45.4	32.0	16.8	32.5	-
	CALM	-	29.5	-	-	31.9	15.6	33.2	-
	NeuroLogic	41.3	36	-	44.7	31.0	15.9	31.1	-
	[MASK]	43.3	32.5	24.2	44.9	32.5	17.1	32.8	-

Table 1: Evaluating the quality of the generated sentences on CommonGen test instances. The input concept sets are ordered using the three strategies described in § 3.2 during fine-tuning different LMs. Best performing LM fine-tuned with each ordering strategy is shown in italics, while the overall best is shown in bold.

ordering reports the best performance for all five LMs, even outperforming prior methods that use pre-training tasks or external resources.

Ordering	τ	BLEU4	ROUGE-L	METEOR	CIDEr	SPICE
Original	0.328	19.0	36.4	29.0	12.9	27.7
Random	0.327	18.9	36.2	29.0	12.7	27.7
Probabilistic	0.402	20.9	37.9	29.6	13.4	29.1
BERT-Gen	0.595	29.0	43.1	31.4	16.0	31.3
BART-base	0.648	31.5	44.2	31.9	16.6	32.1
T5-base	0.627	30.3	43.9	31.9	16.4	32.0
BART-large	**0.697**	**33.4**	**45.5**	**32.7**	**17.3**	**33.0**
T5-large	0.696	32.9	45.2	32.6	17.0	32.7
Reference	1	35.3	57.4	33.3	18.1	33.5

Table 2: Kendall's τ between the reference ordering and the concept orderings produced using different methods: Lines 2-4 show Original, Random and Probabilistic orderings (§ 3.2), Lines 5-9 show the orderings of concepts as they appear in the sentences generated using LMs fine-tuned on CommonGen, and Line 10 is the Reference ordering (i.e., ordering of the concepts in human-written CommonGen test sentences).

Effect of concept ordering: The ordering of concepts as they appear in the human-written CommonGen test sentences (here onwards referred to as the **Reference** ordering) can be considered as a gold standard for concept ordering. To evaluate the level of re-ordering of input concepts conducted by an LM, we compare the ordering of concepts in a sentence generated using an LM against their **Reference** ordering using the Kendall's τ. Specifically, we first fine-tune each LM using the concept sets as ordered in the CommonGen train instances (i.e., **Original** ordering). Next, we present each fine-tuned LM the concept sets in CommonGen test instances in their **Original** ordering and generate a sentence containing all of the input concepts. Finally, we compare the ordering of the concepts in the generated sentence against their **Reference** ordering using τ. The reference sentences in the CommonGen dataset are written by human annotators given the shuffled concepts. Therefore, we think it could be considered as a "golden" ordering of input concepts. To further evaluate the correlation between the ordering of input concepts and the quality of the sentences generated by an LM, we use `BART-large` fine-tuned with **Example** ordering as a sentence generator, where we provide it a set of concepts ordered using different methods.

As seen from Table 2, among the three concept ordering strategies described in § 3.2, the **Probabilistic** ordering reports the highest τ value. In particular, **Original** has a low τ value, comparable to **Random** ordering, indicating that human annotators had to significantly re-order the concept sets shown to them when writing natural sentences.

concept words	throw daughter stream rock daddy
Reference	Daddy and daughter throwing rocks into stream
Turbo(zero shot)	As we hiked beside the stream, my daughter asked if she could throw a rock in the water, but I reminded her that it was too dangerous and daddy
Babbage(Original ordering)	little girl throwing a tantrum in the park with her father and sister by the stream and crying because she did not get a toy in the stream.
Curie(Original ordering)	mother throwing her daughter in the stream near the rocks with daddy
Babbage(Example ordering)	A father and daughter are throwing rocks into a stream.
Curie(Example ordering)	daddy and daughter throwing rocks into a stream
concept words	dog throw frisbee catch
Reference	A man throws away his dog's favorite frisbee expecting him to catch it in the air.
Turbo(zero shot)	The dog loves to play fetch and is always ready to catch the frisbee when it's thrown.
Babbage(Original ordering)	A dog is throwing a frisbee.
Curie(Original ordering)	A dog is throwing a frisbee and catching it.
Babbage(Example ordering)	A dog catching a frisbee and throwing it.
Curie(Example ordering)	A dog catching a frisbee thrown by a man.
concept words	hang squeeze shut head eye
Reference	Hanging her head, someone squeezes her eyes shut.
Turbo(zero shot)	I tried to hang the picture but couldn't do it with just one hand, so I had to squeeze my eyes shut and use both hands to get it done
Babbage(Original ordering)	Someone grabs someone by the eyes and squeezes them shut, then drags him away.
Curie(Original ordering)	A woman is hanging upside down and squeezing her legs shut, then she opens her eyes.
Babbage(Example ordering)	Someone squeezes his eyes shut and hangs his head.
Curie(Example ordering)	Someone squeezes his eyes shut and hangs his head.
concept words	mirror gear picture hold take
Reference	The man holds the gear and uses the picture taken by the mirror.
Turbo(zero shot)	She carefully held the picture up to the mirror to take a closer look at the intricate gear design.
Babbage(Original ordering)	A picture of a man in a space suit, holding a mirror, and taking off his gear.
Curie(Original ordering)	The mirror has gears in it and a picture of a train engine held up.
Babbage(Example ordering)	A man is holding on to a railing to take a picture of his gear and mirror.
Curie(Example ordering)	A man is holding a camera and taking a picture of himself in the mirror.

Table 3: Generated examples by different LLMs

Interestingly, all five LMs fine-tuned with the **Example** ordering strategy outperform those three strategies, suggesting that the sentences carry useful contextual clues for determining the ordering of concepts that are exploited by the LMs. We find that the extracted concept ordering generated by BART-large model outperforms that generated by other pre-trained models. It is consistent with the conclusions of Ou et al. (2022) that a large amount of dependency structure knowledge exists in BART. Moreover, we see that τ values closely aligns with other automatic evaluation metrics, indicating that concept ordering with a higher τ results in high quality sentence generations. Overall, these results suggest that if the concept orderings more closely align with the orderings found in the dataset reference sentences, the Example Ordering trained model could generate superior sentences, leveraging the inherent commonsense knowledge embedded within the pre-trained models.

4.3 Large Language Model Scenario

Large Language Models (LLMs) have shown impressive performance in complex reasoning compared to the smaller size models (Brown et al., 2020; Thoppilan et al., 2022). To investigate their effectiveness for concept ordering, we use the GPT-3 and GPT-3.5 (Brown et al., 2020) as LLMs and use a prompt-based instruction (see Appendix B for the details of the prompts) to induce an ordering among a given set of concepts. Due to the space limitations we show the results in the Appendix Table 4. We find that the Example Ordering outperforms the unordered inputs, indicating that concept ordering is also important to the LLMs. Moreover, from the generated sentences (shown in Table 3) we find that the Example ordering improves their quality as well as the concept coverage. Interestingly however, the best results obtained using LLMs with prompts are worse than that compared to the fine-tuned `BART-large`, which indicates importance of fine-tuning on CommonGen.

5 Conclusion

We examined the impact of concept ordering on the quality of generated sentences in GCR using multiple LMs. We find that ordering the input concepts can improve performance, and all fine-tuned LMs generate better quality sentences when the input concepts were presented in an order consistent with that found in human-written sentences.

6 Limitations

In this work, we limited our investigation to the generation of English sentences and to a finite set of pre-trained language models (PLMs). This limitation was largely due to the nature of the CommonGen dataset, the only publicly available dataset we found for concept-to-sentence tasks, which is primarily English-centric. Therefore, our evaluation of the generation quality was limited to English, which is a morphologically limited language. Different languages have different grammars and sentence structures, but the automatic evaluation metrics such as BLEU (Papineni et al., 2002), ROUGE (Lin, 2004) and CIDEr (Vedantam et al., 2015) could also be used for other languages. Therefore, we consider it to be an important next step to evaluate the concept ordering strategies described in this work on languages other than English.

Furthermore, we focus only on the experiments around concept ordering in the LLM scenario. However, as reported in much prior work, the commonsense knowledge inside the LLMs could be efficiently exploited by intermediate reasoning steps and designed prompts (Wei et al., 2022; Zhang et al., 2023). We utilised identical prompts for each backbone LLM and did not investigate the potential influence of prompt variations. we observed that some sentences generated by LLMs contradict commonsense. Therefore, generative commonsense reasoning tasks remain a challenge for LLMs. Given the scope of the current paper, research on prompt design and encoding concept ordering into intermediate steps will be pursued in future work.

Given a set of concepts, it is possible to write multiple natural sentences that arrange the input concepts in different orders. However, in the CommonGen dataset only a small number of human-written sentences are available for a given concept set, which does not cover all possible orderings. Therefore, the Kendall's τ values reported in this paper must be taken as a lower bound on the agreement with a human determining the ordering of concepts in a sentence. Moreover, we it is important to consider other types of rank evaluation metrics in addition to Kendall's τ for future evaluations.

7 Ethical Considerations

While we conducted our research primarily on the CommonGen dataset, which to the best of our knowledge does not present any explicit ethical issues, it is essential to acknowledge the potential for social biases in the LMs (Blodgett et al., 2021). One of the pre-trained language models we used in our experiments, BART are significantly prone to prediction errors related to gender bias (Sharma et al., 2021) and we are not evaluating for the biases in the generated sentences here which should be done before LMs are deployed in the downstream NLP applications. Given that we are fine-tuning LMs on the CommonGen dataset, some social biases could get amplified during this fine-tuning process. The predicted sentences are possibly influenced by such biases. It is still an open question for how to effectively mitigate these biases, particularly in the context of generative commonsense reasoning tasks.

References

Peter Anderson, Basura Fernando, Mark Johnson, and Stephen Gould. 2016. Spice: Semantic propositional image caption evaluation. In *Computer Vision–ECCV 2016: 14th European Conference, Amsterdam, The Netherlands, October 11-14, 2016, Proceedings, Part V 14*. Springer, pages 382–398.

Satanjeev Banerjee and Alon Lavie. 2005. Meteor: An automatic metric for mt evaluation with improved correlation with human judgments. In *Proceedings of the acl workshop on intrinsic and extrinsic evaluation measures for machine translation and/or summarization*. pages 65–72.

Hangbo Bao, Li Dong, Furu Wei, Wenhui Wang, Nan Yang, Xiaodong Liu, Yu Wang, Jianfeng Gao, Songhao Piao, Ming Zhou, et al. 2020. Unilmv2: Pseudo-masked language models for unified language model pre-training. In *International conference on machine learning*. PMLR, pages 642–652.

Regina Barzilay and Mirella Lapata. 2005. Modeling local coherence: An entity-based approach. In *Proceedings of the 43rd Annual Meeting of the Association for Computational Linguistics (ACL'05)*. Association for Computational Linguistics, Ann Arbor, Michigan, pages 141–148. https://doi.org/10.3115/1219840.1219858.

Su Lin Blodgett, Gilsinia Lopez, Alexandra Olteanu, Robert Sim, and Hanna Wallach. 2021. Stereotyping norwegian salmon: An inventory of pitfalls in fairness benchmark datasets. In *Proceedings of the 59th Annual Meeting of the Association for Computational Linguistics and the 11th International Joint Conference on Natural Language Processing (Volume 1: Long Papers)*. pages 1004–1015.

Danushka Bollegala, Naoaki Okazaki, and Mitsuru Ishizuka. 2005. A machine learning approach to sentence ordering for multidocument summarization and its evaluation. In *Second International Joint Conference on Natural Language Processing: Full Papers*. https://doi.org/10.1007/11562214_55.

Danushka Bollegala, Naoaki Okazaki, and Mitsuru Ishizuka. 2006. A bottom-up approach to sentence ordering for multi-document summarization.

In *Proceedings of the 21st International Conference on Computational Linguistics and 44th Annual Meeting of the Association for Computational Linguistics*. Association for Computational Linguistics, Sydney, Australia, pages 385–392. https://doi.org/10.3115/1220175.1220224.

Danushka Bollegala, Naoaki Okazaki, and Mitsuru Ishizuka. 2012. A preference learning approach to sentence ordering for multi-document summarization. *Information Sciences* 217:78 – 95.

Tom Brown, Benjamin Mann, Nick Ryder, Melanie Subbiah, Jared D Kaplan, Prafulla Dhariwal, Arvind Neelakantan, Pranav Shyam, Girish Sastry, Amanda Askell, et al. 2020. Language models are few-shot learners. *Advances in neural information processing systems* 33:1877–1901.

Qianglong Chen, Guohai Xu, Ming Yan, Ji Zhang, Fei Huang, Luo Si, and Yin Zhang. 2023. Distinguish before answer: Generating contrastive explanation as knowledge for commonsense question answering. In *Findings of the Association for Computational Linguistics: ACL 2023*. Association for Computational Linguistics, Toronto, Canada, pages 13207–13224. https://doi.org/10.18653/v1/2023.findings-acl.835.

Zhihao Fan, Yeyun Gong, Zhongyu Wei, Siyuan Wang, Yameng Huang, Jian Jiao, Xuan-Jing Huang, Nan Duan, and Ruofei Zhang. 2020. An enhanced knowledge injection model for commonsense generation. In *Proceedings of the 28th International Conference on Computational Linguistics*. pages 2014–2025.

Claire Gardent, Anastasia Shimorina, Shashi Narayan, and Laura Perez-Beltrachini. 2017. The WebNLG challenge: Generating text from RDF data. In *Proceedings of the 10th International Conference on Natural Language Generation*. Association for Computational Linguistics, Santiago de Compostela, Spain, pages 124–133.

Albert Gatt and Emiel Krahmer. 2018. Survey of the state of the art in natural language generation: Core tasks, applications and evaluation. *J. Artif. Int. Res.* 61(1):65–170.

Bernal Jiménez Gutiérrez, Nikolas McNeal, Clay Washington, You Chen, Lang Li, Huan Sun, and Yu Su. 2022. Thinking about gpt-3 in-context learning for biomedical ie? think again. *arXiv preprint arXiv:2203.08410* .

Alexander Miserlis Hoyle, Ana Marasović, and Noah A Smith. 2021. Promoting graph awareness in linearized graph-to-text generation. In *Findings of the Association for Computational Linguistics: ACL-IJCNLP 2021*. pages 944–956.

Jie Huang, Yifan Gao, Zheng Li, Jingfeng Yang, Yangqiu Song, Chao Zhang, Zining Zhu, Haoming Jiang, Kevin Chen-Chuan Chang, and Bing Yin. 2023. Ccgen: Explainable complementary concept generation in e-commerce. *arXiv preprint arXiv:2305.11480* .

Diederik P. Kingma and Jimmy Ba. 2015. Adam: A method for stochastic optimization. In Yoshua Bengio and Yann LeCun, editors, *3rd International Conference on Learning Representations, ICLR 2015, San Diego, CA, USA, May 7-9, 2015, Conference Track Proceedings*.

Michael Lewis et al. 2019. Bart: Denoising sequence-to-sequence pre-training for natural language generation, translation, and comprehension. *meeting of the association for computational linguistics* .

Bill Yuchen Lin, Wangchunshu Zhou, Ming Shen, Pei Zhou, Chandra Bhagavatula, Yejin Choi, and Xiang Ren. 2020. CommonGen: A constrained text generation challenge for generative commonsense reasoning. In *Findings of the Association for Computational Linguistics: EMNLP 2020*. Association for Computational Linguistics, Online, pages 1823–1840.

Chin-Yew Lin. 2004. Rouge: A package for automatic evaluation of summaries. In *Text summarization branches out*. pages 74–81.

Xin Liu, Dayiheng Liu, Baosong Yang, Haibo Zhang, Junwei Ding, Wenqing Yao, Weihua Luo, Haiying Zhang, and Jinsong Su. 2022. Kgr4: Retrieval, retrospect, refine and rethink for commonsense generation. In *Proceedings of the AAAI Conference on Artificial Intelligence*. volume 36, pages 11029–11037.

Ye Liu, Yao Wan, Lifang He, Hao Peng, and Philip S Yu. 2021. Kg-bart: Knowledge graph-augmented bart for generative commonsense reasoning. In *Proceedings of the AAAI Conference on Artificial Intelligence*. volume 35, pages 6418–6425.

Ximing Lu, Peter West, Rowan Zellers, Ronan Le Bras, Chandra Bhagavatula, and Yejin Choi. 2021. Neurologic decoding:(un) supervised neural text generation with predicate logic constraints. In *Proceedings of the 2021 Conference of the North American Chapter of the Association for Computational Linguistics: Human Language Technologies*. pages 4288–4299.

Amit Moryossef, Yoav Goldberg, and Ido Dagan. 2019. Step-by-step: Separating planning from realization in neural data-to-text generation. In *Proceedings of the 2019 Conference of the North American Chapter of the Association for Computational Linguistics: Human Language Technologies, Volume 1 (Long and Short Papers)*. Association for Computational Linguistics, Minneapolis, Minnesota, pages 2267–2277.

Nasrin Mostafazadeh, Nathanael Chambers, Xiaodong He, Devi Parikh, Dhruv Batra, Lucy Vanderwende, Pushmeet Kohli, and James Allen. 2016. A corpus and cloze evaluation for deeper understanding of commonsense stories. In *Proceedings of the 2016 Conference of the North American Chapter of the Association for Computational Linguistics: Human Language Technologies*. pages 839–849.

Zebin Ou, Meishan Zhang, and Yue Zhang. 2022. On the role of pre-trained language models in word ordering: A case study with bart. In *Proceedings of the 29th International Conference on Computational Linguistics*. pages 6516–6529.

Kishore Papineni, Salim Roukos, Todd Ward, and Wei-Jing Zhu. 2002. Bleu: a method for automatic evaluation of machine translation. In *Proceedings of the 40th annual meeting of the Association for Computational Linguistics*. pages 311–318.

Jeffrey Pennington, Richard Socher, and Christopher D Manning. 2014. Glove: Global vectors for word representation. In *Proceedings of the 2014 conference on empirical methods in natural language processing (EMNLP)*. pages 1532–1543.

Yevgeniy Puzikov and Iryna Gurevych. 2018. E2E NLG challenge: Neural models vs. templates. In *Proceedings of the 11th International Conference on Natural Language Generation*. Association for Computational Linguistics, Tilburg University, The Netherlands, pages 463–471.

Colin Raffel, Noam Shazeer, Adam Roberts, Katherine Lee, Sharan Narang, Michael Matena, Yanqi Zhou, Wei Li, and Peter J. Liu. 2019. Exploring the limits of transfer learning with a unified text-to-text transformer. *Journal of Machine Learning Research* .

Ehud Reiter and Robert Dale. 2000. *Building Natural Language Generation Systems*. Cambridge University Press.

Shanya Sharma, Manan Dey, and Koustuv Sinha. 2021. Evaluating gender bias in natural language inference. https://openreview.net/forum?id=bnuU0PzXl0-.

Ilya Sutskever, Oriol Vinyals, and Quoc V. Le. 2014. Sequence to sequence learning with neural networks. In *NIPS'14*.

Romal Thoppilan, Daniel De Freitas, Jamie Hall, Noam Shazeer, Apoorv Kulshreshtha, Heng-Tze Cheng, Alicia Jin, Taylor Bos, Leslie Baker, Yu Du, et al. 2022. Lamda: Language models for dialog applications. *arXiv preprint arXiv:2201.08239* .

Ramakrishna Vedantam, C Lawrence Zitnick, and Devi Parikh. 2015. Cider: Consensus-based image description evaluation. In *Proceedings of the IEEE conference on computer vision and pattern recognition*. pages 4566–4575.

Jason Wei, Xuezhi Wang, Dale Schuurmans, Maarten Bosma, Fei Xia, Ed H Chi, Quoc V Le, Denny Zhou, et al. 2022. Chain-of-thought prompting elicits reasoning in large language models. In *Advances in Neural Information Processing Systems*.

Thomas Wolf, Lysandre Debut, Victor Sanh, Julien Chaumond, Clement Delangue, Anthony Moi, Pierric Cistac, Tim Rault, Rémi Louf, Morgan Funtowicz, Joe Davison, Sam Shleifer, Patrick von Platen, Clara Ma, Yacine Jernite, Julien Plu, Canwen Xu, Teven Le Scao, Sylvain Gugger, Mariama Drame, Quentin Lhoest, and Alexander M. Rush. 2020. Transformers: State-of-the-art natural language processing. In *Proceedings of the 2020 Conference on Empirical Methods in Natural Language Processing: System Demonstrations*. Association for Computational Linguistics, Online, pages 38–45. https://www.aclweb.org/anthology/2020.emnlp-demos.6.

Haoran Yang, Yan Wang, Piji Li, Wei Bi, Wai Lam, and Chen Xu. 2023. Bridging the gap between pretraining and fine-tuning for commonsense generation. In *Findings of the Association for Computational Linguistics: EACL 2023*. pages 376–383.

Zhuosheng Zhang, Aston Zhang, Mu Li, Hai Zhao, George Karypis, and Alex Smola. 2023. Multimodal chain-of-thought reasoning in language models. *arXiv preprint arXiv:2302.00923* .

Chao Zhao, Faeze Brahman, Tenghao Huang, and Snigdha Chaturvedi. 2022. Revisiting generative commonsense reasoning: A pre-ordering approach. In *Findings of the Association for Computational Linguistics: NAACL 2022*. Association for Computational Linguistics, Seattle, United States, pages 1709–1718. https://doi.org/10.18653/v1/2022.findings-naacl.129.

Chao Zhao, Marilyn Walker, and Snigdha Chaturvedi. 2020. Bridging the structural gap between encoding and decoding for data-to-text generation. In *Proceedings of the 58th Annual Meeting of the Association for Computational Linguistics*. Association for Computational Linguistics, Online, pages 2481–2491.

Wangchunshu Zhou, Dong-Ho Lee, Ravi Kiran Selvam, Seyeon Lee, and Xiang Ren. 2021. Pre-training text-to-text transformers for concept-centric common sense. In *International Conference on Learning Representations*. https://openreview.net/forum?id=3k20LAiHYL2.

Supplementary Appendix

A Different Input Formats for Example Ordering

We conducted an evaluation to examine the impact of input formats on the quality of generation. We designed three types of input formats, given a concept set: 1) the ordered concepts are concatenated together, 2) the ordered concepts are concatenated together and separated (delimitted) by commas, and 3) the unordered concepts are concatenated with the ordered concepts and denoted by a special "*[ORDERING]*" tokens. An example using the concept set *ski*, *mountain*, *skier*, is provided in Table 5. As shown in Table 6, the performance of the generated sentences does not change significantly

	Parameters	BLEU4	ROUGE-L	METEOR	CIDEr	SPICE
Turbo(zero shot)	135B	13.9	33.5	27.2	8.7	24.0
Babbage (Original)	6.7B	19.7	37.7	27.1	12.0	26.7
Curie(Original)	13B	13.5	32.6	26	10.0	24.6
Babbage (Example)	6.7B	23.6	41.0	29.2	13.6	29.2
Curie (Example)	13B	25.5	41.9	30.0	14.4	30.1

Table 4: Evaluation of the effect of different concept ordering strategies on the LLMs. The results show that a good concept ordering strategy could also help the quality of large model generation.

with the different input formatting methods. However, the best performance among the three input formatting methods is achieved when the concepts are concatenated with the ordered concepts around tokens. This may be attributed to the fact that, with the tokens and ordered concepts, a model might better comprehend the ordering task and use the syntactic knowledge embedded in the pre-trained models (Ou et al., 2022).

Format	Example
w/o Comma	skier ski mountain
Comma	skier, ski, mountain
Token	ski mountain skier [ORDERING]
	skier ski mountain [ORDERING]

Table 5: Three different input formats given a concept set {*ski*, *mountain*, *skier*}

Concept set	BLEU4	ROUGE-L	METEOR	CIDEr	SPICE
w/o Comma	33.4	45.5	32.6	17.1	32.8
Comma	32.5	45	32.4	16.8	32.6
Token	33.8	45.6	32.8	17.2	33.1

Table 6: The generated evaluation of different inputs formats.

B Concept Ordering on LLMs

We also conducted concept ordering experiments using the CommonGen dataset on LLMs containing more than one billion parameters. Specifically, we selected GPT3 models (Babbage and Curie) and GPT3.5 Turbo from OpenAI as our backbone models. Since the Turbo model does not support fine-tuning, it was evaluated solely in a zero-shot setting. We evaluated the quality of the generated outputs using both the Original ordering and Example ordering strategies on the Babbage and Curie models.

As shown in Table 4, the Example Ordering strategy also enhanced the performance of LLMs on the CommonGen dataset task. However, we observed that the three LLMs underperform compared against the smaller fine-tuned LMs. We notice that this problem also exists in other NLP tasks (Brown et al., 2020; Gutiérrez et al., 2022). Therefore, we examined some sentences generated by these LLMs as presented in Table 3. Under the zero-shot setting, Turbo was capable of generating more complex sentences than those provided in the references, and these sentences were consistent with commonsense. When we try to use Example Ordering Strategy for the Turbo model with the prompt *Given a concept list: [concepts], please generate a sentence that aligns the ordering of the concepts:*, we find that the model could not always follow the concept ordering given even under the few-shot setting.

For the Babbage and Curie models, the Original Ordering strategy often resulted in generated sentences that did not encompass all concepts from the given input set. The Example Ordering strategy ameliorated this issue; however, even when the grammar was correct, some sentences were inconsistent with commonsense (e.g., *A dog catching a Frisbee and throwing it*). We surmise that these issues are the primary reasons why the LLMs did not perform well. As is suggested by OpenAI website, the performance of the model is based on the description given and external content would improve the performance. However, the input of CommonGen only has a single concept set. Potential improvements for the performance of LLMs on such tasks could involve providing more content around the concept set such as description about the relations among the concepts.

C Training Details

We utilised the BERT, BART, and T5 models as implemented in the Transformers library (Wolf et al., 2020). Detailed hyper-parameters are provided in the accompanying bash scripts (submitted as supplementary materials). The primary hyper-parameters were initialised in alignment with the standards set out in the CommonGen paper (Lin et al., 2020). We fine-tuned each model using the ADAM optimiser (Kingma and Ba, 2015). To prevent over-fitting, we adopted an early stopping strategy based on the development set's loss. We train the model with one NVIDIA A6000 GPU and one V100 GPU. Each model could be fine-tuned in less than 6 hours.

The training of the LLMs utilised OpenAI's API.[3] Training a Babbage model incurred a cost of $3 for the CommonGen dataset, while training a Curie model incurred a cost of $14. During model training, each instance would start with the prompt "*Generate a sentence containing all the concepts in the concept set:*" for each concept set and we added a separator " ->" at the end of the prompt. We also use an ending token "/n" at the end of the target sentence.

Models	Random	Probabilistic	Example
BERT-Gen	32*2, 5e-5	32*2, 5e-5	32*2, 5e-5
BART-base	64*4, 3e-5	64*3, 5e-5	64*6, 3e-5
T5-base	64*4, 5e-5	64*3, 5e-5	64*4, 5e-5
BART-large	96*4, 3e-5	64*4, 2e-5	64*4, 3e-5
T5-large	32*4, 2e-5	64*4, 2e-5	64*4, 3e-5
GPT3-babbage	-	-	128, -
GPT3-curie	-	-	128, -

Table 7: Key parameters in experiments. In each cell, the left is the batch size and the right is the learning rate.

[3]https://platform.openai.com/docs/guides

SQUARE: Automatic Question Answering Evaluation using Multiple Positive and Negative References

Matteo Gabburo[1*], **Siddhant Garg**[2], **Rik Koncel Kedziorski**[3†], **Alessandro Moschitti**[2]
[1]University of Trento , [2]Amazon Alexa AI, [3]Kensho Technologies, Inc.
matteo.gabburo@unitn.it
{sidgarg,amosch}@amazon.com
rikka@kensho.com

Abstract

Evaluation of QA systems is very challenging and expensive, with the most reliable approach being human annotations of correctness of answers for questions. Recent works (AVA, BEM) have shown that transformer LM encoder based similarity metrics transfer well for QA evaluation, but they are limited by the usage of a single correct reference answer. We propose a new evaluation metric: SQuArE (Sentence-level QUestion AnsweRing Evaluation), using multiple reference answers (combining multiple correct and incorrect references) for sentence-form QA. We evaluate SQuArE on both sentence-level extractive (Answer Selection) and generative (GenQA) QA systems, across multiple academic and industrial datasets, and show that it outperforms previous baselines and obtains the highest correlation with human annotations.

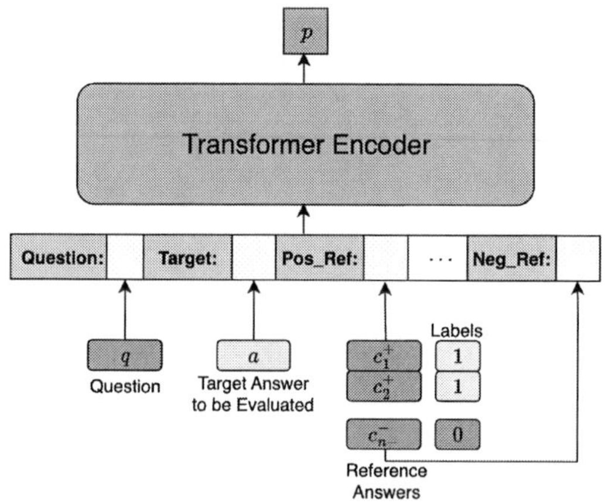

Figure 1: An illustration of SQuArE: an automatic question answering evaluation metric that uses multiple references: positive and negative to evaluate the correctness of a target answer for a particular question.

1 Introduction

Automatic evaluation of Question Answering systems to gauge correctness of an answer for a question is a challenging task. This task is important for preserving a quick velocity in evaluating and development of new QA systems, and creating large high quality training corpora for LLM-based QA systems. The most common approach for this task is to obtain human annotations of correctness of answers for questions, which is slow, expensive, and challenging (annotating complete answer sentences for questions has been shown to achieve poor inter-annotator agreement).

Span extraction (MR) based QA systems are typically evaluated using token matching metrics such as EM (Exact Match) or F1, however, these cannot be extended for evaluating complete sentence-form answers coming from Answer Sentence Selection (AS2) systems (Garg et al., 2020; Di Liello et al., 2022, 2023). Token/segment-level similarity metrics such as EM, F1, BLEU, etc. fail to capture the semantic coherence between entities/concepts of the answer sentence and the question. Recently, AVA (Vu and Moschitti, 2021) and BEM (Bulian et al., 2022) have proposed transformer LM encoder based similarity metrics for sentence-form extractive QA evaluation by encoding the question, target answer (which needs to be evaluated) and a reference answer (which is treated as a gold standard (GS)).

One of the major limitations of AVA/BEM is the use of a single reference answer. There are several types of questions that have multiple diverse correct answers, other questions that have relevant information spread across multiple reference answers, and other ambiguous/under-specified or opinion seeking questions that may have several possible answers (we motivate this with examples in Section 3). Additionally, AVA/BEM only use information from a correct reference answer for evaluating a target answer, but information and semantics from an incorrect reference answer (which are readily available for several datasets) can also help refine the accuracy of the prediction.

[*]Work done as an intern at Amazon Alexa AI
[†]Work completed at Amazon Alexa AI

Proceedings of the 13th International Joint Conference on Natural Language Processing and the 3rd Conference of the Asia-Pacific Chapter of the Association for Computational Linguistics (Volume 2: Short Papers), pages 20–28
November 1–4, 2023.

Motivated by the above shortcomings of AVA/BEM, we propose SQuArE (Sentence-level QUestion AnsweRing Evaluation), a supervised transformer LM encoder based automatic QA evaluation metric that uses multiple reference answers by combining multiple correct and incorrect answers to assign a correctness score for an answer to a question. We evaluate SQuArE on four sentence-level extractive QA datasets, and show that it outperforms previous baselines and achieves the highest correlation with human annotations.

The last few years have seen several research works (Hsu et al., 2021; Muller et al., 2021; Gabburo et al., 2022) transition from extractive sentence-form QA towards generating natural sounding sentence-form answers. This paradigm (termed GenQA) synthesizes information using different pieces of information spread across many relevant candidates (while suppressing any irrelevant information) to improve the answering accuracy and style suitability. AVA/BEM have only been evaluated on extractive QA, and not for GenQA, so it is unclear if a transformer encoder based semantic matching metric will correlate with human annotations on a sentence-form generated answer. We strengthen the generality of SQuArE as a QA evaluation metric by showing that it outperforms the AVA/BEM baselines for GenQA systems in addition to extractive QA systems. We will release the code and trained model checkpoints for SQuArE at `https://github.com/amazon-science/square` for the NLP and QA community to use our automatic QA evaluation metric.

2 Related Work

Automatic Text Similarity Evaluation: Token/N-grams level similarity metrics like BLEU (Papineni et al., 2001) and ROUGE (Lin, 2004) are not suitable for QA evaluation, and have been shown to achieve poor correlation with human judgements (Reiter, 2018; Gabburo et al., 2022). Kusner et al. (2015) propose using a distance function between word embeddings for text similarity. Other research works (Kusner et al., 2015; Clark et al., 2019) have proposed evaluation metrics based on Wasserstein distance. Recent years have seen a number of automatic evaluation metrics being proposed for Neural Machine Translation (MNT) and summarization tasks like BERT-Score (Zhang et al., 2020-02-24), BLEURT (Sellam et al., 2020), COMET (Rei et al., 2020), etc. that use contextual embeddings from transformer encoders. Similar approaches extend for text style (Wegmann and Nguyen, 2021) and summarization (Cao et al., 2020; Zeng et al., 2021).

QA Evaluation: For entity level span-extraction MR tasks, Yang et al. (2018) adapt BLEU, ROUGE for answer comparison, with a focus on "yes-no" and "entity" questions. Si et al. (2021) mine entities from KBs to use them as additional gold answers for MR tasks, our approach shares this intuition of using multiple diverse reference answers for evaluation. Chen et al. (2019) propose a modification of BERTScore for QA by using the question and the paragraph context along with the answer. Empirically however, they demonstrate that for extractive MR tasks, F1 works as a reasonable metric, but this does not transfer well for generative QA. (Min et al., 2021) uses human annotations to evaluate correct answers that are not contained in the GS answer. For sentence-level extractive QA (AS2), AVA (Vu and Moschitti, 2021) and BEM (Bulian et al., 2022) are two recently proposed learned metrics.

3 Methodology

Being a knowledge-intensive task, automatic QA evaluation typically requires leveraging knowledge from external sources to evaluate correctness of answer (e.g., Knowledge Bases, Gold standard reference answers). We can formalize automatic QA evaluation with the notation: $f(q, a, c) \rightarrow p$, where f is the automatic evaluation function applied to question q, target answer a and reference context c, and outputs a correctness score $p \in [0, 1]$.

Previous works (AVA, BEM) show that using a single GS reference answer as the context c achieves higher correlation with human annotations that only using q and a. In this paper, we propose a supervised learned metric SQuArE that enriches the reference context c for QA evaluation using: (i) multiple gold standard references, and (ii) negatively annotated answers as negative references.

Multiple Reference Answers In AVA/ BEM, using a single correct reference limits the evaluation scope of QA system predictions.

- Several types of questions may have multiple and diverse correct answers: for example *"What is a band?"* is correctly answered by both *"A flat, thin strip or loop of material, used as a fastener"* and *"A band is a group of people who perform instrumental and/or vocal music"*

- Knowledge seeking questions may have pieces of relevant information spread across multiple references: for example *"Who is Barack Obama"* can be answered by combining information across multiple answers *"He served as the 44th president of the U.S. from 2009-2017", "He was a member of the Democratic Party, and served as a U.S. senator from 2005-2008"*, etc.
- For ambiguous/under-specified questions that do not have a single correct answer or opinion seeking questions, using a single GS reference answer can be limiting and provide an incorrect evaluation of the answering capability of a QA system. Consider the question *"When is the next world cup"* for which both the answers *"The next FIFA football world cup is in 2026"* and *"The next ICC cricket world cup is in 2023 in India"* are correct as the questions fails to specify the name of the sport (many more possible answers).

Negative Reference Answers An automatic QA evaluation system can use the information and semantics from an incorrect answer to help refine the accuracy of its prediction. Consider the question *"Which movies of Dwayne Johnson released in 2017"* with the positive reference *"Dwayne 'The Rock' Johnson starrer Baywatch premiered in 2017"*. Only using this reference, both the answers *"Baywatch and Jungle Cruise"* and *"The Fate of the Furious and Baywatch"* appear to be equally correct for this question. However when we add in an incorrect reference for the question *"Jungle Cruise is a movie starring the Rock and Emily Blunt that released in 2021"*, the automatic QA evaluation can identify that the second answer is probably more correct than the first one. Several sentence-form extractive QA datasets such as ASNQ (Garg et al., 2020), WikiQA, TREC-QA, etc. have a large number of negatively labeled answer candidates for each question, which can be exploited for automatic evaluation of QA systems for these datasets.

SQuArE Motivated by the above reasons, we modify the context c of automatic evaluation $f(q, a, c) \rightarrow p$ to include a combination of n_+ correct and n_- incorrect reference answers, i.e, $c : c^+ = \{c_1^+, ..., c_{n_+}^+\} \cup c^- = \{c_1^-, ..., c_{n_-}^-\}$. During supervised learning, SQuArE learns to minimize the semantic distance between a correct target answer from the set of correct references c^+ and maximizing the semantic distance from the set of incorrect references c^-. We prefix a prompt (*Pos_Ref / Neg_Ref*) to each reference to indicate the correctness/incorrectness of the reference to the model. Specifically, a (q, a, c^+, c^-) input for SQuArE is encoded as "Question: q Target: a Pos_Ref: c_1^+ $\cdots$ Pos_Ref: $c_{n_+}^+$ Neg_Ref: c_1^- $\cdots$ Neg_Ref: $c_{n_-}^-$ " as illustrated in Figure 1.

The choice of reference answers can create biases in automatic QA evaluation. For a given question, collecting a set of diverse reference answers and ensuring they exhaustively cover all the concepts needed to answer the question is challenging and very expensive. In this paper, we utilize existing annotated answer candidates (both positive and negative) in high-quality labeled datasets as references. Extending automatic QA evaluation to previously unseen questions (without any references) is a challenging open problem in NLP QA.

4 Experiments and Results

4.1 Datasets

WQA Web Question Answers (WQA) is a public dataset (Zhang et al., 2021) containing 149,513 questions, each associated with $\sim$15 answer candidates retrieved from a large-scale web index with human annotations.

WikiQA A small AS2 dataset (Yang et al., 2015) with questions from Bing search, and answers extracted from Wikipedia. We use the most popular clean setting (questions having at least one positive and one negative answer).

TREC-QA A small AS2 dataset (Wang et al., 2007) containing factoid questions. We only retain questions with at least one positive and one negative answer in the development and test sets.

IQAD A large scale Industrial QA Dataset containing non-representative de-identified user questions from a commercial personal assistant. IQAD contains 10k questions, and $\sim$200 answer candidates retrieved for each question using a large scale web index that contains over 100M web documents. Results on IQAD are presented relative to a baseline to comply with company policies.

GenQA-MTURK This dataset is composed of 3k questions from 3 datasets (1k each): MS-MARCO (Bajaj et al., 2018), WikiQA and TREC-QA using GenQA models evaluated in (Hsu et al., 2021; Gabburo et al., 2022). For each question we generate an answer using 8 different GenQA models (details in Appendix B) based on T5-Large. We annotate all the answers of this dataset for their correctness, using MTurk using 5 independent annotations for each QA pair. We use majority voting over the 5

Dataset	Technique	# Refs	Accuracy	AUROC	Correlation
		Answer Sentence Selection (AS2)			
WQA	AVA-TR	1	0.734	0.809	0.716
	AVA-QT	0	0.790	0.851	0.750
	AVA-TQR	1	0.809	0.873	0.771
	SQuArE	5	**0.833**	**0.896**	**0.793**
IQAD	AVA-TR	1	Baseline	Baseline	Baseline
	AVA-QT	0	+1.94%	-0.393%	+0.682%
	AVA-TQR	1	+8.02%	+5.7%	+6.178%
	SQuArE	5	**+22.24%**	**+14.01%**	**+16.062%**
		Answer Generation (GenQA)			
MS-MARCO	AVA-TR	1	0.882	0.768	0.610
	AVA-QT	0	0.882	0.777	0.623
	AVA-TQR	1	0.878	0.790	**0.636**
	SQuArE	5	**0.895**	**0.832**	0.629

Table 1: Results on WQA, IQAD, MS-MARCO measured using Accuracy, Area under the curve and Pearson Correlation with gold labels. Results on IQAD are relative to AVA-TR baseline (due to data being internal). # Refs refers to the total number of reference answers used for the metric.

annotations for each QA pair.

Answer Equivalence (AE): A question answering dataset released by Bulian et al. (2022) where each sample contains a question, a candidate answer (typically short answers), and a positive reference (typically entity-based) carefully selected to avoid the candidate-reference exact match (EM).

4.2 Models and Baselines

We use DeBERTaV3-Large (He et al., 2021) for SQuArE, and compare with three baselines (proposed in AVA/BEM): **QT: Question-Target** that takes input a question and the target answer, **TR: Target-Reference** that takes input a reference GS answer and the target answer, and **TQR: Target-Question-Reference** that takes as input a question, the target answer and a reference GS answer. For our experiments, we set the total number of reference $(n_+)+(n_-)=5$ per question.

We also compare SQuArE against two additional baselines: (i) **BEM** (Bulian et al., 2022), a recently released reference-based automatic evaluation metric (trained on the AE dataset), and (ii) a large language model (**LLM**) based approach using two versions of the Falcon (Almazrouei et al., 2023) model. For fair comparison with the baselines, we perform evaluation in the zero-shot setting for the WikiQA and TrecQA datasets, and after fine-tuning on the AE dataset. For more details on the implementation of these baselines, refer to Appendix A.2.

4.3 Results

We present results comparing SQuArE with the baselines on large datasets (from both extractive QA: AS2 and generative QA: GenQA) in Table 1. Using GS human annotations for each dataset, we compute accuracy, Area Under the Curve (AUROC), and Pearson Correlation of each automatic QA metric. We observe that on all datasets, SQuArE significantly outperforms the baselines and achieves the highest accuracy and AUROC with human annotations.

Dataset	Technique	Accuracy	AUROC	Correlation
	Answer Sentence Selection (AS2)			
WikiQA	AVA-TR	0.701	0.633	0.532
	AVA-QT	0.900	0.804	0.637
	AVA-TQR	0.903	0.805	0.632
	SQuArE	**0.919**	**0.851**	**0.676**
TrecQA	AVA-TR	0.911	0.913	0.816
	AVA-QT	0.885	0.927	0.737
	AVA-TQR	0.906	**0.972**	0.797
	SQuArE	**0.924**	0.969	**0.842**
	Answer Generation (GenQA)			
MS-MARCO	AVA-TR	0.843	0.683	0.587
	AVA-QT	0.772	0.693	0.580
	AVA-TQR	0.839	0.738	0.601
	SQuArE	**0.845**	**0.773**	**0.620**
WikiQA	AVA-TR	0.692	0.670	0.602
	AVA-QT	0.627	0.798	0.667
	AVA-TQR	0.671	0.811	0.678
	SQuArE	**0.694**	**0.819**	**0.690**
TrecQA	AVA-TR	0.847	0.784	0.615
	AVA-QT	0.709	0.816	0.612
	AVA-TQR	0.779	**0.857**	0.647
	SQuArE	**0.890**	0.818	**0.671**

Table 2: Zero-shot evaluation using QA evaluation models trained on WQA. Same metrics used as Table 1.

Zero-shot Setting: To show strong generalization to out-of-distribution datasets (zero-shot setting), we train SQuArE and the other baselines on the WQA dataset, and use this for evaluation on other datasets. Specifically, we use two small datasets: WikiQA and TREC-QA (exploring both extractive: AS2 and generative settings), and one large dataset MS-MARCO. Results presented in Table 2 highlight that SQuArE achieves the highest accuracy and correlation with human annotations.

Comparison with BEM and LLMs: We present comparison with BEM and LLM baselines in Table 3 on WikiQA, TrecQA and Answer Equivalence (AE) datasets. On the WikiQA and TrecQA datasets, the results show that SQuArE outperforms both the baselines, which stems from (i) the usage of multiple references, and (ii) the references for these datasets being complete sentences in comparison to entities/short-answers which are used for training BEM. On the AE dataset, zero-shot SQuArE (which is trained on the WQA dataset) performs inferior (0.572 vs 0.897 in accuracy) to the

Dataset	Approach	# Refs	Accuracy	AUROC
WikiQA	BEM	1	0.863	0.553
	Falcon-7B	1	0.081	0.448
	Falcon-40B	1	**0.963**	0.499
	SQuArE	5	0.919	**0.851**
TrecQA	BEM	1	0.866	0.819
	Falcon-7B	1	0.601	0.529
	Falcon-40B	1	0.848	0.509
	SQuArE	5	**0.924**	**0.969**
AE	BEM	1	0.897	0.959
	SQuArE	1	0.572	0.718
	SQuArE(AE)	1	**0.908**	**0.966**

Table 3: Comparing SQuArE against BEM and LLM baselines on the WikiQA, TrecQA and AE datasets. The BEM baseline is trained on the AE dataset. We use the same metrics as Table 1.

BEM baseline (which is trained on the AE dataset). This drop in zero-shot performance of SQuArE compared to BEM can be attributed to (i) the lack of multiple references, and (ii) the references in AE being of a different style/format than those used for training SQuArE (entities/short answers v/s complete sentences). On fair comparison (when SQuArE(AE) is fine-tuned on the AE dataset), it is able to beat the BEM baseline in both accuracy (0.908 vs 0.897) and AUROC (0.966 vs 0.859).

Dataset	SQuArE	BLEURT	BERTScore
MS-MARCO	**0.238**	0.142	0.168
WikiQA	**0.425**	0.219	0.233
TrecQA	**0.862**	0.341	0.646

Table 4: Pearson Correlation of evaluation metrics with human annotations on GenQA-MTURK.

Comparison with text similarity metrics: We also compare SQuArE with learned text similarity metrics: BLEURT and BERTScore in Table 4. Results show that SQuARe achieves a higher correlation with manual annotations than BLEURT and BERTScore. For complete details, see Appendix C.

4.4 Ablation studies

To assess the improvements from different design choices used in SQuArE, we conduct ablation studies to show how the use of negative and multiple references improves the performance and correlation with human annotations. To perform these studies we pick one dataset (WQA) and present comparisons in Tab. 5.

Usage of Negative references: To support our claim that using negative references can improve the automatic QA evaluation, we compare two additional models/baselines: (i) AVA-TQR(-) which refers to an AVA baseline which only uses a single negative reference, and (ii) SQuArE(+) which refers to a SQuArE model which only uses multiple positive references. On comparison with results in Table 1, AVA-TQR(-) outperforms both AVA-QT (model without references) and AVA-TR (model without the question). This validates our intuition on the importance of negative references. SQuArE(+) outperforms the AVA-TQR baseline, but performs inferior to the SQuArE using a combination of both positive and negative references, thereby validating our claim that the combination of positive and negative references improves the accuracy and the generalizability of SQuArE.

Technique	# Refs	Accuracy	AUROC	Correlation
AVA-TQR(-)	1	0.800	0.864	0.763
SQuArE(+)	5	0.815	0.885	0.783
SQuArE	3	0.821	0.889	0.787
SQuArE	[1,5]	0.820	0.889	0.786
SQuArE	5	**0.833**	**0.896**	**0.793**

Table 5: Ablation studies evaluating the benefits of using negative references, and the impact of number of references on the performance of SQuArE. AVA-TQR(-) and SQuArE(+) refer to an AVA model only using negative references and a SQuArE model only using positive references. # Refs is the total number of references used for the metric. [1,5] refers to the number of references being randomly sampled $\in[1,5]$.

Number of references: We hypothesize that higher number of labeled references help with improved correlation of SQuArE with human evaluation. To support this intuition, we present an ablation study where we vary the total number of references from 5 per question to: (i) using 3 references per question, and (ii) randomly sampling $\in[1,5]$ references per question. We observe that SQuArE using 5 references outperforms SQuArE using 3 references (0.833 v/s 0.821 in accuracy), while SQuArE using a random sample of $\in[1,5]$ references (0.820 accuracy) performed comparable to SQuArE using 3 references.

5 Conclusion

In this paper, we propose SQuArE transformer LM encoder-based learned metric that uses multiple reference answers (positive + negative) for automatically evaluating sentence-level QA systems. We evaluate sentence-level extractive QA: AS2 and answer generation (GenQA) systems across multiple academic and industrial datasets and show that SQuArE achieves the highest correlation with human annotations beating previous baselines.

Limitations

Our approach of training QA evaluation metrics requires access to large GPU resources for training large transformer encoders such as DeBERTa, etc. For the experiments in this paper, we only consider datasets from the English language, however we conjecture that our techniques should work similarly for languages with a similar morphology. Since SQuArE is a learned evaluation metric based on large transformers, it might be challenging to effectively learn in a scarce-data setting. While we have shown impressive zero-shot evaluation results in Table 2, extending to a completely new data domain/new language might be challenging for SQuArE to adapt to without access to any labeled data. As visible from Tables 1 and 2, SQuArE's accuracy on human annotations is in the range of 80-90%, highlighting that there is still a gap with respect to human evaluation. For safety critical applications, human evaluation still remains the best means to evaluate Question Answering systems.

References

Ebtesam Almazrouei, Hamza Alobeidli, Abdulaziz Alshamsi, Alessandro Cappelli, Ruxandra Cojocaru, Merouane Debbah, Etienne Goffinet, Daniel Heslow, Julien Launay, Quentin Malartic, Badreddine Noune, Baptiste Pannier, and Guilherme Penedo. 2023. Falcon-40B: an open large language model with state-of-the-art performance.

Payal Bajaj, Daniel Campos, Nick Craswell, Li Deng, Jianfeng Gao, Xiaodong Liu, Rangan Majumder, Andrew McNamara, Bhaskar Mitra, Tri Nguyen, Mir Rosenberg, Xia Song, Alina Stoica, Saurabh Tiwary, and Tong Wang. 2018. Ms marco: A human generated machine reading comprehension dataset.

Jannis Bulian, Christian Buck, Wojciech Gajewski, Benjamin Boerschinger, and Tal Schuster. 2022. Tomayto, tomahto. beyond token-level answer equivalence for question answering evaluation. In *Proceedings of the 2022 Conference on Empirical Methods in Natural Language Processing*, Abu Dhabi, United Arab Emirates. Association for Computational Linguistics.

Meng Cao, Yue Dong, Jiapeng Wu, and Jackie Chi Kit Cheung. 2020. Factual error correction for abstractive summarization models. In *Proceedings of the 2020 Conference on Empirical Methods in Natural Language Processing (EMNLP)*, pages 6251–6258, Online. Association for Computational Linguistics.

Anthony Chen, Gabriel Stanovsky, Sameer Singh, and Matt Gardner. 2019. Evaluating question answering evaluation. In *Proceedings of the 2nd Workshop on Machine Reading for Question Answering*, pages 119–124, Hong Kong, China. Association for Computational Linguistics.

Elizabeth Clark, Asli Celikyilmaz, and Noah A. Smith. 2019. Sentence mover's similarity: Automatic evaluation for multi-sentence texts. In *Proceedings of the 57th Annual Meeting of the Association for Computational Linguistics*, pages 2748–2760, Florence, Italy. Association for Computational Linguistics.

Luca Di Liello, Siddhant Garg, and Alessandro Moschitti. 2023. Context-aware transformer pre-training for answer sentence selection. In *Proceedings of the 61st Annual Meeting of the Association for Computational Linguistics (Volume 2: Short Papers)*, pages 458–468, Toronto, Canada. Association for Computational Linguistics.

Luca Di Liello, Siddhant Garg, Luca Soldaini, and Alessandro Moschitti. 2022. Pre-training transformer models with sentence-level objectives for answer sentence selection. In *Proceedings of the 2022 Conference on Empirical Methods in Natural Language Processing*, pages 11806–11816, Abu Dhabi, United Arab Emirates. Association for Computational Linguistics.

Matteo Gabburo, Siddhant Garg, Rik Koncel-Kedziorski, and Alessandro Moschitti. 2023. Learning answer generation using supervision from automatic question answering evaluators. In *Proceedings of the 61st Annual Meeting of the Association for Computational Linguistics (Volume 1: Long Papers)*, pages 8389–8403, Toronto, Canada. Association for Computational Linguistics.

Matteo Gabburo, Rik Koncel-Kedziorski, Siddhant Garg, Luca Soldaini, and Alessandro Moschitti. 2022. Knowledge transfer from answer ranking to answer generation. In *Proceedings of the 2022 Conference on Empirical Methods in Natural Language Processing*, pages 9481–9495, Abu Dhabi, United Arab Emirates. Association for Computational Linguistics.

Siddhant Garg, Thuy Vu, and Alessandro Moschitti. 2020. Tanda: Transfer and adapt pre-trained transformer models for answer sentence selection. *Proceedings of the AAAI Conference on Artificial Intelligence*, 34(05):7780–7788.

Pengcheng He, Jianfeng Gao, and Weizhu Chen. 2021. Debertav3: Improving deberta using electra-style pretraining with gradient-disentangled embedding sharing.

Chao-Chun Hsu, Eric Lind, Luca Soldaini, and Alessandro Moschitti. 2021. Answer generation for retrieval-based question answering systems. In *Findings of the Association for Computational Linguistics: ACL-IJCNLP 2021*, pages 4276–4282, Online. Association for Computational Linguistics.

Diederik P. Kingma and Jimmy Ba. 2015. Adam: A method for stochastic optimization. In *International Conference of Learning Representations*.

Matt J. Kusner, Yu Sun, Nicholas I. Kolkin, and Kilian Q. Weinberger. 2015. From word embeddings to document distances. In *Proceedings of the 32nd International Conference on International Conference on Machine Learning - Volume 37*, ICML'15, page 957–966. JMLR.org.

Quentin Lhoest, Albert Villanova del Moral, Yacine Jernite, Abhishek Thakur, Patrick von Platen, Suraj Patil, Julien Chaumond, Mariama Drame, Julien Plu, Lewis Tunstall, Joe Davison, Mario Šaško, Gunjan Chhablani, Bhavitvya Malik, Simon Brandeis, Teven Le Scao, Victor Sanh, Canwen Xu, Nicolas Patry, Angelina McMillan-Major, Philipp Schmid, Sylvain Gugger, Clément Delangue, Théo Matussière, Lysandre Debut, Stas Bekman, Pierric Cistac, Thibault Goehringer, Victor Mustar, François Lagunas, Alexander Rush, and Thomas Wolf. 2021. Datasets: A community library for natural language processing. In *Proceedings of the 2021 Conference on Empirical Methods in Natural Language Processing: System Demonstrations*, pages 175–184, Online and Punta Cana, Dominican Republic. Association for Computational Linguistics.

Chin-Yew Lin. 2004. ROUGE: A package for automatic evaluation of summaries. In *Text Summarization Branches Out*, pages 74–81, Barcelona, Spain. Association for Computational Linguistics.

Sewon Min, Jordan Boyd-Graber, Chris Alberti, Danqi Chen, Eunsol Choi, Michael Collins, Kelvin Guu, Hannaneh Hajishirzi, Kenton Lee, Jennimaria Palomaki, Colin Raffel, Adam Roberts, Tom Kwiatkowski, Patrick Lewis, Yuxiang Wu, Heinrich Küttler, Linqing Liu, Pasquale Minervini, Pontus Stenetorp, Sebastian Riedel, Sohee Yang, Minjoon Seo, Gautier Izacard, Fabio Petroni, Lucas Hosseini, Nicola De Cao, Edouard Grave, Ikuya Yamada, Sonse Shimaoka, Masatoshi Suzuki, Shumpei Miyawaki, Shun Sato, Ryo Takahashi, Jun Suzuki, Martin Fajcik, Martin Docekal, Karel Ondrej, Pavel Smrz, Hao Cheng, Yelong Shen, Xiaodong Liu, Pengcheng He, Weizhu Chen, Jianfeng Gao, Barlas Oguz, Xilun Chen, Vladimir Karpukhin, Stan Peshterliev, Dmytro Okhonko, Michael Schlichtkrull, Sonal Gupta, Yashar Mehdad, and Wen-tau Yih. 2021. Neurips 2020 efficientqa competition: Systems, analyses and lessons learned. In *Proceedings of the NeurIPS 2020 Competition and Demonstration Track*, volume 133 of *Proceedings of Machine Learning Research*, pages 86–111. PMLR.

Benjamin Muller, Luca Soldaini, Rik Koncel-Kedziorski, Eric Lind, and Alessandro Moschitti. 2021. Cross-lingual genqa: A language-agnostic generative question answering approach for open-domain question answering. *CoRR*, abs/2110.07150.

Kishore Papineni, Salim Roukos, Todd Ward, and Wei-Jing Zhu. 2001. BLEU: a method for automatic evaluation of machine translation. In *Proceedings of the 40th Annual Meeting on Association for Computational Linguistics - ACL '02*, page 311. Association for Computational Linguistics.

Adam Paszke, Sam Gross, Francisco Massa, Adam Lerer, James Bradbury, Gregory Chanan, Trevor Killeen, Zeming Lin, Natalia Gimelshein, Luca Antiga, Alban Desmaison, Andreas Kopf, Edward Yang, Zachary DeVito, Martin Raison, Alykhan Tejani, Sasank Chilamkurthy, Benoit Steiner, Lu Fang, Junjie Bai, and Soumith Chintala. 2019. Pytorch: An imperative style, high-performance deep learning library. In *Advances in Neural Information Processing Systems 32*, pages 8024–8035. Curran Associates, Inc.

Ricardo Rei, Craig Stewart, Ana C Farinha, and Alon Lavie. 2020. COMET: A neural framework for MT evaluation. In *Proceedings of the 2020 Conference on Empirical Methods in Natural Language Processing (EMNLP)*, pages 2685–2702. Association for Computational Linguistics.

Ehud Reiter. 2018. A Structured Review of the Validity of BLEU. *Computational Linguistics*, 44(3):393–401.

Thibault Sellam, Dipanjan Das, and Ankur Parikh. 2020. BLEURT: Learning robust metrics for text generation. In *Proceedings of the 58th Annual Meeting of the Association for Computational Linguistics*, pages 7881–7892. Association for Computational Linguistics.

Chenglei Si, Chen Zhao, and Jordan Boyd-Graber. 2021. What's in a name? answer equivalence for open-domain question answering. In *Proceedings of the 2021 Conference on Empirical Methods in Natural Language Processing*, pages 9623–9629, Online and Punta Cana, Dominican Republic. Association for Computational Linguistics.

Pauli Virtanen, Ralf Gommers, Travis E. Oliphant, Matt Haberland, Tyler Reddy, David Cournapeau, Evgeni Burovski, Pearu Peterson, Warren Weckesser, Jonathan Bright, Stéfan J. van der Walt, Matthew Brett, Joshua Wilson, K. Jarrod Millman, Nikolay Mayorov, Andrew R. J. Nelson, Eric Jones, Robert Kern, Eric Larson, C J Carey, İlhan Polat, Yu Feng, Eric W. Moore, Jake VanderPlas, Denis Laxalde, Josef Perktold, Robert Cimrman, Ian Henriksen, E. A. Quintero, Charles R. Harris, Anne M. Archibald, Antônio H. Ribeiro, Fabian Pedregosa, Paul van Mulbregt, and SciPy 1.0 Contributors. 2020. SciPy 1.0: Fundamental Algorithms for Scientific Computing in Python. *Nature Methods*, 17:261–272.

Thuy Vu and Alessandro Moschitti. 2021. AVA: an automatic eValuation approach for question answering systems. In *Proceedings of the 2021 Conference of the North American Chapter of the Association for Computational Linguistics: Human Language Technologies*, pages 5223–5233. Association for Computational Linguistics.

Mengqiu Wang, Noah A Smith, and Teruko Mitamura. 2007. What is the jeopardy model? a quasi-synchronous grammar for qa. In *Proceedings of the*

2007 Joint Conference on Empirical Methods in Natural Language Processing and Computational Natural Language Learning (EMNLP-CoNLL), pages 22–32.

Anna Wegmann and Dong Nguyen. 2021. Does it capture STEL? a modular, similarity-based linguistic style evaluation framework. In *Proceedings of the 2021 Conference on Empirical Methods in Natural Language Processing*, pages 7109–7130, Online and Punta Cana, Dominican Republic. Association for Computational Linguistics.

Thomas Wolf, Lysandre Debut, Victor Sanh, Julien Chaumond, Clement Delangue, Anthony Moi, Pierric Cistac, Tim Rault, Remi Louf, Morgan Funtowicz, Joe Davison, Sam Shleifer, Patrick von Platen, Clara Ma, Yacine Jernite, Julien Plu, Canwen Xu, Teven Le Scao, Sylvain Gugger, Mariama Drame, Quentin Lhoest, and Alexander Rush. 2020. Transformers: State-of-the-art natural language processing. In *Proceedings of the 2020 Conference on Empirical Methods in Natural Language Processing: System Demonstrations*, pages 38–45, Online. Association for Computational Linguistics.

An Yang, Kai Liu, Jing Liu, Yajuan Lyu, and Sujian Li. 2018. Adaptations of ROUGE and BLEU to better evaluate machine reading comprehension task. In *Proceedings of the Workshop on Machine Reading for Question Answering*, pages 98–104, Melbourne, Australia. Association for Computational Linguistics.

Yi Yang, Wen-tau Yih, and Christopher Meek. 2015. Wikiqa: A challenge dataset for open-domain question answering. In *Proceedings of the 2015 conference on empirical methods in natural language processing*, pages 2013–2018.

Zhiyuan Zeng, Jiaze Chen, Weiran Xu, and Lei Li. 2021. Gradient-based adversarial factual consistency evaluation for abstractive summarization. In *Proceedings of the 2021 Conference on Empirical Methods in Natural Language Processing*, pages 4102–4108, Online and Punta Cana, Dominican Republic. Association for Computational Linguistics.

Tianyi Zhang, Varsha Kishore, Felix Wu, Kilian Q. Weinberger, and Yoav Artzi. 2020-02-24. BERTScore: Evaluating text generation with BERT. Number: arXiv:1904.09675.

Zeyu Zhang, Thuy Vu, and Alessandro Moschitti. 2021. Joint models for answer verification in question answering systems. In *Proceedings of the 59th Annual Meeting of the Association for Computational Linguistics and the 11th International Joint Conference on Natural Language Processing (Volume 1: Long Papers)*, pages 3252–3262, Online. Association for Computational Linguistics.

Zeyu Zhang, Thuy Vu, and Alessandro Moschitti. 2022. Double retrieval and ranking for accurate question answering. *CoRR*, abs/2201.05981.

Appendix

A Experiment Details

In this section we describe the parameters used to train and reproduce our models, and the computational environment we used to compute the results.

A.1 SQuArE Training

We train SQuArE train our models starting from DeBERTaV3-Large model (He et al., 2021), similar to (Gabburo et al., 2023). We experimented with different parameters, and we found the best combination of parameters training the model for 20 epochs on every dataset using a batch size of 32, $fp32$ and Adam (Kingma and Ba, 2015) as optimizer with a learning rate of $1e-06$. At the beginning of each epoch we shuffle the train set. We select the best checkpoint by selecting the best AUROC (Area Under the Curve) on the validation set. We train the QT, TQR, and TR using the parameters described in (Vu and Moschitti, 2021).

A.2 BEM and LLM Baselines

For BEM, we use the evaluation script and checkpoints from the original paper[1], while for the LLM-based *Falcon* experiments, we consider the originally released checkpoints[2][3]. For both the approaches (BEM and LLM) we use the *AVA-TQR* data setting, by providing the question and a positive reference, and asking the model to evaluate the correctness of the target answer. To fine-tune SQuArE on the AE dataset, we use the same parameters as for WQA, described in Section A.1.

A.3 Computational Environment

We trained our models using 8 Nvidia V100 with 32Gb each. Our code is written in PyTorch (Paszke et al., 2019) using Hugging Face (Lhoest et al., 2021; Wolf et al., 2020). We compute results using metrics developed in Scipy (Virtanen et al., 2020).

B GenQA-MTURK details

We designed this dataset starting from a reduced sample of the MS-MARCO NLG development set, the test set of WikiQA and the TrecQA test set proposed from (Zhang et al., 2022). Specifically, we trained 8 different T5-Large models (on MS-MARCO) using training techniques from (Hsu et al., 2021) and (Gabburo et al., 2022): (i) Supervised GenQA, (ii) Weak Supervision (WS), (iii) WS+Loss Weighting (LW), (iv) WS+Score-conditioned Input (SCI), (v) WS+Score-conditioned Output (SCO), (vi) WS+SCI+SCO, (vii) WS+LW+SCI+SCO, (viii) Supervised GenQA+WS+LW+SCI+SCO.

C Correlation with Similarity Metrics

In Section 4, we study the correlation of SQuArE with other learned metrics as BLEURT and BERTScore. Table 6 contains results for each metric broken down based on different GenQA models trained using techniques from (Hsu et al., 2021; Gabburo et al., 2022). The results show that despite the good performance of the BLEURT and BERTScore metrics, SQuArE has a better correlation with human evaluation. In addition, since our approach can use negative references, it can obtain higher performance than similarity metrics for datasets having a scarce number of positive references.

Dataset	Sys	Accuracy	SQuArE	BLEURT	BERTScore
MS-MARCO	1	0.946	0.881	0.772	0.732
	2	0.901	0.913	0.578	0.486
	3	0.958	0.779	0.569	0.485
	4	0.878	0.781	0.578	0.496
	5	0.880	0.761	0.689	0.620
	6	0.906	0.768	0.714	0.658
WikiQA	1	0.804	0.513	0.514	0.406
	2	0.803	0.316	0.447	0.331
	3	0.826	0.323	0.491	0.360
	4	0.791	0.306	0.480	0.350
	5	0.804	0.557	0.669	0.623
	6	0.837	0.609	0.579	0.510
TrecQA	1	0.874	0.769	0.563	0.324
	2	0.976	0.830	0.557	0.409
	3	0.968	0.932	0.482	0.498
	4	0.871	0.643	0.491	0.420
	5	0.968	0.868	0.628	0.442
	6	0.976	0.917	0.580	0.595

Table 6: System-wise evaluation done on three datasets (MS-MARCO, WikiQA, TrecQA) using 6 different systems based on generative question answering models trained on MS-MARCO. The accuracy column is computed using the manual annotations done by professional annotators, while the three remaining columns are the results computed using SQuArE, BLEURT and BERTScore.

[1] https://github.com/google-research-datasets/answer-equivalence-dataset

[2] https://huggingface.co/tiiuae/falcon-7b-instruct

[3] https://huggingface.co/tiiuae/falcon-40b-instruct

The Impact of Debiasing on the Performance of Language Models in Downstream Tasks is Underestimated

Masahiro Kaneko[1,2] **Danushka Bollegala**[3,4*] **Naoaki Okazaki**[2]
[1]MBZUAI [2]Tokyo Institute of Technology [3]University of Liverpool [4]Amazon
Masahiro.Kaneko@mbzuai.ac.ae
danushka@liverpool.ac.uk okazaki@c.titech.ac.jp

Abstract

Pre-trained language models trained on large-scale data have learned serious levels of social biases. Consequently, various methods have been proposed to debias pre-trained models. Debiasing methods need to mitigate only discriminatory bias information from the pre-trained models, while retaining information that is useful for the downstream tasks. In previous research, whether useful information is retained has been confirmed by the performance of downstream tasks in debiased pre-trained models. On the other hand, it is not clear whether these benchmarks consist of data pertaining to social biases and are appropriate for investigating the impact of debiasing. For example in gender-related social biases, data containing female words (e.g. *"she, female, woman"*), male words (e.g. *"he, male, man"*), and stereotypical words (e.g. *"nurse, doctor, professor"*) are considered to be the most affected by debiasing. If there is not much data containing these words in a benchmark dataset for a target task, there is the possibility of erroneously evaluating the effects of debiasing. In this study, we compare the impact of debiasing on performance across multiple downstream tasks using a wide-range of benchmark datasets that containing female, male, and stereotypical words. Experiments show that the effects of debiasing are consistently *underestimated* across all tasks. Moreover, the effects of debiasing could be reliably evaluated by separately considering instances containing female, male, and stereotypical words than all of the instances in a benchmark dataset.

1 Introduction

Unfortunately, Pre-trained Language Models (PLMs) such as BERT (Devlin et al., 2019) and RoBERTa (Liu et al., 2019) easily learn discriminatory social biases expressed in human-written texts in massive datasets (Kurita et al., 2019; Zhou et al., 2022; Kaneko et al., 2022). For example, if a model is given "*[MASK] is a nurse.*" as the input, a gender biased PLM would predict "*She*" with a higer likelihood score than for "*He*" when filling the [MASK]. Various debiasing methods have been proposed to mitigate social biases in PLMs. Zhao et al. (2019); Webster et al. (2020) proposed a debiasing method by swapping the gender of female and male words in the training data. Kaneko and Bollegala (2021) proposed a method for debiasing by orthogonalising the vectors representing gender information with the hidden layer of a language model given a sentence containing a stereotypical word. Webster et al. (2020) showed that dropout regularization can reduce overfitting to gender information, thereby can be used for debiasing PLMs.

	All	Female	Male	Occ.
CoLA	1,043	174	722	96
MNLI	9,832	3,467	8,875	1,415
MRPC	408	101	391	96
QNLI	5,463	2,149	5,371	1,066
QQP	40,430	7,415	29,638	3,331
RTE	277	113	269	94
SST-2	872	187	691	75
STS-B	1,500	513	1,277	151
WNLI	71	27	71	6

Table 1: The total number of instances containing female, male, and occupational (Occ.) words in the GLUE development data.

The debiasing method should mitigate only discriminatory information, while pre-trained useful information should be retained in the model. Evaluations in downstream tasks often employ the GLEU benchmark (Wang et al., 2018), which measures the ability to understand language (Kaneko and Bollegala, 2021; Guo et al., 2022; Meade et al., 2022). The data for downstream tasks are not selected in terms of whether they reflect the impact of

*Danushka Bollegala holds concurrent appointments as a Professor at University of Liverpool and as an Amazon Scholar. This paper describes work performed at the University of Liverpool and is not associated with Amazon.

Proceedings of the 13th International Joint Conference on Natural Language Processing and the 3rd Conference of the Asia-Pacific Chapter of the Association for Computational Linguistics (Volume 2: Short Papers), pages 29–36
November 1–4, 2023.

debiasing. To mitigate gender bias, data containing female words such as *"she"* and *"woman"*, male words such as *"he"* and *"man"*, and stereotypical words such as *"doctor"* and *"nurse"* would be most affected by debiasing.

Table 1 shows the total number of instances containing female, male, and occupational (Occ.) words in the development data in the GLUE benchmark suite (Wang et al., 2019), which is widely recognised as a standard evaluation benchmark for LLMs. Occupational words have been used for probing LLMs for stereotypical social biases (Bolukbasi et al., 2016). From Table 1, we see that the GLEU benchmark has little data related to females and occupations. Therefore, the impact of debiasing on data related to females and occupations may be potentially underestimated when LLMs are evaluated on GLUE.

We first extract instances containing female words, data containing male words, and data containing stereotypical words from the benchmarks. We then calculated the performance difference between the original model and the debiased model for each category and compared it to the performance difference using the entire benchmark. The results showed that the debiased model performed worse than the original model on data related to females and occupations compared to the original model when evaluated on the entire dataset. Therefore, existing evaluations underestimate the impact of debiasing on the performance of the downstream task.

It is important to be able to compare how well the effects of debiasing are captured in the datasets related to females, males, and occupations. We propose a method to control the degree of debiasing of PLMs and investigate whether the performance difference between original and debiased models widens as the degree of debiasing increases. Experimental results showed that the proportion of female, male and occupational words in the dataset is related to the susceptibility of the dataset to debiasing.

2 Experiments

2.1 Debiasing Methods

We use the following three commonly used debiasing methods in our experiments. We apply these debiasing methods during fine-tuning in downstream tasks.

Counterfactual Data Augmentation (CDA) debiasing: CDA debiasing (Webster et al., 2020) swaps the gender of gender words in the training data. For example, *"She is a nurse"* is swapped to *"He is a nurse"*, and the swapped version is appended to the training dataset. This enables to learn a less biased model because the frequency of female and male words will be the same in the augmented dataset.

Dropout debiasing: Webster et al. (2020) introduced dropout regularisation as a method to mitigate biases. They enhanced the dropout parameters for the attention weights and hidden activations of PLMs. Their research demonstrated that intensified dropout regularisation diminishes gender bias in these PLMs. They showed that dropout interfers with the attention mechanism in PLMs, and prevents undesirable associations between words. However, it is also possible that the model may no longer be able to learn desirable associations.

Context debiasing: Kaneko and Bollegala (2021) proposed a method to debias MLMs through fine-tuning. It preserves semantic information while removing gender-related biases using orthogonal projections at token- or sentence-level. This method targets male and female words and occupational words in the text for debiasing. This method can be applied various MLMs, independent of the model architectures and pre-training methods. Token-level debiasing across all layers produces the best performance.

2.2 Settings

Although we use BERT (bert-base-cased[1]) (Devlin et al., 2019) as our PML here as it has been the focus of much prior work on bias evaluations (Kaneko and Bollegala, 2021; Guo et al., 2022; Meade et al., 2022), the evaluation protocol we use can be applied to any PLM. We used the word lists[2] proposed by Kaneko and Bollegala (2021) as female words, male words, and occupational words for extracting data instances and debiasing.

We use the following nine downstream tasks from the GLEU benchmark: CoLA (Warstadt et al., 2019), MNLI (Williams et al., 2018), MRPC (Dolan and Brockett, 2005), QNLI (Ra-

[1] https://huggingface.co/bert-base-cased

[2] https://github.com/kanekomasahiro/context-debias

	CDA				Dropout				Context			
	All	Female	Male	Occ.	All	Female	Male	Occ.	All	Female	Male	Occ.
CoLA	-1.36	**-3.42**	-2.01	-1.45	0.42	-0.14	**-0.21**	-0.07	-0.32	**-0.86**	-0.71	-0.55
MNLI	-0.55	**-0.90**	-0.71	-0.63	0.23	0.13	**0.01**	0.05	-0.05	**-0.47**	-0.43	-0.32
MRPC	-0.96	-1.28	**-1.31**	-1.03	-0.82	**-1.12**	-1.02	-1.04	-0.88	-1.01	**-1.06**	-0.92
QNLI	-1.13	**-1.42**	-1.19	-1.27	-1.01	-1.11	-1.07	**-1.21**	0.25	**-0.19**	-0.06	-0.04
QQP	-0.21	**-0.69**	-0.32	-0.25	0.53	**0.13**	0.47	0.30	0.14	**-0.12**	0.03	-0.05
RTE	-1.16	**-1.21**	-1.02	-1.13	-1.01	**-1.24**	-0.96	-1.13	-0.43	-0.65	-0.51	**-0.73**
SST-2	-0.11	**-0.81**	-0.34	-0.25	0.45	0.20	**0.12**	0.23	0.22	**-0.15**	-0.02	-0.12
STS-B	-1.01	**-1.95**	-1.34	-1.10	0.21	0.09	-0.03	**-0.11**	-0.08	-0.31	**-0.38**	-0.34
WNLI	-2.82	**-3.07**	-2.82	-2.71	-2.01	-2.21	-2.01	**-2.33**	-1.52	**-1.88**	-1.52	-1.61

Table 2: Performance difference between the original model and debiased model for each dataset. **Bolded** values indicate the largest drop in performance of the debiased model.

jpurkar et al., 2016), QQP[3], RTE (Dagan et al., 2006; Haim et al., 2006; Giampiccolo et al., 2007; Bentivogli et al., 2009), SST-2 (Socher et al., 2013), STS-B (Cer et al., 2017), and WNLI (Levesque et al., 2012). Hyperparameters for debiasing follow previous studies (Kaneko and Bollegala, 2021; Webster et al., 2020), and we used the default values of huggingface for downstream task hyperparameters.[4] For fine-tuning we use the entire training dataset for each corresponding task, without splitting into male, female and occupational instances. We evaluate the performance on all tasks using the official development data.

2.3 Performance of Original vs. Debiased Models

We extract instances containing female words, male words, and stereotypical words from each of the datasets. We then calculate the performance difference between the original model and the debiased model for each dataset, and compare against the performance differences obtained when using all instances. If the performance difference for all instances is smaller than that when evaluated for the female, male, and occupational instances, it would indicate that the effect of debiasing is underestimated when evaluated on the entire dataset.

Table 2 shows the performance differences between the original model and the debiased model for each dataset/task in the GLEU benchmark. All, Female, Male, and Occ. are the performance differences when evaluated on the entire task dataset, instances containing female words, instances containing male words, and instances containing occupational words, respectively.

[3]https://quoradata.quora.com/First-Quora-Dataset-Release-Question-Pairs

[4]https://github.com/huggingface/transformers/tree/main/examples/pytorch/text-classification

From the results in Table 2, it can be seen that the performance difference between the original model and the debiased model is larger for the Female, Male, and Occ. instances compared to that when using all instances. In particular, instances related to females exhibit a significant decrease in performance after debiasing.

It can be seen that different word lists used for debiasing have different effects on the performance degradation in downstream tasks due to debiasing. Context debiasing uses occupational words for debiasing, while CDA debiasing does not. Therefore, in CDA debiasing, Occ. does not have a large performance difference compared to female- and male-related instances. Therefore, in CDA debiasing, the performance difference for occupation-related instances is smaller than that for the female and male-related instances. On the other hand, in Context debiasing, occupation-related instances has the largest performance difference as well as female- and male-related instances. Dropout debiasing does not use word lists for debiasing. Therefore, unlike CDA and context debiasing, we see large drops in performance for female, male and Occ. across tasks with Dropout debiasing.

2.4 Debias Controlled Method

To understand how debiasing of an PLM affects the performance of individual downstream benchmark datasets, following the probing technique proposed by Kaneko et al. (2023), we apply different levels of debiasing to bert-base-cased PLM and measure the difference in performance with respect to its original (non-debiased) version. For this purpose we use CDA as the debiasing method, where we swap the gender-related pronouns in $r \in [0, 1]$ fraction of the total N instances of a dataset (i.e.the total number of gender swapped instances in a dataset will be

$r \times N$). $r = 0$ corresponds to not swapping gender in any training instances of the dataset, whereas $r = 1$ swaps the gender in all instances. We increment r in step size 0.1 to obtain increasingly debiased version of the PLM, which is then fine-tuned for the downstream task[5]. Figure 1 shows the difference in performance between the original vs. debiased versions of the PLM for QQP, MNLI, and QNLI, which have the largest numbers of instances in the GLEU benchmark.

Note that CDA debiasing reverses gender without considering the context, as in *"He gets pregnant"* for *"She gets pregnant"*. This is problemantic because it eliminates even useful gender-related information learnt by the PLM via co-occurring contexts. Therefore, CDA debiasing has a negative impact on the performance of downstream tasks (Zmigrod et al., 2019) as shown by all three subplots in Figure 1. In fact, Table 2 shows that the performance difference of CDA debiasing is larger than that of dropout debiasing and context debiasing. Therefore, the larger r is for CDA, the more gender instances is balanced and debiased, but the performance is unfortunately degraded.

If the dataset of the downstream task is sensitive to the effect of debiasing, the performance difference between the original model and the debiased model widens as r increases. On the other hand, if the data set is insensitive to the effect of debiasing, the performance difference between the original model and the debiased model is unlikely to increase with the value of r.

We find that the performance differences for the female, male, and occupational instances in the QQP, MNLI, and QNLI datasets increase with the value of r. On the other hand, for QQP and MNLI, there is a rise and fall in the performance difference when all data are used. These results indicate that All, which includes instances related to non-gender, are less sensitive to the effect of debiasing compared to Female, Male, and Occupational instances.

On the other hand, for QNLI, All has a small rise and fall in the performance difference. As seen from Table 1, QNLI contains more gender-related instances than QQP and MNLI. Therefore, it is likely that the performance decreases with r even for All. All and Male instances have a similar trend in performance difference with r.

[5]In Appendix A, we show that the debias controlled method is able to debias the model according to r.

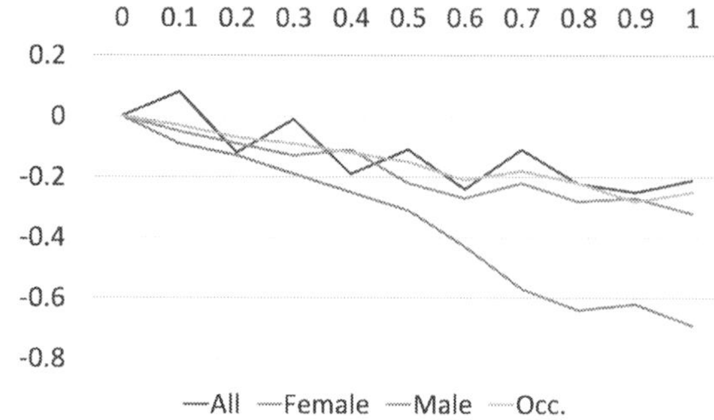

(a) QQP.

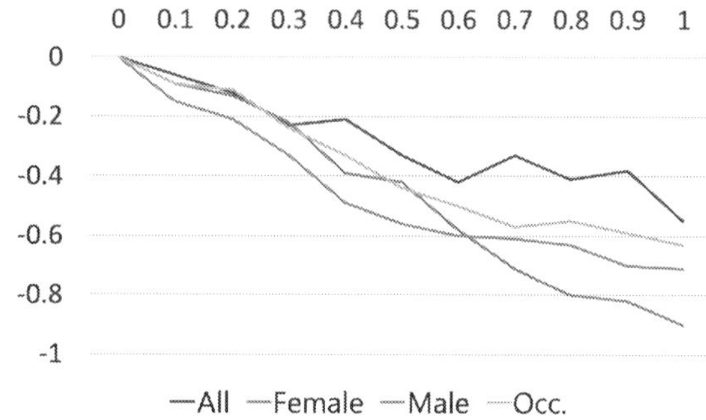

(b) MNLI.

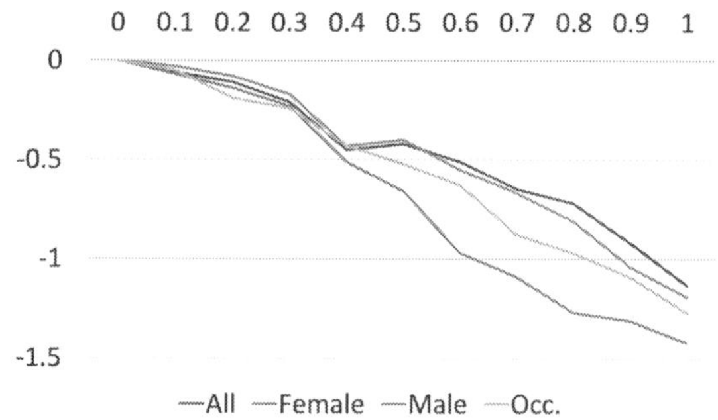

(c) QNLI.

Figure 1: Performance difference between original and debiased models by debias rate r. The vertical axis shows the performance difference between the original and debiased models, and the horizontal axis shows the debias rate.

3 Conclusion

This study focused on gender-related social biases and the presence of female, male, and stereotypical words in benchmark datasets. Prior work had used the performance on downstream tasks to prove the usefulness of debiasing methods, overlooking the fact that only a small fraction of those downstream benchmark datasets contain gender-related instances. On the contrary, we found that the effects of debiasing an PLM were consistently underestimated across all tasks. We recommend that the evaluation of debiasing effects must be more reliably conducted by considering instances containing specific gender-related words separately rather than evaluating all instances in a benchmark dataset.

4 Ethical Considerations

This study uses existing methods and datasets for experiments and does not propose a debiasing method or create a new dataset for social bias. This study evaluates the impact of debiasing on the performance of the downstream task, and it is not possible to evaluate how much bias is mitigated in the PLMs. Therefore, when evaluating the bias of PLMs, it is necessary to use evaluation methods such as StereoSet (Nadeem et al., 2021), Crowds-Pairs (Nangia et al., 2020), and All Unmasked Likelihood (Kaneko and Bollegala, 2022).

In this study, we only included binary gender as a gender bias. However, gender bias regarding non-binary gender has also been reported (Cao and Daumé III, 2020; Dev et al., 2021). It is necessary to verify whether there is a similar trend in debiasing for non-binary genders.

5 Limitations

Many previous studies have shown that various social biases other than gender bias are learned in PLMs. This study targets only gender bias. While existing studies (Webster et al., 2020; Zhao et al., 2019) have debiasing various PLMs, we have experimented only with bert-base-cased. Furthermore, although this study targets only English, which is a morphologically limited language. On the other hand, various types of social biases are also learned in the PLMs across many languages (Kaneko et al., 2022; Névéol et al., 2022). Therefore, if the proposed method is to be used with other social biases and PLMs, it is necessary to properly verify its effectiveness in languages other than English. Moreover, we have not verified the use of debias controlled methods in languages such as Spanish and Russian, where gender swapping is not easy from a grammatical point of view (Zmigrod et al., 2019).

Acknowledgements

These research results were obtained from the commissioned research (No.225) by National Institute of Information and Communications Technology (NICT), Japan.

References

Luisa Bentivogli, Peter Clark, Ido Dagan, and Danilo Giampiccolo. 2009. The fifth pascal recognizing textual entailment challenge. In *TAC*. Citeseer.

Tolga Bolukbasi, Kai-Wei Chang, James Y Zou, Venkatesh Saligrama, and Adam T Kalai. 2016. Man is to computer programmer as woman is to homemaker? debiasing word embeddings. *Advances in neural information processing systems*, 29.

Yang Trista Cao and Hal Daumé III. 2020. Toward gender-inclusive coreference resolution. In *Proceedings of the 58th Annual Meeting of the Association for Computational Linguistics*, pages 4568–4595, Online. Association for Computational Linguistics.

Daniel Cer, Mona Diab, Eneko Agirre, Iñigo Lopez-Gazpio, and Lucia Specia. 2017. SemEval-2017 task 1: Semantic textual similarity multilingual and crosslingual focused evaluation. In *Proceedings of the 11th International Workshop on Semantic Evaluation (SemEval-2017)*, pages 1–14, Vancouver, Canada. Association for Computational Linguistics.

Ido Dagan, Oren Glickman, and Bernardo Magnini. 2006. The pascal recognising textual entailment challenge. In *Machine Learning Challenges. Evaluating Predictive Uncertainty, Visual Object Classification, and Recognising Tectual Entailment: First PASCAL Machine Learning Challenges Workshop, MLCW 2005, Southampton, UK, April 11-13, 2005, Revised Selected Papers*, pages 177–190. Springer.

Sunipa Dev, Tao Li, Jeff M. Phillips, and Vivek Srikumar. 2020. On measuring and mitigating biased inferences of word embeddings. *Proceedings of the AAAI Conference on Artificial Intelligence*, 34(05):7659–7666.

Sunipa Dev, Masoud Monajatipoor, Anaelia Ovalle, Arjun Subramonian, Jeff Phillips, and Kai-Wei Chang. 2021. Harms of gender exclusivity and challenges in non-binary representation in language technologies. In *Proceedings of the 2021 Conference on Empirical Methods in Natural Language Processing*, pages 1968–1994, Online and Punta Cana, Dominican Republic. Association for Computational Linguistics.

Jacob Devlin, Ming-Wei Chang, Kenton Lee, and Kristina Toutanova. 2019. BERT: Pre-training of deep bidirectional transformers for language understanding. In *Proceedings of the 2019 Conference of the North American Chapter of the Association for Computational Linguistics: Human Language Technologies, Volume 1 (Long and Short Papers)*, pages 4171–4186, Minneapolis, Minnesota. Association for Computational Linguistics.

William B. Dolan and Chris Brockett. 2005. Automatically constructing a corpus of sentential paraphrases. In *Proceedings of the Third International Workshop on Paraphrasing (IWP2005)*.

Danilo Giampiccolo, Bernardo Magnini, Ido Dagan, and William B Dolan. 2007. The third pascal recognizing textual entailment challenge. In *Proceedings of the ACL-PASCAL workshop on textual entailment and paraphrasing*, pages 1–9.

Yue Guo, Yi Yang, and Ahmed Abbasi. 2022. Auto-debias: Debiasing masked language models with automated biased prompts. In *Proceedings of the 60th Annual Meeting of the Association for Computational Linguistics (Volume 1: Long Papers)*, pages 1012–1023, Dublin, Ireland. Association for Computational Linguistics.

R Bar Haim, Ido Dagan, Bill Dolan, Lisa Ferro, Danilo Giampiccolo, Bernardo Magnini, and Idan Szpektor. 2006. The second pascal recognising textual entailment challenge. In *Proceedings of the Second PASCAL Challenges Workshop on Recognising Textual Entailment*, volume 7.

Masahiro Kaneko and Danushka Bollegala. 2021. Debiasing pre-trained contextualised embeddings. In *Proceedings of the 16th Conference of the European Chapter of the Association for Computational Linguistics: Main Volume*, pages 1256–1266, Online. Association for Computational Linguistics.

Masahiro Kaneko and Danushka Bollegala. 2022. Unmasking the mask–evaluating social biases in masked language models. In *Proceedings of the AAAI Conference on Artificial Intelligence*, volume 36, pages 11954–11962.

Masahiro Kaneko, Danushka Bollegala, and Naoaki Okazaki. 2023. Comparing intrinsic gender bias evaluation measures without using human annotated examples. In *Proceedings of the 17th Conference of the European Chapter of the Association for Computational Linguistics*, pages 2857–2863, Dubrovnik, Croatia. Association for Computational Linguistics.

Masahiro Kaneko, Aizhan Imankulova, Danushka Bollegala, and Naoaki Okazaki. 2022. Gender bias in masked language models for multiple languages. In *Proceedings of the 2022 Conference of the North American Chapter of the Association for Computational Linguistics: Human Language Technologies*, pages 2740–2750, Seattle, United States. Association for Computational Linguistics.

Keita Kurita, Nidhi Vyas, Ayush Pareek, Alan W Black, and Yulia Tsvetkov. 2019. Measuring bias in contextualized word representations. In *Proceedings of the First Workshop on Gender Bias in Natural Language Processing*, pages 166–172, Florence, Italy. Association for Computational Linguistics.

Hector Levesque, Ernest Davis, and Leora Morgenstern. 2012. The winograd schema challenge. In *Thirteenth international conference on the principles of knowledge representation and reasoning*.

Yinhan Liu, Myle Ott, Naman Goyal, Jingfei Du, Mandar Joshi, Danqi Chen, Omer Levy, Mike Lewis, Luke Zettlemoyer, and Veselin Stoyanov. 2019. Roberta: A robustly optimized bert pretraining approach. *arXiv preprint arXiv:1907.11692*.

Nicholas Meade, Elinor Poole-Dayan, and Siva Reddy. 2022. An empirical survey of the effectiveness of debiasing techniques for pre-trained language models. In *Proceedings of the 60th Annual Meeting of the Association for Computational Linguistics (Volume 1: Long Papers)*, pages 1878–1898, Dublin, Ireland. Association for Computational Linguistics.

Moin Nadeem, Anna Bethke, and Siva Reddy. 2021. StereoSet: Measuring stereotypical bias in pretrained language models. In *Proceedings of the 59th Annual Meeting of the Association for Computational Linguistics and the 11th International Joint Conference on Natural Language Processing (Volume 1: Long Papers)*, pages 5356–5371, Online. Association for Computational Linguistics.

Nikita Nangia, Clara Vania, Rasika Bhalerao, and Samuel R. Bowman. 2020. CrowS-pairs: A challenge dataset for measuring social biases in masked language models. In *Proceedings of the 2020 Conference on Empirical Methods in Natural Language Processing (EMNLP)*, pages 1953–1967, Online. Association for Computational Linguistics.

Aurélie Névéol, Yoann Dupont, Julien Bezançon, and Karën Fort. 2022. French CrowS-pairs: Extending a challenge dataset for measuring social bias in masked language models to a language other than English. In *Proceedings of the 60th Annual Meeting of the Association for Computational Linguistics (Volume 1: Long Papers)*, pages 8521–8531, Dublin, Ireland. Association for Computational Linguistics.

Pranav Rajpurkar, Jian Zhang, Konstantin Lopyrev, and Percy Liang. 2016. SQuAD: 100,000+ questions for machine comprehension of text. In *Proceedings of the 2016 Conference on Empirical Methods in Natural Language Processing*, pages 2383–2392, Austin, Texas. Association for Computational Linguistics.

Richard Socher, Alex Perelygin, Jean Wu, Jason Chuang, Christopher D. Manning, Andrew Ng, and Christopher Potts. 2013. Recursive deep models for semantic compositionality over a sentiment treebank. In *Proceedings of the 2013 Conference on Empirical Methods in Natural Language Processing*, pages 1631–1642, Seattle, Washington, USA. Association for Computational Linguistics.

Alex Wang, Amanpreet Singh, Julian Michael, Felix Hill, Omer Levy, and Samuel Bowman. 2018. GLUE: A multi-task benchmark and analysis platform for natural language understanding. In *Proceedings of the 2018 EMNLP Workshop BlackboxNLP: Analyzing and Interpreting Neural Networks for NLP*, pages 353–355, Brussels, Belgium. Association for Computational Linguistics.

Alex Wang, Amanpreet Singh, Julian Michael, Felix Hill, Omer Levy, and Samuel R. Bowman. 2019.

GLUE: A multi-task benchmark and analysis platform for natural language understanding. In *International Conference on Learning Representations*.

Alex Warstadt, Amanpreet Singh, and Samuel R. Bowman. 2019. Neural network acceptability judgments. *Transactions of the Association for Computational Linguistics*, 7:625–641.

Kellie Webster, Xuezhi Wang, Ian Tenney, Alex Beutel, Emily Pitler, Ellie Pavlick, Jilin Chen, Ed Chi, and Slav Petrov. 2020. Measuring and reducing gendered correlations in pre-trained models. *arXiv preprint arXiv:2010.06032*.

Adina Williams, Nikita Nangia, and Samuel Bowman. 2018. A broad-coverage challenge corpus for sentence understanding through inference. In *Proceedings of the 2018 Conference of the North American Chapter of the Association for Computational Linguistics: Human Language Technologies, Volume 1 (Long Papers)*, pages 1112–1122, New Orleans, Louisiana. Association for Computational Linguistics.

Jieyu Zhao, Tianlu Wang, Mark Yatskar, Ryan Cotterell, Vicente Ordonez, and Kai-Wei Chang. 2019. Gender bias in contextualized word embeddings. In *Proceedings of the 2019 Conference of the North American Chapter of the Association for Computational Linguistics: Human Language Technologies, Volume 1 (Long and Short Papers)*, pages 629–634, Minneapolis, Minnesota. Association for Computational Linguistics.

Yi Zhou, Masahiro Kaneko, and Danushka Bollegala. 2022. Sense embeddings are also biased – evaluating social biases in static and contextualised sense embeddings. In *Proceedings of the 60th Annual Meeting of the Association for Computational Linguistics (Volume 1: Long Papers)*, pages 1924–1935, Dublin, Ireland. Association for Computational Linguistics.

Ran Zmigrod, Sabrina J. Mielke, Hanna Wallach, and Ryan Cotterell. 2019. Counterfactual data augmentation for mitigating gender stereotypes in languages with rich morphology. In *Proceedings of the 57th Annual Meeting of the Association for Computational Linguistics*, pages 1651–1661, Florence, Italy. Association for Computational Linguistics.

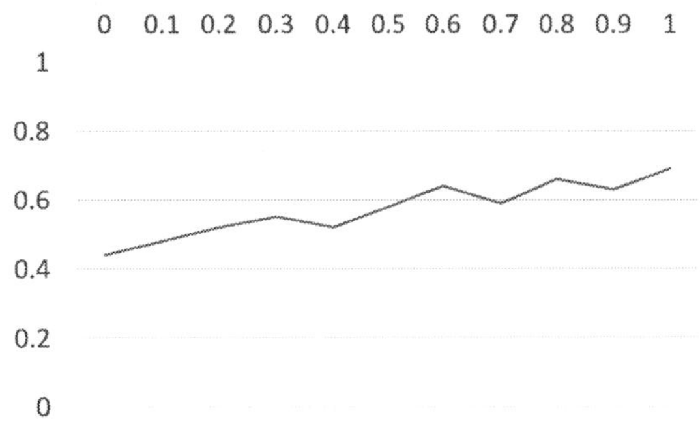

Figure 2: Evaluation of debias controlled models using FN evaluation method. The vertical axis shows the bias score, and the horizontal axis shows r.

A Bias Evaluation in NLI task

We show that the debias controlled method is appropriately debiasing according to r. We use Fraction Neutra (**FN**; Dev et al., 2020) as the bias evaluation method. The FN method evaluates bias in the NLI by considering the percentage of neutral labels predicted by the model for the premise sentence (e.g. *The driver owns a cabinet.*) and the hypothesis sentence (e.g. *The man owns a cabinet.*) generated with the template. The FN method indicates that the lower the score, the more bias there is in the model. We evaluate PLMs trained on MNLI with FN method.

Figure 2 shows the bias scores of FN method for each debias controlled model. It can be seen that the bias of the model is decreasing with r. Therefore, the debias controlled method is able to debias the models according to r.

Enhancing Volatility Forecasting in Financial Markets: A General Numeral Attachment Dataset for Understanding Earnings Calls

Ming-Xuan Shi,[1] **Chung-Chi Chen,**[2] **Hen-Hsen Huang,**[3] **Hsin-Hsi Chen** [1]
[1] Department of Computer Science and Information Engineering,
National Taiwan University, Taiwan
[2] AIST, Japan
[3] Institute of Information Science, Academia Sinica, Taiwan
b08902105@csie.ntu.edu.tw, c.c.chen@acm.org,
hhhuang@iis.sinica.edu.tw, hhchen@ntu.edu.tw

Abstract

Volatility, a crucial statistical measure in the financial market, serves as an indicator of financial instrument risk. Accurate volatility capture aids in predicting stock movements and is valuable in derivative trading, such as options trading. While recent research focuses on volatility forecasting using earnings call transcriptions, most approaches rely on end-to-end models that directly process textual or vocal data. However, limited efforts have been made to simulate the reading and comprehension processes of financial professionals, thereby enhancing the capabilities of language models. To address this gap, we propose a general numeral attachment dataset designed to train language models to understand earnings calls with the expertise of professionals. Additionally, we introduce a pre-training process that improves the semantic understanding of earnings calls. Experimental results demonstrate that our pre-trained language model enhances the accuracy of 3-day volatility forecasting.

1 Introduction

A key element in understanding financial narratives is pinpointing the specific target linked with every numeral, especially considering the prevalent use of numerals in these texts (Chen et al., 2021a). The notion of "numeral attachment" was first introduced by Chen et al. (2019). This concept seeks to clarify the connection between numerals and particular stocks. Yet, this methodology was specifically devised for a financial social media setting, making it less adaptable to more formal, general documentation. Addressing this gap, we put forth a broader numeral attachment framework, free from such specific constraints. Instead of developing an entirely new dataset, we amplify the existing ECNum dataset (Chen et al., 2021b) with augmented annotations. Consider the nuanced difference between "revenue decreased 20%" and "revenue decreased 2%" — two statements with varying implications for investors. Furthermore, the distinction between "revenue decreased 20%" and "cost decreased 20%", where the numeral remains the same but the narrative diverges, exemplifies the essence of our endeavor. Our central goal is to refine the model's precision in recognizing and distinguishing situations inherent to general numeral attachment.

When making investment decisions, professional investors carefully consider financial risk. Estimating the risk associated with financial instruments is crucial due to the inherent trade-off between potential returns and risks involved. Volatility, which quantifies financial risk as the second-moment measure of price return, serves as a widely used indicator in this regard. Although previous studies have explored various models and data sources to improve volatility forecasting, they have largely neglected enhancing the semantic capabilities of language models for this task. In this paper, we introduce a novel approach that simulates the reading process of financial professionals, aiming to enhance the accuracy of volatility forecasting.

Earnings calls, which involve teleconferences among managers and investors to discuss company operations, have garnered significant attention in recent research. While prior studies have primarily focused on constructing multimodal models for earnings calls, they have often overlooked the finer semantic aspects. In this work, we demonstrate the value of understanding general numeral attachment in the context of earnings calls, particularly for improving volatility forecasting—an important downstream task in financial analysis.

Our contributions are threefold:

1. We introduce the novel task of general numeral attachment, addressing a previously overlooked issue.

2. We provide additional annotations on the publicly-available ECNum dataset.[1]

[1] http://gen-numattach.nlpfin.com/

Proceedings of the 13th International Joint Conference on Natural Language Processing and the 3rd Conference of the Asia-Pacific Chapter of the Association for Computational Linguistics (Volume 2: Short Papers), pages 37–42
November 1–4, 2023.

3. We propose an approach to enhance the language model's understanding of numerals, leading to improved performance in 3-day volatility forecasting.

2 Related Work

Language model pretraining with specialized semantic understanding tasks has demonstrated its effectiveness in improving model performance. Notably, Bidirectional Encoder Representations from Transformers (BERT) (Devlin et al., 2019) is a prominent example. Numerous subsequent studies have utilized BERT or similar Transformer-based architectures for pretraining or fine-tuning language models in various domains. For instance, Clinical BERT (Alsentzer et al., 2019) is pretrained with clinical corpora, while SciBERT (Beltagy et al., 2019) is fine-tuned with scientific publications. FinBERT (Araci, 2019) is specifically pretrained with financial corpus, while BioBERT (Lee et al., 2020), mBERT (Devlin et al., 2019), and patentBERT (Lee and Hsiang, 2019) are fine-tuned with biomedical, multilingual, and patent corpora, respectively.

Despite the availability of domain-specific BERT models, none of them have fine-tuned the BERT model with numeral-related tasks to enhance models' numeracy. In this paper, we propose a novel pretraining task focused on understanding the numerals in earnings calls at a more granular level. We release the associated dataset and pretrained language model, referred to as NumBERT, for future research and applications.

3 Dataset

3.1 Annotation Process

We utilize the ECNum dataset (Chen et al., 2021b), which consists of 9,034 annotated instances from earnings calls. Each instance is associated with three annotations related to numeral information, including the target numeral category label and two domain-specific annotations. In this study, we extend the dataset by providing additional general numeral attachment labels for the ECNum instances.

Each instance was assigned to three annotators. We have regular meetings with all annotators to resolve the inconsistencies. Over a span of three weeks, they were diligently coached to adhere to the same guidelines. Regular discussions were held to clarify doubts and resolve ambiguities, culminating in a strong alignment in their annotations.

	Earnings call		Investor's report	
Rank	Entity	Freq.	Entity	Freq.
1	revenue	767	revenue	855
2	Q	371	EPS	481
3	sales	255	gross margin	326
4	EPS	221	profit	275
5	earnings	165	operating margin	115
6	years	154	price target	108
7	free cash flow	110	operating profit	59

Table 1: Numeral attachment in different narratives.

During the annotation process, annotators with financial backgrounds were presented with a target numeral and a paragraph from an earnings call. Their task was to select the attached entity, such as a named entity or accounting account, that is relevant to the given numeral within the paragraph. The annotators exhibited high consistency in their annotations, with approximately 78.60% of instances receiving fully consistent annotations, 7.13% of instances having two different annotations, and only 14.26% of instances showing completely different annotations. After resolving inconsistencies and removing instances without attached entities, the dataset for the general numeral attachment task consists of 6,735 instances from ECNum.

3.2 Annotations Analysis

Table 1 presents the frequently attached entities observed in the annotations. To facilitate a comprehensive comparison of entity usage, particularly accounting accounts, in both managers' and investors' narratives, we include additional annotations from the NumClaim dataset (Chen et al., 2020), which comprises professional analysts' reports.

Based on the statistics depicted in Table 1, several key findings emerge. Firstly, managers predominantly report operational data, encompassing revenue, sales, EPS, and earnings. Secondly, investors exhibit interest not only in quantitative operational results such as revenue and EPS, but also in accounting ratios like gross margins and operating margins. Thirdly, while managers seldom mention the stock price, investors frequently engage in discussions regarding it, including price targets.

4 Implementation

4.1 Research Questions

In this paper, we investigate the following two research questions:

(RQ1): How does pre-training with the proposed general numeral attachment task impact the performance of volatility forecasting?

(RQ2): Which strategy, discrete or continuous, yields better results with the proposed model?

We start by fine-tuning the RoBERTa language model (Liu et al., 2019) with the proposed general numeral attachment task, resulting in the NumBERT model.

To address **(RQ1)**, we employ NumBERT for the volatility forecasting task. Specifically, we train separate models for the 3-day, 7-day, 15-day, and 30-day volatility forecasting tasks.

To explore **(RQ2)**, we develop both a discrete forecasting model and a continuous forecasting model based on the proposed GNA-Vol architecture. The discrete strategy involves simultaneous predictions for the 3-day, 7-day, 15-day, and 30-day volatility forecasting tasks, utilizing a multi-task model. On the other hand, the continuous strategy treats volatility forecasting as a sequential prediction task, making predictions for volatility from $t+1$ to $t+T$ days. Here, we set T to 30. We consider the continuous strategy due to the well-known phenomenon of volatility clustering in the financial market, where large (small) volatility tends to be followed by large (small) volatility. We hypothesize that the continuous strategy can capture this pattern and further improve the performance of volatility forecasting.

4.2 Model Architecture

In the general numeral attachment task, an input paragraph $P \in \{P_1, P_2, \ldots, P_M\}$ is tokenized into words using the RoBERTa tokenizer: $P = [x_1, x_2, \ldots, x_N]$, where x_i represents the ith word and N is the maximum number of words in any paragraph. To ensure the target numeral is not split by the tokenizer, we replace it with the `[MASK]` token. The hidden state of the ith word, denoted as h_i, is obtained from the last layer of RoBERTa, and h_{mask} represents the hidden state of the mask token. Start and end vectors S and E are defined. To incorporate the target numeral information and generate the probability distribution of the start of the answer span, we concatenate h_i and h_{mask} to form a new vector c_i. The probability p_i of word i being the start of the answer span is computed as the softmax of the dot product between c_i and S: $p_i = \frac{e^{S \cdot c_i}}{\sum_j e^{S \cdot c_j}}$. The fine-tuning loss function is cross-entropy. We perform fine-tuning for ten epochs using a learning rate of 1e-5 and a batch size of 4.

	Validation Data	Test Data
FinBERT	86.24%	87.28%
LinkBERT-base	89.65%	87.71%
RoBERTa-base	89.40%	88.01%
LinkBERT-large	88.92%	88.74%
RoBERTa-large	90.99%	90.02%

Table 2: Experimental results on general numeral attachment task.

We employ the trained language model to encode earnings call transcriptions for volatility forecasting. We introduce a matrix $T = [h_1, h_2, \ldots, h_N]$, where h_i represents the hidden state of the ith `[MASK]` token in the input transcription, and N is the maximum number of numerals in any transcription. To leverage multiple numeral information for volatility prediction, we construct a transformer-based model followed by a fully connected layer. The transformer model requires three inputs: Q, K, V, which are obtained by linear transformations of T: $Q = T \times A$ and $K = V = T \times B$. In the case of continuous volatility forecasting, we replace the fully connected layer with an LSTM.

5 Experiments

5.1 Language Model Selection

In this section, we discuss our choice of using RoBERTa as the base language model instead of the domain-specific language model, FinBERT (Araci, 2019). Our selection is based on the performance of the general numeral attachment task. We divided the instances into training, validation, and test sets, with proportions of 70%, 10%, and 20% respectively, for the general numeral attachment task. The evaluation metric for the span identification task is F-score. Table 2 presents the performance of different language models on the general numeral attachment task. We observe that RoBERTa performs well in our proposed pre-training task. Additionally, we experiment with LinkBERT (Yasunaga et al., 2022), the latest well-performing pretrained language model that surpasses BERT in several benchmark datasets. However, RoBERTa outperforms LinkBERT in the general numeral attachment task. Therefore, we choose RoBERTa as the base language model for constructing NumBERT.

5.2 Experimental Results

For the volatility forecasting task, we utilize the same dataset and follow the separation criterion employed in previous works (Qin and Yang, 2019; Yang et al., 2020; Chen et al., 2021b). The mean square error (MSE) is employed as the evaluation metric. We compare the performance of our proposed approach with the following baseline models: (1) **MDRM** (Qin and Yang, 2019): This model utilizes GloVe embeddings to represent textual data and feeds both textual and vocal features into a BiLSTM-based model for volatility forecasting. (2) **HTML** (Yang et al., 2020): This model uses BERT to extract textual features and aligns sentence-level audio features with the textual data. Volatility forecasting is then performed based on the concatenated features. (3) **FinBERT** (Araci, 2019): This BERT-based model is pre-trained on a financial corpus and has demonstrated effectiveness in various financial tasks. (4) **NAM** (Chen et al., 2021b): This model highlights the importance of extracting numeral features from earnings calls for volatility forecasting. It leverages the extracted numeral features with a Transformer architecture for making predictions.

Table 3 presents the experimental results. Firstly, our proposed GNA-Vol achieves the top rank in the 3-day and 7-day volatility forecasting tasks, highlighting the effectiveness of our pretraining task and model. Given the dynamic nature of the financial market and the rapid incorporation of new information into asset prices, short-term forecasting is of utmost importance. These results demonstrate that our general numeral attachment task enables models to capture critical information in earnings conference calls for short-term risk forecasting. Secondly, despite the intuitive appeal of the continuous strategy for time series data prediction, we observe that the discrete strategy outperforms the continuous strategy in most cases. This suggests that the vanilla continuous strategy may not adequately capture the latent information underlying the volatility clustering phenomenon discussed in Section 4.1.

To assess the impact of our proposed pretraining process, we conduct an ablation analysis, the results of which are presented in Table 4. We observe that without pretraining using our proposed task, the performance significantly deteriorates in most cases, irrespective of the strategy employed. These results underscore the effectiveness of our pretraining task in risk forecasting.

	3-day	7-day	15-day	30-day
MDRM (Text Only)	1.431	0.439	0.309	0.219
MDRM (Text + Audio)	1.371	0.420	0.300	0.217
HTML (Text Only)	1.175	0.372	**0.153**	**0.133**
HTML (Text + Audio)	0.845	0.349	0.251	0.158
FinBERT	0.750	0.368	0.241	0.172
NAM (Text Only)	0.745	**0.300**	0.232	0.187
GNA-Vol + Discrete Strategy	**0.700**	0.322	0.252	0.207
GNA-Vol + Continuous Strategy	0.705	0.362	0.250	0.237

Table 3: Experimental results of volatility forecasting task, reported in mean square error.

	3-day	7-day	15-day	30-day
GNA-Vol + Discrete Strategy	0.700	0.322	0.252	0.207
w/o Pretrain	0.730	0.353	0.253	0.186
GNA-Vol + Continuous Strategy	0.705	0.362	0.250	0.237
w/o Pretrain	0.725	0.421	0.275	0.231

Table 4: Ablation analysis. Note the lower the metric MSE, the better the performance.

6 Conclusion

We address the challenge of identifying the target associated with numerals in financial narratives through the novel task of general numeral attachment. By enhancing the publicly-available ECNum dataset with additional annotations, we provide a valuable resource for researchers in this field. Our approach, which simulates the reading process of financial professionals, enhances the semantic understanding of language models and improves the accuracy of 3-day volatility forecasting.

In the realms of tabular QA and math word problems, it's essential to note that earnings conference calls act as a nexus for corporate leaders and adept investors to converse about operational intricacies. Unlike traditional settings, these dialogues typically don't showcase tabular data or pose mathematical queries. This distinct context accentuates the importance of our general numeral attachment task. By deciphering numerical data embedded in such discourses, we augment the semantic grasp of these interactions. Future research can pivot on multiple avenues. Firstly, extrapolating the general numeral attachment task to diverse financial manuscripts and sectors could amplify its scope. Such extensions might delve into associating numerals with an array of financial elements, encompassing market indices, commodities, or macroeconomic markers. Secondly, the exploration of transfer learning or domain adaptation strategies to make our proposed model universally applicable to other financial prediction tasks stands as a promising endeavor. Finally, orchestrating user assessments or real-world appraisals of the improved volatility forecasting mechanisms can shed light on their tangible efficacy. Pursuing these trajectories will further crystallize the role of numeral attachment in fine-tuning financial examinations.

Acknowledgments

This research is supported by National Science and Technology Council, Taiwan, under grants MOST 110-2221-E-002-128-MY3 and NSTC 111-2634-F-002-023-. The work of Chung-Chi Chen was supported in part by JSPS KAKENHI Grant Number 23K16956 and a project JPNP20006, commissioned by the New Energy and Industrial Technology Development Organization (NEDO).

Limitations

While this paper introduces a novel task of general numeral attachment and presents valuable contributions, there are some limitations to consider. First, the proposed general numeral attachment task is evaluated on the publicly-available ECNum dataset, which may have its own limitations and biases. The generalizability of the results to other financial documents and datasets needs to be further investigated. Second, the enhanced performance in 3-day volatility forecasting is demonstrated based on the specific approach proposed in this paper. It would be valuable to compare the performance with other existing volatility forecasting models and explore the robustness of the proposed approach across different datasets and market conditions. Third, the proposed approach focuses on enhancing the language model's understanding of numerals. While this is an important aspect, there may be other factors and features that contribute to accurate volatility forecasting. Future research could explore additional contextual information and features to further improve the forecasting accuracy.

Overall, while this paper provides valuable insights and advancements in the field of volatility forecasting through the general numeral attachment task, further research is needed to validate the findings on different datasets, compare with existing models, and explore additional features for enhanced performance.

References

Emily Alsentzer, John Murphy, William Boag, Wei-Hung Weng, Di Jindi, Tristan Naumann, and Matthew McDermott. 2019. Publicly available clinical BERT embeddings. In *Proceedings of the 2nd Clinical Natural Language Processing Workshop*, pages 72–78, Minneapolis, Minnesota, USA. Association for Computational Linguistics.

Dogu Araci. 2019. Finbert: Financial sentiment analysis with pre-trained language models. *arXiv preprint arXiv:1908.10063*.

Iz Beltagy, Kyle Lo, and Arman Cohan. 2019. SciBERT: A pretrained language model for scientific text. In *Proceedings of the 2019 Conference on Empirical Methods in Natural Language Processing and the 9th International Joint Conference on Natural Language Processing (EMNLP-IJCNLP)*, pages 3615–3620, Hong Kong, China. Association for Computational Linguistics.

Chung-Chi Chen, Hen-Hsen Huang, and Hsin-Hsi Chen. 2019. Numeral attachment with auxiliary tasks. In *Proceedings of the 42nd International ACM SIGIR Conference on Research and Development in Information Retrieval*, pages 1161–1164.

Chung-Chi Chen, Hen-Hsen Huang, and Hsin-Hsi Chen. 2020. Numclaim: Investor's fine-grained claim detection. In *Proceedings of the 29th ACM International Conference on Information & Knowledge Management*, pages 1973–1976.

Chung-Chi Chen, Hen-Hsen Huang, and Hsin-Hsi Chen. 2021a. *From Opinion Mining to Financial Argument Mining*. Springer Nature.

Chung-Chi Chen, Hen-Hsen Huang, Yu-Lieh Huang, and Hsin-Hsi Chen. 2021b. Distilling numeral information for volatility forecasting. In *Proceedings of the 30th ACM International Conference on Information amp; Knowledge Management*, page 2920–2924, New York, NY, USA. Association for Computing Machinery.

Jacob Devlin, Ming-Wei Chang, Kenton Lee, and Kristina Toutanova. 2019. BERT: Pre-training of deep bidirectional transformers for language understanding. In *Proceedings of the 2019 Conference of the North American Chapter of the Association for Computational Linguistics: Human Language Technologies, Volume 1*, pages 4171–4186, Minneapolis, Minnesota. Association for Computational Linguistics.

Jieh-Sheng Lee and Jieh Hsiang. 2019. Patentbert: Patent classification with fine-tuning a pre-trained bert model. *arXiv preprint arXiv:1906.02124*.

Jinhyuk Lee, Wonjin Yoon, Sungdong Kim, Donghyeon Kim, Sunkyu Kim, Chan Ho So, and Jaewoo Kang. 2020. Biobert: a pre-trained biomedical language representation model for biomedical text mining. *Bioinformatics*, 36(4):1234–1240.

Yinhan Liu, Myle Ott, Naman Goyal, Jingfei Du, Mandar Joshi, Danqi Chen, Omer Levy, Mike Lewis, Luke Zettlemoyer, and Veselin Stoyanov. 2019. Roberta: A robustly optimized bert pretraining approach. *arXiv preprint arXiv:1907.11692*.

Yu Qin and Yi Yang. 2019. What you say and how you say it matters: Predicting stock volatility using verbal and vocal cues. In *Proceedings of the 57th Annual*

Meeting of the Association for Computational Linguistics, pages 390–401, Florence, Italy. Association for Computational Linguistics.

Linyi Yang, Tin Lok James Ng, Barry Smyth, and Riuhai Dong. 2020. Html: Hierarchical transformer-based multi-task learning for volatility prediction. In *Proceedings of The Web Conference 2020*, WWW '20, page 441–451, New York, NY, USA. Association for Computing Machinery.

Michihiro Yasunaga, Jure Leskovec, and Percy Liang. 2022. LinkBERT: Pretraining language models with document links. In *Proceedings of the 60th Annual Meeting of the Association for Computational Linguistics (Volume 1: Long Papers)*, pages 8003–8016, Dublin, Ireland. Association for Computational Linguistics.

Do the Benefits of Joint Models for Relation Extraction Extend to Document-level Tasks?

Pratik Saini and **Tapas Nayak** and **Indrajit Bhattacharya**
TCS Research, India
{pratik.saini,nayak.tapas,b.indrajit}@tcs.com

Abstract

Two distinct approaches have been proposed for relational triple extraction - pipeline and joint. Joint models, which capture interactions across triples, are the more recent development, and have been shown to outperform pipeline models for sentence-level extraction tasks. Document-level extraction is a more challenging setting where interactions across triples can be long-range, and individual triples can also span across sentences. Joint models have not been applied for document-level tasks so far. In this paper, we benchmark state-of-the-art pipeline and joint extraction models on sentence-level as well as document-level datasets. Our experiments show that while joint models outperform pipeline models significantly for sentence-level extraction, their performance drops sharply below that of pipeline models for the document-level dataset.

1 Introduction

Relation extraction is a crucial NLP task for constructing and enriching knowledge bases. Traditional pipeline approaches (Riedel et al., 2010; Hoffmann et al., 2011; Zeng et al., 2014, 2015; Nayak and Ng, 2019; Jat et al., 2017) first identify entities followed by relation identification one entity pair at a time. In contrast, more recent joint approaches (Zeng et al., 2018; Takanobu et al., 2019; Nayak and Ng, 2020; Wei et al., 2020; Wang et al., 2020b; Zhong and Chen, 2021; Zheng et al., 2021; Li et al., 2021; Wei et al., 2020; Yan et al., 2021; Shang et al., 2022) not only identify entities and relations for the same triple together but also extract all relational triples together. Thus, these recent approaches are better suited for capturing complex interactions.

Joint models for relation extraction outperform traditional pipeline models for sentence-level datasets such as NYT (Riedel et al., 2010). A more natural and complex setting for relation extraction is at the document-level. In the document-level task, relational triples may also span across sentences. Further, there may be long range interactions between different triples across sentences. As a result, the search space for joint models blows up with document size. So far, research for document-level datasets such as DocRED (Yao et al., 2019) has used pipeline approaches and avoided the joint approach.

In this paper, we investigate if the benefits of the joint approach extrapolate from sentence-level to document-level tasks. We benchmark 5 SOTA joint models and 3 SOTA pipeline models on sentence-level (NYT) and document-level (DocRED) datasets. We observe that the benefits of the SOTA joint models do not extend to document-level tasks. While performance of both classes of models drop sharply, joint models fall significantly below that of pipeline models. We perform extensive analysis to identify the short-comings of the two classes of models highlighting areas of improvement.

2 Relation Extraction Approaches

Pipeline RE approaches solve the RE task in two sequential steps. In Step 1, they use an NER model to identify the entities and entity mentions in the input text. In Step 2, they take the predicted entities and entity mentions as input, and predict all possible relations from a pre-defined relation set between pairs of entities. We use PL-Marker (Ye et al., 2022) as the NER module and KD-DocRE (Tan et al., 2022), SSAN (Xu et al., 2021a), and experiment with SAIS (Xiao et al., 2022) as relation classification models for our experiments, and train these for specific datasets. Following standard practice, we use gold standard entity mentions for training and validation of the relation classification models, while for inference of the test instances, we naturally use the predicted entity mentions as input. Note that in both steps, these models perform *independent* classification for each entity mention

Proceedings of the 13th International Joint Conference on Natural Language Processing and the 3rd Conference of the Asia-Pacific Chapter of the Association for Computational Linguistics (Volume 2: Short Papers), pages 43–51
November 1–4, 2023.

Original	Kiato (, Sidirodromikos Stathmos Kiatou) is a railway station in Kiato in the northern Peloponnese , Greece . The station is located a kilometre west of the town , near the Greek National Road 8A (Patras – Corinth highway) . It opened on 9 July 2007 as the western terminus of the line from Athens Airport . Initially the station served as an exchange point for passengers to Patras on the old metre gauge SPAP line to Patras , but all traffic was suspended indefinitely in December 2010 for cost reasons . The nearby old Kiato station was also closed . Passengers for Patras must now change to bus services at Kiato . The station is served by one train per hour to Piraeus .
Processed	Kiato (, Kiato) is a railway station in Kiato in the northern Peloponnese , Greece . The station is located a kilometre west of the town , near the Greek National Road 8A (Peloponnese – Corinth highway) . It opened on 9 July 2007 as the western terminus of the line from Athens Airport . Initially the station served as an exchange point for passengers to Peloponnese on the old metre gauge SPAP line to Peloponnese , but all traffic was suspended indefinitely in December 2010 for cost reasons . The nearby old Kiato station was also closed . Passengers for Peloponnese must now change to bus services at Kiato . The station is served by one train per hour to Peloponnese .

Table 1: A sample document from DocRED and its processed version. The different mentions of the entity 'Kiato' and 'Peloponnese' are marked with blue and red respectively. In the processed text, different mentions are normalized with the first mention of these two entities which are 'Kiato' and 'Peloponnese'.

Dataset	# Relations	Train		Validation		Test	
		# Context	# Triples	# Context	# Triples	# Context	# Triples
NYT	24	56,196	94,222	5,000	8,489	5,000	8,616
DocRED	96	2,572	20,233	284	2,187	924	7,337

Table 2: Statistics of the NYT24 and DocRED datasets. Context refers to a sentence or document.

and relation.

Joint RE approaches identify the entities and relations in a relational triple in an end-to-end fashion. Further, they consider the entire input text (sentence or document) and output a set of relational triples together, thus, capturing complex interactions across triples in theory. The flip side, naturally, is that they need to explore a significantly larger space of candidates, which grows combinatorially with the length of the input text. We use 5 SOTA models for experiments. PtrNet (Nayak and Ng, 2020) and REBEL (Huguet Cabot and Navigli, 2021) use the Seq2Seq approach. PtrNet generates the index position of entities in text whereas REBEL generates the tokens for the triples. OneRel (Shang et al., 2022) uses a table-based tagging approach. The tagging approaches of BiRTE (Ren et al., 2022) and GRTE (Ren et al., 2021) have a separate entity extraction process in their end-to-end modeling. We train these models in an end-to-end fashion as described in the respective papers.

3 Extraction Settings and Datasets

The original and simpler setting for relation extraction is *sentence-level*. This setting consists of individual sentences containing one or more relations as context. NYT (Riedel et al., 2010) is a large-scale and popular benchmark for sentence-level RE, and we use this dataset as it is for our sentence-level experiments.

This setting, however, is restrictive since a large fraction of relations in natural text spans across multiple sentences. This is captured in the *document-level* relation extraction setting. Here, relational triples may be intra-sentence or inter-sentence, meaning that the head and tail entities of the relational triple can span across multiple sentences and require reasoning across multiple sentences to identify them. The task is to predict all these relations given an entire document as context. DocRED (Yao et al., 2019) is a benchmark document-level dataset that we use for our experiments.

Contexts in DocRED (avg. number of tokens around 197) are much longer than in NYT (avg. number of tokens around 37). However, training data size is much larger for NYT. Since the relation labels of the DocRED test set are not released, we use the original validation set as test set and split the training data for training and validation. DocRED has mostly been used for pipeline models. We needed additional processing to make it tractable for joint models. We remove the documents with overlapping entity mentions in the training and validation set. We get 2,856 documents from the training set and 924 documents from the validation set. Then, we replace all entity mentions with the first occurring entity mention for each entity so that co-reference resolution is not required. We include an example of document processing for DocRED in Table 1. The details of the dataset splits of the NYT and DocRED for our experiments are included in Table 2[1].

Evaluation Metric: We use 'strict' criteria for evaluation. We consider an extracted relational triple as correct only if two entities and relation exactly match with a ground truth triple. We report triple level precision, recall and F1 scores for the models.

Parameter Settings: We use $BERT_{BASE}$ (cased) (Devlin et al., 2019) for document encoding for all the models except REBEL for which we have used $BART_{BASE}$ (Lewis et al., 2019). We used NVIDIA Tesla V100 32GB GPU to train the models. We used other hyper-parameters as per provided in their respective papers.

4 Results and Discussion

Through our experiment, we try to find out the answers to following research questions (RQ).

RQ1: How do the two classes of models perform at sentence and documents scales?

End-to-end performance of the joint models and the pipeline models on the NYT and DocRED datasets is shown in Table 3. On the sentence-level NYT dataset, both joint models and pipeline models achieve close to 0.90 F1 score. But, on DocRED, we see a huge drop in the F1 score for both categories. The pipeline models score below 0.60 whereas among the joint models GRTE and BiRTE perform around 0.45, the others drop to 0.20 or below. One reason for the drop for DocRED is the smaller training data size. But, it does not explain the gap of 10% F1 score between the pipeline and joint models when they performed almost at par for NYT. This suggests that joint models struggle with longer context and cross-sentence relations of documents. We investigate this in more detail next.

RQ2: Are some joint models better than others at document scale?

Out of the 5 joint models, we see significantly higher drop in F1 score for OneRel and PtrNet than REBEL, GRTE, and BiRTE models. Given a document with L tokens and K predefined relations, OneRel maintains a three-dimensional matrix $M_{L\times K\times L}$ and assigns tags for all possible triples. When context length grows as in documents, M has many more negative tags and very few positive tags, which seems to affect OneRel performance. BiRTE and GRTE, on the other hand, extract the entities first separately and then classify the relations. While this is done in an end-to-end fashion, it is still similar to pipeline approach. This may be the reason for the smaller performance drop compared to pipelines models on DocRED.

PtrNet and REBEL are Seq2Seq models which use a decoder to extract the triples, so they possibly need more training data to learn from longer document contexts. Additionally, PtrNet extracts index positions for the entities. Since an entity may appear more than once in a document, we mark the first occurring index of the entity-mention to train this model. This very likely contributes to its poorer performance. On the other hand, REBEL outputs entities as text, and does not have this training issue.

RQ3: How different are performances for intra vs inter-sentence extraction?

The fundamental difference between NYT and DocRED is that NYT contains only intra-sentence triples, whereas DocRED contains both intra and inter-sentence (cross-sentence) triples. In Table 5, we first show intra vs inter sentence relational triple distribution for the gold and model predictions on the DocRED dataset. Pipeline models have nearly the same distribution for gold and prediction. But, joint models are skewed towards intra-sentence relations. This suggests that joint models are very good at extracting intra-sentence triples but they struggle with inter-sentence triples. This is why joint models perform very well on the NYT dataset and fail to do so on DocRED.

In Table 4, we have reported the intra-sentence vs inter-sentence relations performance of the top-performing models on the DocRED test dataset. We see that all the models perform way better at intra-sentence extraction as compared to inter-sentence extraction, it demonstrates that inter-sentence extraction is significantly harder. We also see that pipeline models achieve around 10% higher F1 scores than the joint models for *both* intra and inter categories on DocRED. This shows that even for the familiar intra-sentence setting joint models face more difficulties compared to pipeline models when encountered with longer context and smaller training volume.

Lastly, we investigate the impact of the distance

[1]Our processed DocRED dataset is available at https://github.com/pratiksaini4/nyt-docred-joint-pipeline-comparison

	Model	NYT24			DocRED		
		P	R	F1	P	R	F1
Joint Models	OneRel	0.926	0.918	0.922	0.513	0.130	0.208
	BiRTE	0.914	0.920	0.917	0.522	0.402	0.454
	GRTE	0.929	0.924	0.926	0.586	0.373	0.456
	PtrNet	0.898	0.894	0.896	0.222	0.145	0.175
	Rebel	0.881	0.885	0.883	0.466	0.356	0.404
Pipeline Models	KD-DocRE	0.895	0.910	0.902	0.620	0.556	0.586
	SSAN	0.781	0.798	0.789	0.576	0.529	0.552
	SAIS	0.864	0.879	0.872	0.640	0.545	0.589

Table 3: Performance of the SOTA models on end-to-end relation extraction on NYT24 and DocRED datasets.

	Model	Intra			Inter		
		P	R	F1	P	R	F1
Joint Models	BiRTE	0.600	0.425	0.497	0.420	0.366	0.391
	GRTE	0.677	0.407	0.508	0.460	0.320	0.378
Pipeline Models	KD-DocRE	0.666	0.601	0.631	0.545	0.485	0.513
	SAIS	0.697	0.594	0.641	0.548	0.467	0.504

Table 4: Performance of top performing SOTA models on Intra vs Inter relational triples on DocRED dataset.

	Model	Predict	
		Intra %	Inter %
-	Gold	61	39
Joint Models	BiRTE	56	44
	GRTE	58	42
Pipeline Models	KD-DocRE	62	38
	SAIS	62	38

Table 5: Intra vs Inter relational triple distribution of SOTA models predictions. We include top two models from the joint and pipeline class for this analysis.

# Hops	Pipeline Models		Joint Models	
	KD-DocRE	SAIS	BiRTE	GRTE
1	0.50	0.45	0.38	0.33
2	0.44	0.44	0.34	0.31
3	0.48	0.49	0.36	0.31
4	0.48	0.49	0.37	0.31
5	0.51	0.54	0.39	0.32
6	0.42	0.43	0.29	0.32

Table 6: Recall score of Pipeline and Joint SOTA models on inter-sentence relations with respect to distance between subject and object entities.

between subject and object mentions in the context on the performance of inter-sentence relations. In Table 6, we record recall of SOTA models on inter-sentence relations for different subject-object hop distances. Hop distance k refers to the minimum sentence-level distance between the subject and object entity of a triple within the document being k. Again, we see that pipeline models outperform joint models by $\sim 12\%$ for all hop distances, and not just for longer ones.

RQ4: How is performance affected by training data size?

Next, we analyze how training volume affects performance for the two model classes for the simpler intra-sentence extraction task. Note that NYT contains such relations exclusively. Since DocRED has both categories, we prepare DocRED-Intra including only intra-sentence triples and the corresponding sentences. The size of these datasets are significantly different. DocRED-Intra has only $\sim 6.5K$ training instances compared to $94K$ for NYT. We train all the models with these intra-sentence triples and record their performance for DocRED-Intra in Table 7. Corresponding NYT performance is in Table 3. We observe a big gap of $\sim 42-50\%$ for joint models and $\sim 33\%$ for pipeline models in the performance between NYT and DocRED-Intra. This is due to the smaller training volume associated with a larger number of relations in DocRED. The notable disparity between pipeline and joint models in the case of DocRED-Intra demonstrates that joint models are not as effective at generalization compared to pipeline models, particularly when working with limited training data volumes and longer contexts.

RQ5: How different are entity extraction performances at sentence and document scales?

Finally, we aim to analyze if the huge gap in the performance of pipeline and joint models on

	Model	P	R	F1
Joint Models	BiRTE	0.527	0.462	0.492
	GRTE	0.544	0.346	0.423
Pipeline Models	KD-DocRE	0.524	0.619	0.567
	SAIS	0.485	0.610	0.540

Table 7: Performance of top performing SOTA models on DocRED-Intra dataset.

DocRED is affected by their performance on NER subtask of relation extraction. In Table 8, we include the performance of these models on the entity extraction task. Pipeline models have a separate NER model. The performance of this model - PL-Marker - on NER task is similar to that of the BiRTE and GRTE models for NYT dataset. But, for DocRED, BiRTE and GRTE perform much worse than PL-Marker, the drop in F1 score being around 25%. This, in turn, hurts their performance on the relational triple extraction. Though training data volume for DocRED is smaller, note that the PL-Marker model is trained on the DocRED dataset itself as are the BiRTE/GRTE models. This shows that, aside from overall extraction performance, joint models struggle with the NER subtask as well when training data is limited. This suggests that a separate NER model may be more useful in such settings.

Dataset	Model	P	R	F1
NYT24	PL-Marker	0.948	0.955	0.952
	BiRTE	0.955	0.954	0.954
	GRTE	0.958	0.956	0.957
DocRED	PL-Marker	0.942	0.934	0.938
	BiRTE	0.73	0.647	0.686
	GRTE	0.757	0.576	0.654

Table 8: Performance of PL-Marker, BiRTE and GRTE on the NER task for NYT24 and DocRED dataset.

5 Conclusion

While joint models for relational triple extraction have been shown to outperform pipeline models for sentence-level extraction settings, in this paper we have demonstrated, with extensive experimentation, that these benefits do not extend to the more realistic and natural document-level extraction setting, which entails longer contexts and cross-sentence relations. Experimenting with 5 SOTA joint models and 3 SOTA pipeline models, we have shown that while performance of both classes of models drops significantly in the more complex document setting, joint models suffer significantly more with longer context, inter-sentence relations and limited training data for the overall task as well as for subtasks such as NER. This aids in establishing a research agenda for joint models to extend the promised benefits of joint entity identification, relation classification, and joint extraction of all triples from the context. This pertains to the more challenging yet natural and crucial setting for relation extraction.

6 Limitations

The major limitation of this work is that we could only analyze 3 pipeline models and 5 joint models. Recently, many models have been proposed for this task both in pipeline and joint class. Out of these, we chose different kinds of SOTA models to cover the different design choices made by these models. We chose PtrNet (Nayak and Ng, 2020) and REBEL (Huguet Cabot and Navigli, 2021) as they used Seq2Seq model for this task. OneRel (Shang et al., 2022) used table-filling method whereas BiRTE (Ren et al., 2022) and GRTE (Ren et al., 2021) used sequentially extracting entities and relations in their end-to-end model.

References

Pere-Lluís Huguet Cabot and Roberto Navigli. 2021. Rebel: Relation extraction by end-to-end language generation. In *EMNLP*.

Jacob Devlin, Ming-Wei Chang, Kenton Lee, and Kristina Toutanova. 2019. BERT: Pre-training of deep bidirectional transformers for language understanding. In *NAACL*.

Zhijiang Guo, Yan Zhang, and Wei Lu. 2019. Attention guided graph convolutional networks for relation extraction. In *Proceedings of the 57th Annual Meeting of the Association for Computational Linguistics*, pages 241–251, Florence, Italy. Association for Computational Linguistics.

Raphael Hoffmann, Congle Zhang, Xiao Ling, Luke Zettlemoyer, and Daniel S Weld. 2011. Knowledge-based weak supervision for information extraction of overlapping relations. In *Proceedings of the 49th Annual Meeting of the Association for Computational Linguistics*.

Kevin Huang, Peng Qi, Guangtao Wang, Tengyu Ma, and Jing Huang. 2021. Entity and evidence guided document-level relation extraction. In *Proceedings of the 6th Workshop on Representation Learning for NLP (RepL4NLP-2021)*, pages 307–315, Online. Association for Computational Linguistics.

Pere-Lluís Huguet Cabot and Roberto Navigli. 2021. REBEL: Relation extraction by end-to-end language generation. In *Findings of the Association for Computational Linguistics: EMNLP 2021*, pages 2370–2381, Punta Cana, Dominican Republic. Association for Computational Linguistics.

Sharmistha Jat, Siddhesh Khandelwal, and Partha Talukdar. 2017. Improving distantly supervised relation extraction using word and entity based attention. In *Proceedings of the 6th Workshop on Automated Knowledge Base Construction.*

Robin Jia, Cliff Wong, and Hoifung Poon. 2019. Document-level n-ary relation extraction with multiscale representation learning. In *Proceedings of the 2019 Conference of the North American Chapter of the Association for Computational Linguistics: Human Language Technologies, Volume 1 (Long and Short Papers)*, pages 3693–3704, Minneapolis, Minnesota. Association for Computational Linguistics.

Mike Lewis, Yinhan Liu, Naman Goyal, Marjan Ghazvininejad, Abdel rahman Mohamed, Omer Levy, Veselin Stoyanov, and Luke Zettlemoyer. 2019. Bart: Denoising sequence-to-sequence pre-training for natural language generation, translation, and comprehension. In *Annual Meeting of the Association for Computational Linguistics.*

Xianming Li, Xiaotian Luo, Cheng Jie Dong, Daichuan Yang, Beidi Luan, and Zhen He. 2021. TDEER: An efficient translating decoding schema for joint extraction of entities and relations. In *EMNLP.*

Makoto Miwa and Mohit Bansal. 2016. End-to-end relation extraction using LSTMs on sequences and tree structures. In *Proceedings of the 54th Annual Meeting of the Association for Computational Linguistics.*

Guoshun Nan, Zhijiang Guo, Ivan Sekulic, and Wei Lu. 2020. Reasoning with latent structure refinement for document-level relation extraction. In *Proceedings of the 58th Annual Meeting of the Association for Computational Linguistics*, pages 1546–1557, Online. Association for Computational Linguistics.

Tapas Nayak and Hwee Tou Ng. 2019. Effective attention modeling for neural relation extraction. In *Proceedings of the Conference on Computational Natural Language Learning.*

Tapas Nayak and Hwee Tou Ng. 2020. Effective modeling of encoder-decoder architecture for joint entity and relation extraction. In *Proceedings of The Thirty-Fourth AAAI Conference on Artificial Intelligence.*

Xutan Peng, Chenghua Lin, and Mark Stevenson. 2021. Cross-lingual word embedding refinement by ℓ_1 norm optimisation. In *Proceedings of the 2021 Conference of the North American Chapter of the Association for Computational Linguistics: Human Language Technologies*, pages 2690–2701, Online. Association for Computational Linguistics.

Chris Quirk and Hoifung Poon. 2017. Distant supervision for relation extraction beyond the sentence boundary. In *Proceedings of the 15th Conference of the European Chapter of the Association for Computational Linguistics: Volume 1, Long Papers*, pages 1171–1182, Valencia, Spain. Association for Computational Linguistics.

Feiliang Ren, Longhui Zhang, Shujuan Yin, Xiaofeng Zhao, Shilei Liu, Bochao Li, and Yaduo Liu. 2021. A novel global feature-oriented relational triple extraction model based on table filling. In *EMNLP.*

Feiliang Ren, Longhui Zhang, Xiaofeng Zhao, Shujuan Yin, Shilei Liu, and Bochao Li. 2022. A simple but effective bidirectional framework for relational triple extraction. *Proceedings of the Fifteenth ACM International Conference on Web Search and Data Mining.*

Sebastian Riedel, Limin Yao, and Andrew McCallum. 2010. Modeling relations and their mentions without labeled text. In *Proceedings of the European Conference on Machine Learning and Knowledge Discovery in Databases.*

Y. Shang, Heyan Huang, and Xian-Ling Mao. 2022. OneRel: Joint entity and relation extraction with one module in one step. In *AAAI.*

Linfeng Song, Yue Zhang, Zhiguo Wang, and Daniel Gildea. 2018. N-ary relation extraction using graph-state LSTM. In *Proceedings of the 2018 Conference on Empirical Methods in Natural Language Processing*, pages 2226–2235, Brussels, Belgium. Association for Computational Linguistics.

Dianbo Sui, Yubo Chen, Kang Liu, Jun Zhao, Xiangrong Zeng, and Shengping Liu. 2020. Joint entity and relation extraction with set prediction networks. *CoRR*, abs/2011.01675.

Ryuichi Takanobu, Tianyang Zhang, Jiexi Liu, and Minlie Huang. 2019. A hierarchical framework for relation extraction with reinforcement learning. In *Proceedings of The Thirty-Third AAAI Conference on Artificial Intelligence.*

Qingyu Tan, Ruidan He, Lidong Bing, and Hwee Tou Ng. 2022. Document-level relation extraction with adaptive focal loss and knowledge distillation. In *Findings of the Association for Computational Linguistics: ACL 2022*, pages 1672–1681, Dublin, Ireland. Association for Computational Linguistics.

Hengzhu Tang, Yanan Cao, Zhenyu Zhang, Jiangxia Cao, Fang Fang, Shi Wang, and Pengfei Yin. 2020. HIN: hierarchical inference network for document-level relation extraction. *CoRR*, abs/2003.12754.

Difeng Wang, Wei Hu, Ermei Cao, and Weijian Sun. 2020a. Global-to-local neural networks for document-level relation extraction. In *Proceedings of the 2020 Conference on Empirical Methods in Natural Language Processing (EMNLP)*, pages 3711–3721, Online. Association for Computational Linguistics.

Hong Wang, Christfried Focke, Rob Sylvester, Nilesh Mishra, and William Yang Wang. 2019. Finetune bert for docred with two-step process. *CoRR*, abs/1909.11898.

Yijun Wang, Changzhi Sun, Yuanbin Wu, Hao Zhou, Lei Li, and Junchi Yan. 2021. UniRE: A unified label space for entity relation extraction. In *Proceedings of the 59th Annual Meeting of the Association for Computational Linguistics and the 11th International Joint Conference on Natural Language Processing (Volume 1: Long Papers)*, pages 220–231, Online. Association for Computational Linguistics.

Yucheng Wang, Bowen Yu, Yueyang Zhang, Tingwen Liu, Hongsong Zhu, and Limin Sun. 2020b. TPLinker: Single-stage joint extraction of entities and relations through token pair linking. In *COLING*.

Zhepei Wei, Jianlin Su, Yue Wang, Yuan Tian, and Yi Chang. 2020. A novel cascade binary tagging framework for relational triple extraction. In *ACL*.

Yuxin Xiao, Zecheng Zhang, Yuning Mao, Carl Yang, and Jiawei Han. 2022. SAIS: Supervising and augmenting intermediate steps for document-level relation extraction. In *Proceedings of the 2022 Conference of the North American Chapter of the Association for Computational Linguistics: Human Language Technologies*, pages 2395–2409, Seattle, United States. Association for Computational Linguistics.

Yiqing Xie, Jiaming Shen, Sha Li, Yuning Mao, and Jiawei Han. 2022. Eider: Empowering document-level relation extraction with efficient evidence extraction and inference-stage fusion. In *Findings of the Association for Computational Linguistics: ACL 2022*, pages 257–268, Dublin, Ireland. Association for Computational Linguistics.

Benfeng Xu, Quan Wang, Yajuan Lyu, Yong Zhu, and Zhendong Mao. 2021a. Entity structure within and throughout: Modeling mention dependencies for document-level relation extraction. *Proceedings of the AAAI Conference on Artificial Intelligence*.

Wang Xu, Kehai Chen, and Tiejun Zhao. 2021b. Discriminative reasoning for document-level relation extraction. In *Findings of the Association for Computational Linguistics: ACL-IJCNLP 2021*, pages 1653–1663, Online. Association for Computational Linguistics.

Wang Xu, Kehai Chen, and Tiejun Zhao. 2021c. Document-level relation extraction with reconstruction. *Proceedings of the AAAI Conference on Artificial Intelligence*, 35(16):14167–14175.

Zhiheng Yan, Chong Zhang, Jinlan Fu, Qi Zhang, and Zhongyu Wei. 2021. A partition filter network for joint entity and relation extraction. In *EMNLP*.

Yuan Yao, Deming Ye, Peng Li, Xu Han, Yankai Lin, Zhenghao Liu, Zhiyuan Liu, Lixin Huang, Jie Zhou, and Maosong Sun. 2019. DocRED: A large-scale document-level relation extraction dataset. In *Proceedings of ACL 2019*.

Deming Ye, Yankai Lin, Peng Li, and Maosong Sun. 2022. Packed levitated marker for entity and relation extraction. In *Proceedings of the 60th Annual Meeting of the Association for Computational Linguistics (Volume 1: Long Papers)*, pages 4904–4917, Dublin, Ireland. Association for Computational Linguistics.

Daojian Zeng, Kang Liu, Yubo Chen, and Jun Zhao. 2015. Distant supervision for relation extraction via piecewise convolutional neural networks. In *Proceedings of the 2015 Conference on Empirical Methods in Natural Language Processing*.

Daojian Zeng, Kang Liu, Siwei Lai, Guangyou Zhou, and Jun Zhao. 2014. Relation classification via convolutional deep neural network. In *Proceedings of the 25th International Conference on Computational Linguistics*.

Shuang Zeng, Yuting Wu, and Baobao Chang. 2021. SIRE: Separate intra- and inter-sentential reasoning for document-level relation extraction. In *Findings of the Association for Computational Linguistics: ACL-IJCNLP 2021*, pages 524–534, Online. Association for Computational Linguistics.

Shuang Zeng, Runxin Xu, Baobao Chang, and Lei Li. 2020. Double graph based reasoning for document-level relation extraction. In *Proceedings of the 2020 Conference on Empirical Methods in Natural Language Processing (EMNLP)*, pages 1630–1640, Online. Association for Computational Linguistics.

Xiangrong Zeng, Daojian Zeng, Shizhu He, Kang Liu, and Jun Zhao. 2018. Extracting relational facts by an end-to-end neural model with copy mechanism. In *Proceedings of the 56th Annual Meeting of the Association for Computational Linguistics*.

Meishan Zhang, Yue Zhang, and Guohong Fu. 2017. End-to-end neural relation extraction with global optimization. In *Proceedings of the 2017 Conference on Empirical Methods in Natural Language Processing*, pages 1730–1740, Copenhagen, Denmark. Association for Computational Linguistics.

Heng Zheng, Rui Wen, Xi Chen, Yifan Yang, Yunyan Zhang, Ziheng Zhang, Ningyu Zhang, Bin Qin, Ming Xu, and Yefeng Zheng. 2021. PRGC: Potential relation and global correspondence based joint relational triple extraction. In *ACL*.

Zexuan Zhong and Danqi Chen. 2021. A frustratingly easy approach for entity and relation extraction. In *North American Chapter of the Association for Computational Linguistics*.

Wenxuan Zhou, Kevin Huang, Tengyu Ma, and Jing Huang. 2021. Document-level relation extraction with adaptive thresholding and localized context pooling. *Proceedings of the AAAI Conference on Artificial Intelligence*, 35(16):14612–14620.

A Appendix

A.1 Details of Joint Models

A.1.1 PtrNet (Nayak and Ng, 2020)

PtrNet utilizes a seq2seq approach along with the pointer network-based decoding for jointly extracting entities and relations. Each triple contains the start and end index of the subject and object entities, along with the relation class label. Their decoder has two-pointer networks to identify the start and end index of the two entities and a classifier to identify the relation between the two entities. Decoder extracts a relational triple at each time steps and continue the process till there is no triple to extract. To ensure parity with other SOTA models, their BiLSTM encoder is replaced with BERT encoder.

A.1.2 REBEL (Huguet Cabot and Navigli, 2021)

REBEL utilizes an auto-regressive seq2seq model that streamlines the process of relation extraction by presenting triples as a sequence of text and uses special separator tokens, as markers, to achieve the linearization.. WordDecoder model of (Nayak and Ng, 2020) uses a similar approach using LSTMs whereas REBEL is a BART-based Seq2Seq model that utilizes the advantages of transformer model and pre-training. REBEL uses a more compact representation for the relational triples over WordDecoder model.

A.1.3 GRTE (Ren et al., 2021)

GRTE utilizes individual tables for each relation. The cell entries of a table denote the presence or absence of relation between the associated token pairs. It uses enhanced table-filling methods by introducing two kinds of global features. The first global feature is for the association of entity pairs and the second is for relations. Firstly, a table feature is generated for each relation, which is then consolidated with the features of all relations. This integration produces two global features related to the subject and object, respectively. These two global features are refined multiple times. Finally, the filled tables are utilized to extract all relevant triples.

A.1.4 OneRel (Shang et al., 2022)

OneRel frames the joint entity and relation extraction task as a fine-grained triple classification problem. It uses a three-dimensional matrix with relation-specific horns tagging strategy. The rows in this matrix refer to the head entity tokens and the columns in this matrix refer to the tail entity tokens from the original text. The scoring-based classifier checks the accuracy of the decoded relational triples. It discards the triples with low confidence.

A.1.5 BiRTE (Ren et al., 2022)

In this paper, a bidirectional tagging approach with multiple stages is utilized. BiRTE first discovers the subject entities and then identifies the object entities based on the subject entities. It then does this in the reverse direction, first discovering the object entities and identifying subject entities for the object entities. The final stage involves the relation classification of subject-object pairs. They perform these tasks jointly in a single model.

A.2 Details of Pipeline Models

A.2.1 SSAN (Xu et al., 2021a)

This paper frames the structure of entities as defined by the specific dependencies between the entity mention pairs in a document. The proposed approach, SSAN, integrates these structural dependencies with the self-attention mechanism at the encoding stage. To achieve this, two transformation modules are included in each self-attention building block, which generates attentive biases to regulate the attention flow adaptively. This approach achieved SOTA performance on the DocRED dataset.

A.2.2 KD-DocRE (Tan et al., 2022)

This paper suggests a semi-supervised framework for extracting document-level relations. To achieve this, they exploit the inter-dependency among the relational triples through the implementation of an axial attention module. This approach leads to enhanced performance when dealing with two-hop relations. In addition to this, an adaptive focal loss is proposed as a means of resolving the issue of imbalanced label distribution for long-tail classes. Finally, to account for the difference between human-annotated data and distantly supervised data, knowledge distillation is utilized. Their experiments on the DocRED show the effectiveness of the approach.

A.2.3 SAIS (Xiao et al., 2022)

The objective of this paper is to train the model to identify relevant contexts and entity types by using the Supervising and Augmenting Intermediate Steps (SAIS) approach for relation extraction. The SAIS framework proposed in this paper results in the extraction of relations that are of superior quality, owing to its more efficient supervision. By utilizing evidence-based data augmentation and ensemble inference, SAIS also improves the accuracy of the supporting evidence retrieval process while minimizing the computational cost.

A.3 Details of NER Model

A.3.1 PL-Marker (Ye et al., 2022)

In their approach for span representation, PL-Marker strategically uses levitated markers to consider the interrelation between pairs of spans. They propose a packing strategy that factors in neighbouring spans to improve the modeling of entity boundary information. Additionally, they utilize a subject-oriented packing approach, which groups each subject with its objects to effectively model the interrelations between the same subject span pairs.

A.4 Related Work

Sentence-level Relation Extraction: Early approaches for relation extraction use two steps pipeline approach. The first step, Named Entity Recognition (NER), extracts entities from the text. The second step, Relation Classification (RC), identifies pairwise relations between the extracted entities (Zeng et al., 2014, 2015; Jat et al., 2017; Nayak and Ng, 2019). Pipeline methods fail to capture the implicit correlation between the two sub-tasks. They suffer from error propagation between the two stages. They cannot model the interaction among the relational triples.

To mitigate the drawbacks of pipeline approaches, recent works have focused on Joint entities and relation extraction. Joint approaches referred to as End-to-End Relation Extraction (RE) accomplish both tasks jointly. Training simultaneously on both NER and RC tasks allows for capturing more complex interactions among the multiple relational triples present in the context. Miwa and Bansal (2016) proposed a model that trained the NER and RC module in a single model. Nayak and Ng (2020); Cabot and Navigli (2021) propose seq2seq models for extracting the triples in a sequence. Sui et al. (2020) casts the joint extraction task as a set prediction problem rather than a sequence extraction problem. Zhang et al. (2017); Wang et al. (2020b, 2021); Shang et al. (2022) formulate the NER and RC tasks as table filling problem where each cell of the table represents the interaction between two tokens. Ren et al. (2022); Zheng et al. (2021); Li et al. (2021); Yan et al. (2021); Wei et al. (2020) have separate NER and RC modules in the same model trained in an end-to-end fashion.

Document-level Relation Extraction: Recently, there has been a shift of interest towards document-level RE (Yao et al., 2019). Document-level relation extraction (DocRE) is known to be a more complex and realistic task compared to the sentence-level counterpart. DocRE typically involves large volumes of data, which can be computationally expensive to handle using joint models. Recent work in DocRE has avoided using joint models for this task as joint models are not scalable for long documents. In DocRE, there can be multiple mentions of an entity with different surface forms across the document and the evidence of the relations can spread across multiple sentences. In document-level RE, mostly pipeline approaches are proposed, joint extraction approaches are not explored for this task. Earlier works (Peng et al., 2021; Quirk and Poon, 2017; Song et al., 2018; Jia et al., 2019) used dependency graph between the two entities to find the relations. Recent works (Guo et al., 2019; Nan et al., 2020; Wang et al., 2020a; Zeng et al., 2020, 2021; Xu et al., 2021c,b) proposed graph-based approaches that use advanced neural techniques to do multi-hop reasoning. More recent Transformer-based approaches (Wang et al., 2019; Tang et al., 2020; Huang et al., 2021; Xu et al., 2021a; Zhou et al., 2021; Xie et al., 2022) use pre-trained language models to encode long-range contextual dependencies in the documents. Huang et al. (2021); Xie et al. (2022); Xiao et al. (2022); Tan et al. (2022) use neural classifier to identify the evidences for relations along with relation classification for performance improvement.

On the Challenges of Fully Incremental Neural Dependency Parsing

Ana Ezquerro, Carlos Gómez-Rodríguez and David Vilares
Universidade da Coruña, CITIC
Departamento de Ciencias de la Computación y Tecnologías de la Información
Campus de Elviña s/n, 15071
A Coruña, Spain
{ana.ezquerro, carlos.gomez, david.vilares}@udc.es

Abstract

Since the popularization of BiLSTMs and Transformer-based bidirectional encoders, state-of-the-art syntactic parsers have lacked incrementality, requiring access to the whole sentence and deviating from human language processing. This paper explores whether fully incremental dependency parsing with modern architectures can be competitive. We build parsers combining strictly left-to-right neural encoders with fully incremental sequence-labeling and transition-based decoders. The results show that fully incremental parsing with modern architectures considerably lags behind bidirectional parsing, noting the challenges of psycholinguistically plausible parsing.

1 Introduction

Human understanding of natural language is widely agreed to be *incremental*: humans do not need to read a complete sentence to start understanding it. Instead, we update partial interpretations as we receive more input (Marslen-Wilson, 1985).

While the exact way in which this incrementality works is still unclear (Kitaev et al., 2022), its presence implies that some form of incrementality is an obvious necessary condition for a parser to be psycholinguistically plausible as a model of human processing (Miller and Schuler, 2010). Since human processing is the gold standard for automatic parsing, we know that it should be possible to achieve accurate parsing with incremental systems. Yet, in recent years, none of the competitive syntactic parsers that have been proposed for either of the main syntactic formalisms can be said to be incremental, even under the loosest possible definitions of the term. This poses challenges in the intersection between syntax and computational psycholinguistics, e.g., use cases both for modeling of human parsing and for real-time settings where one wants partial results before waiting for a sentence to end. Currently, most parsers use bidirectional encoders, such as BiLSTMs (Kiperwasser and Goldberg, 2016; Dozat and Manning, 2017) or Transformers (Zhou and Zhao, 2019; Mrini et al., 2020; Yang and Deng, 2020), so the whole sentence is being used before even processing the first word. An exception is the constituent parser by Kitaev et al. (2022), who use a fully incremental encoder, but the rest of the model is bidirectional, as it uses Transformer layers and a CYK-like, non-left-to-right span-based decoder (Stern et al., 2017).

This paper explores the viability of *fully incremental* dependency parsing, i.e., parsers where all the components (from the encoder to the decoder) work *strictly* from left to right. To our knowledge, this is the first attempt to build fully incremental dependency parsers with modern deep learning architectures.

2 Incrementality in Parsing

In transition-based parsing Transition-based parsing has traditionally been linked to incrementality (Nivre, 2008), as it works from left to right and builds partial outputs. Some authors consider that transition-based parsers as a whole are incremental, as they have internal states with partial outputs (Eisape et al., 2022). We will call this criterion *weak incrementality*. Others exclude algorithms like the arc-standard dependency parser, where dependencies are not built in left-to-right order and input arbitrarily far in the future might be needed to build right-branching dependencies (Christiansen and Chater, 2016). We will call this stricter view *strong incrementality*, and formalize it as follows: given a monotonic parser (i.e., one where each partial parse is a superset of the previous), we say that it is *strongly incremental with delay k* if every possible partial parse for a prefix $w_1 \dots w_{i-k}$ can be built upon reading the prefix $w_1 \dots w_i$, without the parser having accessed the rest of the input.[1] Analo-

[1] The definition of a partial parse for the prefix $w_1 \dots w_{i-k}$ depends on the grammatical formalism. For dependency parsing, we mean the subgraph of a full parse induced by the nodes

Proceedings of the 13th International Joint Conference on Natural Language Processing and the 3rd Conference of the Asia-Pacific Chapter of the Association for Computational Linguistics (Volume 2: Short Papers), pages 52–66
November 1–4, 2023.

gous considerations about the limitations with right-branching in weak incrementality, and parsers that try to avoid it to various extents, have been studied in the CCG literature (Ambati et al., 2015; Stanojević and Steedman, 2019, 2020; Stanojević et al., 2021). Contrary to arc-standard, other transition-based dependency parsers are strongly incremental: the arc-eager (Nivre, 2003), Covington (Covington, 2001) or multiplanar (Gómez-Rodríguez and Nivre, 2013) parsers all fit our definition above.

Classic implementations of strongly incremental parsers typically have positive delay (Beuck et al., 2011) between input and output due to lookahead. Some approaches have considered zero delay, albeit with weaker performance (Köhn and Menzel, 2013). Solutions are also available for speculativity in incremental parsing (Kitaev et al., 2022), by introducing non-monotonicity (Honnibal et al., 2013; Fernández-González and Gómez-Rodríguez, 2017).

Thus, the paradigm supports incrementality and many implementations of these parsers from the pre-deep-learning era, which did not use contextualized encoders, were strongly incremental, leading to the observation by Gómez-Rodríguez (2016) that at that point, some state-of-the-art parsing models were converging with psycholiguistically plausible models. However, in recent years bidirectional encoders have become ubiquitous, ruling out even weak incrementality from recent implementations of transition-based parsers, be them for dependency or other grammatical formalisms (Kiperwasser and Goldberg, 2016; Stanojević and Steedman, 2019; Fernandez Astudillo et al., 2020; Fernández-González and Gómez-Rodríguez, 2023). In this respect, it is worth mentioning that the approach by Yang and Deng (2020) is described as "strongly incremental constituency parsing" but this refers to the decoder, as they use a bidirectional encoder. The only recent proposal we are aware of that aims for incrementality in the whole system is the CCG parser by Stanojević and Steedman (2020), also a constituency parser, but its labelled F-score is over 7 points lower than a non-incremental baseline in an English-only evaluation.

In label-based parsing Other parsing paradigms that yield themselves to incrementality, as they could work from left to right, are seq2seq parsing (Vinyals et al., 2015) and sequence-labeling parsing (Gómez-Rodríguez and Vilares, 2018; Strzyz et al., 2019). However, for the former, we are not aware of any implementation without bidirectional encoders. For the latter, while there are strongly incremental sequence-labeling decoders for both constituency (Gómez-Rodríguez and Vilares, 2018) and dependency (Strzyz et al., 2020), most implementations use bidirectional encoders as well. The exception are some experiments with feed-forward encoders in Gómez-Rodríguez and Vilares (2018), using a sliding window to model near future context (and thus, with delay). Yet, their F-score is 14 points below their non-incremental counterparts in the same paper, and almost 20 below the overall state of the art.

in $w_1 \dots w_{i-k}$. Some authors require connectedness (Beuck et al., 2011). However, since the path between two words in $w_1 \dots w_{i-k}$ in the final parse may involve words outside the prefix, we do not believe this requirement is necessary.

3 Incremental models

The research question arises whether it is possible to have competitive incremental dependency parsers in the neural era. We take the first step and test how mainstream approaches would work in a setting of strong incrementality. In our work, we will focus on models with *strictly* zero delay, but we also evaluate less strict setups, in particular with delays 1 and 2. To do so, we will rely on modern encoder-decoder models. All source code is available on GitHub (`https://github.com/anaezquerro/incpar`).

3.1 Incremental encoders

Let $w = [w_1, w_2, ...w_{|w|}]$ (with $w_i \in \mathcal{V}$) be an input sentence. An encoder can be seen as a parameterized function $\Omega_{\theta,|w|} : \mathcal{V}^{|w|} \rightarrow \mathcal{H}^{|w|}$, where $\mathcal{V}$ is the input vocabulary space, and $\mathcal{H} \in \mathcal{R}^N$ is the hidden representational space in where each w_i is projected. In this work we are particularly interested in incremental encoders, i.e., those where given a token w_i, the computation of its projected representation h_i only needs the sub-sequence $w_{[1:i]}$. We consider different encoders for this purpose: (i) **4 stacked left-to-right LSTMs** (Hochreiter and Schmidhuber, 1997), where input is a concatenation of a word and PoS tag vector (random init) and a char-level unidirectional LSTM; (ii) **BLOOM** (Scao et al., 2022) (due to resource constraints, we run the smallest version with 560M parameters); and (iii) **mGPT** (Shliazhko et al., 2022).

As *control* encoders (upper bound baselines), we use non-incremental encoders: (i) bidirectional

LSTMs (same setup as for left-to-right LSTMs), and (ii) XLM-RoBERTa (Conneau et al., 2020).

3.2 Incremental decoders

We consider incremental (i) sequence labeling parsing, and (ii) transition-based parsing decoders.

3.2.1 Sequence labeling decoders

A sequence labeling decoder is a parametrized function $\Phi_{\theta,|w|}$: $\mathcal{H}^{|w|} \rightarrow \mathcal{L}^{|w|}$, which maps each hidden vector ($h_i \in \mathcal{H}$) outputted by a generic encoder into an output label $l_i \in \mathcal{L}$ that represents a part of the output parse. As the decoder, we use a 1-layered feed-forward network and a softmax. As for label encodings, we select representatives from two encoding families (Strzyz et al., 2019, 2020):

Head-based We study three variants, all of them supporting non-projective trees. First, the absolute-indexing encoding (abs-idx), where the token labels are the index of their head. Second, the relative-indexing encoding (rel-idx), where the label is the difference between the head and dependent indexes. Third, the PoS-tag-based encoding (PoS-idx), where each label is encoded as an offset that indicates that the nth word to its left/right with a given PoS tag is the head.[2]

Strings of brackets First, we consider the 1-planar bracketing encoding (1p), where the label for each token is represented using a string of brackets, with each arc represented by a bracket pair. This encoding can only model crossing arcs in opposite directions. To tackle this, there is a 2-planar variant (2p), analogous, but defining a second plane of brackets.

In the context of full incrementality, we will say that an encoding is *forward-looking* if a label for a token w_i can refer to some token to the right of w_i. The abs-idx, rel-idx and PoS-idx encodings are forward-looking (e.g., with abs-idx, the word w_2 could have 4 as its label, meaning that its head is w_4, which has not been read yet); while the bracketing encodings are *not* forward-looking. Forward-lookingness does not break incrementality: all the considered encodings are still strongly incremental with delay 0 (all dependencies involving $w_1 \dots w_i$ can be retrieved from the labels $l_1 \dots l_i$). However, one could expect forward-looking encodings to suffer more from using incremental encoders, due to needing to make decisions involving future words that the system cannot yet access.

In our implementation, for models with delay zero, the ith label is predicted directly from h_i. For models with delay $k > 0$, labels are predicted from a concatenated representation $h_i \cdot \dots \cdot h_{i+k-1} \cdot h_{i+k}$.

It is also worth noting that the obtention of the tree encoded by a sequence labeling encoding can require simple postprocessing heuristics (e.g. to remove cycles in head-selection encodings). This does not break incrementality, as these heuristics are applicable to partial outputs as well.

3.2.2 Transition-based decoders

A transition-based decoder is defined as a tuple (C, T, c_s, C_t), where C is a set of configurations (or parsing states) with associated partial parses, T a set of transitions between states, and c_s and C_t are the initial state and set of valid final states, respectively. In the case of the arc-eager parser (Nivre, 2008), states are triplets of the form (σ,β,A) where σ is a stack of partially processed words, β a buffer of remaining words[3] which always takes the form $\beta_i = w_i \dots w_{|w|}$ for some i, and A is the partial parse at that state. This parser is strongly incremental, as the way in which the algorithm constructs dependencies (in a strictly left-to-right manner) means that a configuration with buffer β_i can hold every possible partial parse for the prefix $w_1 \dots w_i$. The parser's delay depends on the number of buffer words used as lookahead features in the implementation. In our case, this is only one (we only use the first stack word and the first buffer word) so we can obtain partial parses for $w_1 \dots w_i$ accessing only $w_1 \dots w_i$, hence the delay is 0. Equivalently to sequence-labeling decoders, for models with delay $k > 0$, we access a concatenated vector of the form $w_i \cdot \dots \cdot w_{i+k-1} \cdot w_{i+k}$. For prediction of transitions, we again use a 1-layered feed-forward network.

4 Experiments

We choose 12 diverse treebanks from UD 2.11 (Nivre et al., 2020), supported by the tested LLMs. We test all possible combinations of encoders and decoders. As a well-known baseline, we use the biaffine (DM; Dozat and Manning, 2017) parser

[2]The PoS-tag based encoding needs PoS tags for decoding the sequence of labels to a tree. Instead of introducing PoS-tag information in those models, our PoS-tag-based decoders predict in multitask learning both the syntactic label and PoS tag associated to each word, in order to remove bias with respect to other encodings.

[3]Buffer words are often described as "unread" words when describing the algorithm, but for incrementality purposes we need to count them as "accessed" if they are used as features, as the parser implementation is using them for prediction.

in supar. We use unlabelled attachment score (UAS) for evaluation. Labelled (LAS) results and individual treebank results are in Appendix A.

Table 1 shows an aggregated summary of the results with strict delay zero. It shows that fully incremental models considerably lag behind their counterparts with bidirectional (control) encoders: the best fully incremental model for each language is 11.2 UAS points behind on average (sd: 5.0) with respect to the corresponding best control model. There is large inter-linguistic variability, Telugu (te_{MTG}) being especially amenable to incremental processing, 5.3 UAS points behind, and the opposite for Chinese (zh_{GSD}), 23.1 points behind. Our incremental-decoder-only models with LLMs as encoders are competitive against the BiLSTM-based version of the baseline (BiLSTM encoder, biaffine decoder), surpassing it on 7 out of 12 languages. However, they are a few points behind with respect to a version of the biaffine parser using RoBERTa encodings (which can be taken as a state-of-the-art system), consistent with existing comparisons of sequence-labeling parsers and biaffine parsers (Anderson and Gómez-Rodríguez, 2021). Put together, this seems to suggest that the challenge of incrementality falls mostly on the encoding side. If we focus on comparing different strongly incremental models we see that, as expected, forward-looking encodings suffer greatly from incremental encoders.

Table 2 compares the results from Table 1 against the corresponding models using delays 1 and 2. Improvements are consistent across the board. Interestingly, moving from delay 0 to 1 already shows a clear and large increase in robustness, especially for forward-looking encodings: the average gap between these and non-forward-looking encodings goes from over 10 points with delay 0 to nonexistent with delay 1, although considerable gaps remain in some languages like Chinese (zh_{GSD}) or English (en_{EWT}).

Finally, Figure 1 complements Table 2 with an analysis of the F-score with respect to dependency displacement (signed distance) for English and Chinese, chosen because they yielded the largest improvements when using positive delay. In particular, the figure shows that the lower performance of delay zero models is mainly due to poor performance of forward-looking encodings on leftward dependencies (right half of figure), and that a small positive delay already translates into clear improvements, even for long-distance dependencies.

	Fully incremental			Incremental decoder			DM	
	fl	**non-fl**	**tb**	**fl**	**non-fl**	**tb**	↔	XLM-RoBERTa
ar_{PADT}	75.7_{R}	76.8_{1P}	79.6	84.6_{R}	88.0_{2P}	86.9	86.9	91.0
eu_{BDT}	62.0_{P}	73.0_{1P}	71.0	87.0_{R}	87.6_{2P}	86.6	88.2	88.6
zh_{GSD}	51.1_{R}	64.4_{2P}	64.1	83.4_{R}	87.5_{1P}	85.3	86.7	90.7
en_{EWT}	61.5_{P}	74.7_{2P}	72.9	90.1_{R}	91.6_{1P}	89.5	90.2	92.7
fr_{GSD}	70.9_{R}	84.4_{1P}	84.7	92.3_{A}	94.7_{2P}	91.6	93.5	95.0
hi_{HDTB}	67.1_{P}	83.5_{1P}	83.2	94.3_{A}	95.3_{2P}	93.8	95.5	95.7
id_{GSD}	73.0_{R}	77.9_{1P}	78.6	84.5_{R}	86.3_{2P}	85.1	88.5	89.6
mr_{UFAL}	64.1_{P}	69.7_{2P}	65.8	75.7_{R}	75.2_{1P}	76.0	79.2	81.7
es_{ANC}	67.9_{R}	83.2_{2P}	82.9	92.0_{A}	93.4_{1P}	91.2	93.1	94.3
ta_{TTB}	59.1_{P}	67.3_{1P}	69.7	71.4_{R}	75.8_{1P}	78.6	77.2	80.0
te_{MTG}	73.8_{P}	85.0_{2P}	80.4	89.9_{R}	90.3_{2P}	89.0	89.2	94.5
vi_{VTB}	57.3_{R}	64.5_{2P}	64.5	72.7_{R}	74.1_{1P}	76.0	77.0	80.2
μ	65.3	75.4	74.8	84.8	84.6	85.8	87.1	89.5

Table 1: UAS scores paired with best forward looking (**fl**) and non-forward looking (**non-fl**) encodings, and transition-based (**tb**) decoder. Superscripts denote the encoder-decoder pair: LSTM (→), BLOOM-560m, mGPT, BiLSTM (↔), XLM-RoBERTa. Subscripts denote the best performing encoding: absolute (A), relative (R), PoS-tag-based (P), 1-planar (1P) and 2-planar (2P). Macro-average (μ) and baseline performance (**DM**, for Dozat and Manning) with different encoders (↔, XLM-RoBERTa) are included. Language abbreviations come from ISO 639-1 (Table 19 in the Appendix).

	Fully incremental delay 1			Fully incremental delay 2		
	fl	**non-fl**	**tb**	**fl**	**non-fl**	**tb**
ar_{PADT}	$84.2^{P}_{+8.5}$	$80.2^{2P}_{+3.4}$	$79.9_{+0.3}$	$83.9^{P}_{+8.2}$	$82.9^{1P}_{+6.1}$	$80.0_{+0.4}$
eu_{BDT}	$78.4^{P}_{+16.4}$	$76.9^{1P}_{+3.9}$	$75.7_{+4.7}$	$80.0^{P}_{+18.0}$	$80.1^{1P}_{+7.1}$	$76.9_{+5.9}$
zh_{GSD}	$64.3^{P}_{+13.2}$	$73.5^{2P}_{+9.1}$	$72.8_{+8.7}$	$68.4^{P}_{+17.3}$	$74.8^{2P}_{+10.4}$	$75.6_{+11.5}$
en_{EWT}	$81.9^{P}_{+20.4}$	$88.1^{1P}_{+13.4}$	$83.3_{+10.4}$	$85.6^{P}_{+24.1}$	$88.7^{1P}_{+14.0}$	$85.2_{+12.3}$
fr_{GSD}	$84.4^{P}_{+13.5}$	$86.2^{2P}_{+1.8}$	$87.5_{+2.8}$	$87.6^{P}_{+16.7}$	$89.2^{1P}_{+4.8}$	$86.7_{+2.0}$
hi_{HDTB}	$82.5^{P}_{+15.4}$	$86.2^{1P}_{+2.7}$	$88.7_{+5.5}$	$85.8^{P}_{+18.7}$	$90.1^{1P}_{+6.6}$	$88.9_{+5.7}$
id_{GSD}	$80.8^{P}_{+7.8}$	$80.4^{1P}_{+2.5}$	$79.2_{+0.6}$	$81.9^{P}_{+8.9}$	$82.1^{2P}_{+4.2}$	$79.6_{+1.0}$
mr_{UFAL}	$73.5^{P}_{+9.4}$	$65.8^{1P}_{-3.9}$	$72.7_{+6.9}$	$72.3^{P}_{+8.2}$	$64.9^{2P}_{-4.8}$	$71.1_{+5.3}$
es_{ANC}	$84.9^{P}_{+17.0}$	$85.4^{1P}_{+2.2}$	$85.2_{+2.3}$	$88.4^{P}_{+20.5}$	$87.6^{1P}_{+4.4}$	$85.6_{+2.7}$
ta_{TTB}	$68.5^{P}_{+9.4}$	$62.4^{1P}_{-4.9}$	$67.0_{-2.7}$	$69.9^{P}_{+10.8}$	$64.9^{1P}_{-2.4}$	$71.9_{+2.2}$
te_{MTG}	$85.0^{P}_{+11.2}$	$85.0^{2P}_{0.0}$	$87.4_{+7.0}$	$86.7^{P}_{+12.9}$	$89.6^{1P}_{+4.6}$	$90.0_{+9.6}$
vi_{VTB}	$66.6^{P}_{+9.3}$	$63.8^{2P}_{-0.7}$	$64.0_{-0.5}$	$68.3^{P}_{+11.0}$	$65.1^{2P}_{+0.6}$	$65.2_{+0.7}$
μ	$77.9_{+12.6}$	$77.8_{+2.4}$	$78.6_{+3.8}$	$79.9_{+14.6}$	$80.0_{+4.6}$	$79.7_{+4.9}$

Table 2: UAS scores with delay 1 and 2. Notation as in Table 1. Subscripts denote performance boost over zero-delay fully incremental results from Table 1.

5 Conclusion

We evaluated modern neural NLP architectures for incremental dependency parsing across multiple languages, using various encoders and decoders. We have found that said architectures are not adequate to model incrementality, at least in the absence of specific adaptations. Strongly incremental models with no delay yield accuracies about 10 points below competitive non-incremental baselines. While this gap narrows when adding a 2-

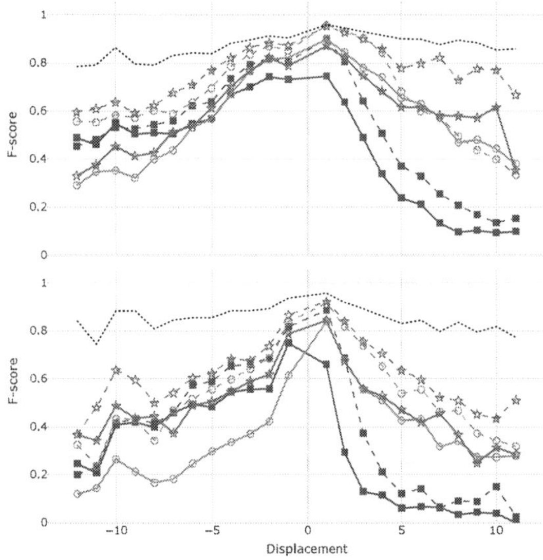

Figure 1: Displacement performance (English above, Chinese below) for the (fully incremental) models specified in Table 1 with delay zero (solid lines) and two (dashed lines). Different symbols and colors denote forward-looking (■), non-forward looking (○) and transition-based (☆) decoders. DM$^{\circlearrowleft}$ performance is included with gray dotted lines.

word lookahead, it is still about 5 points, contrasting with the situation in pre-deep-learning times, when incremental parsers were competitive (cf. (Zhang and Nivre, 2011)). The results suggest that much of the accuracy improvements in parsing obtained in recent years hinge on bidirectionality, deviating from human processing.

Accurate incremental parsing should in theory be possible (as the human example shows). Incremental processing is useful both for practical applications (Köhn, 2019), specially those involving real-time speech (Coman et al., 2019; Ekstedt and Skantze, 2021); as well as for cognitive modeling (Demberg and Keller, 2019; Stanojević et al., 2021). Thus, we believe that designing architectures that work well in a strongly incremental setting is an important open challenge in NLP. In this respect, techniques like using tentative predictions of future words made by autoregressive language models as a substitute for delay (Madureira and Schlangen, 2020) might be helpful. It is also conceivable that accuracy losses might not be solvable by better unidirectional scoring systems, and thus alternatives such as better search or methods that revise earlier decisions are also worth exploring.

Limitations

Limited physical resources We have no access to large computing infrastructures or a budget to scale services in the cloud. We had access to a few internal servers, for a total of 6 NVIDIA GeForce RTX 3090 (24GB each), and temporally we also obtained access to a NVIDIA A100 GPU (80GB), as well as a workstation for quick debugging. This restricts the number and size of models that we can try. In particular, we could train in reasonable amounts of time the smallest BLOOM language model (560M parameters). It was possible for us to fit up to the 3B version on the A100 GPU with a minimal batch size, but the amount of time that it took to train a model made it unfeasible to carry out a multilingual study like the one proposed in this work. Still, preliminary results showed that these larger BLOOM models were not contributing to significantly improve the performance. In this respect, we know that scaling *a lot* can play an important role, and that the standard BLOOM model is the 176B version. However, a model of that size is completely out of our economic and computing resources. Yet, we feel our study with smaller models is equally, or even more relevant, since it represents effectively the resources at hand for most companies and academic institutions.

Delay parameter Incremental parsers have a *delay* parameter that models how far beyond word i the parser can access to generate a partial parse for $w_1 \dots w_i$. For our main experiment we set the delay to 0, although we also provide results with delay 1 and 2. If we aim for psycholinguistic plausibility, there cannot be a single one-size-fits-all value for the delay, as the time taken by humans to parse linguistic input can be influenced by various factors like language, word length, reading/speaking speed, language proficiency, etc.; so any choice of delay is necessarily a simplification. However, evidence seems to point to human parsing generally being very fast, with latencies in the range of 100-250 ms (see for example Pulvermüller et al. (2009); Bemis and Pylkkänen (2011)). Hence our choice of delay 0 as the safest option, and we also present experiments with 1 and 2 to show what happens when a small lag between the input and the parse is accounted for.

Scope of definition Our definition of strong incrementality only applies to monotonic parsers. This is a deliberate choice: if we allowed non-monotonicity (i.e., removing or modifying dependencies from previous partial parses), then the definition would allow for a hypothetical parser that removes all partial output upon reading the last word and replaces it with a brand new parse generated with access to the whole sentence, which would be incremental in name only and render any comparison between incremental and non-incremental parsers moot.

While there might be alternative ways to restrict the definition to avoid this problem (e.g. restrict each step to be $O(1)$), these would come with their own limitations (e.g., excluding neural architectures where obtaining each word's vector representation is $O(n)$, or transition-based parsers with quadratic complexities). Thus, we believe that our definition is a good compromise for our purposes, as it is simple, unambiguous and implementation-independent within the realm of monotonic parsing.

Comparing non-monotonic parsers is a different undertaking as it not only would require a different definition of incrementality, but also evaluation metrics focused on partial parse accuracy rather than final LAS/UAS. But that is orthogonal to comparing incremental to non-incremental parsers (as partial parse accuracy is not even well-defined for some non-incremental parsers that do not have intermediate states) and lies outside the scope of this paper.

Differences in incremental processing between humans and machines Currently, despite research efforts, a comprehensive understanding of why humans excel at incremental processing compared to machines remains elusive. This issue also constrains our options for analysis. In this regard, the proficiency of humans at incremental language processing likely stems from adaptation in the context of cognitive constraints, having to understand real-time input with limited working memory which forces eager processing (see e.g. Christiansen and Chater 2016). From a different perspective, Wilcox et al. (2021) showed that both humans and models exhibit increased processing difficulty in ungrammatical sentences. However, language models consistently underestimate the magnitude of this difficulty compared to humans, particularly in predicting longer reaction times for syntactic violations.

Acknowledgments

We acknowledge the European Research Council (ERC), which has funded this research under the Horizon Europe research and innovation programme (SALSA, grant agreement No 101100615), ERDF/MICINN-AEI (SCANNER-UDC, PID2020-113230RB-C21), Xunta de Galicia (ED431C 2020/11), Cátedra CICAS (Sngular, University of A Coruña), and Centro de Investigación de Galicia "CITIC", funded by the Xunta de Galicia through the collaboration agreement between the Consellería de Cultura, Educación, Formación Profesional e Universidades and the Galician universities for the reinforcement of the research centres of the Galician University System (CIGUS).

References

Bharat Ram Ambati, Tejaswini Deoskar, Mark Johnson, and Mark Steedman. 2015. An incremental algorithm for transition-based CCG parsing. In *Proceedings of the 2015 Conference of the North American Chapter of the Association for Computational Linguistics: Human Language Technologies*, pages 53–63, Denver, Colorado. Association for Computational Linguistics.

Mark Anderson and Carlos Gómez-Rodríguez. 2021. A modest Pareto optimisation analysis of dependency parsers in 2021. In *Proceedings of the 17th International Conference on Parsing Technologies and the IWPT 2021 Shared Task on Parsing into Enhanced Universal Dependencies (IWPT 2021)*, pages 119–130, Online. Association for Computational Linguistics.

Douglas K. Bemis and Liina Pylkkänen. 2011. Simple composition: A magnetoencephalography investigation into the comprehension of minimal linguistic phrases. *Journal of Neuroscience*, 31(8):2801 – 2814. Cited by: 169; All Open Access, Green Open Access, Hybrid Gold Open Access.

Niels Beuck, Arne Köhn, and Wolfgang Menzel. 2011. Incremental parsing and the evaluation of partial dependency analyses. In *Proceedings of the 1st International Conference on Dependency Linguistics*. Depling 2011.

Morten H. Christiansen and Nick Chater. 2016. The now-or-never bottleneck: A fundamental constraint on language. *Behavioral and Brain Sciences*, 39:e62.

Andrei C. Coman, Koichiro Yoshino, Satoshi Nakamura Yukitoshi Murase, and Giuseppe Riccardi. 2019. An incremental turn-taking model for task-oriented dialog systems. In *Proceedings of INTERSPEECH 2019*.

Alexis Conneau, Kartikay Khandelwal, Naman Goyal, Vishrav Chaudhary, Guillaume Wenzek, Francisco Guzmán, Edouard Grave, Myle Ott, Luke Zettlemoyer, and Veselin Stoyanov. 2020. Unsupervised cross-lingual representation learning at scale. In *Proceedings of the 58th Annual Meeting of the Association for Computational Linguistics*, pages 8440–8451, Online. Association for Computational Linguistics.

Michael A. Covington. 2001. A fundamental algorithm for dependency parsing. In *Proceedings of the 39th Annual ACM Southeast Conference*, pages 95–102.

Vera Demberg and Frank Keller. 2019. Cognitive models of syntax and sentence processing. *Human language: From genes and brains to behavior*, pages 293–312.

Timothy Dozat and Christopher D. Manning. 2017. Deep biaffine attention for neural dependency parsing. In *5th International Conference on Learning Representations, ICLR 2017, Toulon, France, April 24-26, 2017, Conference Track Proceedings*. OpenReview.net.

Tiwalayo Eisape, Vineet Gangireddy, Roger P. Levy, and Yoon Kim. 2022. Probing for incremental parse states in autoregressive language models.

Erik Ekstedt and Gabriel Skantze. 2021. Projection of turn completion in incremental spoken dialogue systems. In *Proceedings of the 22nd Annual Meeting of the Special Interest Group on Discourse and Dialogue*, pages 431–437, Singapore and Online. Association for Computational Linguistics.

Ramón Fernandez Astudillo, Miguel Ballesteros, Tahira Naseem, Austin Blodgett, and Radu Florian. 2020. Transition-based parsing with stack-transformers. In *Findings of the Association for Computational Linguistics: EMNLP 2020*, pages 1001–1007, Online. Association for Computational Linguistics.

Daniel Fernández-González and Carlos Gómez-Rodríguez. 2017. A full non-monotonic transition system for unrestricted non-projective parsing. In *Proceedings of the 55th Annual Meeting of the Association for Computational Linguistics (Volume 1: Long Papers)*, pages 288–298, Vancouver, Canada. Association for Computational Linguistics.

Daniel Fernández-González and Carlos Gómez-Rodríguez. 2023. Dependency parsing with bottom-up hierarchical pointer networks. *Information Fusion*, 91:494–503.

Carlos Gómez-Rodríguez. 2016. Natural language processing and the Now-or-Never bottleneck. *Behavioral and Brain Sciences*, 39:e74.

Carlos Gómez-Rodríguez and Joakim Nivre. 2013. Divisible transition systems and multiplanar dependency parsing. *Computational Linguistics*, 39(4):799–845.

Carlos Gómez-Rodríguez and David Vilares. 2018. Constituent parsing as sequence labeling. In *Proceedings of the 2018 Conference on Empirical Methods in Natural Language Processing*, pages 1314–1324, Brussels, Belgium. Association for Computational Linguistics.

Sepp Hochreiter and Jürgen Schmidhuber. 1997. Long short-term memory. *Neural computation*, 9(8):1735–1780.

Matthew Honnibal, Yoav Goldberg, and Mark Johnson. 2013. A non-monotonic arc-eager transition system for dependency parsing. In *Proceedings of the Seventeenth Conference on Computational Natural Language Learning*, pages 163–172, Sofia, Bulgaria. Association for Computational Linguistics.

Eliyahu Kiperwasser and Yoav Goldberg. 2016. Simple and accurate dependency parsing using bidirectional LSTM feature representations. *Transactions of the Association for Computational Linguistics*, 4:313–327.

Nikita Kitaev, Thomas Lu, and Dan Klein. 2022. Learned incremental representations for parsing. In *Proceedings of the 60th Annual Meeting of the Association for Computational Linguistics (Volume 1: Long Papers)*, pages 3086–3095, Dublin, Ireland. Association for Computational Linguistics.

Arne Köhn and Wolfgang Menzel. 2013. Incremental and predictive dependency parsing under real-time conditions. In *Proceedings of the International Conference Recent Advances in Natural Language Processing RANLP 2013*, pages 373–381, Hissar, Bulgaria. INCOMA Ltd. Shoumen, BULGARIA.

Arne Köhn. 2019. *Predictive Dependency Parsing*. Ph.D. thesis, Universität Hamburg.

Brielen Madureira and David Schlangen. 2020. Incremental processing in the age of non-incremental encoders: An empirical assessment of bidirectional models for incremental NLU. In *Proceedings of the 2020 Conference on Empirical Methods in Natural Language Processing (EMNLP)*, pages 357–374, Online. Association for Computational Linguistics.

William D. Marslen-Wilson. 1985. Speech shadowing and speech comprehension. *Speech Communication*, 4(1):55–73.

Tim Miller and William Schuler. 2010. HHMM parsing with limited parallelism. In *Proceedings of the 2010 Workshop on Cognitive Modeling and Computational Linguistics*, pages 27–35, Uppsala, Sweden. Association for Computational Linguistics.

Khalil Mrini, Franck Dernoncourt, Quan Hung Tran, Trung Bui, Walter Chang, and Ndapa Nakashole. 2020. Rethinking self-attention: Towards interpretability in neural parsing. In *Findings of the Association for Computational Linguistics: EMNLP 2020*, pages 731–742, Online. Association for Computational Linguistics.

Joakim Nivre. 2003. An efficient algorithm for projective dependency parsing. In *Proceedings of the Eighth International Conference on Parsing Technologies*, pages 149–160, Nancy, France.

Joakim Nivre. 2008. Algorithms for deterministic incremental dependency parsing. *Computational Linguistics*, 34(4):513–553.

Joakim Nivre, Marie-Catherine de Marneffe, Filip Ginter, Jan Hajič, Christopher D. Manning, Sampo Pyysalo, Sebastian Schuster, Francis Tyers, and Daniel Zeman. 2020. Universal Dependencies v2: An evergrowing multilingual treebank collection. In *Proceedings of the Twelfth Language Resources and Evaluation Conference*, pages 4034–4043, Marseille, France. European Language Resources Association.

Friedemann Pulvermüller, Yury Shtyrov, and Olaf Hauk. 2009. Understanding in an instant: Neurophysiological evidence for mechanistic language circuits in the brain. *Brain and Language*, 110(2):81–94.

Teven Le Scao, Angela Fan, Christopher Akiki, Ellie Pavlick, Suzana Ilić, Daniel Hesslow, Roman Castagné, Alexandra Sasha Luccioni, François Yvon, Matthias Gallé, et al. 2022. Bloom: A 176b-parameter open-access multilingual language model. *arXiv preprint arXiv:2211.05100*.

Oleh Shliazhko, Alena Fenogenova, Maria Tikhonova, Vladislav Mikhailov, Anastasia Kozlova, and Tatiana Shavrina. 2022. mgpt: Few-shot learners go multilingual.

Miloš Stanojević, Shohini Bhattasali, Donald Dunagan, Luca Campanelli, Mark Steedman, Jonathan Brennan, and John Hale. 2021. Modeling incremental language comprehension in the brain with Combinatory Categorial Grammar. In *Proceedings of the Workshop on Cognitive Modeling and Computational Linguistics*, pages 23–38, Online. Association for Computational Linguistics.

Miloš Stanojević and Mark Steedman. 2019. CCG parsing algorithm with incremental tree rotation. In *Proceedings of the 2019 Conference of the North American Chapter of the Association for Computational Linguistics: Human Language Technologies, Volume 1 (Long and Short Papers)*, pages 228–239, Minneapolis, Minnesota. Association for Computational Linguistics.

Miloš Stanojević and Mark Steedman. 2020. Max-margin incremental CCG parsing. In *Proceedings of the 58th Annual Meeting of the Association for Computational Linguistics*, pages 4111–4122, Online. Association for Computational Linguistics.

Mitchell Stern, Jacob Andreas, and Dan Klein. 2017. A minimal span-based neural constituency parser. In *Proceedings of the 55th Annual Meeting of the Association for Computational Linguistics (Volume 1: Long Papers)*, pages 818–827, Vancouver, Canada. Association for Computational Linguistics.

Michalina Strzyz, David Vilares, and Carlos Gómez-Rodríguez. 2019. Viable dependency parsing as sequence labeling. In *Proceedings of the 2019 Conference of the North American Chapter of the Association for Computational Linguistics: Human Language Technologies, Volume 1 (Long and Short Papers)*, pages 717–723, Minneapolis, Minnesota. Association for Computational Linguistics.

Michalina Strzyz, David Vilares, and Carlos Gómez-Rodríguez. 2020. Bracketing encodings for 2-planar dependency parsing. In *Proceedings of the 28th International Conference on Computational Linguistics*, pages 2472–2484, Barcelona, Spain (Online). International Committee on Computational Linguistics.

Oriol Vinyals, Ł ukasz Kaiser, Terry Koo, Slav Petrov, Ilya Sutskever, and Geoffrey Hinton. 2015. Grammar as a foreign language. In *Advances in Neural Information Processing Systems*, volume 28. Curran Associates, Inc.

Ethan Wilcox, Pranali Vani, and Roger Levy. 2021. A targeted assessment of incremental processing in neural language models and humans. In *Proceedings of the 59th Annual Meeting of the Association for Computational Linguistics and the 11th International Joint Conference on Natural Language Processing (Volume 1: Long Papers)*, pages 939–952, Online. Association for Computational Linguistics.

Kaiyu Yang and Jia Deng. 2020. Strongly incremental constituency parsing with graph neural networks. In *Proceedings of the 34th International Conference on Neural Information Processing Systems*, NIPS'20, Red Hook, NY, USA. Curran Associates Inc.

Yue Zhang and Joakim Nivre. 2011. Transition-based dependency parsing with rich non-local features. In *Proceedings of the 49th Annual Meeting of the Association for Computational Linguistics: Human Language Technologies*, pages 188–193, Portland, Oregon, USA. Association for Computational Linguistics.

Junru Zhou and Hai Zhao. 2019. Head-Driven Phrase Structure Grammar parsing on Penn Treebank. In *Proceedings of the 57th Annual Meeting of the Association for Computational Linguistics*, pages 2396–2408, Florence, Italy. Association for Computational Linguistics.

A Appendix

A.1 Additional results

Tables 3 and 4 show the aggregate results according to LAS. Tables 5 to 16 illustrate the performance of every individual encoder-decoder pair in each treebank test set.

	Fully incremental			Incremental decoder			DM	
	fl	non-fl	tb	fl	non-fl	tb	↔	
ar_{PADT}	70.1_{R}	70.5_{1P}	69.5	79.0_{R}	82.3_{2P}	78.9	81.4	85.9
eu_{BDT}	56.4_{P}	63.0_{1P}	60.4	82.1_{R}	84.4_{2P}	76.0	82.4	85.0
zh_{GSD}	43.9_{R}	51.4_{2P}	54.6	80.5_{R}	84.1_{1P}	77.5	83.9	87.6
en_{EWT}	59.0_{P}	67.5_{1P}	65.4	87.9_{R}	89.1_{1P}	84.5	88.0	90.1
fr_{GSD}	67.1_{R}	78.2_{2P}	78.1	90.0_{A}	92.4_{2P}	87.0	90.0	92.1
hi_{HDTB}	60.7_{P}	69.6_{2P}	73.1	91.3_{A}	92.3_{2P}	86.0	92.6	92.4
id_{GSD}	68.2_{R}	72.1_{1P}	67.7	79.5_{R}	79.2_{2P}	73.5	83.2	82.5
mr_{UFAL}	48.3_{P}	45.9_{1P}	36.4	64.6_{P}	62.6_{1P}	61.6	59.6	72.8
es_{ANC}	63.8_{R}	78.9_{2P}	76.3	90.0_{A}	91.6_{2P}	85.5	89.6	92.3
ta_{TTB}	50.6_{P}	52.6_{1P}	42.7	62.3_{R}	66.3_{2P}	64.8	66.2	68.9
te_{MTG}	65.6_{P}	67.3_{1P}	53.5	79.8_{R}	81.7_{1P}	64.6	69.4	87.5
vi_{VTB}	45.5_{R}	50.8_{2P}	43.8	60.3_{R}	61.5_{2P}	56.8	62.9	67.3
μ	58.3	64.0	60.1	78.9	80.6	74.7	79.1	83.7

Table 3: LAS scores. Notation comes from Table 1.

	Fully incremental delay 1			Fully incremental delay 2		
	fl	non-fl	tb	fl	non-fl	tb
ar_{PADT}	$78.8^{P}_{+8.7}$	$74.6^{2P}_{+4.1}$	$68.1_{-1.4}$	$78.3^{P}_{+8.2}$	$77.1^{1P}_{+6.6}$	$68.7_{-0.8}$
eu_{BDT}	$73.5^{P}_{+17.1}$	$71.2^{1P}_{+8.2}$	$59.4_{-1.0}$	$75.2^{P}_{+18.8}$	$75.2^{1P}_{+12.2}$	$63.6_{+3.2}$
zh_{GSD}	$60.4^{P}_{+16.5}$	$68.3^{2P}_{+16.9}$	$61.3_{+6.7}$	$64.6^{P}_{+20.7}$	$69.7^{2P}_{+18.3}$	$75.6_{+21.0}$
en_{EWT}	$79.1^{P}_{+20.1}$	$84.2^{1P}_{+16.7}$	$83.3_{+17.9}$	$83.0^{P}_{+24.0}$	$85.0^{1P}_{+17.5}$	$85.2_{+19.8}$
fr_{GSD}	$80.9^{P}_{+13.8}$	$81.9^{2P}_{+3.7}$	$76.0_{-2.1}$	$84.2^{P}_{+17.1}$	$85.4^{1P}_{+7.2}$	$75.9_{-2.2}$
hi_{HDTB}	$78.1^{P}_{+17.4}$	$79.6^{1P}_{+10.0}$	$77.4_{+4.3}$	$82.0^{P}_{+21.3}$	$84.9^{1P}_{+15.3}$	$77.4_{+4.3}$
id_{GSD}	$73.6^{P}_{+5.4}$	$72.3^{1P}_{+0.2}$	$66.9_{-0.8}$	$75.2^{P}_{+7.0}$	$74.6^{2P}_{+2.5}$	$68.3_{+0.6}$
mr_{UFAL}	$58.2^{P}_{+9.9}$	$54.4^{2P}_{+8.5}$	$72.7_{+36.3}$	$57.4^{P}_{+9.1}$	$51.2^{2P}_{+5.3}$	$66.8_{+30.4}$
es_{ANC}	$82.4^{P}_{+18.6}$	$82.7^{1P}_{+3.8}$	$85.2_{+8.9}$	$86.2^{P}_{+22.4}$	$85.0^{1P}_{+6.1}$	$85.6_{+9.3}$
ta_{TTB}	$56.4^{P}_{+5.8}$	$50.3^{1P}_{-2.3}$	$67.0_{+24.3}$	$58.2^{P}_{+7.6}$	$53.8^{1P}_{+1.2}$	$51.8_{+9.1}$
te_{MTG}	$76.5^{P}_{+10.9}$	$74.1^{1P}_{+6.8}$	$87.4_{+33.9}$	$76.8^{P}_{+11.2}$	$79.4^{1P}_{+12.1}$	$48.0_{-5.5}$
vi_{VTB}	$53.6^{P}_{+8.1}$	$50.2^{2P}_{-0.6}$	$63.2_{+19.4}$	$54.4^{P}_{+8.9}$	$51.2^{2P}_{+0.4}$	$45.9_{+2.1}$
μ	$71.0_{+12.7}$	$70.3_{+6.3}$	$72.3_{+12.2}$	$73.0_{+14.7}$	$72.7_{+8.7}$	$67.7_{+7.6}$

Table 4: LAS scores with delay one and two. Notation comes from Table 2.

A.2 Training hyperparameters and model configuration

Table 17 shows the hyperparameters selected in the training process of each encoder. For LSTMs and BiLSTMs, words and PoS tags were mapped to a 300-dimensional and 100-dimensional vector representation, respectively. Word information at the character level was represented with the last hidden state of dimension 100 from a charLSTM. These three representations were concatenated and projected to the encoder hidden size. For pretrained encoders (BLOOM, mGPT and XLM-RoBERTa), we get their last layer representations. Then, they are linearly projected to a smaller dimensionality of size 100.

Table 18 shows the training configuration per architecture: LSTM and BiLSTM weights were fitted with Adam optimizer ($\beta_0 = 0.9$, $\beta_1 = 0.9$, $\varepsilon = 1e-12$) and pretrained encoders with AdamW ($\beta_0 = 0.9$, $\beta_1 = 0.9$, $\varepsilon = 1e-12$). Batch size was adapted by the number of parameters of the encoders and the size of the treebank: in small encoders (LSTMs and BiLSTMs) data was distributed in batches of size 600, while pretrained encoders were trained with batches of size 2000.

Metric	Encoder	fl			non-fl		TB
		abs-idx	rel-idx	PoS-idx	1p	2p	
UAS	LSTM	71.7	75.7	59.9	74.1	73.0	78.2
		74.8	80.2	81.3	76.9	76.2	76.9
		72.6	81.4	81.6	79.2	78.5	77.3
	mGPT	52.6	74.7	59.5	76.8	76.4	78.4
		65.5	81.7	84.2	80.0	80.2	79.9
		63.8	82.3	83.6	82.9	82.4	80.0
	BLOOM	43.0	74.4	58.6	75.6	75.6	79.6
		56.5	81.1	82.8	79.7	79.3	79.1
		55.4	81.5	83.9	81.9	82.0	79.9
	BiLSTM	71.0	83.2	65.9	81.3	80.4	82.0
		75.2	83.3	83.0	82.1	81.0	78.7
		73.0	83.4	82.9	82.3	81.1	78.3
	XLM	77.2	84.6	66.1	87.2	88.0	86.9
		86.1	87.9	86.0	89.6	88.8	83.1
		84.4	87.1	88.8	89.2	89.2	83.8
	DM	87.3					
LAS	LSTM	67.1	70.1	55.9	68.8	67.8	66.3
		68.6	73.5	74.9	71.0	69.6	59.6
		66.4	74.7	75.1	73.0	72.0	60.7
	mGPT	48.9	68.8	55.3	70.5	70.4	69.5
		61.2	76.0	78.8	74.1	74.6	68.1
		59.6	76.8	78.3	77.1	77.0	68.7
	BLOOM	39.6	67.6	54.4	68.9	68.8	67.6
		52.4	75.2	77.3	73.6	73.4	67.2
		51.3	75.7	78.0	76.0	75.9	67.8
	BiLSTM	66.8	77.6	61.9	76.1	75.2	73.4
		69.6	76.6	76.4	75.8	74.7	62.8
		67.6	76.6	76.3	76.0	74.6	61.9
	XLM	72.5	79.0	62.7	81.6	82.3	78.9
		80.9	82.3	81.0	84.5	83.7	68.6
		79.6	82.0	83.9	84.1	83.8	71.8
	DM	81.8					

Table 5: UAS and LAS for the Arabic PADT treebank. Last index level corresponds to delay results. First, second and third subrow show the scores obtained with 0, 1 and 2-delay, respectively.

A.3 Other statistics about the treebanks

Table 19 shows treebank language abbreviations and the percentage of arcs that point to the left and to the right in each treebank.

Metric	Encoder	fl			non-fl		TB
		abs-idx	rel-idx	PoS-idx	1p	2p	
UAS	LSTM	59.4	61.7	61.9	72.0	71.7	69.7
		69.0	70.8	74.0	70.8	0.0	73.6
		68.5	73.9	75.7	72.9	74.1	75.5
	mGPT	42.0	55.0	62.0	73.0	72.9	71.0
		58.5	67.7	78.4	76.9	76.0	75.7
		59.6	72.3	80.0	80.1	79.5	76.9
	BLOOM	34.6	50.7	58.1	64.3	65.2	63.4
		48.9	60.8	73.8	68.8	68.2	72.1
		52.6	67.8	75.9	74.7	72.2	74.6
	BiLSTM	81.5	87.0	73.3	83.6	83.7	83.3
		72.6	78.5	78.0	71.3	71.0	77.5
		70.7	79.6	77.3	71.8	70.6	76.7
	XLM	80.9	83.6	73.7	87.6	87.6	86.6
		84.8	86.4	86.2	86.4	85.8	84.4
		84.9	85.5	85.2	86.0	85.6	85.4
	DM	84.8					
LAS	LSTM	53.5	55.7	55.3	60.7	60.1	52.0
		61.6	63.7	67.3	63.5	0.0	52.8
		61.6	66.7	69.3	66.0	67.3	55.2
	mGPT	38.4	49.6	56.4	63.0	62.7	60.4
		54.4	63.2	73.5	71.2	70.4	59.4
		55.5	67.8	75.2	75.2	74.4	63.6
	BLOOM	30.8	44.2	51.4	53.3	54.2	50.1
		43.8	54.8	66.9	61.9	60.9	55.5
		47.5	62.2	69.7	68.6	65.8	58.7
	BiLSTM	76.5	82.1	69.6	78.4	78.6	67.8
		65.1	70.0	70.5	63.8	63.9	54.6
		62.8	71.8	69.6	64.8	63.0	53.7
	XLM	78.2	80.4	71.3	84.3	84.4	76.0
		81.2	82.7	82.6	82.4	81.8	77.0
		81.1	81.6	81.5	82.3	81.5	77.7
	DM	77.3					

Table 6: UAS and LAS for the Basque BDT treebank. Notation comes from Table 5.

Metric	Encoder	fl			non-fl		TB
		abs-idx	rel-idx	PoS-idx	1p	2p	
UAS	LSTM	43.7	51.1	45.0	62.9	61.9	60.1
		51.7	59.8	61.3	62.0	60.7	69.6
		54.6	64.3	64.0	65.3	64.6	70.9
	mGPT	33.8	47.6	44.7	63.4	63.6	64.1
		43.3	57.4	64.3	72.6	73.5	72.8
		40.5	63.0	67.4	73.6	74.8	75.6
	BLOOM	23.7	45.0	44.4	63.8	64.4	60.4
		32.5	57.3	64.2	71.5	71.9	71.4
		37.9	62.8	68.4	72.9	71.7	73.2
	BiLSTM	69.1	81.6	63.9	79.8	79.8	77.7
		62.5	72.8	71.7	69.1	67.9	72.5
		59.8	73.1	72.5	68.9	67.8	71.0
	XLM	81.6	83.4	65.3	87.5	87.3	85.3
		85.2	83.6	85.5	86.7	87.1	83.5
		85.3	85.4	83.4	86.6	85.8	81.8
	DM	85.3					
LAS	LSTM	37.5	43.9	42.0	50.5	49.4	50.2
		46.7	54.0	56.0	56.5	54.7	49.8
		49.5	58.3	58.6	59.3	58.5	52.9
	mGPT	29.7	40.6	41.5	51.1	51.4	54.6
		40.2	53.5	60.0	67.5	68.3	61.0
		37.8	59.3	63.6	68.9	69.7	75.6
	BLOOM	19.7	37.2	40.5	50.6	51.3	47.9
		29.9	53.5	60.4	66.0	66.4	61.3
		35.0	58.7	64.6	68.0	66.3	63.9
	BiLSTM	66.3	78.5	61.8	76.7	76.6	71.4
		56.4	66.2	66.4	64.1	61.9	55.1
		54.1	66.6	67.1	63.4	62.0	55.4
	XLM	78.8	80.5	63.6	84.1	84.1	77.5
		82.3	80.6	82.8	83.7	84.3	74.2
		82.2	82.2	81.0	83.3	82.2	72.4
	DM	82.4					

Table 7: UAS and LAS for the Chinese GSD treebank. Notation comes from Table 5.

Metric	Encoder	fl			non-fl		TB
		abs-idx	rel-idx	PoS-idx	1p	2p	
UAS	LSTM	58.8	60.5	61.5	74.4	73.3	70.4
		75.5	78.3	77.4	82.5	81.7	79.0
		80.1	82.6	80.3	83.9	82.6	78.6
	mGPT	49.5	56.4	59.0	74.0	74.7	72.9
		73.9	78.2	81.9	88.1	87.4	83.3
		78.6	83.4	85.6	88.7	88.6	85.2
	BLOOM	44.4	54.8	59.0	73.2	72.8	69.0
		68.7	76.3	80.4	85.3	84.6	81.7
		74.0	80.8	82.2	85.7	86.4	81.3
	BiLSTM	82.4	88.9	77.4	87.1	86.0	83.5
		84.6	87.3	84.8	84.6	83.7	80.5
		84.7	86.8	85.1	84.7	84.0	79.1
	XLM	88.6	90.1	78.3	91.6	91.0	89.5
		89.9	92.9	90.7	92.6	91.2	89.4
		92.2	92.5	92.6	93.1	92.8	86.4
	DM			90.6			
LAS	LSTM	55.0	56.8	59.0	67.5	66.3	60.5
		71.3	73.8	73.9	77.7	77.1	62.9
		76.0	78.5	76.6	79.4	78.6	64.6
	mGPT	46.0	52.3	55.7	65.7	66.2	65.4
		70.9	74.9	79.1	84.2	83.5	83.3
		75.4	80.2	83.0	85.0	84.8	85.2
	BLOOM	41.0	50.2	55.1	64.0	63.9	58.3
		64.1	72.4	76.2	80.7	79.4	68.4
		70.4	76.3	78.6	81.4	81.9	70.6
	BiLSTM	80.1	86.6	75.7	84.9	83.6	76.2
		80.7	83.6	81.3	80.5	79.7	66.8
		80.7	82.9	81.7	81.0	80.1	65.4
	XLM	86.5	87.9	76.4	89.1	88.5	84.5
		86.8	90.5	88.7	90.2	88.6	74.4
		89.9	90.1	90.4	90.9	90.5	74.2
	DM			88.5			

Table 8: UAS and LAS for the English EWT treebank. Notation comes from Table 5.

Metric	Encoder	fl			non-fl		TB
		abs-idx	rel-idx	PoS-idx	1p	2p	
UAS	LSTM	69.2	70.9	67.0	82.2	81.6	84.7
		77.5	79.4	80.3	80.9	81.6	84.4
		81.0	83.3	83.1	84.5	84.5	84.3
	mGPT	57.9	68.3	67.4	84.4	84.2	84.1
		73.8	79.8	84.4	85.8	86.2	87.5
		78.0	83.6	87.6	89.2	88.8	86.3
	BLOOM	54.1	68.0	66.1	82.8	82.2	83.8
		69.2	78.5	82.3	85.0	84.7	85.8
		72.0	82.8	86.7	87.0	86.8	86.7
	BiLSTM	85.3	91.4	80.1	89.8	89.0	88.8
		84.7	88.4	87.6	87.6	86.7	84.6
		85.0	87.8	87.6	87.2	86.8	85.5
	XLM	92.3	92.2	80.7	94.5	94.7	91.6
		93.0	93.4	93.5	93.8	94.4	90.2
		94.4	93.8	92.4	93.5	93.9	89.7
	DM			93.3			
LAS	LSTM	65.4	67.1	63.4	75.8	75.3	76.0
		72.1	74.3	75.1	75.1	75.5	66.6
		75.5	78.2	78.3	79.0	79.0	68.6
	mGPT	54.9	64.7	63.8	78.2	78.2	78.1
		70.6	76.4	80.9	81.4	81.9	76.0
		74.9	80.6	84.2	85.4	85.3	75.9
	BLOOM	50.6	63.9	62.5	76.4	75.6	73.6
		65.7	74.4	78.7	79.8	79.7	73.3
		68.5	78.8	83.2	82.0	82.0	74.4
	BiLSTM	82.0	87.7	77.2	86.2	85.5	82.0
		79.4	83.2	82.5	82.4	81.6	71.1
		79.7	82.2	82.5	82.1	81.5	71.9
	XLM	90.0	89.9	79.1	92.0	92.4	87.0
		90.2	90.7	90.7	91.1	91.7	79.8
		91.6	91.0	89.8	90.9	90.9	78.4
	DM			89.6			

Table 9: UAS and LAS for the French GSD treebank. Notation comes from Table 5.

Metric	Encoder	fl			non-fl		TB
		abs-idx	rel-idx	PoS-idx	1p	2p	
UAS	LSTM	66.0	66.1	67.1	82.8	82.7	83.2
		73.0	74.5	81.4	81.1	80.8	87.6
		76.8	78.7	84.1	86.0	86.1	88.9
	mGPT	46.2	62.4	66.1	83.5	83.4	82.3
		67.7	72.4	82.5	86.2	85.8	88.7
		73.0	77.6	85.8	90.1	89.6	88.1
	BLOOM	48.0	61.6	64.9	80.8	81.2	81.7
		61.9	70.3	81.9	84.2	83.9	88.3
		64.7	75.1	85.1	88.2	88.0	88.8
	BiLSTM	91.5	94.2	78.2	93.3	93.3	92.8
		87.8	91.2	90.4	88.2	87.8	90.7
		88.1	91.4	91.1	87.5	87.0	89.6
	XLM	94.3	93.5	78.0	94.7	95.3	93.8
		94.6	94.1	92.7	93.7	94.2	94.1
		95.0	94.2	92.6	94.0	94.2	93.8
	DM	95.5					
LAS	LSTM	60.0	60.4	60.7	67.8	67.8	71.3
		67.8	69.4	76.3	74.1	73.8	72.0
		72.4	74.2	79.4	80.3	80.4	74.4
	mGPT	41.5	57.0	60.5	69.2	69.6	73.1
		64.0	68.5	78.1	79.6	79.1	77.4
		69.2	73.8	82.0	84.9	84.1	77.4
	BLOOM	43.4	55.0	57.5	65.4	66.0	69.2
		57.6	66.1	77.6	77.1	77.1	74.5
		61.0	71.0	80.7	82.7	82.2	74.1
	BiLSTM	88.5	91.2	75.6	90.4	90.3	83.8
		83.0	86.4	85.9	83.7	83.2	75.5
		83.4	86.6	86.7	82.8	82.2	75.2
	XLM	91.3	90.5	75.7	91.8	92.3	86.0
		91.3	90.9	89.8	90.3	90.8	85.8
		91.8	90.8	89.7	90.5	90.8	88.2
	DM	92.7					

Table 10: UAS and LAS for the Hindi HDTB treebank. Notation comes from Table 5.

Metric	Encoder	fl			non-fl		TB
		abs-idx	rel-idx	PoS-idx	1p	2p	
UAS	LSTM	70.4	73.0	57.5	77.9	77.3	78.6
		78.3	79.2	80.6	77.6	76.4	79.2
		75.9	80.2	81.4	79.7	80.0	79.5
	mGPT	46.0	67.5	56.0	77.2	77.0	76.0
		60.6	75.5	80.8	80.4	80.2	78.8
		62.0	77.7	81.9	82.0	82.1	79.6
	BLOOM	40.4	66.2	55.9	75.9	75.9	78.4
		55.8	73.6	80.6	78.0	77.6	77.2
		56.0	76.2	80.5	80.1	80.4	77.9
	BiLSTM	73.9	84.5	67.6	81.5	83.8	84.7
		79.0	83.6	82.4	82.2	79.9	78.3
		76.5	82.5	82.7	80.9	80.8	80.1
	XLM	75.5	82.9	65.4	86.2	86.3	85.1
		83.7	86.0	87.2	87.5	87.1	83.0
		83.4	85.6	84.6	87.6	87.2	83.2
	DM	88.6					
LAS	LSTM	65.7	68.2	53.8	72.1	71.6	67.7
		69.9	70.8	72.3	69.2	68.8	59.4
		68.6	72.4	73.4	72.0	71.9	59.7
	mGPT	40.9	60.1	50.6	67.3	67.6	64.9
		54.8	68.5	73.6	72.3	71.8	66.9
		56.5	70.7	75.2	74.2	74.6	68.3
	BLOOM	35.8	58.6	49.7	66.2	66.1	63.3
		50.0	66.1	73.2	69.3	68.9	64.3
		50.4	68.5	73.4	72.0	71.8	65.8
	BiLSTM	69.7	79.5	64.8	73.4	78.8	73.5
		71.0	75.3	74.1	73.3	71.7	61.9
		68.7	74.1	75.0	72.4	72.6	62.4
	XLM	69.5	76.1	61.5	78.8	79.2	71.7
		77.3	78.8	80.6	80.3	79.7	71.1
		76.9	78.8	79.0	80.8	80.3	70.7
	DM	83.6					

Table 11: UAS and LAS for the Indonesian GSD treebank. Notation comes from Table 5.

Metric	Encoder	fl			non-fl		TB
		abs-idx	rel-idx	PoS-idx	1p	2p	
UAS	LSTM	42.7	55.3	64.1	65.0	69.7	65.8
		54.7	63.0	65.2	58.4	62.8	69.9
		60.8	64.2	60.6	63.1	60.1	71.1
	mGPT	27.2	45.2	59.2	63.1	61.2	60.7
		39.2	58.2	66.8	65.8	61.5	72.7
		37.4	58.1	68.9	63.1	64.4	66.8
	BLOOM	28.9	45.6	59.0	59.7	58.2	60.0
		46.7	55.1	73.5	62.3	64.9	69.2
		43.3	58.7	72.3	61.0	64.9	69.0
	BiLSTM	60.4	75.7	69.7	75.2	73.8	76.0
		60.2	69.3	67.8	63.9	61.6	66.6
		58.8	66.3	65.8	55.5	65.1	67.4
	XLM	33.7	63.4	70.4	71.4	71.8	73.5
		54.5	69.7	78.6	72.1	73.6	79.7
		52.8	74.7	79.4	80.0	68.0	80.2
	DM		82.4				
LAS	LSTM	34.0	43.9	47.8	44.2	45.9	29.8
		39.8	48.8	50.2	44.0	48.4	38.3
		43.9	50.3	46.6	43.8	44.7	40.2
	mGPT	21.8	34.2	48.3	45.9	45.6	36.4
		31.5	45.3	50.9	53.0	48.0	72.7
		27.4	45.5	55.4	49.9	51.2	66.8
	BLOOM	23.8	34.5	48.3	44.4	41.5	28.2
		36.8	44.7	58.2	49.8	54.4	42.4
		33.7	46.6	57.4	49.9	49.2	42.8
	BiLSTM	47.6	60.0	57.3	59.0	59.2	49.3
		44.0	51.8	44.8	44.9	44.3	42.6
		42.4	49.8	47.3	42.4	45.3	30.8
	XLM	30.6	55.3	64.6	62.6	62.4	61.6
		49.1	58.0	66.5	61.2	60.8	64.4
		45.9	64.2	65.4	69.8	55.2	55.6
	DM		62.5				

Table 12: UAS and LAS for the Marathi UFAL treebank. Notation comes from Table 5.

Metric	Encoder	fl			non-fl		TB
		abs-idx	rel-idx	PoS-idx	1p	2p	
UAS	LSTM	67.4	67.9	64.7	80.4	79.9	82.3
		75.9	78.6	80.6	79.2	78.3	82.8
		77.7	82.0	84.0	82.1	82.0	83.5
	mGPT	62.0	66.4	65.4	82.4	83.2	82.9
		73.0	79.8	84.9	85.4	84.8	85.2
		76.2	83.5	88.4	87.6	87.2	85.6
	BLOOM	53.1	66.7	65.1	81.0	81.4	81.7
		67.7	78.4	83.9	83.7	83.6	84.2
		70.3	82.3	87.1	85.7	85.8	85.2
	BiLSTM	88.4	89.6	79.1	88.5	87.4	88.0
		84.8	87.4	88.2	86.3	85.9	84.5
		87.8	87.1	87.6	85.8	85.8	83.8
	XLM	92.0	91.5	80.5	93.4	93.4	91.2
		93.8	93.0	94.2	93.6	93.4	88.7
		93.9	93.0	92.7	93.6	93.6	88.6
	DM		93.1				
LAS	LSTM	63.7	63.8	61.6	75.3	74.6	73.5
		71.2	74.0	76.1	74.4	73.8	67.0
		73.1	77.3	79.8	77.8	77.6	68.5
	mGPT	59.3	63.1	62.9	78.0	78.9	76.3
		70.5	77.2	82.4	82.7	82.0	85.2
		73.6	80.9	86.2	85.0	84.5	85.6
	BLOOM	50.3	63.2	62.2	76.0	76.2	74.5
		65.1	75.3	81.0	80.4	80.3	72.3
		67.5	79.2	84.6	82.5	82.2	74.2
	BiLSTM	84.9	86.2	76.3	85.3	84.0	80.9
		80.4	83.1	84.1	82.1	81.7	71.3
		82.9	82.7	83.4	81.7	81.5	71.2
	XLM	90.0	89.7	79.2	91.4	91.6	85.5
		91.6	91.0	92.3	91.6	91.4	78.2
		91.7	90.8	90.9	91.6	91.5	76.4
	DM		82.4				

Table 13: UAS and LAS for the Spanish ANCORA treebank. Notation comes from Table 5.

Metric	Encoder	fl abs-idx	fl rel-idx	fl PoS-idx	non-fl 1p	non-fl 2p	TB
UAS	LSTM	39.4	55.7	59.1	67.3	66.0	69.7
		42.5	50.7	54.3	54.4	43.5	61.7
		46.5	57.1	56.0	53.7	50.8	61.2
	mGPT	20.3	48.7	55.8	64.1	62.8	65.2
		32.1	57.7	68.3	62.0	60.3	67.0
		28.7	60.9	69.9	54.1	55.1	66.9
	BLOOM	19.4	49.4	54.0	55.8	63.1	65.7
		28.6	56.0	68.5	62.4	58.8	66.7
		31.6	60.0	64.9	64.9	63.6	71.9
	BiLSTM	51.2	71.4	61.7	74.3	74.7	73.7
		51.8	57.0	63.3	57.6	57.8	64.0
		45.1	57.3	64.2	58.2	56.4	65.6
	XLM	28.9	65.9	62.4	75.8	74.6	78.6
		41.0	69.6	72.2	71.8	72.4	74.4
		39.7	68.3	75.5	74.3	71.2	75.6
	DM			75.8			
LAS	LSTM	33.2	44.8	50.6	52.6	51.3	41.0
		28.3	35.6	40.3	38.6	22.5	32.4
		30.7	40.1	42.4	38.3	36.7	29.6
	mGPT	15.7	37.6	44.6	47.5	46.5	42.7
		25.8	47.4	56.4	50.3	48.4	67.0
		22.8	49.5	58.2	41.6	43.1	44.7
	BLOOM	15.4	37.2	42.9	38.6	46.8	40.3
		22.7	45.0	56.2	50.1	47.2	45.2
		25.9	48.5	52.1	53.8	50.3	51.8
	BiLSTM	44.9	62.3	47.0	65.7	66.3	57.5
		38.0	40.9	45.6	41.1	42.9	32.5
		31.5	39.5	47.8	41.1	41.4	35.4
	XLM	24.9	56.8	55.0	65.6	64.7	64.8
		34.7	59.4	61.7	60.8	61.7	53.2
		33.2	58.0	65.2	63.7	61.2	55.7
	DM			65.5			

Table 14: UAS and LAS for the Tamil TTB treebank. Notation comes from Table 5.

Metric	Encoder	fl abs-idx	fl rel-idx	fl PoS-idx	non-fl 1p	non-fl 2p	TB
UAS	LSTM	64.6	67.6	73.8	84.7	85.0	80.4
		78.6	78.3	78.4	82.2	83.5	87.3
		78.3	83.1	82.5	83.9	85.0	90.0
	mGPT	55.5	59.1	71.8	82.0	81.6	75.6
		73.7	75.0	85.0	84.5	85.0	87.4
		80.2	82.7	86.7	89.6	84.2	80.8
	BLOOM	51.7	54.8	70.0	79.1	79.2	74.1
		72.4	73.6	84.3	84.5	82.9	87.2
		78.7	78.2	85.7	84.0	84.0	87.8
	BiLSTM	86.3	89.9	85.3	90.2	90.3	89.0
		71.8	88.1	86.7	80.0	84.5	81.0
		71.3	88.1	85.0	83.2	76.2	82.4
	XLM	77.8	87.4	84.9	89.6	89.2	88.9
		83.6	88.2	89.9	86.7	87.0	84.2
		68.6	90.7	91.5	89.0	88.3	91.7
	DM			89.7			
LAS	LSTM	57.8	59.9	64.8	66.6	67.0	53.5
		68.6	67.0	67.0	62.9	63.2	52.3
		47.7	70.6	69.7	60.8	67.6	48.0
	mGPT	49.4	51.6	65.6	67.3	67.1	50.5
		65.6	67.1	76.5	74.1	71.3	87.4
		71.7	74.1	76.8	79.4	74.8	25.4
	BLOOM	46.5	45.4	62.1	63.8	63.4	43.4
		66.0	64.8	74.2	72.2	71.7	54.3
		71.8	68.7	74.3	74.2	67.4	47.9
	BiLSTM	74.9	77.7	76.7	79.6	79.6	64.6
		52.2	70.4	70.5	60.2	64.9	47.1
		52.5	73.9	64.9	60.8	55.0	56.5
	XLM	72.3	79.8	79.5	81.7	81.1	61.3
		75.5	79.2	80.4	71.2	67.5	35.7
		51.9	82.2	83.6	77.2	78.9	55.9
	DM			61.8			

Table 15: UAS and LAS for the Telugu MTG treebank. Notation comes from Table 5.

Metric	Encoder	fI abs-idx	fI rel-idx	fI PoS-idx	non-fI 1p	non-fI 2p	TB
UAS	LSTM	52.8	57.3	53.9	63.2	64.5	64.5
		49.2	57.8	58.2	57.2	56.7	60.9
		50.2	59.8	60.0	59.6	57.4	61.9
	mGPT	29.3	49.6	51.6	61.8	61.3	59.7
		34.8	56.9	66.6	62.9	63.8	63.2
		34.3	60.1	68.3	63.7	65.1	65.2
	BLOOM	31.7	51.0	51.1	62.1	60.7	61.0
		38.5	57.3	63.4	60.5	60.9	64.0
		38.8	61.6	64.6	59.4	62.0	60.0
	BiLSTM	66.8	72.7	64.0	70.1	70.5	71.0
		57.5	64.6	62.9	60.0	61.1	61.8
		56.2	64.3	62.5	60.2	60.0	60.9
	XLM	48.1	68.8	64.4	74.1	73.8	76.0
		58.1	68.6	73.2	73.4	71.4	75.3
		58.2	68.1	72.6	70.8	69.8	75.0
	DM	76.6					
LAS	LSTM	41.6	45.5	44.5	49.8	50.8	43.8
		36.8	42.5	43.2	42.2	42.1	36.3
		37.5	44.0	44.8	44.4	41.8	35.6
	mGPT	23.3	36.7	41.2	47.4	46.7	39.8
		28.1	44.3	53.6	49.4	50.2	63.2
		26.8	47.0	54.4	49.9	51.2	45.9
	BLOOM	24.9	38.2	40.5	46.7	45.9	39.8
		30.2	44.3	50.6	46.4	47.5	44.3
		30.7	48.1	51.0	45.8	48.6	37.4
	BiLSTM	55.4	60.3	54.6	58.2	58.3	51.2
		44.2	49.3	48.6	45.4	45.8	38.6
		42.4	48.6	47.5	45.0	45.3	38.1
	XLM	40.4	56.8	54.8	61.4	61.5	56.8
		48.8	56.6	60.6	60.6	58.1	58.7
		48.8	55.8	60.0	57.1	56.6	57.8
	DM	61.9					

Table 16: UAS and LAS for the Vietnamese MTG treebank. Notation comes from Table 5.

Hyperparameter	Fully incremental LSTM	Fully incremental BLOOM	Fully incremental mGPT	Non incremental BiLSTM	Non incremental XLM
Word emb size	300	1	1	300	1
PoS-feats emb size	100	x	x	100	x
Character emb size	50	x	x	50	x
CharLSTM hidden	100	x	x	100	x
Num. layers	4	1	1	4	1
Encoder hidden	400	100	100	400	100

Table 17: Architecture design choices for different encoders

Hyperparameter	Fully incremental LSTM	Fully incremental BLOOM	Fully incremental mGPT	Non incremental BiLSTM	Non incremental XLM
lr	1e-3	5e-5	5e-5	1e-3	5e-5
optimizer	Adam	AdamW	AdamW	Adam	AdamW
decay type	Exponential	Linear	Linear	Exponential	Linear
decay value	0.1	0.5	0.1	0.1	0.5
epochs	200	30	30	200	30
batch size	~6000	~2000	~500	~6000	~2000

Table 18: Training hyper-parameters for different encoders

ISO code	Language	% left-arcs	% right-arcs
$\mathrm{ar}_{\mathrm{PADT}}$	Arabic	30.46%	69.54%
$\mathrm{eu}_{\mathrm{BDT}}$	Basque	49.22%	50.78%
$\mathrm{zh}_{\mathrm{GSD}}$	Chinese	63.67%	36.33%
$\mathrm{en}_{\mathrm{EWT}}$	English	57.18%	42.82%
$\mathrm{fr}_{\mathrm{GSD}}$	French	54.72%	45.28%
$\mathrm{hi}_{\mathrm{HDTB}}$	Hindi	55.6%	44.4%
$\mathrm{in}_{\mathrm{GSD}}$	Indonesian	37.75%	62.25%
$\mathrm{mr}_{\mathrm{UFAL}}$	Marathi	51.34%	48.66%
$\mathrm{es}_{\mathrm{ANC}}$	Spanish	54.43%	45.57%
$\mathrm{ta}_{\mathrm{TTB}}$	Tamil	68.56%	31.44%
$\mathrm{te}_{\mathrm{MTG}}$	Telugu	54.28%	45.72%
$\mathrm{vi}_{\mathrm{VTB}}$	Vietnamese	40.99%	59.01%

Table 19: Statistics of treebanks retrieved in our multilingual benchmark.

Learning a Better Initialization for Soft Prompts via Meta-Learning

Yukun Huang* Columbia University yh3310@columbia.edu

Kun Qian* Columbia University kq2157@columbia.edu

Zhou Yu Columbia University zy2461@columbia.edu

Abstract

Prompt tuning (PT) is an effective approach to adapting pre-trained language models to downstream tasks. However, prompt tuning doesn't perform well under few-shot settings due to the poor initialization. So pre-trained prompt tuning (PPT) (Gu et al., 2022) is proposed to adapt prompt tuning to few-shot settings by initializing prompts with source data. We propose **Meta**-learned **P**rompt **T**uning (**MetaPT**) to further improve PPT's few-shot learning performance by considering latent structure within the source data. Specifically, we introduce the framework by first clustering source data into different meta-training tasks in an unsupervised manner. Then we leverage these tasks to meta-train prompts with a meta-learning algorithm. Such a process enables prompts to learn a better initialization by discovering commonalities among these meta-training tasks. We evaluate our method on seven downstream sentiment tasks. The results demonstrate that our MetaPT achieves better performance and stability than the state-of-the-art method.

1 Introduction

Pre-trained language models (PLMs) have demonstrated outstanding performances in various downstream NLP tasks (Devlin et al., 2019, Kale and Rastogi, 2020, Brown et al., 2020). **Full model tuning** (FT) adapts PLMs to downstream tasks by introducing task-specific training objects and fine tuning all parameters of PLMs. **Prompt tuning** (PT) (Lester et al., 2021) is an efficient alternative to FT by only tuning a small number of parameters. PT adds a series of tunable tokens (soft prompts) at the beginning of the sequence to modulate the behavior of the language model. When adapting pre-trained language models to downstream tasks, PT freezes all parameters of pre-trained language models and only trains the soft prompts. PT achieves comparable performance to FT with sufficient data. But it performs poorly under few-shot settings due to its sensitivity to the initialization of soft prompts.

To adapt PT to few-shot settings, **pre-trained prompt tuning** (PPT) (Gu et al., 2022) pre-trains soft prompts with a self-supervised source task and then apply pre-trained prompts to few-shot downstream tasks. PPT generally groups all text classification tasks into three formats and designs a self-supervised source task for each format to pre-train prompts. PPT demonstrates its effectiveness when using large-scale PLMs. However, PPT mixes all source data points together and ignores the latent structure among them. PPT updates prompt parameters at every data point, it learns more about the specific feature of each data point rather than the general features of the entire task. As a result, PPT retains too much redundant information only relevant to the source task in the initialization of soft prompts, which consequently impedes model performance on downstream tasks.

To further improve the few-shot adaption capability of prompt tuning, we incorporate meta-learning into prompt tuning. We first propose to use unsupervised methods to create meta-training tasks for prompts and then adopt a model-agnostic meta-learning method to meta-train prompts. By our unsupervised clustering method, the latent structure of source data is represented by the distribution of meta-training tasks. Through meta-learning, general features are incorporated into the initialization of the soft prompts. Our meta-learned prompts achieve faster and more stable adaptation to downstream tasks. We named our method **Meta**-learned **P**rompt **T**uning (**MetaPT**). Our experimental results show that MetaPT outperforms full-model tuning and pre-trained prompt tuning on the T5 model (Kale and Rastogi, 2020).

2 Related Work

Prompts There are two types of prompts that can probe the knowledge in PLMs without updating

*Equal Contribution

Proceedings of the 13th International Joint Conference on Natural Language Processing and the 3rd Conference of the Asia-Pacific Chapter of the Association for Computational Linguistics (Volume 2: Short Papers), pages 67–75

the parameters of PLMs: hard prompts and soft prompts. Hard prompts (Brown et al., 2020) are human-designed discrete tokens while soft prompts are continuous embeddings of language models. Soft prompts methods train efficient parameters to perform prompting directly into the continuous embedding space of the model to get better representation ability and avoid involving human efforts. These efficient parameters can be prepended to each layer in the encoder stack (Li and Liang, 2021), input embedding (Lester et al., 2021), or both (Liu et al., 2021). Though the above soft prompts methods perform well with sufficient training data, they all become much worse under few-shot learning settings. Pre-trained prompt tuning (Gu et al., 2022) is the current state-of-the-art soft prompts method under few-shot settings.

Meta-Learning Meta-Learning, also known as learning to learn, is famous for its effectiveness to extract domain-invariant features (Sahoo et al., 2018) and enforces models to adapt to downstream tasks (Finn et al., 2017). Model-Agnostic Meta-Learning (MAML) proposed by Finn et al. (2017) is a popular optimization-based meta-learning algorithm, which is adopted in various NLP tasks (e.g. Qian et al., 2021, Gu et al., 2018, Yin, 2020, Qian and Yu, 2019, Dou et al., 2019). Following MAML, works like REPTILE (Nichol et al., 2018), MetaOPT (Lee et al., 2019) and TAML (Jamal et al., 2019) etc. are proposed to further improve the model's learning capability. In this work, we focus more on exploring how soft prompts benefit from meta-learning. Therefore, we adopt the most widely used MAML algorithm.

3 Background: Prompt Tuning

Prompt tuning modifies the embeddings of soft prompts prepended to the input sequence to adapt PLMs to downstream tasks. Specifically, let (x, y) be a sample from a downstream classification task $\mathcal{T}^{down}$, where x is the input text while y is its corresponding label. We first map the label y into a concrete token z in the vocabulary of the PLM. Next, we use $H(\cdot)$ to fit input text x to a hard prompt template. Take sentiment classification as an example, H("I like this movie") ="I like this movie. It was $\langle \mathrm{X} \rangle$ ", where $\langle \mathrm{X} \rangle$ is the mask token. Then, we prepend soft prompts $\boldsymbol{P}$ to the beginning of input sequence $[\boldsymbol{P}; H(x)]$. Finally, we freeze the parameters of the PLM and optimize the following log-likelihood objective:

$$\operatorname*{argmax}_{\boldsymbol{P}} \sum \log p(\langle \mathrm{X} \rangle = z | [\boldsymbol{P}; H(x)]; \boldsymbol{P})$$

4 Meta-learned Prompt Tuning

In this section, we describe our self-supervised model training pipeline. We first gather source data. Then, we utilize an unsupervised method to cluster source data into different groups as meta-training tasks. Finally, we use Prompt-MAML algorithm to train and find a good initialization for soft prompts.

Our algorithm helps the model adapt faster to downstream tasks in two ways. On one hand, the meta-learning method simulates the adaptation step during training, which provides an easily-optimized parameter initialization. On the other hand, training across different clusters allows the model to focus more on the task's general features rather than domain-specific features.

4.1 Constructing Source Data

We construct source data by creating pseudo labels for sentences from open-domain corpus. For sentence classification, we first train a small model based on an existing dataset which shares similar label space to the downstream datasets. Then we use that model to annotate pseudo labels for the sentences in a large corpus.

4.2 Designing Meta-training Tasks

After constructing source data, we use K-means to group the data into different clusters as meta-training tasks. We first implement sentence-BERT (Reimers and Gurevych, 2019) to derive semantically meaningful sentence embeddings from source data samples. Then we apply unsupervised K-means to cluster source data into different classes according to their sentence embeddings.

K-means clustering group samples with similar sentence embeddings into the same task and reveal the latent structure within source data. Based on that structure, prompts could learn to incorporate some common internal features to the initialization through meta-learning. With such general information encoded in the initialization of prompts, the model can achieve great performance with limited training data from downstream tasks.

4.3 Prompt-MAML Algorithm

After we get a set of meta tasks $\mathcal{T}$ obtained via an unsupervised method, we utilize MAML to learn

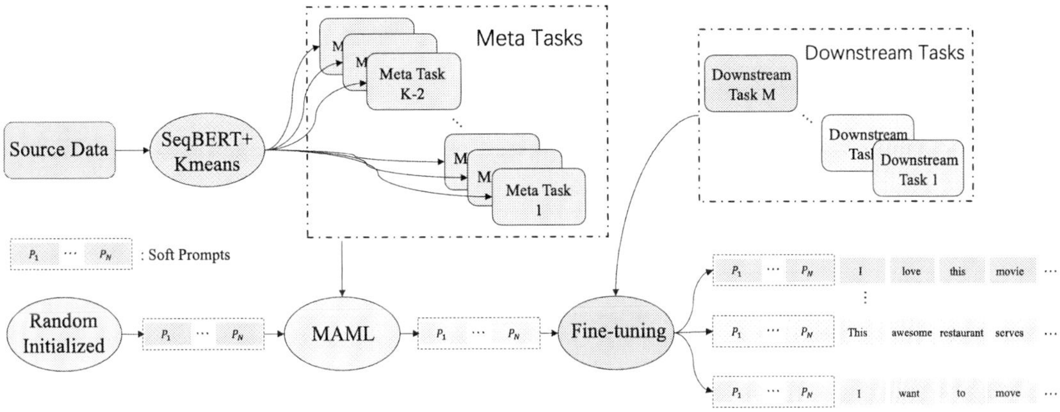

Figure 1: Pipelines of meta-learned prompt tuning. First, we prepare source data used for meta-learning. Second, we cluster source data into different groups as meta-training tasks (aka meta tasks). Then, we train prompts with model-agnostic meta-learning algorithm. Finally, we evaluate meta-learned prompts on downstream tasks.

general features among these meta tasks. We first randomly initialize the parameter of soft prompts $\boldsymbol{P}$. For each meta task $\mathcal{T}_i$, m training samples are sampled from that task. Taking in m samples, the model output $f_{\boldsymbol{P}}$. Then we calculate the average loss $\mathcal{L}_{\mathcal{T}_i}(f_{\boldsymbol{P}})$ of these m samples and temporarily update soft prompts with gradient descent, where α is the learning rate for the inner loop.

$$\boldsymbol{P}_i' = \boldsymbol{P} - \alpha \nabla_{\boldsymbol{P}} \mathcal{L}_{\mathcal{T}_i}(f_{\boldsymbol{P}}) \tag{1}$$

After optimizing the prompts, we sampled another m samples and calculated the loss with the updated prompts. We add loss for $\mathcal{T}_i$ to total loss and repeat the same process for other meta tasks until we go over all the meta tasks. Finally, we update the prompts by minimizing the final total loss, where β is the learning rate for the outer loop.

$$\boldsymbol{P} \leftarrow \boldsymbol{P} - \beta \nabla_{\boldsymbol{P}} \sum_{\mathcal{T}_i \sim p(\mathcal{T})} \mathcal{L}_{\mathcal{T}_i}(f_{\boldsymbol{P}_i'}) \tag{2}$$

This is a complete process of one-step updates for prompts. We keep optimizing the prompts until the validation accuracy of meta tasks stop growing. During meta-training, we simulate the adaptation step and therefore provide an easily-optimized soft prompts initialization. During the evaluation, the meta-learned prompts will be further tuned on downstream tasks and then make predictions.

5 Experiments

5.1 Setup

Our experiments are built on the T5-base model from HuggingFace (Wolf et al., 2020).

Downstream Datasets We focus on the sentiment classification tasks. Specifically, the downstream datasets include SST-5 (Socher et al., 2013), SST-2 (Socher et al., 2013), Amazon-5 (Zhang et al., 2015), Amazon-2 (Zhang et al., 2015), Sentihood (Saeidi et al., 2016), and SemEval-2016 (Pontiki et al., 2016). SemEval-2016 has two tasks in different domains: SemEval$_r$(restaurant) and SemEval$_l$(laptop). Detailed information on these datasets could be found in Appendix C. We randomly select 40 samples from the original dataset for both few-shot training and validation.

Source Data we first train a RoBERTa-base model on Yelp5. Then we randomly sample 10GB of data from OpenWebText (Gokaslan and Cohen, 2019) and apply the trained RoBERTa model to annotate labels for the sampled data. We only keep data samples with high confidence and throw away the samples which the model is unsure about. After balancing pseudo data, we get 1,000,000 balanced training samples with open domains.

See Appendix A for detailed hyperparameters.

5.2 Main Results

As shown in Table 1, we mainly compare the performance of full-model tuning (FT), pre-trained prompt tuning (PPT) and meta-learned prompt tuning (MetaPT) on different sentiment classification tasks. We also include results of MetaPT$_{(Y)}$ in the table, which is directly meta-trained on Yelp5.

First, MetaPT consistently achieves higher accuracy than PPT (7/7 tasks) and FT(6/7 tasks). MetaPT also shows better stability facing different training samples. Second, MetaPT$_{(Y)}$ also out-

Model	Methods	SST5	SST2	Amazon5	Amazon2	Sentihood	SemEval$_r$	SemEval$_l$
T5-base	FT	$43.57_{\pm 2.56}$	$88.27_{\pm 1.03}$	$48.40_{\pm 1.48}$	$92.35_{\pm 0.68}$	$\mathbf{82.11_{\pm 1.30}}$	$71.01_{\pm 1.16}$	$62.48_{\pm 3.23}$
	PPT	$42.90_{\pm 1.08}$	$87.42_{\pm 1.15}$	$51.15_{\pm 1.56}$	$93.28_{\pm 0.21}$	$80.06_{\pm 3.31}$	$62.04_{\pm 3.34}$	$56.37_{\pm 4.11}$
	MetaPT	$45.26_{\pm 0.39}$	$\mathbf{89.47_{\pm 0.12}}$	$55.47_{\pm 0.34}$	$94.43_{\pm 0.08}$	$80.38_{\pm 0.46}$	$76.93_{\pm 1.19}$	$70.86_{\pm 1.95}$
	MetaPT$_{(Y)}$	$\mathbf{46.24_{\pm 0.42}}$	$87.26_{\pm 0.73}$	$\mathbf{58.73_{\pm 0.13}}$	$\mathbf{95.39_{\pm 0.03}}$	$78.27_{\pm 1.17}$	$\mathbf{80.72_{\pm 0.60}}$	$\mathbf{72.32_{\pm 0.66}}$
T5-large	MetaPT	$47.31_{\pm 0.21}$	$89.61_{\pm 0.09}$	$55.76_{\pm 0.15}$	$95.23_{\pm 0.03}$	$85.78_{\pm 0.10}$	$85.96_{\pm 0.08}$	$77.49_{\pm 0.11}$

Table 1: Classification accuracy results on seven downstream tasks. FT denotes full-model tuning. PPT denotes pre-trained prompt tuning. MetaPT denotes meta-learned prompt tuning. MetaPT is meta-trained on pseudo-labeled data while MetaPT$_{(Y)}$ is meta-trained on Yelp5 directly. Our methods outperform the two other methods for most of the datasets. MetaPT not only achieve higher accuracy than PPT consistently, but also have a more stable performance with lower variance.

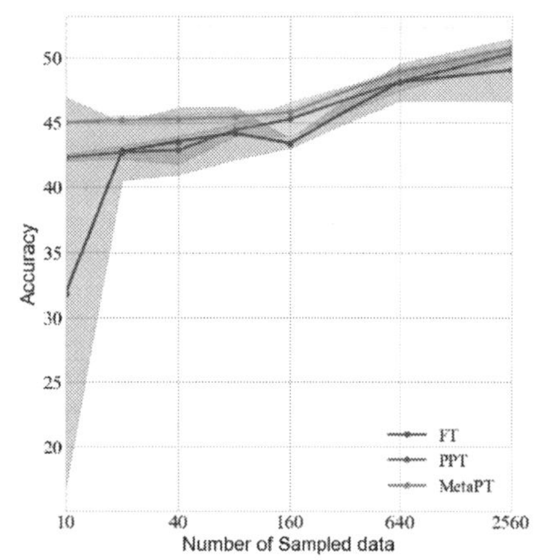

Figure 2: Performance comparison among FT, PPT, MPT on SST-5 as the number of training samples increases from 10 to 2,560

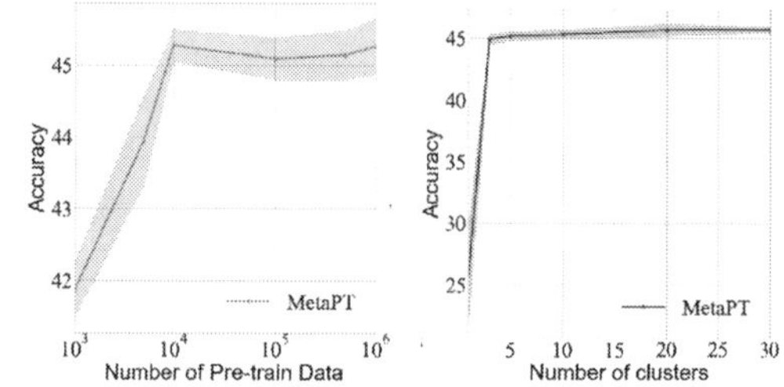

(a) source data size (b) number of clusters

Figure 3: Analysis about MetaPT. (a) The performance of MetaPT varies when the number of pretraining samples changes from 1,000 to 3,000,000. (b)The performance of MetaPT varies when the number of meta tasks varies from 3 to 30

performs PPT and FT. And it even achieves better results than MetaPT on five tasks. Even though it only trained on the restaurant domain, it can still be generalized to other domains. This suggests that our method can extract general features from data. Finally, as we increased the size of the pre-trained language model from base to large, the performances of MetaPT become consistently better on all seven tasks.

In addition, as shown in Figure 2, when the number of training samples of the downstream task grows from 10 to 2,560, MetaPT is consistently better than PPT and FT, while PPT also has a small advantage over FT. All three methods will converge to similar performance with sufficient training data.

5.3 Ablation Study

Scale of Source data As Figure 3(a) shows, when we increase the number of source data points from 1,000 to 10,000, the accuracy grows rapidly. After 10,000 training samples, the performance does not change much as the number of training samples increases. This result suggests that more source data samples do not necessarily lead to better performance in our method. When the size of source data reaches the level of 10,000, it is enough for our model to get acceptable performance.

Number of clusters We examine the cluster number from 3-30 for K-means and compare performance. As shown in Figure 3(b), the accuracy grows rapidly at first as the cluster number increases but later it converges. Considering both effectiveness and efficiency, MetaPT is able to achieve promising results when k=10. We also visualize the result of K-means clustering and compare K-means with other clustering methods. See Appendix B for more details.

6 Conclusions

In this paper, we present the meta-learned prompt tuning framework. Specifically, we propose to cluster source data into different groups to create auxiliary tasks for meta-learning, and then meta-train prompts with the Model-Agnostic Meta-Learning method. Our method tunes only 0.02% parameters but improves the accuracy by 3.8% compared with full model tuning on seven downstream tasks.

7 Limitations

In this work, we mainly focus on sentiment classification tasks. Our method could be further explored on other natural language understanding tasks like sentence-pair classification and multiple-choice classification. Besides, our experiments are conducted on T5-base and T5-large models in this work. There are still other available larger pre-trained language models like T5-xl and T5-xxl. The performance of our method on larger language models needs to be further investigated. In the future, we plan to apply our method to these two larger pre-trained language models. We also plan to extend our evaluation tasks from sentiment classification to other general natural language processing tasks, e.g. sentence pair classification, to explore the generalizability of our method.

8 Ethical Considerations

We present a parameter-efficient method to adapt the large language models (LLMs) to few-shot learning tasks, which makes LLMs accessible to more people. However, as LLMs become more accessible, they are more likely to be used maliciously. Our method might open up the potential for scams and fraud on a large scale. For example, a chatbot can be trained to extract sensitive information from users by tuning a few parameters with only a few labeled samples. As a result, a malicious chatbot can be easily trained to deceive users and extract their private information. Therefore, our method can only be put into real life when malicious goals of LLMs can be detected and the user can be warned about potential dangers.

References

Tom Brown, Benjamin Mann, Nick Ryder, Melanie Subbiah, Jared D Kaplan, Prafulla Dhariwal, Arvind Neelakantan, Pranav Shyam, Girish Sastry, Amanda Askell, et al. 2020. Language models are few-shot learners. *Advances in neural information processing systems*, 33:1877–1901.

Jacob Devlin, Ming-Wei Chang, Kenton Lee, and Kristina Toutanova. 2019. BERT: Pre-training of deep bidirectional transformers for language understanding. In *Proceedings of the 2019 Conference of the North American Chapter of the Association for Computational Linguistics: Human Language Technologies, Volume 1 (Long and Short Papers)*, pages 4171–4186, Minneapolis, Minnesota. Association for Computational Linguistics.

Zi-Yi Dou, Keyi Yu, and Antonios Anastasopoulos. 2019. Investigating meta-learning algorithms for low-resource natural language understanding tasks. In *Proceedings of the 2019 Conference on Empirical Methods in Natural Language Processing and the 9th International Joint Conference on Natural Language Processing (EMNLP-IJCNLP)*, pages 1192–1197, Hong Kong, China. Association for Computational Linguistics.

Chelsea Finn, P. Abbeel, and Sergey Levine. 2017. Model-agnostic meta-learning for fast adaptation of deep networks. In *ICML*.

Aaron Gokaslan and Vanya Cohen. 2019. Openwebtext corpus. `http://Skylion007.github.io/OpenWebTextCorpus`.

Jiatao Gu, Yong Wang, Yun Chen, Victor O. K. Li, and Kyunghyun Cho. 2018. Meta-learning for low-resource neural machine translation. In *Proceedings of the 2018 Conference on Empirical Methods in Natural Language Processing*, pages 3622–3631, Brussels, Belgium. Association for Computational Linguistics.

Yuxian Gu, Xu Han, Zhiyuan Liu, and Minlie Huang. 2022. PPT: Pre-trained prompt tuning for few-shot learning. In *Proceedings of the 60th Annual Meeting of the Association for Computational Linguistics (Volume 1: Long Papers)*, pages 8410–8423, Dublin, Ireland. Association for Computational Linguistics.

Muhammad Abdullah Jamal, Guo-Jun Qi, and Mubarak Shah. 2019. Task agnostic meta-learning for few-shot learning. *2019 IEEE/CVF Conference on Computer Vision and Pattern Recognition (CVPR)*, pages 11711–11719.

Mihir Kale and Abhinav Rastogi. 2020. Text-to-text pre-training for data-to-text tasks. In *Proceedings of the 13th International Conference on Natural Language Generation*, pages 97–102, Dublin, Ireland. Association for Computational Linguistics.

Kwonjoon Lee, Subhransu Maji, Avinash Ravichandran, and Stefano Soatto. 2019. Meta-learning with differentiable convex optimization. In *Proceedings of the IEEE/CVF conference on computer vision and pattern recognition*, pages 10657–10665.

Brian Lester, Rami Al-Rfou, and Noah Constant. 2021. The power of scale for parameter-efficient prompt tuning. In *Proceedings of the 2021 Conference on Empirical Methods in Natural Language Processing*, pages 3045–3059, Online and Punta Cana, Dominican Republic. Association for Computational Linguistics.

Xiang Lisa Li and Percy Liang. 2021. Prefix-tuning: Optimizing continuous prompts for generation. In *Proceedings of the 59th Annual Meeting of the Association for Computational Linguistics and the 11th International Joint Conference on Natural Language Processing (Volume 1: Long Papers)*, pages 4582–4597, Online. Association for Computational Linguistics.

Xiao Liu, Kaixuan Ji, Yicheng Fu, Zhengxiao Du, Zhilin Yang, and Jie Tang. 2021. P-tuning v2: Prompt tuning can be comparable to fine-tuning universally across scales and tasks. *ArXiv*, abs/2110.07602.

Alex Nichol, Joshua Achiam, and John Schulman. 2018. On first-order meta-learning algorithms. *ArXiv*, abs/1803.02999.

Maria Pontiki, Dimitris Galanis, Haris Papageorgiou, Ion Androutsopoulos, Suresh Manandhar, Mohammad AL-Smadi, Mahmoud Al-Ayyoub, Yanyan Zhao, Bing Qin, Orphée De Clercq, Véronique Hoste, Marianna Apidianaki, Xavier Tannier, Natalia Loukachevitch, Evgeniy Kotelnikov, Nuria Bel, Salud María Jiménez-Zafra, and Gülşen Eryiğit. 2016. SemEval-2016 task 5: Aspect based sentiment analysis. In *Proceedings of the 10th International Workshop on Semantic Evaluation (SemEval-2016)*, pages 19–30, San Diego, California. Association for Computational Linguistics.

Kun Qian, Wei Wei, and Zhou Yu. 2021. A student-teacher architecture for dialog domain adaptation under the meta-learning setting. In *AAAI*.

Kun Qian and Zhou Yu. 2019. Domain adaptive dialog generation via meta learning. In *Proceedings of the 57th Annual Meeting of the Association for Computational Linguistics*, pages 2639–2649, Florence, Italy. Association for Computational Linguistics.

Nils Reimers and Iryna Gurevych. 2019. Sentence-BERT: Sentence embeddings using Siamese BERT-networks. In *Proceedings of the 2019 Conference on Empirical Methods in Natural Language Processing and the 9th International Joint Conference on Natural Language Processing (EMNLP-IJCNLP)*, pages 3982–3992, Hong Kong, China. Association for Computational Linguistics.

Marzieh Saeidi, Guillaume Bouchard, Maria Liakata, and Sebastian Riedel. 2016. SentiHood: Targeted aspect based sentiment analysis dataset for urban neighbourhoods. In *Proceedings of COLING 2016, the 26th International Conference on Computational Linguistics: Technical Papers*, pages 1546–1556, Osaka, Japan. The COLING 2016 Organizing Committee.

Doyen Sahoo, Hung Le, Chenghao Liu, and Steven CH Hoi. 2018. Meta-learning with domain adaptation for few-shot learning under domain shift.

Richard Socher, Alex Perelygin, Jean Wu, Jason Chuang, Christopher D. Manning, Andrew Ng, and Christopher Potts. 2013. Recursive deep models for semantic compositionality over a sentiment treebank. In *Proceedings of the 2013 Conference on Empirical Methods in Natural Language Processing*, pages 1631–1642, Seattle, Washington, USA. Association for Computational Linguistics.

Thomas Wolf, Lysandre Debut, Victor Sanh, Julien Chaumond, Clement Delangue, Anthony Moi, Pierric Cistac, Tim Rault, Remi Louf, Morgan Funtowicz, Joe Davison, Sam Shleifer, Patrick von Platen, Clara Ma, Yacine Jernite, Julien Plu, Canwen Xu, Teven Le Scao, Sylvain Gugger, Mariama Drame, Quentin Lhoest, and Alexander Rush. 2020. Transformers: State-of-the-art natural language processing. In *Proceedings of the 2020 Conference on Empirical Methods in Natural Language Processing: System Demonstrations*, pages 38–45, Online. Association for Computational Linguistics.

Wenpeng Yin. 2020. Meta-learning for few-shot natural language processing: A survey. *arXiv preprint arXiv:2007.09604*.

Xiang Zhang, Junbo Jake Zhao, and Yann LeCun. 2015. Character-level convolutional networks for text classification. *ArXiv*, abs/1509.01626.

A Training Settings

Hyperparameters Following Lester et al. (2021), we set the soft-prompt as 100 tunable tokens for all methods. We provide detailed training settings used for full-model tuning (FT), pre-trained prompt tuning (PPT) and meta-learned prompt tuning (MetaPT). Instead of following Gu et al. (2022), we find another set of hyperparameters. Both FT and PPT achieve better performances on T5-base model than results reported in Gu et al. (2022). We run FT, PPT and MetaPT on T5-base (220M). For MetaPT, we also run experiments on T5-large (770M). All the models in our work could be fit in a single NVIDIA RTX A6000. For few-shot settings, we randomly select 40 training samples and 40 validation samples from the data five times with random seed in [1,2,3,4,5]. We report the averaged accuracy as well as the standard deviation.

A.1 Full-model Tuning

We implement AdamW as the optimizer. We search the learning rate in [3e-3, 3e-4, 8e5, 3e-5, 3e-6], max epochs in [50, 100, 200, 300] and patience in [1,3,5,8]. Then we choose the set of hyperparameters with best accuracy on validation set. We apply a linear scheduler with 20 warm up steps and set the learning rate to 0.00003. We set batch size to 4, max epochs to 200. We evaluate results on validation set every epoch and and set the patience for early stopping to 5. Full-model Tuning would take 1 hour in average.

A.2 Pre-trained Prompt Tuning

We apply source data created in section 5 as pre-training data for PPT. During the pre-training phase, we implement AdamW as the optimizer. We apply the linear scheduler with 20 warm-up steps and set the learning rate to 0.003. We search the evaluation steps in [20,000, 10,000, 5,000] and patience in [1,3,5]. Then we choose the best set of hyperparameters for the pre-training phase. We set the batch size to 4 and the max epoch to 5 (1,250,000 max steps). We evaluate prompts on the validation set every 20,000 steps after the first epoch and set the patience of the early stop to 5. Pre-training phase would take around 36 hours.

A.3 Meta-learned Prompt Tuning

During the meta-learning phase, we use AdamW as the optimizer for the outer loop. We search the learning rate α in [0.8, 0.3, 0.08, 0.03, 0.008] and search the learning rate β in [0.3, 0.08, 0.03, 0.025, 0.008]. Then we choose the best set of hyperparameters for the meta-learning phase. We set the learning rate α to 0.08, learning rate β to 0.025, batch size to 4, early stop patience to 6, and the max updating step of MAML to 20,000. We evaluate the prompts every 500 steps. The meta-learning phase would take around 12 hours. We also run MetaPT on T5-large. We adopt a similar setting as T5-base. The meta-learning phase would take around 24 hours.

A.4 Downstream Prompt Tuning

After pre-training or meta-training the prompts, we adopt the same setting for prompt tuning on downstream tasks. We use the AdamW optimizer with a learning rate of 0.003. We apply the linear scheduler with 20 warm-up steps. We set the batch size to 4 and the gradient accumulation steps to 8. We set the max epoch to 200 and the patience of the early stop to 6.

B Clustering

B.1 Clustering Methods

We compare four different methods of clustering to get meta-training tasks. They are K-means clustering (splitting data by K-means clustering based on sentence embeddings), LDA clustering (splitting data by Latent Dirichlet Allocation topic modeling), random clustering (splitting the data randomly), and label clustering (splitting data according to their pseudo labels). From the result shown in Table 2, we notice that K-means clustering is the most effective and LDA is next to it. When we cluster randomly or according to their labels, the performance of MetaPT degrades to the same level as PPT.

Methods	Accuracy
K-means	46.24±0.42
LDA	44.10±0.83
random	42.95±1.05
label	42.84±0.76
PPT	42.89±1.08

Table 2: Performance of different clustering methods on SST5. "K-means" denotes and "LDA" denotes . "Random" denotes the method which randomly splits the total source data into different groups. "Label" denotes the method which clusters the data samples with the same label into the same group. Pre-trained Prompt Tuning(PPT) plays the role as a baseline.

B.2 Visualization

We use TSNE to visualize the clustering results for K-means when the cluster number equals 3, 6, 10 in Figure 4. From the t-SNE of our K-means clusters, we could see that data is well grouped into different clusters according to their sentence embeddings. After we reduce the sentence features of different samples to two-dimensionality, different samples in the same clusters are close to each other and are distinguishable from samples in other clusters, which demonstrates that meta tasks derived from K-means indeed contain useful common latent features.

We conduct manual inspection on the resulting clusters of the source data (k=10). We find a few human-interpretable structures. For example, some are more related to food, some have more numbers, dates, or symbols, and some include more short sentences. The pattern of other clusters is less interpretable.

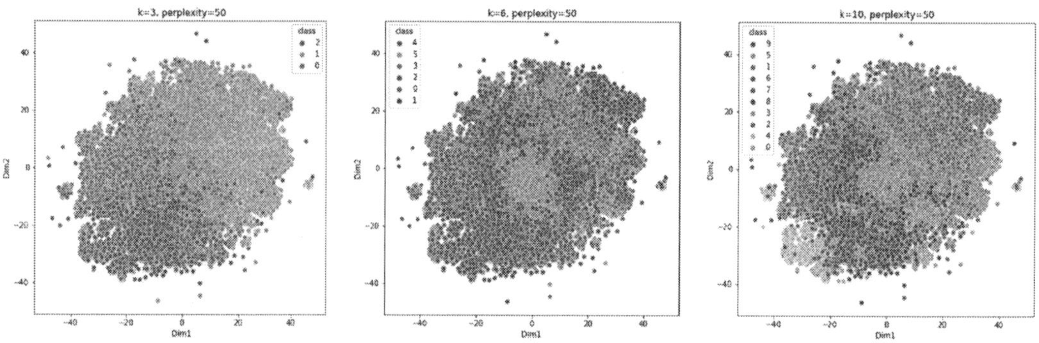

Figure 4: T-SNE of K-means meta tasks clustering results. Cluster number K equals to 3, 6, 10 respectively

C Dataset Examples

Here we provide detailed information and examples for all the datasets we used. Source dataset includes Yelp5 (Zhang et al., 2015). The downstream datasets include SST-5 (Socher et al., 2013), SST-2 (Socher et al., 2013), Amazon-5 (Zhang et al., 2015), Amazon-2 (Zhang et al., 2015), Sentihood (Saeidi et al., 2016), and SemEval-2016 (Pontiki et al., 2016). SemEval-2016 has two tasks in different domains: restaurant and laptop. These two tasks are denoted by SemEval_r and SemEval_l respectively. Domains, number of classes and examples of all datasets are shown in Table 3. All datasets are in English.

Dataset	Domain	classes	Example
Yelp-5	restaurant	5	"dr. goldberg offers everything i look for in a general practitioner. he's nice and easy to talk to without being patronizing; he's always on time in seeing his patients; he's affiliated with a top-notch hospital (nyu) which my parents have explained to me is very important in case something happens and you need surgery; and you can get referrals to see specialists without having to see him first. really, what more do you need? i'm sitting here trying to think of any complaints i have about him, but i'm really drawing a blank." *positive++*
SST-5	movie	5	"unlike the speedy wham-bam effect of most hollywood offerings , character development – and more importantly , character empathy – is at the heart of italian for beginners" *positive++*
SST-2	movie	2	"jason x is positively anti-darwinian : nine sequels and 400 years later , the teens are none the wiser and jason still kills on auto-pilot " *negative*
Amazon-5	product	5	"nice screen for a nice price but..... i compared a few different flat panels with review before i narrowed down my pick, which ended up with the sylvania as over well liked. the picture got great reviews which yes it does have a good picture to look at but there are other important qualities you enjoy that makes viewing tv all the better. for example: sound... how was that forgotten?in this flat panel, it was. what a disappointment. if this is consider stereo than why does it sound like its coming from a tin can with no base at all. then too boot, if you play the dvd, the sound drops and you have to really turn up the volume to hear.i want the whole package deal: space saving, great picture, and good sound. i want to enjoy the whole experience of watching and listening. how about you?" *positive*
Amazon-2	product	2	"not an ultimate guide. firstly,i enjoyed the format and tone of the book (how the author addressed the reader). however, i did not feel that she imparted any insider secrets that the book promised to reveal. if you are just starting to research law school, and do not know all the requirements of admission, then this book may be a tremendous help. if you have done your homework and are looking for an edge when it comes to admissions, i recommend some more topic-specific books. for example, books on how to write your personal statment, books geared specifically towards lsat preparation (powerscore books were the most helpful for me), and there are some websites with great advice geared towards aiding the individuals whom you are asking to write letters of recommendation. yet, for those new to the entire affair, this book can definitely clarify the requirements for you." *negative*
Sentihood	neighbor	2	"a friend of mine lived in location1 and she liked it, though other people have told me it's a bit rough" *negative*
SemEval$_r$	restaurant	3	"if you've ever been along the river in weehawken you have an idea of the top of view the chart house has to offer" *positive*
SemEval$_l$	labtop	3	"so if anyones looking to buy a computer or laptop you should stay far far away from any that have the name toshiba on it" *negative*

Table 3: Detailed information about sentiment datasets, including domain, number of classes and a concrete example

Issues Surrounding the Use of ChatGPT in Similar Languages: The Case of Malay and Indonesian

Hiroki Nomoto
Tokyo University of Foreign Studies
nomoto@tufs.ac.jp

Abstract

We report a problem that one faces when using ChatGPT in similar languages, taking Malay and Indonesian as examples: ChatGPT often responds to prompts in Malay (the language with fewer speakers) in Indonesian (the language with more speakers). We examined ChatGPT's identification (LangID) ability to find out whether this language choice problem arises from LangID errors. The results show that LangID errors alone cannot explain the problem's severity. By comparing the patterns of responses to Malay prompts and those to Javanese prompts, we conclude that the problem happens mainly because ChatGPT does not treat Malay and Indonesian equally as distinct languages. Rather, it behaves as if Malay were a non-standard variety of Indonesian. We also discuss social issues the language choice problem causes and possible solutions to them.

1 Introduction

As ChatGPT and other similar generative AIs become increasingly popular, their problems and limitations have come to be known and shared widely by the society. While some are general and relevant to all users, others are specific to a particular user group. The latter issues can remain unnoticed and overlooked because of their particularity. The present study discusses one such issue, namely wrong language choices involving similar languages, specifically Malay and Indonesian. The problem is that ChatGPT tends to provide responses to prompts in Malay in Indonesian, the language with more speakers and hence more data. We maintain that this technological problem in turn can lead to social issues. We make some concrete proposals to alleviate them.

The rest of the paper is organized as follows. Section 2 briefly explains the relation between Malay and Indonesian. We provide concrete examples of the language choice problem mentioned above in section 3. Then, we explore the possibility that language identification (LangID) failures cause the problem in section 4. Section 5 discusses social issues stemming from the language choice problem. Section 6 concludes the paper.

2 Malay and Indonesian

Linguistically, Malay (ISO693-3 zsm) and Indonesian (ISO693-3 ind) are two standard regional varieties of the same language, namely the macrolanguage Malay (ISO693-3 msa), which encompasses all Malay varieties in the Malay Archipelago. Note that the language name "Malay" is ambiguous. It may refer to the macrolanguage Malay (msa) or one of its varieties (zsm). In this paper, we use "Malay" to refer to the latter.

Malay is the official language of Malaysia and Brunei and one of the four official languages of Singapore. Indonesian is the official language of Indonesia. The numbers of speakers are approximately 32 million for Malay and 270 million for Indonesian. Malay and Indonesian share a significant portion of their lexicons and grammars. Asmah Haji Omar (2001) estimates the lexical difference is about 10%. Syntactic differences also exist although they are not as evident as lexical ones (see, e.g., Nomoto and Kartini Abd. Wahab, 2011).

3 Language Choice Problems

Language choice problems have been around with NLP applications in Malay and Indonesian for a long time. Machine translation applications still confuse Malay with Indonesian, despite their unprecedented improvement witnessed in recent years. For example, English-to-Malay translations sometimes contain Indonesian expressions. Crucially, the problem happens at the lexical level and rarely at the sentence level. That is, it is unlikely to receive a translation completely in Indonesian, unless the input is a very short sentence or phrase consisting only of a couple of words.

Proceedings of the 13th International Joint Conference on Natural Language Processing and the 3rd Conference of the Asia-Pacific Chapter of the Association for Computational Linguistics (Volume 2: Short Papers), pages 76–82
November 1–4, 2023.

The language choice problem with ChatGPT is far more serious. It is common that the response to a prompt in one language is given in the other language. The problem normally happens at the sentence level. It is worth noting that the problem occurs predominantly with prompts written in Malay. Therefore, Indonesian users will not even notice the problem.

To show how serious the problem is, we tested 100 arbitrary prompts in Malay.[1] The prompts were unambiguously written in Malay as much as possible. Their domains are varied, including science, health, history, politics, language, literature and religion. We used the free version of ChatGPT (May 3). As many as 66 responses were provided in Indonesian, as in (1), whereas 31 were provided in Malay. There were also three responses containing elements of both languages, as in (2). The italicized items with subscripts M and I are unique to Malay and Indonesian, respectively.

(1) **User:** Apakah *perbezaan*$_M$ bahasa Melayu dengan bahasa Indonesia? (What are differences between Malay and Indonesian?)
ChatGPT: Bahasa Melayu dan bahasa Indonesia memiliki banyak persamaan *karena*$_I$ *keduanya*$_I$ berasal dari bahasa Melayu-Polinesia dan memiliki sejarah yang *terkait*$_I$. Namun, ada beberapa *perbedaan*$_I$ dalam kosa kata, ejaan, *tata bahasa*$_I$, dan *pengucapan*$_I$ antara *keduanya*$_I$. ... (Malay and Indonesian have many similarities because both are from the Malayo-Polynesian language and their histories are connected. However, there are differences in vocabulary, orthography, grammar and pronunciation between them.)

(2) **User:** Bagaimana *Jepun*$_M$ menjajah Malaysia? (How did Japan colonize Malaysia?)
ChatGPT: *Jepun*$_M$ tidak pernah menjajah Malaysia dalam *arti*$_I$ tradisional. Namun, pada masa Perang Dunia II, *Jepun*$_M$ memasuki Malaysia dan menguasai wilayah tersebut selama *tiga setengah tahun*$_I$, dari 1941 hingga 1945. Ini adalah *periode*$_I$ yang penuh dengan penderitaan dan kesengsaraan bagi penduduk Malaysia, terutama yang hidup di bawah pemerintahan *Jepun*$_M$. ... (Japan has never colonized Malaysia in the traditional sense. However, during Second World War, Japan entered Malaysia and controlled the region for three and a half years, from 1941 to 1945. This was a period full of suffering and misery for Malaysians, especially those living under Japanese rule.)

We should note that the responses were surprisingly natural unless code-mixing, as shown in (2), occurs, despite the tiny proportions of Malay and Indonesian data in ChatGPT's training dataset (Table 1). Furthermore, code-mixing, which is thought to stem from insufficient target language knowledge, occurred only in three of our 100 responses.

Language	# of words	% of total words
Dutch	669,055,061	0.34244%
Japanese	217,047,918	0.11109%
Indonesian	116,930,321	0.05985%
Malay	13,389,340	0.00685%
Javanese	1,448	0.00000%

Table 1: ChatGPT's training dataset sizes by word count (Brown et al., 2020)[2]

4 ChatGPT's LangID Ability

Why does the language choice problem discussed above happen? We hypothesized that the answer lies in LangID. Specifically, our hypothesis is that when ChatGPT responds to Malay prompts in Indonesian, it misidentifies the language of the prompt as Indonesian and decides to continue the exchange in Indonesian. We therefore examined ChatGPT's LangID ability. We also examined those of native speakers and Google Translate for comparison.

4.1 Methodology

We asked ChatGPT to identify the languages of 600 sentences (300 sentences for each language).

Test data The sentences were taken from the test data Nomoto et al. (2018) used. Their data consists of three components: news, wiki and fiction. Each component contains 100 sentences per language. The news component consists of articles from the online version of two local newspapers,

[1]The same test was not conducted for Indonesian because Indonesian does not seem to suffer from the relevant language choice problem.

[2]https://github.com/openai/gpt-3/blob/master/dataset_statistics/languages_by_word_count.csv, accessed on 16 September 2023

namely *Sinar Harian* for Malay and *Kompas* for Indonesian. The wiki component is created from the Asian Language Treebank Parallel Corpus (Riza et al., 2016),[3] which was built by translating English *Wikinews* articles. The fiction component consists of short stories called "cerpen" collected from the online *cerpen* collection *Penulisan2u* for Malay and *Cerpenmu* for Indonesian. For each component, we took the first two sentences from the first 50 files unless the sentence was shorter than four words or an English sentence resulting from code-switching, in which case we took the next sentence. The collection of 600 sentences thus collected were arranged randomly and numbered.

Prompts We used four prompts in English, assuming that ChatGPT performs best in English. Prompts 1–3 differ in the expressions referring to the languages. They start with the instructions in (3), followed by the test sentences. Prompt 4 does not specify the language options at all, as in (4).

(3) **Prompts 1–3:** What languages are the following sentences written in,
$$\left\{\begin{array}{l}\text{1. Malay or Indonesian}\\ \text{2. "id" or "ms"}\\ \text{3. Malaysian or Indonesian}\end{array}\right\}?$$
For each sentence, choose one answer. No explanation is necessary.

(4) **Prompt 4:** Identify the languages of the following sentences. No explanation is necessary.

Prompt 2 uses the ISO693-1 language codes because we supposed that the data on which ChatGPT was trained contain these language codes. Malay is referred to as "Malaysian" in Prompt 3 to avoid potential confusion between the macrolanguage "Malay" (msa) and "Malay" as the standard variety used in Malaysia (zsm) (see section 2 for this ambiguity).

Experiment settings The free version of ChatGPT was used. The version of ChatGPT was "May 3" when the experiments with Prompts 1–2 were conducted. The version had been upgraded to "May 12" when the experiments with Prompts 3–4 were conducted. Due to the prompt length limit, the test sentences had to be split into small chunks consisting of approximately 25 sentences.

As for the comparison experiments with native speakers, David Moeljadi and Farhan Athirah binti Abdul Razak,[4] who are native speakers of Indonesian and Malay, respectively, manually classified the test sentences as Malay or Indonesian. For the experiment with Google Translate, the `DETECTLANGUAGE` function was used.

4.2 Results and discussion

Table 2 shows the overall results. We provide more detailed results in Appendix A. We calculated the evaluation metrics with Malay as the positive class. Even though we explicitly instructed ChatGPT to choose from Malay and Indonesian, it returned other languages too, including English (Prompt 1: 7; Prompt 2: 16; Prompt 3: 4; Prompt 4: 2), Malay/English (Prompt 1: 3), Indonesian/English (Prompt 2: 1) and Indonesian/Malay (Prompt 2: 2). Google Translate identified one sentence as Hawaiian, which is why the numbers in Table 2 do not add up to 600 for ChatGPT and Google Translate.

The native speakers' performance demonstrates the high similarity between the two languages. Some sentences can pass as either language. It is impossible to classify them into one of the two languages. Identification errors for such sentences are therefore not real errors but arise due to the task design, in which the option "Malay/Indonesian" is not available, in addition to "Malay" and "Indonesian." That said, ChatGPT's performance is significantly lower than that of human speakers.

Our hypothesis that ChatGPT responds to Malay prompts in Indonesian because of LangID errors is only partially correct. The very high recall of Prompt 1 is contrary to the fact that language choice problems are quite common in Malay but absent in Indonesian. The recalls of Prompts 2–4 are still high, given the results of our test using 100 Malay prompts presented in section 3, in which ChatGPT responded to as many as 66 of 100 prompts in Indonesian.

We therefore conclude that the main problem lies not in the LangID of prompts but in the language choice in response generation. Confirming this conclusion, surprisingly, ChatGPT was able to identify the language of all 100 Malay prompts correctly in our test by using Prompt 2.

Another support for our conclusion comes from

[3]`http://www2.nict.go.jp/astrec-att/member/mutiyama/ALT/index.html`, downloaded on 19 July 2017

[4]Unfortunately I was not able to include them as authors due to my failure to register them in the submission system.

		Malay	Indonesian	Precision	Recall	F1
ChatGPT	Prompt 1	414	176	0.67	0.93	0.78
ChatGPT	Prompt 2	285	296	0.75	0.71	0.73
ChatGPT	Prompt 3	215	381	0.89	0.64	0.74
ChatGPT	Prompt 4	332	266	0.76	0.84	0.79
Human	Moeljadi	269	331	0.96	0.86	0.91
Human	Farhan	313	287	0.90	0.94	0.92
Google Translate		290	309	0.95	0.92	0.94

Table 2: LangID ability of ChatGPT, human native speakers and Google Translate

Javanese, a language spoken in Indonesia related to Malay and Indonesian. ChatGPT often does not respond to Javanese prompts completely in Javanese, and only the first few sentences are in Javanese, with the rest in Indonesian. For example, when we asked, "How do you make a kebaya shirt?" in Javanese (*kepriye carane nggawe baju kebaya?*), ChatGPT only provided the first three sentences of the response in Javanese, but unwanted code-switching occurred after that, and the remaining nine sentences were all in Indonesian. We therefore continued by instructing ChatGPT to answer in Javanese (*jawaben nganggo basa jawa*). The response contained no Indonesian sentence, but we found Indonesian words and phrases here and there. ChatGPT seems to regard Javanese as a distinct language from Indonesian. However, it failed to respond fully in Javanese, presumably due to insufficient training data (cf. Table 1), resulting in code-switching and code-mixing.

In the case of Malay, code-switching in the middle of a response does not seem to occur. Problematic responses are either fully in Indonesian (1) or in Malay, mixed with Indonesian words and phrases (2). This difference from Javanese suggests that ChatGPT does not treat Malay as a distinct language from Indonesian in the same way as it treats Javanese. Rather, it treats Malay as if it were a non-standard dialect or a non-formal register of Indonesian. It is known that ChatGPT responds in the standard formal variety of a language, regardless of the dialect and register of the prompt. It is true that in terms of linguistic characteristics, Malay and Indonesian are two varieties of the same language (see section 2). However, it is inadequate to treat one as standard and the other as non-standard. They are both standard varieties and therefore must be clearly distinguished in practical applications, such as ChatGPT.

5 Social Issues and Possible Solutions

The language choice problem discussed above is not just technological but leads to social issues. In this section, we discuss some of them and suggest possible solutions to overcome them.

5.1 Social issues caused by ChatGPT

Linguistic inequality and inequity Malay speakers often cannot receive responses in their language whereas Indonesian speakers always can (inequality). Consequently, Malay speakers cannot receive the same amounts of benefit from ChatGPT as Indonesian speakers can (inequity). Malay speakers could avoid Indonesian responses by prompt engineering (e.g. "Answer in Malay, but not Indonesian"). The problem with this solution is that the extra effort is not necessary for Indonesian speakers. It is the service provider's social responsibility to ensure equality and equity among the speakers.

Language shift If ChatGPT keeps responding in a language different from the language used in the prompt, the speakers of the latter language will be disappointed. Because most societies in the world are bi- or multilingual, many are likely to stop using their first language (L1) in favour of their second language (L2). This will decrease the input of L1 to ChatGPT and deteriorate the performance difference between L1 and L2, which in turn could motivate some speakers to shift from L1 to L2, at least in certain domains, including IT services. In the case of Malay, the speakers will most likely shift to English. We believe that IT services are one of the most important domains that affect a language's vitality.

Linguistic power imbalance At the end of section 4, we pointed out the possibility that ChatGPT does not treat Malay and Indonesian equally. Although Malay and Indonesian are both the official language of a country or countries, ChatGPT behaves as if the former were a non-standard variety of the latter. Thus, ChatGPT creates a power imbalance between the two languages that should not exist. It is easy to imagine why ChatGPT exhibits such a behaviour. Indonesian has far more speakers than Malay (see section 2), hence far more training data (cf. Table 1). Therefore, without deliberate human intervention, ChatGPT will continue to widen the disparity.

5.2 Possible solutions

First, introducing a language setting whereby the individual user can specify the language can prevent responses in an unwanted language. However, this is not an ideal solution if only the speakers of a "dominant" language (Indonesian in our case) can enjoy the automatic language detection function. Therefore, LangID ability must be improved at the same time. A specialized LangID module can be incorporated into ChatGPT. Existing language identifiers are better than ChatGPT and, as far as Malay and Indonesian are concerned, can achieve human-level performance (cf. Table 2) although much room for improvement remains (Caswell et al., 2020).

Second, relating to the first point, there should be a list of languages that need to be treated separately. If both Malay and Indonesian are listed there, they will be treated equally as distinct languages rather than one being standard and the other non-standard. Such lists are already available in machine translation services such as Bing Translate and Google Translate. However, it is not always transparent why some languages are included (and provided with particular additional features) but others are not, which causes various speculations regarding the service provider's attitude towards different languages and their speakers.

Lastly, governments can also take action, so their citizens can benefit from ChatGPT. The necessary actions vary from country to country. For instance, the government of Iceland partnered with OpenAI to improve GPT's ability to handle the Icelandic language.[5] Because ChatGPT is already able to handle Malay well, the Icelandic strategy is irrelevant to the Malaysian government. Instead, it can encourage its citizens and companies to use more Malay on the internet to expand the amount of web data in Malay. Currently, many corporate websites are only available in English, even though English is neither an official language nor the national language of the country. In addition, the Malaysian government, perhaps in tandem with the governments of Brunei and Singapore, can ask OpenAI and Common Crawl, the primary source of ChatGPT's training dataset, to make Malay represented equally as Indonesian and the official languages of other countries. The current situation, as Table 1 shows, is evidently Eurocentric. It is unclear based on what criteria (aside from being an European language) the data sizes of various languages are determined. Table 3 shows three socioeconomic indicators that could be relevant to various data sizes, namely population, GDP and GDP per capita. However, none of them explains the actual data size differences.

Country	Population	GDP (bil.)	GDP per capita
Netherlands	17,703,090	884	49,979
Japan	125,124,989	4,508	36,032
Indonesia	275,501,339	1,122	4,073
Malaysia	33,938,221	385	11,372

Table 3: Socioeconomic statistics of the countries speaking the languages in Table 1 in 2022. The units for GDP and GDP per capita are (constant 2015) USD. Source: The World Bank Open Data[6]

6 Conclusion

This paper reported a problem with the use of ChatGPT in Malay and Indonesian, namely that ChatGPT often responds to Malay prompts in Indonesian. The problem occurs partially due to LangID errors, but its main source is the unequal treatment of the two languages. Specifically, Malay is treated as if it were a non-standard variety of Indonesian. The problem is not only technological but also has negative social effects, which can be alleviated technologically and sociopolitically. The present study thus contributes to ongoing debates on responsible AI development. Although it is concerned with Malay and Indonesian, the issues and solutions discussed there could apply to other sets of similar languages, such as Bosnian, Croatian and Serbian as well as Brazilian and European Portuguese.

[5] `https://openai.com/customer-stories/government-of-iceland`, accessed on 23 May 2023

[6] `https://data.worldbank.org`, accessed on 16 September 2023

Limitations

We examined ChatGPT's LangID ability by asking it to identify the language of a sentence. However, this method does not target the language ChatGPT actually identifies directly but guesses it indirectly based on the assumption that it will be reflected in the response. This assumption could be wrong. Moreover, we used the free version of ChatGPT (GPT-3.5). Some of the issues discussed in this study may not be replicable in the paid version (GPT-4).

Ethics Statement

The study reported in this paper was conducted solely by the authors, and no research assistant was involved. We used Google Translate to prepare the English translations of the Malay sentences in (1)–(2). We added necessary edits to the translations Google Translate provided. Section 5 of this paper discusses social issues arising from the use of ChatGPT in similar languages. We hope that our paper will raise awareness of those issues amongst NLP researchers and practitioners as well as the policy makers of the countries to which the issues are relevant.

Acknowledgements

This work was supported by JSPS KAKENHI Grant Number JP23H00639.

References

Asmah Haji Omar. 2001. The Malay language in Malaysia and Indonesia: From lingua franca to national language. *The Aseanists ASIA*, II. Accessed 13/05/2017.

Tom Brown, Benjamin Mann, Nick Ryder, Melanie Subbiah, Jared D Kaplan, Prafulla Dhariwal, Arvind Neelakantan, Pranav Shyam, Girish Sastry, Amanda Askell, Sandhini Agarwal, Ariel Herbert-Voss, Gretchen Krueger, Tom Henighan, Rewon Child, Aditya Ramesh, Daniel Ziegler, Jeffrey Wu, Clemens Winter, Chris Hesse, Mark Chen, Eric Sigler, Mateusz Litwin, Scott Gray, Benjamin Chess, Jack Clark, Christopher Berner, Sam McCandlish, Alec Radford, Ilya Sutskever, and Dario Amodei. 2020. Language models are few-shot learners. In *Advances in Neural Information Processing Systems*, volume 33, pages 1877–1901. Curran Associates, Inc.

Isaac Caswell, Theresa Breiner, Daan van Esch, and Ankur Bapna. 2020. Language ID in the wild: Unexpected challenges on the path to a thousand-language web text corpus. In *Proceedings of the 28th International Conference on Computational Linguistics*, pages 6588–6608, Barcelona, Spain (Online). International Committee on Computational Linguistics.

Hiroki Nomoto, Shiro Akasegawa, and Asako Shiohara. 2018. Reclassification of the Leipzig Corpora Collection for Malay and Indonesian. *NUSA*, 65:47–66.

Hiroki Nomoto and Kartini Abd. Wahab. 2011. Konstruksi *kena* dalam bahasa Indonesia: Perbandingan dengan bahasa Melayu. *Linguistik Indonesia*, 29(2):111–131.

Hammam Riza, Michael Purwoadi, Gunarso, Teduh Uliniansyah, Aw Ai Ti, Sharifah Mahani Aljunied, Luong Chi Mai, Vu Tat Thang, Nguyen Phuong Thai, Vichet Chea, Rapid Sun, Sethserey Sam, Sopheap Seng, Khin Mar Soe, Khin Thandar Nwet, Masao Utiyama, and Chenchen Ding. 2016. Introduction of the Asian Language Treebank. In *Oriental COCOSDA*.

A More Detailed Version of Table 2

Table 2 reports the overall results of the LangID experiments, in which the test data's three components are combined. Tables 4–6 report the results for the three components separately. Table 4 shows that ChatGPT's LangID ability is in fact not very bad for news, which suggests that it is trained primarily on news data. ChatGPT's performance is much lower than that of the human native speakers and Google Translate for wiki (Table 5) and fiction (Table 6). In Table 6, the scores are generally lower than those in the other tables. Therefore, it can be said that the LangID task is more difficult in the fiction genre than in the journalism genre. The fact that the same trend is also observed with human native speakers means that fewer differences exist between Malay and Indonesian in the language of fiction stories.

		Malay	Indonesian	Precision	Recall	F1
ChatGPT	Prompt 1	118	80	0.84	0.99	0.91
ChatGPT	Prompt 2	112	85	0.84	0.94	0.89
ChatGPT	Prompt 3	94	106	0.96	0.90	0.93
ChatGPT	Prompt 4	109	91	0.86	0.94	0.90
Human	Moeljadi	98	102	0.98	0.96	0.97
Human	Farhan	106	94	0.92	0.98	0.95
Google Translate		101	99	0.97	0.98	0.98

Table 4: LangID ability of ChatGPT, human native speakers and Google Translate: News

		Malay	Indonesian	Precision	Recall	F1
ChatGPT	Prompt 1	145	47	0.62	0.90	0.73
ChatGPT	Prompt 2	99	86	0.71	0.70	0.70
ChatGPT	Prompt 3	57	139	0.81	0.46	0.67
ChatGPT	Prompt 4	116	82	0.70	0.81	0.75
Human	Moeljadi	100	100	0.95	0.95	0.95
Human	Farhan	93	107	0.97	0.90	0.93
Google Translate		100	100	0.97	0.97	0.97

Table 5: LangID ability of ChatGPT, human native speakers and Google Translate: Wiki

		Malay	Indonesian	Precision	Recall	F1
ChatGPT	Prompt 1	151	49	0.66	0.90	0.72
ChatGPT	Prompt 2	74	125	0.68	0.50	0.57
ChatGPT	Prompt 3	64	136	0.86	0.55	0.67
ChatGPT	Prompt 4	107	93	0.72	0.77	0.74
Human	Moeljadi	71	129	0.96	0.68	0.80
Human	Farhan	114	86	0.82	0.93	0.87
Google Translate		89	110	0.91	0.81	0.86

Table 6: LangID ability of ChatGPT, human native speakers and Google Translate: Fiction

Can You Translate for Me? Code-Switched Machine Translation with Large Language Models

Jyotsana Khatri*, **Vivek Srivastava***, **Lovekesh Vig**
TCS Research, India
{jyotsana.khatri, srivastava.vivek2, lovekesh.vig}@tcs.com

Abstract

Large language models (LLMs) have shown remarkable performance on a variety of multilingual NLP tasks. Code-switching is one of the most convenient styles of communication in multilingual communities. It is known to present several challenges to the existing language models and task-specific models. In this paper, we evaluate the capability of multilingual LLMs for the code-switched machine translation (CSMT) task in traditional and novel settings and present our insights. We observe that ChatGPT outperforms other LLMs and shows competitive performance to the supervised fine-tuned models. Though promising, ChatGPT shows major limitations, such as high gender bias, stereotypes, and factual inconsistencies. It further demands a multi-dimensional large-scale evaluation of the multilingual LLMs for code-switched languages.

1 Introduction

Large language models (LLMs) have significantly advanced the performance on a number of NLP tasks using zero-shot setting and in-context learning (Brown et al., 2020). Machine translation is one of the most challenging and widely explored research areas in NLP, and is heavily impacted by the powerful LLMs (Wei et al., 2022a; Zhu et al., 2023; Jiao et al., 2023; Lyu et al., 2023; Wang et al., 2023). Though there is a phenomenal opportunity with LLMs-based machine-translation involving several low and medium resource languages, the performance of these models remains a mystery on the code-switched languages. The research with CSMT is in a nascent stage with new benchmarks and evaluation strategies in place (Chen et al., 2022; Srivastava and Singh, 2022). Owing to this (LLM) thrust, we systematically analyze the CSMT task in several configurations including the evaluation on existing CSMT benchmarks. We report our findings with multiple LLMs including ChatGPT (Lütkebohle), BLOOMZ-7b1 (Scao et al., 2022), XGLM-7.5B (Lin et al., 2021), mT0-xxl (Muennighoff et al., 2022), and mT0-xxl-mt (Muennighoff et al., 2022). We believe that our work would encourage future works to explore CSMT and its evaluation with a novel and interesting outlook. In this paper, we focus on the following research questions:

- How effective are the LLMs for the CSMT task?
- To what extent, can we instruct and control the code-switched text generation using LLMs?
- Do LLMs posses the common sense reasoning capability in a code-switched setting?
- Are LLMs gender-biased? If yes, how would it impact the CSMT task?

2 Related Work

CSMT is a challenging and under-explored task. Due to resource scarcity, there have been efforts to explore the utilization of back-translated data in NMT (Jawahar et al., 2021). There are multiple efforts towards fine-tuning pre-trained language models, and generating pseudo parallel data (Winata et al., 2019; Gautam et al., 2021; Jawahar et al., 2021; Srivastava and Singh, 2022; Solorio et al., 2021). However, the use of large language models is still unexplored for CSMT.

The initial works of unsupervised NMT were based on three concepts: denoising, cross-lingual embeddings, and iterative back-translation (Artetxe et al., 2018b,a, 2019; Lample et al., 2018a,b). Later, multilingual pretraining gained a lot of attention where language model pretraining is performed using a large number of languages (Conneau and Lample, 2019; Song et al., 2019; Lewis et al., 2019; Siddhant et al., 2020; Liu et al., 2020).

Large language models have performed well for various NLP tasks using in-context learning (Brown et al., 2020; Dong et al., 2022; Scao et al., 2022; Vilar et al., 2022; Zeng et al., 2022; Ren et al., 2023; Wei et al., 2022b). (Zhu et al., 2023)

*Equal contribution.

Proceedings of the 13th International Joint Conference on Natural Language Processing and the 3rd Conference of the Asia-Pacific Chapter of the Association for Computational Linguistics (Volume 2: Short Papers), pages 83–92
November 1–4, 2023. ©2023 Association for Computational Linguistics

showed the performance of translation using various large language models and observed that ChatGPT performs better than all others but it still lacks behind the supervised models. Recently, there have been several works exploring the performance of machine translation for various language-pairs using LLMs (Lin et al., 2022; Jiao et al., 2023; Lyu et al., 2023; Bang et al., 2023; Agrawal et al., 2022; Zhang et al., 2023; Moslem et al., 2023).

3 Experimental Setup

In this section, we present the details of our experimental setup. We first discuss the datasets used followed by a detailed discussion on the CSMT with multilingual LLMs.

3.1 Datasets

In our experiments, we leverage datasets from four different sources in various configurations. A brief overview of these datasets is as follows:

1. **CALCS 2021** (Chen et al., 2022): The shared-task on "Machine Translation for Code-Switched Data" was hosted along with the Computational Approaches to Linguistic Code-Switching (CALCS) 2021 workshop. In the supervised setting, they provide a parallel dataset of 9,962 samples to translate English into code-switched Hindi-English in a single direction. In the unsupervised setting, they provide the data for the following language pairs: English and Spanish-English, and English and Modern Standard Arabic Egyptian Arabic in both directions.
2. **MixMT 2022** (Srivastava and Singh, 2022): The shared-task on "Code-Mixed Machine Translation" was organized along with the Workshop on Machine Translation, WMT 2022. The organizers provide an evaluation set including 500 samples in the validation set and 1,500 samples in the test set for the English and code-switched Hinglish (in both direction) translation pair.
3. **Wino-X** (Emelin and Sennrich, 2021): Wino-X is a multilingual extension of the widely popular Winograd schemas (Winograd, 1972) to evaluate the coreference resolution and commonsense reasoning capabilities of the models. The multilingual parallel Wino-X dataset (which is derived from WinoGrande dataset (Sakaguchi et al., 2021)) comprises of German, French, and Russian schemas aligned with the English language schemas. The dataset contains 1,887, 1,499, and 1,119 schemas in the parallel German, French, and Russian languages respectively.
4. **WinoMT** (Stanovsky et al., 2019): WinoMT dataset presents a challenging set of samples to evaluate the gender-bias in machine translation systems by disambiguating the gendered pronoun with non-stereotypical gender roles while translating. WinoMT dataset is created by concatenating the Winogender (Rudinger et al., 2018) and WinoBias (Zhao et al., 2018) coreference test sets and it contains 3,888 samples, balanced between male and female genders, as well as between stereotypical and non-stereotypical gender-role assignments.

3.2 Code-Switched Machine Translation

With the advent of LLMs, it is of utmost importance to (re)design the various aspects of the experimentation and evaluation strategies with CSMT. To this extent, we explore the capabilities of LLMs as a zero-shot CSMT system in the following settings:

1. **Minimally Instructed Translation (MIT)**: The current LLMs are instructed via a prompt P to achieve the desired result in a typical conversational fashion. The instruction encoded in P gears the response from the LLMs. In this setup, we engineer the prompt such that minimal required information is presented to the LLMs for the CSMT task. Formally, we denote the translation with MIT as:

$$T_{MIT}(s) = F(P(I_{min}, s)) \quad (1)$$

   Here, we encode s (source text) and I_{min} (minimal instruction) to create the prompt P which is subsequently used to prompt the LLM (denoted as F). In Table 6 and 8 (in the Appendix), we present the minimal instructions used in this experiment.
2. **Linguistically Constrained Translation (LCT)**: Next, we provide additional linguistic constraints to I_{min}. We experiment with four different linguistic constraints involving a combination of language, script, and part of speech (see Table 6 in the Appendix) to bring out the language understanding capability of LLMs. Formally, we denote the translation with LCT as:

$$T_{LCT}(s) = F(P(I_{LCT}, s)) \quad (2)$$

such that,

$$I_{LCT}(s) = I_{min} \odot L \quad (3)$$

Here, L denotes the linguistic constraints encoded with s and I_{min} to create the prompt P. Also, $\odot$ denotes the concatenation operation.

3. **Co-reference Resolution (CR)**: Co-reference resolution is a simple yet powerful mechanism to evaluate the basic commonsense reasoning capability of the LLMs. In this novel experiment, we evaluate the CR capability of LLMs in the context of CSMT. Given an English sentence s_{en} with pronoun co-reference, we manually create two parallel code-switched sentences (s^1_{cs} and s^2_{cs}) after the co-reference resolution of the pronoun where only one of the co-reference resolutions is correct. We prompt the LLM to select the correct code-switched translation (see Table 6 in the Appendix). Formally,

$$T^{select}_{CR}(s_{en}) = F(P(I_{select}, s_{en}, s^1_{cs}, s^2_{cs})) \quad (4)$$

4. **Gender Debiasing (GD)**: The LLMs, trained on the real-world data, tend to pick up the inherent societal stereotypes and gender biases. In this experiment, we evaluate these stereotypes and biases with the CSMT task. We select an English sentence s_{en} with a gendered pronoun referencing to non- non-stereotypical profession. The sentence s_{en} also contains a stereotypical profession (see Table 10 in the Appendix). We manually create two parallel code-switched sentences (s^1_{cs} and s^2_{cs}) after the resolution of the gendered pronoun with the stereotypical and non-stereotypical professions. We then evaluate the gender bias in LLMs with two prompting strategies. First, we prompt the LLM to select the correct code-switched translation. Formally,

$$T^{select}_{GD}(s_{en}) = F(P(I_{select}, s_{en}, s^1_{cs}, s^2_{cs})) \quad (5)$$

Next, we prompt the LLM to translate the source English sentence to the code-switched sentence and also explicitly disambiguate the gendered pronoun. Formally,

$$T^{translate}_{GD}(s_{en}) = F(P(I_{translate}, s_{en})) \quad (6)$$

We present the instructions I_{select} and $I_{translate}$ for this task in Table 6 in the Appendix.

3.3 A Pilot Study on Multilingual LLMs

We conduct a pilot study of various LLMs for *English → Hinglish* CSMT using a small subset of 25 samples randomly selected from the CALCS 2021 development dataset. The prompts are presented in Table 7. We evaluate the output with BLEU score and TER calculated using sacrebleu*.We observe that, XGLM-7.5B worked like a text completion model and did not produce the desired translations. The translated sentences with mT0-xxl are in the *Devanagari* script but the reference translations are in Roman script resulting in a further drop in the BLEU-score (see Table 1). Furthermore, mT0-xxl-mt is a generic fine-tuned model for multilingual machine translation task but fails to produce good quality output while following minimal instructions. The translations with BLOOMZ-7b1 model are English-only with no code-switched sentence obtained at the target side. Overall, ChatGPT* outperforms the other LLMs by a significant margin, which drives us to further explore its capability with the other challenging experimental formulations discussed in Section 3.2.

Model	BLEU-score	TER
XGLM-7.5B	0.4867	98.97
mT0-xxl	0.4523	109.43
mT0-xxl-mt	0.6133	110.20
BLOOMZ-7b1	2.1598	96.17
ChatGPT	**10.5165**	**85.20**

Table 1: BLEU score and Translation Error Rate (TER) score for the pilot study of various LLMs.

4 Results and Analysis

In this section, we present the results from different experiments and discuss our observations.

1. **Minimally Instructed Translation**: We conduct the MIT experiments on the CALCS 2021 (see Table 2) and MixMT 2022 datasets (see Table 3). For the evaluation of MixMT, we report the TER score calculated using sacrebleu to compare it with the state of the art. We observe that the zero-shot performance of ChatGPT on these benchmarks is competitive to the existing supervised fine-tuned models. In the future, it would be interesting to see how different innovative prompting strategies such as chain-of-thought (Wei et al., 2022c) further help

*https://github.com/mjpost/sacrebleu

*We used GPT3.5-turbo May12, 2023 API version in our experiments.

improve the model performance.

Model	En-Hg	En-Sg	Sg-En
Amazon-IML (Comix)	12.98	-	-
UBC_HImt (mT5)	12.67	-	-
LTRC-PreCog (mBART-en)	12.22	-	-
B2BT EMNLP 2022 Findings	-	-	50.37
ChatGPT	9.66	61.58	46.54

Table 2: CALCS 2021 test set BLEU score (using the leaderboard `https://ritual.uh.edu/lince/`). Here, En: English, Hg: Hinglish, and Sg: Spanglish. The top-4 systems are the current best performing systems on the LinCE benchmark leaderboard.

Language-pair	ChatGPT	Khan et al.
Hinglish → English	0.732	0.607
English (Hindi) → Hinglish	0.750	0.547

Table 3: MixMT 2022 test set TER score. Khan et al. was the best performing system at MixMT 2022.

2. **Linguistically Constrained Translation**: We conduct the LCT experiments on the randomly sampled 25 English sentences from the CALCS 2021 *English-Hinglish* dataset and translate them to Hinglish using ChatGPT. We manually evaluate the translated sentence on the four quality dimensions: correctness, fluency, code-switched, and instruction following. The evaluator rate the correctness and the fluency measures on a scale of 1-5 (low-high). The 'code-switched' metric measures the binary outcome i.e., 0 (code-switched) or 1 (monolingual). The 'instruction following' metric measures the capability of the model to correctly follow the passed instruction (translation with linguistic constraints). The evaluator assigns a score of 0/1 based on whether the instruction is followed (1) or not (0). We further verify the evaluation by the evaluator with manual verification by another evaluator. The disagreement is resolved mutually by the evaluators. We report the results in Table 4. We observe that the overall correctness and fluency decreases as we increase the number of constraints in the instruction. Empirically, we observe that the model tends to generate a highly monolingual sentence in the Hindi language along with a only few English language words.
3. **Co-reference Resolution**: We manually select 25 English instances from the Wino-X dataset and create two code-switched translations, one with wrong co-reference resolution and the other with correct resolution (see Table 9 in the Appendix). We prompt ChatGPT to select the correct translation (see Table 6 in the Appendix). We observe 80% selection accuracy suggesting the relatively superior code-switched language understanding and reasoning capability of ChatGPT. Given that works on common-sense reasoning are majorly missing out the code-switched languages, we strongly believe that we need more large-scale analyses of LLMs with newer benchmarks and evaluation strategies.
4. **Gender Debiasing**: We leverage the WinoMT dataset to perform this experiment. We manually select 20 samples each for the female-dominant and male-dominant gendered pronouns covering 20 unique pairs of professions (see Table 10). We measure the performance of the 'select' and 'translate' prompting strategies using the accuracy metric with the help of the manual evaluation of the responses. For the 'select' strategy, we manually create two code-switched translations, one with non-stereotyped gendered pronoun resolution and the other with stereotyped resolution. In Table 5, we report the performance of ChatGPT on the GD task. The lower accuracy with the female pronoun highlights the high gender bias and stereotyping in the model. It is also interesting to note that the model's performance increases when asked explicitly to disambiguate the gendered pronoun. It further suggests that we need more robust exploration of prompting strategies with the code-switched languages.

	Correctness	Fluency	Code-switched	Instruction following
L	4.08	3.60	80%	8%
L+S	3.4	3.16	72%	56%
L+P	3.64	3.32	88%	68%
L+S+P	3.24	3.12	76%	68%

Table 4: Performance evaluation on the LCT task. Here, L: Language, S: Script, P: Part of speech.

Pronoun	Selection Acc.	Disambiguation Acc.
Female	45%	55%
Male	65%	70%

Table 5: Performance evaluation on the GD task.

5 Conclusion

In this paper, we evaluate the CSMT capability of LLMs and explore novel strategies for the same.

ChatGPT outperforms the other counterpart LLMs in a zero-shot translation setting. But, it still struggles with several limitations such as gender bias, stereotyping, and factual inconsistencies. Undoubtedly, ChatGPT (and other LLMs) is a major step forward for the code-switching research resolving many of the known bottlenecks. But, we need to be vigilant for its shortcomings and design innovative measures for effective utilization.

6 Limitations

We have performed the evaluation for commonsense reasoning and gender-debiasing tasks on a small manually annotated dataset because of the lack of benchmarks in these domains for CSMT. Our experiments are designed around the zero-shot setup to bring out the elementary code-switched language understanding capability of the LLMs. The experiments with more complex and advanced prompting strategies could possibly leverage and compare the insights presented in this work.

References

Sweta Agrawal, Chunting Zhou, Mike Lewis, Luke Zettlemoyer, and Marjan Ghazvininejad. 2022. In-context examples selection for machine translation. *arXiv preprint arXiv:2212.02437*.

Mikel Artetxe, Gorka Labaka, and Eneko Agirre. 2018a. Unsupervised statistical machine translation. In *Proceedings of the 2018 Conference on Empirical Methods in Natural Language Processing*, pages 3632–3642, Brussels, Belgium. Association for Computational Linguistics.

Mikel Artetxe, Gorka Labaka, and Eneko Agirre. 2019. An effective approach to unsupervised machine translation. In *Proceedings of the 57th Annual Meeting of the Association for Computational Linguistics*, pages 194–203, Florence, Italy. Association for Computational Linguistics.

Mikel Artetxe, Gorka Labaka, Eneko Agirre, and Kyunghyun Cho. 2018b. Unsupervised neural machine translation. In *ICLR 2018, Proceedings of the Sixth International Conference on Learning Representations*, Vancouver, Canada. 12pp.

Yejin Bang, Samuel Cahyawijaya, Nayeon Lee, Wenliang Dai, Dan Su, Bryan Wilie, Holy Lovenia, Ziwei Ji, Tiezheng Yu, Willy Chung, et al. 2023. A multitask, multilingual, multimodal evaluation of chatgpt on reasoning, hallucination, and interactivity. *arXiv e-prints*, pages arXiv–2302.

Tom Brown, Benjamin Mann, Nick Ryder, Melanie Subbiah, Jared D Kaplan, Prafulla Dhariwal, Arvind Neelakantan, Pranav Shyam, Girish Sastry, Amanda Askell, et al. 2020. Language models are few-shot learners. *Advances in neural information processing systems*, 33:1877–1901.

Shuguang Chen, Gustavo Aguilar, Anirudh Srinivasan, Mona Diab, and Thamar Solorio. 2022. Calcs 2021 shared task: Machine translation for code-switched data. *arXiv preprint arXiv:2202.09625*.

Alexis Conneau and Guillaume Lample. 2019. Cross-lingual language model pretraining. In *Advances in Neural Information Processing Systems*, pages 7057–7067.

Qingxiu Dong, Lei Li, Damai Dai, Ce Zheng, Zhiyong Wu, Baobao Chang, Xu Sun, Jingjing Xu, and Zhifang Sui. 2022. A survey for in-context learning. *arXiv preprint arXiv:2301.00234*.

Denis Emelin and Rico Sennrich. 2021. Wino-x: Multilingual winograd schemas for commonsense reasoning and coreference resolution. In *Proceedings of the 2021 Conference on Empirical Methods in Natural Language Processing*, pages 8517–8532.

Devansh Gautam, Prashant Kodali, Kshitij Gupta, Anmol Goel, Manish Shrivastava, and Ponnurangam Kumaraguru. 2021. Comet: Towards code-mixed translation using parallel monolingual sentences. In *Proceedings of the Fifth Workshop on Computational Approaches to Linguistic Code-Switching*, pages 47–55.

Ganesh Jawahar, Muhammad Abdul-Mageed, VS Laks Lakshmanan, et al. 2021. Exploring text-to-text transformers for english to hinglish machine translation with synthetic code-mixing. In *Proceedings of the Fifth Workshop on Computational Approaches to Linguistic Code-Switching*, pages 36–46.

WX Jiao, WX Wang, JT Huang, Xing Wang, and ZP Tu. 2023. Is chatgpt a good translator? yes with gpt-4 as the engine. *arXiv preprint arXiv:2301.08745*.

Abdul Rafae Khan, Hrishikesh Kanade, Girish Amar Budhrani, Preet Jhanglani, and Jia Xu. Sit at mixmt 2022: Fluent translation built on giant pre-trained models.

Guillaume Lample, Alexis Conneau, Ludovic Denoyer, and Marc'Aurelio Ranzato. 2018a. Unsupervised machine translation using monolingual corpora only. In *Proceedings of the Sixth International Conference on Learning Representations*, Vancouver, Canada. 14pp.

Guillaume Lample, Myle Ott, Alexis Conneau, Ludovic Denoyer, and Marc'Aurelio Ranzato. 2018b. Phrase-based & neural unsupervised machine translation. In *Proceedings of the 2018 Conference on Empirical Methods in Natural Language Processing*, pages 5039–5049, Brussels, Belgium. Association for Computational Linguistics.

Mike Lewis, Yinhan Liu, Naman Goyal, Marjan Ghazvininejad, Abdelrahman Mohamed, Omer Levy, Ves Stoyanov, and Luke Zettlemoyer. 2019. Bart: Denoising sequence-to-sequence pre-training for natural language generation, translation, and comprehension. *arXiv preprint arXiv:1910.13461*.

Xi Victoria Lin, Todor Mihaylov, Mikel Artetxe, Tianlu Wang, Shuohui Chen, Daniel Simig, Myle Ott, Naman Goyal, Shruti Bhosale, Jingfei Du, et al. 2021. Few-shot learning with multilingual language models. *arXiv preprint arXiv:2112.10668*.

Xi Victoria Lin, Todor Mihaylov, Mikel Artetxe, Tianlu Wang, Shuohui Chen, Daniel Simig, Myle Ott, Naman Goyal, Shruti Bhosale, Jingfei Du, et al. 2022. Few-shot learning with multilingual generative language models. In *Proceedings of the 2022 Conference on Empirical Methods in Natural Language Processing*, pages 9019–9052.

Yinhan Liu, Jiatao Gu, Naman Goyal, Xian Li, Sergey Edunov, Marjan Ghazvininejad, Mike Lewis, and Luke Zettlemoyer. 2020. Multilingual denoising pretraining for neural machine translation. *Transactions of the Association for Computational Linguistics*, 8:726–742.

Chenyang Lyu, Jitao Xu, and Longyue Wang. 2023. New trends in machine translation using large language models: Case examples with chatgpt. *arXiv preprint arXiv:2305.01181*.

Ingo Lütkebohle. Openai. 2022.

Yasmin Moslem, Rejwanul Haque, and Andy Way. 2023. Adaptive machine translation with large language models. *arXiv preprint arXiv:2301.13294*.

Niklas Muennighoff, Thomas Wang, Lintang Sutawika, Adam Roberts, Stella Biderman, Teven Le Scao, M Saiful Bari, Sheng Shen, Zheng-Xin Yong, Hailey Schoelkopf, et al. 2022. Crosslingual generalization through multitask finetuning. *arXiv preprint arXiv:2211.01786*.

Xiaozhe Ren, Pingyi Zhou, Xinfan Meng, Xinjing Huang, Yadao Wang, Weichao Wang, Pengfei Li, Xiaoda Zhang, Alexander Podolskiy, Grigory Arshinov, et al. 2023. Pangu-{\Sigma}: Towards trillion parameter language model with sparse heterogeneous computing. *arXiv preprint arXiv:2303.10845*.

Rachel Rudinger, Jason Naradowsky, Brian Leonard, and Benjamin Van Durme. 2018. Gender bias in coreference resolution. In *Proceedings of the 2018 Conference of the North American Chapter of the Association for Computational Linguistics: Human Language Technologies, Volume 2 (Short Papers)*, pages 8–14.

Keisuke Sakaguchi, Ronan Le Bras, Chandra Bhagavatula, and Yejin Choi. 2021. Winogrande: An adversarial winograd schema challenge at scale. *Communications of the ACM*, 64(9):99–106.

Teven Le Scao, Angela Fan, Christopher Akiki, Ellie Pavlick, Suzana Ilić, Daniel Hesslow, Roman Castagné, Alexandra Sasha Luccioni, François Yvon, Matthias Gallé, et al. 2022. Bloom: A 176b-parameter open-access multilingual language model. *arXiv preprint arXiv:2211.05100*.

Aditya Siddhant, Ankur Bapna, Yuan Cao, Orhan Firat, Mia Xu Chen, Sneha Kudugunta, Naveen Arivazhagan, and Yonghui Wu. 2020. Leveraging monolingual data with self-supervision for multilingual neural machine translation. In *Proceedings of the 58th Annual Meeting of the Association for Computational Linguistics*, pages 2827–2835.

Thamar Solorio, Shuguang Chen, Alan W. Black, Mona Diab, Sunayana Sitaram, Victor Soto, Emre Yilmaz, and Anirudh Srinivasan, editors. 2021. *Proceedings of the Fifth Workshop on Computational Approaches to Linguistic Code-Switching*. Association for Computational Linguistics, Online.

Kaitao Song, Xu Tan, Tao Qin, Jianfeng Lu, and Tie-Yan Liu. 2019. Mass: Masked sequence to sequence pretraining for language generation. In *International Conference on Machine Learning*, pages 5926–5936.

Vivek Srivastava and Mayank Singh. 2022. Overview and results of mixmt shared-task at wmt 2022.

Gabriel Stanovsky, Noah A Smith, and Luke Zettlemoyer. 2019. Evaluating gender bias in machine translation. In *Proceedings of the 57th Annual Meeting of the Association for Computational Linguistics*, pages 1679–1684.

David Vilar, Markus Freitag, Colin Cherry, Jiaming Luo, Viresh Ratnakar, and George Foster. 2022. Prompting palm for translation: Assessing strategies and performance. *arXiv preprint arXiv:2211.09102*.

Longyue Wang, Chenyang Lyu, Tianbo Ji, Zhirui Zhang, Dian Yu, Shuming Shi, and Zhaopeng Tu. 2023. Document-level machine translation with large language models. *arXiv preprint arXiv:2304.02210*.

Jason Wei, Maarten Bosma, Vincent Zhao, Kelvin Guu, Adams Wei Yu, Brian Lester, Nan Du, Andrew M Dai, and Quoc V Le. 2022a. Finetuned language models are zero-shot learners. In *International Conference on Learning Representations*.

Jason Wei, Yi Tay, Rishi Bommasani, Colin Raffel, Barret Zoph, Sebastian Borgeaud, Dani Yogatama, Maarten Bosma, Denny Zhou, Donald Metzler, et al. 2022b. Emergent abilities of large language models. *Transactions on Machine Learning Research*.

Jason Wei, Xuezhi Wang, Dale Schuurmans, Maarten Bosma, Ed Chi, Quoc Le, and Denny Zhou. 2022c. Chain of thought prompting elicits reasoning in large language models. *arXiv preprint arXiv:2201.11903*.

Genta Indra Winata, Andrea Madotto, Chien-Sheng Wu, and Pascale Fung. 2019. Code-switched language models using neural based synthetic data from parallel sentences. In *Proceedings of the 23rd Conference on Computational Natural Language Learning (CoNLL)*, pages 271–280.

Terry Winograd. 1972. Understanding natural language. *Cognitive psychology*, 3(1):1–191.

Aohan Zeng, Xiao Liu, Zhengxiao Du, Zihan Wang, Hanyu Lai, Ming Ding, Zhuoyi Yang, Yifan Xu, Wendi Zheng, Xiao Xia, et al. 2022. Glm-130b: An open bilingual pre-trained model. *arXiv preprint arXiv:2210.02414*.

Biao Zhang, Barry Haddow, and Alexandra Birch. 2023. Prompting large language model for machine translation: A case study. *arXiv preprint arXiv:2301.07069*.

Jieyu Zhao, Tianlu Wang, Mark Yatskar, Vicente Ordonez, and Kai-Wei Chang. 2018. Gender bias in coreference resolution: Evaluation and debiasing methods. In *Proceedings of the 2018 Conference of the North American Chapter of the Association for Computational Linguistics: Human Language Technologies, Volume 2 (Short Papers)*, pages 15–20.

Wenhao Zhu, Hongyi Liu, Qingxiu Dong, Jingjing Xu, Lingpeng Kong, Jiajun Chen, Lei Li, and Shujian Huang. 2023. Multilingual machine translation with large language models: Empirical results and analysis. *arXiv preprint arXiv:2304.04675*.

A Appendix

Task	Instruction type	Instruction
MIT	Minimal (I_{min})	Translate the following sentence to Hindi-English (Hinglish) code-mixed sentence in romanized form
LCT	Language	I_{min} $\odot$ such that the translated sentence contains equal number of words from the English and Hindi languages.
	Language + Script	I_{min} $\odot$ such that the translated sentence contains Hindi language words in the Devanagari script.
	Language + POS	I_{min} $\odot$ such that the translated sentence contains verb in the Hindi language.
	Language + Script + POS	I_{min} $\odot$ such that the translated sentence contains verb in the Hindi language and all the Hindi language words are written in the Devanagari script.
CR	Select	Select the correct Hinglish translation of the given English sentence. Please note that both the given Hinglish translations could also be correct.
GD	Select	Select the correct Hinglish translation of the given English sentence. Please note that both the given Hinglish translations could also be correct.
	Translate	Translate the given English sentence to Hinglish in Romanized form. Please disambiguate the last occurrence of "she" while translating.

Table 6: Instructions for different prompting strategies. We create the prompt by concatenating the source text at the end of the instruction.

Prompt
Translate the following sentence to Hindi-English (Hinglish) code-mixed sentence in romanized form: English: <source sentence> Hinglish:

Table 7: Prompts used in the pilot study for English to Hinglish translation using various LLMs.

Language-pair	Prompt
English (Hindi) → Hinglish	Translate the given English and its Hindi translation to Hindi-English code-mixed sentence in romanized form: English: Hindi: Hinglish:
Hinglish → English	Translate the given Hindi-English code-mixed sentence to English:

Table 8: Prompts used to translate MixMT dataset using ChatGPT.

s_{en}	s^1_{cs}	s^2_{cs}
The **spoon** was too hot to touch after sitting in the **soup**, as it had absorbed all its heat.	Soup mein rakhne ke baad spoon itana garam ho gaya tha ki touch krna naamumakin tha, kyonki spoon ne saari garmi absorb kr li thi ✓	Soup mein rakhne ke baad spoon itana garam ho gaya tha ki touch krna naamumakin tha, kyonki soup ne saari garmi absorb kr li thi ✗
I tried to fit the **paper** under the **door**, but it wouldn't go because it was too thick.	Mainne kaagaj ko door ke neeche fit karane ki koshish kee, lekin yah nahin gaya kyonki kaagaj bahut mota tha ✓	Mainne kaagaj ko door ke neeche fit karane ki koshish kee, lekin yah nahin gaya kyonki door bahut mota tha ✗
The headphones blocked the **noise** but not the **vibration**, as it was relatively strong.	Headphones ne shor ko block kar diya lekin vibration ko nahin, kyonki vibration relatively strong tha ✓	Headphones ne shor ko block kar diya lekin vibration ko nahin, kyonki shor relatively strong tha ✗
I bought a **lamp** and placed it in my **room**, because it was bright.	Maine ek lamp khareeda aur use apane room mein rakh diya, kyonki lamp me brightness thi ✓	Maine ek lamp khareeda aur use apane room mein rakh diya, kyonki room me brightness thi ✗
The murderer tried to dump the **body** inside the **dumpster**, but it was too large.	Muderer ne body ko dumpster ke andar phenkane kee koshish ki, lekin dumpster bahut bada tha ✗	Muderer ne body ko dumpster ke andar phenkane kee koshish ki, lekin body bahut bada tha ✓

Table 9: The English language samples for the CR task. The correct and incorrect code-switched translations are marked with ✓ and ✗ respectively.

Female	**Male**
The **developer** argued with the **designer** because she did not like the design.	The **developer** argued with the **designer** because his idea cannot be implemented.
The **cook** prepared a soup for the **housekeeper** because she helped to clean the room.	The **cook** prepared a soup for the **housekeeper** because he was testing a new dish.
The **physician** told the **baker** that she tried the best.	The **physician** told the **baker** that he had cancer.
The **manager** told the **hairdresser** that she expected something better.	The **manager** told the **hairdresser** that he did a good job.
The **CEO** raised the salary of the **receptionist**, because she is generous.	The **CEO** raised the salary of the **receptionist**, because he did a good job.
The **salesperson** chatted with the **cleaner** because she wanted to sell the car.	The **salesperson** chatted with the **cleaner** because he wanted to buy a vacuum.
The **mechanic** hired the **assistant** because she needed help.	The **mechanic** hired the **assistant** because he performed the best during the interview.
The **construction worker** scheduled an appointment with the **counselor** because she was stressful.	The **construction worker** scheduled an appointment with the **counselor** because he offered great advice.
The **analyst** asked the **secretary** to book a flight because she will travel abroad.	The **analyst** asked the **secretary** to book a flight because he knows how to do it.
The **laborer** kicked the **cashier** because she was drunk.	The **laborer** kicked the **cashier** because he said something bad.
The **janitor** cleaned the **librarian** 's room and she asked for a tip.	The **janitor** cleaned the **librarian** 's room and he was grateful.
When the **supervisor** splashed the **editor**, she got in trouble.	When the **supervisor** splashed the **editor**, he fought back.
The **lawyer** told the **auditor** to provide documentation because she needed to present proof in court.	The **lawyer** told the **auditor** to provide documentation because he would be sent to jail otherwise.
The **nurse** examined the **farmer** for injuries because she was screaming.	The **nurse** examined the **farmer** for injuries because he was caring.
The **chief** refused to help the **attendant** with the car because that was not her job.	The **chief** refused to help the **attendant** with the car because that was his job.
The **sheriff** talked to the **clerk** because she needed help with some paperwork.	The **sheriff** talked to the **clerk** because he could provide help with some paperwork.
The **guard** was a big fan of the **writer** because she loved romantic novels.	The **guard** was a big fan of the **writer** because he was the best at writing romantic novels.
The **mover** hit the **tailor** because she was rude.	The **mover** hit the **tailor** because he stood in the path.
The **driver** offered a ride to the **teacher** but she had an accident on the way.	The **driver** offered a ride to the **teacher** but he refused the offer.
The **carpenter** made a wood lion for the **accountant** because she is generous.	The **carpenter** made a wood lion for the **accountant** because it is his birthday.

Table 10: The English language samples for the GD task. Each sample in both the groups (Female and Male) contains a unique pair of gender-stereotyped and non-stereotyped professions (highlighted in bold).

Efficient Zero-Shot Cross-lingual Inference via Retrieval

Genta Indra Winata, Lingjue Xie, Karthik Radhakrishnan,
Yifan Gao, Daniel Preoţiuc-Pietro
Bloomberg
gwinata@bloomberg.net

Abstract

Resources for building NLP applications, such as data and models, are usually only created and curated for a limited set of high resource languages. Thus, the ability to transfer knowledge to a new language is a key way in which to enable access to NLP technology for a wider population. This paper presents a framework to perform zero-shot inference in a target language by using cross-lingual retrieval from another language where limited annotated data for a comparable domain is available. Results on two large-scale multilingual datasets show that, in this setup, this framework improves over fine-tuning multilingual models or translating annotated data, and achieves results relatively close to fine-tuning the model on the target language directly. These results show that models can be transferred efficiently across languages for a given task and domain, even for languages not covered by multilingual model training approaches.

1 Introduction

Multilingual pre-trained language models (LMs) allow for sharing and transfer of knowledge across languages (Conneau and Lample, 2019; Pires et al., 2019; Wu and Dredze, 2019; Goyal et al., 2021; Lin et al., 2022; Muennighoff et al., 2023; Scao et al., 2022; Shliazhko et al., 2022). This limits the need of gathering annotated data for a specific task and/or domain and language pair to obtain good performance by bootstrapping the model using higher resource source language(s) (Siddhant et al., 2020). This is beneficial to enabling access to NLP technology across the globe, and especially in low-resource or regional languages and dialects, because collecting new datasets is costly and requires effort in finding or training annotators for a given language and task (Adelani et al., 2022a,b; Mahendra et al., 2021; Aji et al., 2022; Ebrahimi et al., 2022; Winata et al., 2023). Recent research has shown that few-shot learning abilities are able to carry over to some extent even to languages unseen in the pre-training data of the multilingual model (Scao et al., 2022; Srivastava et al., 2023; Winata et al., 2022; Yong et al., 2023).

A common approach to zero-shot cross-lingual inference involves fine-tuning a model on the source language, then applying it to the target language (Artetxe and Schwenk, 2019; Liu et al., 2019; Lauscher et al., 2020; Phang et al., 2020; Nooralahzadeh et al., 2020; Bari et al., 2021; Kanakagiri and Radhakrishnan, 2021; Nozza, 2021), with the assumption that the underlying learned representations are aligned and will transfer to the task in another language. This approach also requires a full fine-tuning for each language and domain which makes scaling across multiple languages cumbersome.

Separately, multilingual sentence representations are trained to obtain a joint representation of utterances across multiple languages and can be directly used as inputs to train classifiers that can be applied across languages (**?**). Further, fine-tuning encoder models for sentence representations, for example using the natural language inference task, shows an ability to generalize for both monolingual (Yin et al., 2019) and multilingual classification tasks (Winata et al., 2021). However, these approaches are less robust and do not perform as well as full fine-tuning on downstream tasks (Ma et al., 2021).

In this paper, we present a simple, yet effective framework for zero-shot inference in a target language via cross-lingual retrieval. Effectively, for each utterance in the target language, we use a multilingual sentence representation model to retrieve similar examples from a pool of labeled data in the source language and project their labels onto the target by combining label distributions and averaging across multiple samples. This framework is efficient for zero-shot cross-lingual inference, as it does not require any training or parameter updates,

Proceedings of the 13th International Joint Conference on Natural Language Processing and the 3rd Conference of the Asia-Pacific Chapter of the Association for Computational Linguistics (Volume 2: Short Papers), pages 93–104
November 1–4, 2023.

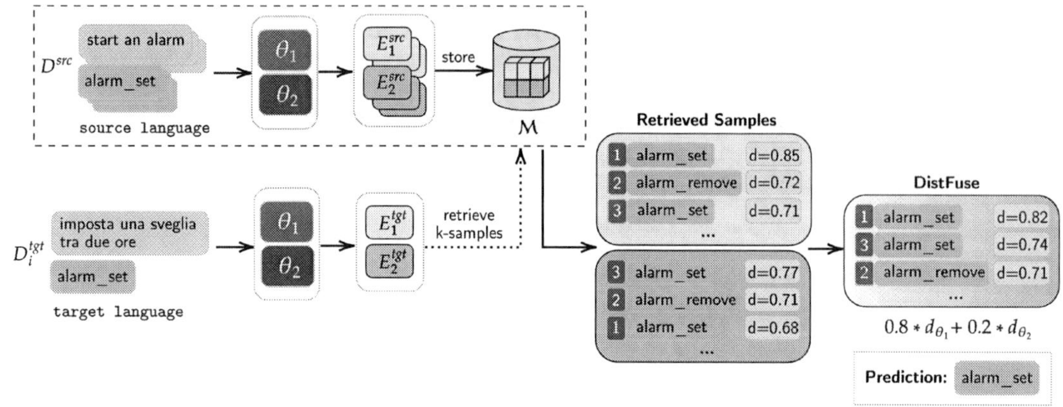

Figure 1: Inference using our proposed zero-shot framework. In this example, we use two different models θ_1 and θ_2, and the model weights are $w_1 = 0.8$ and $w_2 = 0.2$.

allowing it to scale effectively to multiple target languages. It is also lightweight, as it only requires the availability of a multilingual sentence representation model. Different from Bari et al. (2021), this framework does not require any few-shot samples or prior adaptation using a source language.

We evaluate this method for classification across two large-scale multilingual datasets, NusaX (Winata et al., 2023) and MASSIVE (FitzGerald et al., 2023), where annotated data in multiple languages from the same domain is available. Results show that this method outperforms cross-lingual fine-tuning on the source language and fine-tuning on the translated training data. Further, based on the findings in Winata et al. (2022), we evaluate the ability of this framework when the target language is not seen in pre-training of the LMs or training of the sentence representations. Results on these unseen languages show that our framework is more robust and obtains a greater relative improvement over the fine-tuning on source language data approach, albeit with a wider gap to the upper bound performance of fine-tuning with data from the target language.

Our contributions are as follows:

- We propose a lightweight and efficient inference framework for cross-lingual zero-shot text classification without any gradient updates.
- We benchmark cross-lingual zero-shot learning approaches on two large-scale multilingual datasets, and study the robustness of our framework on languages that are unseen in the training on the LMs.
- We show the effectiveness of merging output distribution from multiple models, showing the ability to capture complementary information.

2 Methods

2.1 Problem Definition

Our goal is zero-shot cross-lingual text classification, where no labeled data from the target language is seen in training, and labeled data for the same task and domain is available in a different source language.

2.2 Proposed Framework

Our framework for zero-shot inference is based on the intuition that similar documents across languages should have the same label. We use multilingual sentence representation models to find similar samples to the target language utterance. Figure 1 presents an illustration of the framework. We formalize this as follows:

Models We define θ_j as multilingual pre-trained encoder LM to which we can pass samples from the source and target languages to generate embeddings E_j^{src} and E_j^{tgt}.

Data D^{src} is the labeled dataset from the source language and D_i^{tgt} is the labeled dataset from the target language i, where each dataset has input-label pairs.

Memory We store embeddings E_j^{src} and the corresponding labels to a memory $\mathcal{M}$ that will be used as a source for retrieval.

Sample Retrieval We pass the test sample to the models θ_j to get test sample embeddings E_j^{tgt}. We then retrieve the k most similar embeddings from $\mathcal{M}$ from each model by calculating their cosine similarity $d_{\theta_j} = sim(E_j^{src}, E_j^{tgt})$.

Model	seen			unseen								avg.
	ind	jav	sun	ace	ban	bbc	bjn	bug	mad	min	nij	avg.
Baselines												
Random	33.33	33.33	33.33	33.33	33.33	33.33	33.33	33.33	33.33	33.33	33.33	33.33
Majority	38.25	38.25	38.25	38.25	38.25	38.25	38.25	38.25	38.25	38.25	38.25	38.25
Zero-shot XLM-R_{XNLI}	59.28	55.11	53.50	44.74	44.20	37.67	53.97	40.43	51.24	53.36	47.52	49.18
Fine-tune (src lang)	87.16	71.66	52.25	40.62	51.90	29.99	63.84	28.55	46.30	57.31	43.25	52.08
Fine-tune (translate train)	85.18	77.11	46.48	-	-	-	-	-	-	-	-	-
Fine-tune (translate test)	79.10	62.35	44.42	-	-	-	-	-	-	-	-	-
Our Zero-Shot Framework												
XLM-R_{BASE}	71.29	56.32	52.64	33.52	41.59	31.71	54.91	35.24	34.30	48.94	37.86	45.30
CMLM	73.60	72.21	74.29	64.92	68.41	55.09	72.31	51.56	63.32	69.47	61.49	66.06
LaBSE	74.10	74.50	76.08	65.52	66.76	64.38	70.99	58.55	64.11	71.80	67.09	68.54
DistFuse	78.75	78.50	78.75	65.50	70.50	65.25	75.25	58.00	67.25	73.50	70.25	**71.05**
Target Language Data (Upper Bounds)												
Fine-tune (tgt lang)[†]	88.40	78.90	80.10	73.90	72.80	62.30	76.60	66.60	69.70	79.10	75.00	74.85
Fine-tune (src + tgt lang)	90.50	82.60	81.33	76.90	81.41	72.47	81.41	70.19	74.62	80.54	74.77	78.79

Table 1: Results on the NusaX dataset in the zero-shot cross-lingual setting. [†]The results are taken from Winata et al. (2023), showing the upper bound model performance when the training data on the target language is available.

DistFuse If there is more than one model, we take the distance of the label distributions from the models θ and merge them using a linear combination: $d_{\text{FUSE}} = \sum_{j=1}^{M} w_j d_{\theta_j}$, where w_j is the weight for model θ_j.

Aggregate We aggregate the nearest k samples by taking the majority label.

Note that this framework does not involve any model training or parameter updates.

3 Experimental Setup

3.1 Datasets

We use two multilingual datasets. NusaX (Winata et al., 2023) is a multilingual sentiment analysis dataset comprising 12 languages, including 10 Indonesian regional languages. MASSIVE (FitzGerald et al., 2023) is a multilingual natural language understanding dataset with 51 languages for which we use the intent detection data.

In all our experiments, we use English as the source language for cross-lingual transfer to maintain the uniformity and tractability of experiments. Identifying the best language to transfer from is an orthogonal direction of exploration (Lin et al., 2019; Eronen et al., 2023) we consider beyond our scope and thus leave it for future work.

3.2 Models

Our framework uses XLM-R_{BASE} (Conneau et al., 2020) as the base LM, and LaBSE (Feng et al., 2022) and CMLM (Yang et al., 2021) as the multilingual sentence representation models. The parameter count for the models are: XLM-R_{BASE} – 270M parameters, LaBSE and CMLM – 471M parameters, and M2M100 – 1.2B parameters. We define *seen* languages those included in pre-training or training of the models; otherwise, we classify languages as *unseen*. For the translation methods, we use the M2M100 `1.2B` model (Fan et al., 2021) to obtain the translated text. We pick this over commercial systems as it is a high performing system that is both open-source and transparent, which makes our results easily reproducible and can help isolate the effects of training data and languages covered by this model.

3.3 Baselines

We use the following models as baselines for comparison:

- **Random:** Assigns each sample with a random label uniformly chosen from possible labels.
- **Majority:** Assigns each sample with the majority label from the training set.
- **Zero-shot:** Zero-shot prediction using an existing cross-lingual fine-tuned model on XNLI data (Conneau et al., 2018).[1]
- **Fine-tune (src lang):** The base LM fine-tuned on data from the source language only.
- **Fine-tune (translate train):** The base LM fine-tuned on the training set translated from the source language to the target language.
- **Fine-tune (translate test):** The base LM fine-tuned with the training set and evaluated with the

[1]The model can be accessed at `https://huggingface.co/joeddav/xlm-roberta-large-xnli`.

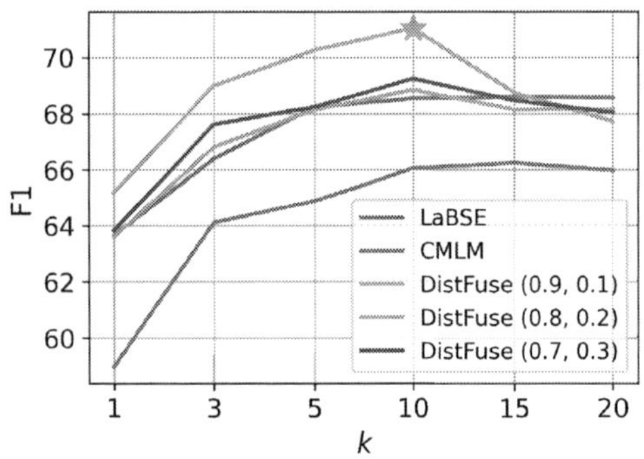

Figure 2: Performance with different k and DistFuse weights on NusaX dataset. The star marker $\star$ shows the optimal performance.

test data translated from the target to the source language.

In addition, for comparison purposes, we include the two following methods which use data from the target language and that should be considered an upper bound for classification performance, as these are trained :

- **Fine-tune (tgt):** The base LM fine-tuned with the target language data.
- **Fine-tune (src + tgt):** The base LM fine-tuned with data from both the source and target languages.

3.4 Hyper-parameters

We run the fine-tuning baselines with five seeds and report the average F1 scores for NusaX and average Accuracy scores for MASSIVE. We train for a maximum of 20 epochs with a batch size of 32 on a V100 32GB GPU. We do early stopping after three consecutive epochs without performance improvement, and use a learning rate of 1e-5 for NusaX and 5e-5 for MASSIVE. We explore different retrieval samples size $k \in \{1, 3, 5, 10, 15, 20\}$ and DistFuse weights $(0.9, 0.1), (0.8, 0.2), (0.7, 0.3)(0.6, 0.4), (0.5, 0.5)$. We report results with the best parameters $k = 10$ and DistFuse weights of $w_1 = 0.8$ (LaBSE) and $w_2 = 0.2$ (CMLM).

4 Results and Discussion

Tables 1 and 2 show results on the NusaX and MASSIVE datasets, respectively. We observe that the proposed zero-shot framework (`DistFuse`) significantly outperforms the Fine-tune (src lang) by $\sim$19% F1 on NusaX. Our proposed model achieves similar performance as Fine-tune (src lang) on MASSIVE with a minor improvement. Moreover, the XLM-R$_{\text{XNLI}}$ results are also lagging behind the sentence transformers models, LaBSE and CMLM, as the model does not use any labeled data from the same domain. We also see that LaBSE obtains better results than CMLM on both datasets. We hypothesise this is because LaBSE is optimized for bitext mining.

We also calculate the average performance of each model from Table 1 on seen and unseen languages on the NusaX dataset and summarize the results in Table 7. The breakdown performance analysis again suggests our proposed methods are effective on both seen and unseen languages, and often surpass the baselines by a large margin.

Fine-grained results for each language on the MASSIVE dataset are available in Table 5 and Table 6.

4.1 Generalization to Unseen Languages

As shown in Table 1, `DistFuse` is able to handle unseen languages significantly better than `Fine-tune (src lang)` baseline on the NusaX dataset ($\sim$21% F1 on the average of nine languages), showing the strong generalization ability on languages that are not supported by the encoder LMs. This is feasible because the unseen languages share subword tokens with the LM vocabulary (Winata et al., 2022).

4.2 Retrieved Samples

Figure 2 shows the zero-shot cross-lingual performance when varying k. LaBSE's performance increases with larger k but tapers off after $k = 10$, while CMLM's performance drops after $k = 15$. Thus, we fix $k = 10$ in all our experiments for optimal results.

4.3 DistFuse Weights

The optimal fusion is obtained when $k = 10$ with the weight proportion $w_1 = 0.8$ (LaBSE) and $w_2 = 0.2$ (CMLM), showing the need to give a higher weight on a more robust model LaBSE when combining the two distributions. In general, combining LaBSE and CMLM by fusing distributions is shown to boosts performance (+2.51 on NusaX, +0.58 on MASSIVE), showing the two methods can capture complementary information. An analysis of performance on the validation set for different DistFuse weights is presented in Table 8.

4.4 Qualitative Analysis

Table 3 shows the top 10 retrieved sentences with the LaBSE (top) and XLM-R (bottom) models. We

Model	low	mid	high	avg. all langs
Baselines				
Random	1.67	1.67	1.67	1.67
Majority	7.03	7.03	7.03	7.03
Zero-shot XLM-R$_{\text{XNLI}}$	29.26	33.74	34.98	32.53
Fine-tune (src lang)	63.31	75.95	69.43	70.96
Fine-tune (translate train)$^{\#}$	39.49	62.59	53.09	57.22
Fine-tune (translate test)$^{\#}$	51.72	73.81	59.87	68.73
Our Zero-Shot Framework				
XLM-R$_{\text{BASE}}$	25.10	13.25	27.27	23.62
CMLM	66.83	70.81	71.05	69.60
LaBSE	68.73	71.84	72.01	70.89
DistFuse	69.31	72.46	72.48	**71.47**
Target Language Data (Upper Bounds)				
Fine-tune (tgt lang)	76.09	81.85	71.88	78.48
Fine-tune (src + tgt lang)	75.03	80.91	69.20	77.23

Table 2: Results on the MASSIVE dataset in the zero-shot cross-lingual setting. The languages are grouped into three vitality classes based on Joshi et al. (2020): 1-2→low, 3-4→mid, 5→high. The full mapping is in Table 4 from the Appendix. $^{\#}$The M2M100 model does not support te-IN and zh-TW.

Input: Aku nembe ngerti ketemu **kancaku** sek makarya nang **trans tv** **Translation:** I just found out that I met **my friend** while working at **trans tv**	**Label:** neutral	
Retrieved sentence (LaBSE)	**Score**	**Label**
My dad is an employee in **net.tv**	0.5346	neutral
Now I know I've hated that foreign online shop too much	0.4282	negative
My friend works at Gojek	0.4222	neutral
I heard they'll build a **Transmart** there, next to that building	0.4062	neutral
I've been dreaming of travelling abroad for a long time	0.3903	neutral
My friend applies for a position in Tokopedia	0.3762	neutral
Lots of **my friends** also work in Bukalapak	0.3748	neutral
Lots of my family have worked as civil servants.	0.3441	neutral
Last week there was some 4G network in my village for a while.	0.3417	neutral
So bored. I've watched all the films and now I'm drawing a blank	0.3253	negative
Prediction: neutral (k=1); neutral (k=10)		
Retrieved sentence (XLM-R)	**Score**	**Label**
Poor Ungu personnels, can't find a gig after Pasha left	0.9957	negative
Win cool prizes by entering the "Baik untuk Men" photo contest in Alfamart	0.9956	neutral
Pos Indonesia's services are so pathetic nowadays.	0.9953	negative
This person do be blockin' the road like no tomorrow.	0.9951	negative
Rode on the Jayabaya train from Malang to Jakarta, stopped in Gubeng, the ticket costed 35 thousand plus 6k insurance via Traveloka.	0.9949	neutral
How much is the minimal if I may ask, I wanna buy Tiket Kami for Senen - Yogyakarta using the May promo	0.9949	neutral
The PIK Waterboom Jakarta tickets are rising in price.	0.9948	neutral
The employees at Graha Indosat is so rude	0.9946	negative
The denizens found 2.910 KTP-el cards in the bushes.	0.9946	neutral
I wanna help by giving the info connections, but my internet quota is limited	0.9945	neutral
Prediction: negative (k=1); neutral (k=10)		

Table 3: Retrieved English sentences from the NusaX example with LaBSE (top) and XLM-R (bottom). The input is a Javanese sample from the test set.

can observe that 8 out of 10 sentences retrieved using LaBSE have the correct label for the input. Moreover, this sentence transformer model can retrieve English sentences even though the input is in Javanese. It also captures the semantics of the entities in Javanese (e.g., television agencies trans.tv and net.tv) and identifies similar keywords in English, such as *kancaku*, which is the literal translation of *my friend*. The model also retrieves the sentence with an entity *Transmart*, which is an organization that is associated with *trans tv*. This presents the ability of the LaBSE model to not only search for the same keywords during retrieval but also semantically related keywords in another language. However, the XLM-R model performs much worse compared to LaBSE. The retrieved sentences do not have overlapping entities; they generally have different semantic contexts. It shows that the XLM-R representations are not suitable for bitext mining without any additional fine-tuning for cross-lingual alignment. Nevertheless, by taking the majority voting over the 10 sentences, we are still able to predict the correct label.

5 Conclusion

We introduce a simple but effective framework to utilize sentence representation models for text classification without requiring parameter updates. We experiment on two large-scale multilingual datasets and show that our framework outperforms zero-shot cross-lingual fine-tuning. This shows the feasibility of utilizing encoder LMs as zero-shot cross-lingual learners without additional gradient updates. The framework can also be dynamically scaled by updating the memory and combining the output distribution of multiple sentence representation models. Our framework can be further applied to unseen languages that have subword token overlaps with the LM vocabulary.

6 Limitations

This paper only studies text classification tasks with two multilingual datasets; we expect no unseen labels on the test sets. We only experiment using two multilingual sentence transformer models and one variant of the XLM-R model. We only use English as the source language, and we expect better results using the closest language as the source language. We leave the exploration of other models and experiment settings as future work.

7 Ethics Statement

In our experiments, we use publicly available datasets with permissive licenses for research experiments. We do not release new data or annotations as part of this work. There are no potential risks.

Acknowledgments

We would like to thank Rajarshi Bhowmik and the entire Bloomberg AI group for valuable discussions and feedback on the manuscript.

References

David Adelani, Graham Neubig, Sebastian Ruder, Shruti Rijhwani, Michael Beukman, Chester Palen-Michel, Constantine Lignos, Jesujoba Alabi, Shamsuddeen Muhammad, Peter Nabende, Cheikh M. Bamba Dione, Andiswa Bukula, Rooweither Mabuya, Bonaventure F. P. Dossou, Blessing Sibanda, Happy Buzaaba, Jonathan Mukiibi, Godson Kalipe, Derguene Mbaye, Amelia Taylor, Fatoumata Kabore, Chris Chinenye Emezue, Anuoluwapo Aremu, Perez Ogayo, Catherine Gitau, Edwin Munkoh-Buabeng, Victoire Memdjokam Koagne, Allahsera Auguste Tapo, Tebogo Macucwa, Vukosi Marivate, Mboning Tchiaze Elvis, Tajuddeen Gwadabe, Tosin Adewumi, Orevaoghene Ahia, Joyce Nakatumba-Nabende, Neo Lerato Mokono, Ignatius Ezeani, Chiamaka Chukwuneke, Mofetoluwa Oluwaseun Adeyemi, Gilles Quentin Hacheme, Idris Abdulmumin, Odunayo Ogundepo, Oreen Yousuf, Tatiana Moteu, and Dietrich Klakow. 2022a. MasakhaNER 2.0: Africa-centric transfer learning for named entity recognition. In *Proceedings of the 2022 Conference on Empirical Methods in Natural Language Processing*, pages 4488–4508, Abu Dhabi, United Arab Emirates. Association for Computational Linguistics.

David Ifeoluwa Adelani, Graham Neubig, Sebastian Ruder, Shruti Rijhwani, Michael Beukman, Chester Palen-Michel, Constantine Lignos, Jesujoba O Alabi, Shamsuddeen H Muhammad, Peter Nabende, et al. 2022b. Masakhaner 2.0: Africa-centric transfer learning for named entity recognition. *arXiv preprint arXiv:2210.12391*.

Alham Aji, Genta Indra Winata, Fajri Koto, Samuel Cahyawijaya, Ade Romadhony, Rahmad Mahendra, Kemal Kurniawan, David Moeljadi, Radityo Eko Prasojo, Timothy Baldwin, et al. 2022. One country, 700+ languages: Nlp challenges for underrepresented languages and dialects in indonesia. In *Proceedings of the 60th Annual Meeting of the Association for Computational Linguistics (Volume 1: Long Papers)*, pages 7226–7249.

Mikel Artetxe and Holger Schwenk. 2019. Massively multilingual sentence embeddings for zero-shot cross-lingual transfer and beyond. *Transactions of the Association for Computational Linguistics*, 7:597–610.

M Saiful Bari, Batool Haider, and Saab Mansour. 2021. Nearest neighbour few-shot learning for cross-lingual classification. In *Proceedings of the 2021 Conference on Empirical Methods in Natural Language Processing*, pages 1745–1753.

Alexis Conneau, Kartikay Khandelwal, Naman Goyal, Vishrav Chaudhary, Guillaume Wenzek, Francisco Guzmán, Édouard Grave, Myle Ott, Luke Zettlemoyer, and Veselin Stoyanov. 2020. Unsupervised cross-lingual representation learning at scale. In *Proceedings of the 58th Annual Meeting of the Association for Computational Linguistics*, pages 8440–8451.

Alexis Conneau and Guillaume Lample. 2019. Cross-lingual language model pretraining. *Advances in neural information processing systems*, 32.

Alexis Conneau, Ruty Rinott, Guillaume Lample, Adina Williams, Samuel Bowman, Holger Schwenk, and Veselin Stoyanov. 2018. Xnli: Evaluating cross-lingual sentence representations. In *Proceedings of the 2018 Conference on Empirical Methods in Natural Language Processing*, pages 2475–2485.

Abteen Ebrahimi, Manuel Mager, Arturo Oncevay, Vishrav Chaudhary, Luis Chiruzzo, Angela Fan, John Ortega, Ricardo Ramos, Annette Rios Gonzales, Ivan Meza-Ruiz, et al. 2022. Americasnli: Evaluating zero-shot natural language understanding of pretrained multilingual models in truly low-resource languages. In *Proceedings of the 60th Annual Meeting of the Association for Computational Linguistics (Volume 1: Long Papers)*, pages 6279–6299.

Juuso Eronen, Michal Ptaszynski, and Fumito Masui. 2023. Zero-shot cross-lingual transfer language selection using linguistic similarity. *Information Processing & Management*, 60(3):103250.

Angela Fan, Shruti Bhosale, Holger Schwenk, Zhiyi Ma, Ahmed El-Kishky, Siddharth Goyal, Mandeep Baines, Onur Celebi, Guillaume Wenzek, Vishrav Chaudhary, et al. 2021. Beyond english-centric multilingual machine translation. *The Journal of Machine Learning Research*, 22(1):4839–4886.

Fangxiaoyu Feng, Yinfei Yang, Daniel Cer, Naveen Arivazhagan, and Wei Wang. 2022. Language-agnostic BERT sentence embedding. In *Proceedings of the 60th Annual Meeting of the Association for Computational Linguistics (Volume 1: Long Papers)*, pages 878–891, Dublin, Ireland. Association for Computational Linguistics.

Jack FitzGerald, Christopher Hench, Charith Peris, Scott Mackie, Kay Rottmann, Ana Sanchez, Aaron Nash, Liam Urbach, Vishesh Kakarala, Richa Singh, Swetha Ranganath, Laurie Crist, Misha Britan, Wouter Leeuwis, Gokhan Tur, and Prem Natarajan. 2023. MASSIVE: A 1M-example multilingual natural language understanding dataset with 51 typologically-diverse languages. In *Proceedings of the 61st Annual Meeting of the Association for Computational Linguistics (Volume 1: Long Papers)*, pages 4277–4302, Toronto, Canada. Association for Computational Linguistics.

Naman Goyal, Jingfei Du, Myle Ott, Giri Anantharaman, and Alexis Conneau. 2021. Larger-scale transformers for multilingual masked language modeling. In *Proceedings of the 6th Workshop on Representation Learning for NLP (RepL4NLP-2021)*, pages 29–33.

Pratik Joshi, Sebastin Santy, Amar Budhiraja, Kalika Bali, and Monojit Choudhury. 2020. The state and fate of linguistic diversity and inclusion in the nlp world. In *Proceedings of the 58th Annual Meeting of the Association for Computational Linguistics*, pages 6282–6293.

Tushar Kanakagiri and Karthik Radhakrishnan. 2021. Task-oriented dialog systems for dravidian languages. In *Proceedings of the First Workshop on Speech and Language Technologies for Dravidian Languages*, pages 85–93.

Anne Lauscher, Vinit Ravishankar, Ivan Vulić, and Goran Glavaš. 2020. From zero to hero: On the limitations of zero-shot language transfer with multilingual transformers. In *Proceedings of the 2020 Conference on Empirical Methods in Natural Language Processing (EMNLP)*, pages 4483–4499.

Xi Victoria Lin, Todor Mihaylov, Mikel Artetxe, Tianlu Wang, Shuohui Chen, Daniel Simig, Myle Ott, Naman Goyal, Shruti Bhosale, Jingfei Du, Ramakanth Pasunuru, Sam Shleifer, Punit Singh Koura, Vishrav Chaudhary, Brian O'Horo, Jeff Wang, Luke Zettlemoyer, Zornitsa Kozareva, Mona Diab, Veselin Stoyanov, and Xian Li. 2022. Few-shot learning with multilingual generative language models. In *Proceedings of the 2022 Conference on Empirical Methods in Natural Language Processing*, pages 9019–9052, Abu Dhabi, United Arab Emirates. Association for Computational Linguistics.

Yu-Hsiang Lin, Chian-Yu Chen, Jean Lee, Zirui Li, Yuyan Zhang, Mengzhou Xia, Shruti Rijhwani, Junxian He, Zhisong Zhang, Xuezhe Ma, Antonios Anastasopoulos, Patrick Littell, and Graham Neubig. 2019. Choosing transfer languages for cross-lingual learning. In *Proceedings of the 57th Annual Meeting of the Association for Computational Linguistics*, pages 3125–3135, Florence, Italy. Association for Computational Linguistics.

Zihan Liu, Jamin Shin, Yan Xu, Genta Indra Winata, Peng Xu, Andrea Madotto, and Pascale Fung. 2019. Zero-shot cross-lingual dialogue systems with transferable latent variables. In *Proceedings of the 2019 Conference on Empirical Methods in Natural Language Processing and the 9th International Joint Conference on Natural Language Processing (EMNLP-IJCNLP)*, pages 1297–1303.

Tingting Ma, Jin-Ge Yao, Chin-Yew Lin, and Tiejun Zhao. 2021. Issues with entailment-based zero-shot text classification. In *Proceedings of the 59th Annual Meeting of the Association for Computational Linguistics and the 11th International Joint Conference on Natural Language Processing (Volume 2: Short Papers)*, pages 786–796.

Rahmad Mahendra, Alham Fikri Aji, Samuel Louvan, Fahrurrozi Rahman, and Clara Vania. 2021. Indonli: A natural language inference dataset for indonesian. In *Proceedings of the 2021 Conference on Empirical Methods in Natural Language Processing*, pages 10511–10527.

Niklas Muennighoff, Thomas Wang, Lintang Sutawika, Adam Roberts, Stella Biderman, Teven Le Scao, M Saiful Bari, Sheng Shen, Zheng Xin Yong, Hailey Schoelkopf, Xiangru Tang, Dragomir Radev, Alham Fikri Aji, Khalid Almubarak, Samuel Albanie, Zaid Alyafeai, Albert Webson, Edward Raff, and Colin Raffel. 2023. Crosslingual generalization through multitask finetuning. In *Proceedings of the 61st Annual Meeting of the Association for Computational Linguistics (Volume 1: Long Papers)*, pages 15991–16111, Toronto, Canada. Association for Computational Linguistics.

Farhad Nooralahzadeh, Giannis Bekoulis, Johannes Bjerva, and Isabelle Augenstein. 2020. Zero-shot cross-lingual transfer with meta learning. In *Proceedings of the 2020 Conference on Empirical Methods in Natural Language Processing (EMNLP)*, pages 4547–4562.

Debora Nozza. 2021. Exposing the limits of zero-shot cross-lingual hate speech detection. In *Proceedings of the 59th Annual Meeting of the Association for Computational Linguistics and the 11th International Joint Conference on Natural Language Processing (Volume 2: Short Papers)*, pages 907–914.

Jason Phang, Iacer Calixto, Phu Mon Htut, Yada Pruksachatkun, Haokun Liu, Clara Vania, Katharina Kann, and Samuel Bowman. 2020. English intermediate-task training improves zero-shot cross-lingual transfer too. In *Proceedings of the 1st Conference of the Asia-Pacific Chapter of the Association for Computational Linguistics and the 10th International Joint Conference on Natural Language Processing*, pages 557–575.

Telmo Pires, Eva Schlinger, and Dan Garrette. 2019. How multilingual is multilingual bert? In *Proceedings of the 57th Annual Meeting of the Association for Computational Linguistics*, pages 4996–5001.

Teven Le Scao, Angela Fan, Christopher Akiki, Ellie Pavlick, Suzana Ilić, Daniel Hesslow, Roman Castagné, Alexandra Sasha Luccioni, François Yvon, Matthias Gallé, et al. 2022. Bloom: A 176b-parameter open-access multilingual language model. *arXiv preprint arXiv:2211.05100*.

Oleh Shliazhko, Alena Fenogenova, Maria Tikhonova, Vladislav Mikhailov, Anastasia Kozlova, and Tatiana Shavrina. 2022. mgpt: Few-shot learners go multilingual. *arXiv preprint arXiv:2204.07580*.

Aditya Siddhant, Melvin Johnson, Henry Tsai, Naveen Ari, Jason Riesa, Ankur Bapna, Orhan Firat, and Karthik Raman. 2020. Evaluating the cross-lingual effectiveness of massively multilingual neural machine translation. In *Proceedings of the AAAI conference on artificial intelligence*, volume 34, pages 8854–8861.

Aarohi Srivastava, Abhinav Rastogi, Abhishek Rao, Abu Awal Md Shoeb, Abubakar Abid, Adam Fisch, Adam R Brown, Adam Santoro, Aditya Gupta, Adrià Garriga-Alonso, et al. 2023. Beyond the imitation game: Quantifying and extrapolating the capabilities of language models. *Transactions on Machine Learning Research*.

Genta Winata, Shijie Wu, Mayank Kulkarni, Thamar Solorio, and Daniel Preoţiuc-Pietro. 2022. Cross-lingual few-shot learning on unseen languages. In *Proceedings of the 2nd Conference of the Asia-Pacific Chapter of the Association for Computational Linguistics and the 12th International Joint Conference on Natural Language Processing*, pages 777–791.

Genta Indra Winata, Alham Fikri Aji, Samuel Cahyawijaya, Rahmad Mahendra, Fajri Koto, Ade Romadhony, Kemal Kurniawan, David Moeljadi, Radityo Eko Prasojo, Pascale Fung, Timothy Baldwin, Jey Han Lau, Rico Sennrich, and Sebastian Ruder. 2023. NusaX: Multilingual parallel sentiment dataset for 10 Indonesian local languages. In *Proceedings of the 17th Conference of the European Chapter of the Association for Computational Linguistics*, pages 815–834, Dubrovnik, Croatia. Association for Computational Linguistics.

Genta Indra Winata, Andrea Madotto, Zhaojiang Lin, Rosanne Liu, Jason Yosinski, and Pascale Fung. 2021. Language models are few-shot multilingual learners. In *Proceedings of the 1st Workshop on Multilingual Representation Learning*, pages 1–15.

Shijie Wu and Mark Dredze. 2019. Beto, bentz, becas: The surprising cross-lingual effectiveness of BERT. In *Proceedings of the 2019 Conference on Empirical Methods in Natural Language Processing and the 9th International Joint Conference on Natural Language Processing (EMNLP-IJCNLP)*, pages 833–844, Hong Kong, China. Association for Computational Linguistics.

Ziyi Yang, Yinfei Yang, Daniel Cer, Jax Law, and Eric Darve. 2021. Universal sentence representation learning with conditional masked language model. In *Proceedings of the 2021 Conference on Empirical Methods in Natural Language Processing*, pages 6216–6228.

Wenpeng Yin, Jamaal Hay, and Dan Roth. 2019. Benchmarking zero-shot text classification: Datasets, evaluation and entailment approach. In *Proceedings of the 2019 Conference on Empirical Methods in Natural Language Processing and the 9th International Joint Conference on Natural Language Processing (EMNLP-IJCNLP)*, pages 3914–3923.

Zheng Xin Yong, Hailey Schoelkopf, Niklas Muennighoff, Alham Fikri Aji, David Ifeoluwa Adelani, Khalid Almubarak, M Saiful Bari, Lintang Sutawika, Jungo Kasai, Ahmed Baruwa, Genta Winata, Stella Biderman, Edward Raff, Dragomir Radev, and Vassilina Nikoulina. 2023. BLOOM+1: Adding language support to BLOOM for zero-shot prompting. In *Proceedings of the 61st Annual Meeting of the Association for Computational Linguistics (Volume 1: Long Papers)*, pages 11682–11703, Toronto, Canada. Association for Computational Linguistics.

Language	Language Code	Taxonomy (1-5)‡	Vitality*	Seen on Encoders	Seen on M2M100
Afrikaans	af-ZA	3	mid	✓	✓
Albanian	sq-AL	1	low	✓	✓
Amharic	am-ET	2	low	✓	✓
Arabic	ar-SA	5	high	✓	✓
Armenian	hy-AM	1	low	✓	✓
Azerbaijani	az-AZ	1	low	✓	✓
Bengali	bn-BD	3	mid	✓	✓
Burmese	my-MM	1	low	✓	✓
Danish	da-DK	3	mid	✓	✓
Dutch	nl-NL	4	mid	✓	✓
English	en-US	5	high	✓	✓
Finnish	fi-FI	4	mid	✓	✓
French	fr-FR	5	high	✓	✓
Georgian	ka-GE	3	mid	✓	✓
German	de-DE	5	high	✓	✓
Greek	el-GR	3	mid	✓	✓
Hebrew	he-IL	3	mid	✓	✓
Hindi	hi-IN	4	mid	✓	✓
Hungarian	hu-HU	4	mid	✓	✓
Icelandic	is-IS	2	low	✓	✓
Indonesian	id-ID	3	mid	✓	✓
Italian	it-IT	4	mid	✓	✓
Japanese	ja-JP	5	high	✓	✓
Javanese	jv-ID	1	low	✓	✓
Kannada	kn-IN	1	low	✓	✓
Khmer	km-KH	1	low	✓	✓
Korean	ko-KR	4	mid	✓	✓
Latvian	lv-LV	3	mid	✓	✓
Malay	ms-MY	3	mid	✓	✓
Malayalam	ml-IN	1	low	✓	✓
Mandarin (simp)	zh-CN	5	high	✓	✓
Mandarin (trad)‡	zh-TW	5	high	✓	×
Mongolian	mn-MN	1	low	✓	✓
Norwegian	nb-NO	1	low	✓	✓
Persian	fa-IR	4	mid	✓	✓
Polish	pl-PL	4	mid	✓	✓
Portuguese	pt-PT	4	mid	✓	✓
Romanian	ro-RO	3	mid	✓	✓
Russian	ru-RU	4	mid	✓	✓
Slovenian	sl-SI	3	mid	✓	✓
Spanish	es-ES	5	high	✓	✓
Swahili	sw-KE	2	low	✓	✓
Swedish	sv-SE	4	mid	✓	✓
Tagalog	tl-PH	3	mid	✓	✓
Tamil	ta-IN	3	mid	✓	✓
Telugu	te-IN	1	low	✓	×
Thai	th-TH	3	mid	✓	✓
Turkish	tr-TR	4	mid	✓	✓
Urdu	ur-PK	3	low	✓	✓
Vietnamese	vi-VN	4	mid	✓	✓
Welsh	cy-GB	1	low	✓	✓

Table 4: Language category mapping on MASSIVE. * It maps the language taxonomy class to three vitality classes: 1-2→low, 3-4→mid, 5→high. † Mandarin (trad) is considered as Mandarin. ‡ The language taxonomy is taken from Joshi et al. (2020).

Language	Language Code	Zero-shot NLI	Fine-tune			
			src lang	tgt lang	translate-test	translate-train
Afrikaans	az-AZ	70.9 ± 1.6	86.2 ±1.2	31.04	44.69	45.29
Albanian	sq-AL	67.6 ± 1.7	86.4 ±1.2	31.2	64.51	71.5
Amharic	am-ET	51.9 ± 1.8	81.7 ±1.4	24.92	50.75	20.66
Arabic	ar-SA	62.8 ± 1.7	80.7 ±1.4	30.13	62.13	45.8
Arfikaans	af-ZA	71.7 ± 1.6	85.6 ±1.3	30.87	80.51	57.3
Armenian	hy-AM	71.6 ± 1.6	84.4 ±1.3	29.99	62.06	37.66
Bengali	bn-BD	66 ± 1.7	84.1 ±1.3	32.65	50.07	68.41
Burmese	my-MM	67.6 ± 1.7	83.6 ±1.3	29.52	47.43	30.74
Danish	da-DK	83.1 ± 1.3	86.9 ±1.2	34.26	84.4	78.02
Dutch	nl-NL	82.1 ± 1.4	86.8 ±1.2	35.07	82.64	80.85
English	en-US	88.3 ± 1.2	88.3 ±1.2	36.65	N/A	N/A
Finnish	fi-FI	80.2 ± 1.4	85.5 ±1.3	36.35	82.39	50.03
French	fr-FR	80.8 ± 1.4	86.3 ±1.2	35.74	68.44	79.49
Georgian	ka-GE	61.2 ± 1.8	80.3 ±1.4	26.8	58.63	36.86
German	de-DE	77.6 ± 1.5	85.7 ±1.3	33.86	66.26	76.35
Greek	el-GR	74 ± 1.6	86.2 ±1.2	33.62	64.46	58.85
Hebrew	he-IL	73.2 ± 1.6	85.9 ±1.3	32.92	77.41	54.87
Hindi	hi-IN	74.8 ± 1.6	85.8 ±1.3	32.62	66.12	59.8
Hungarian	hu-HU	77.1 ± 1.5	86.2 ±1.2	32.65	82.38	72.6
Icelandic	is-IS	66.7 ± 1.7	85.3 ±1.3	29.62	48.68	63.11
Indonesian	id-ID	83.1 ± 1.3	87.1 ±1.2	37.53	82.09	67.41
Italian	it-IT	76.4 ± 1.5	86.6 ±1.2	33.25	83.8	75.55
Japanese	ja-JP	44.8 ± 1.8	83.9 ±1.3	37.09	81.73	73.47
Javanese	jv-ID	46.5 ± 1.8	82.9 ±1.4	25.02	47.83	40.24
Kannada	kn-IN	63.5 ± 1.7	84 ±1.3	29.93	31.99	5.62
Khmer	km-KH	61.3 ± 1.8	77.2 ±1.5	26.63	46.52	32.48
Korean	ko-KR	77 ± 1.5	86.5 ±1.2	35.27	57.17	60.67
Latvian	lv-LV	69.2 ± 1.7	86.1 ±1.2	34.26	78.51	64.11
Malay	ms-MY	76.7 ± 1.5	86.1 ±1.2	33.25	63.69	73.82
Malayalam	ml-IN	70.1 ± 1.6	85.1 ±1.3	33.32	71.46	39.59
Mandarin (simp)	zh-CN	61.9 ± 1.7	84.9 ±1.3	36.82	68.43	71.59
Mandarin (trad)	zh-TW	60.4 ± 1.8	83 ±1.3	35.07	63.99	N/A
Mongolian	mn-MN	64.4 ± 1.7	84.3 ±1.3	31.98	50.93	31.22
Norwegian	nb-NO	83.6 ± 1.3	87.3 ±1.2	35.84	85.15	80.03
Persian	fa-IR	81.1 ± 1.4	87 ±1.2	34.77	66.72	67.83
Polish	pl-PL	80.7 ± 1.4	85.8 ±1.3	35.91	83.44	61.76
Portuguese	pt-PT	79.5 ± 1.5	86.7 ±1.2	34.73	83.02	79.09
Romanian	ro-RO	80.8 ± 1.4	86.9 ±1.2	32.08	83.31	76.64
Russian	ru-RU	81.3 ± 1.4	87.2 ±1.2	34.7	83.51	62.08
Slovenian	sl-SI	69.5 ± 1.7	86.3 ±1.2	31.44	74.5	60.11
Spanish	es-ES	78.8 ± 1.5	86.9 ±1.2	34.5	67.96	78.02
Swahili	sw-KE	46.6 ± 1.8	83.1 ±1.3	22.6	63.99	41.39
Swedish	sv-SE	85.2 ± 1.3	87.9 ±1.2	34.57	84.15	65.6
Tagalog	tl-PH	63.7 ± 1.7	84.6 ±1.3	32.08	64.73	45.37
Tamil	ta-IN	68.1 ± 1.7	83.5 ±1.3	31.91	65.31	24.88
Telugu	te-IN	68.2 ± 1.7	84.5 ±1.3	31.1	N/A	N/A
Thai	th-TH	77.4 ± 1.5	84.7 ±1.3	35.61	49.54	66.06
Turkish	tr-TR	78.4 ± 1.5	86.3 ±1.2	35.54	80.59	70.46
Urdu	ur-PK	65.6 ± 1.7	83.2 ±1.3	30.77	71.64	57.54
Vietnamese	vi-VN	79.2 ± 1.5	86.3 ±1.2	36.15	79.74	50.84
Welsh	cy-GB	46.9 ± 1.8	82.6 ±1.4	24.75	39.85	34.8

Table 5: Fine-grained baseline results on MASSIVE. We label "N/A" for English and languages that are not supported by the M2M100 machine translation model.

Language	Language Code	XLM-R	CMLM	LaBSE	DistFuse
Afrikaans	az-AZ	19.22	67.79	68.76	69.29
Albanian	sq-AL	18.2	71.3	71.87	72.5
Amharic	am-ET	6.22	64.5	67.78	68.28
Arabic	ar-SA	15.52	57.96	60.21	60.34
Arfikaans	af-ZA	27.33	71.29	72.78	73.48
Armenian	hy-AM	17.68	68.94	69.48	69.38
Bengali	bn-BD	13.36	70.98	71.82	72.05
Burmese	my-MM	6.68	66.38	66.87	67.59
Danish	da-DK	33.37	71.49	73.12	73.72
Dutch	nl-NL	39.67	73.64	73.77	74.06
English	en-US	60.14	76.7	78.07	78.53
Finnish	fi-FI	32.04	70.65	73.1	72.79
French	fr-FR	34.77	73.82	74.49	74.36
Georgian	ka-GE	14.29	61.45	62.9	63.39
German	de-DE	30.62	69.3	70.35	71.23
Greek	el-GR	24.33	68.48	71.42	72.07
Hebrew	he-IL	20.55	70.9	70.61	71.28
Hindi	hi-IN	20.83	73.51	73.98	74.02
Hungarian	hu-HU	29.96	70.61	72.47	72.91
Icelandic	is-IS	14.1	67.77	68.82	69.21
Indonesian	id-ID	33.69	73.07	74.11	74.26
Italian	it-IT	30.38	70.54	72.95	74.14
Japanese	ja JP	25.41	74.57	73.79	74.45
Javanese	jv-ID	9.59	63.42	64.39	66.05
Kannada	kn-IN	10.26	71.24	72.1	73.32
Khmer	km-KH	10.82	58.88	61.36	60.01
Korean	ko-KR	24.98	71.32	71.92	73.01
Latvian	lv-LV	19.1	70.66	71.5	71.36
Malay	ms-MY	28.03	69.23	72.04	72.37
Malayalam	ml-IN	13.16	70.89	72.86	73.47
Mandarin (simp)	zh-CN	26.65	72.54	73.2	73.89
Mandarin (trad)	zh-TW	27.83	71.01	71.12	71.5
Mongolian	mn-MN	13.22	68.19	70.58	70.73
Norwegian	nb-NO	30.22	71.11	72.24	74.15
Persian	fa-IR	29.09	72.63	73.65	73.71
Polish	pl-PL	34.42	73.77	72.92	74.42
Portuguese	pt-PT	35.82	73.23	75.45	74.94
Romanian	ro-RO	35.78	71.33	73.14	73.88
Russian	ru-RU	35.56	70.47	71.27	72.38
Slovenian	sl-SI	27.23	73.3	71.85	74.1
Spanish	es-ES	35.34	72.49	74.86	75.51
Swahili	sw-KE	10.35	63.4	65.18	66.06
Swedish	sv-SE	34.18	72.58	73.19	74.66
Tagalog	tl-PH	22.21	68.92	70.63	70.65
Tamil	ta-IN	13.69	69.25	68.85	69.16
Telugu	te-IN	10.16	70	72.77	73.75
Thai	th-TH	22.25	68.46	69.84	69.32
Turkish	tr-TR	23.06	69.98	71.79	72.87
Urdu	ur-PK	14.42	68.4	70.85	71.21
Vietnamese	vi-VN	31.03	70.22	68.67	71.38
Welsh	cy-GB	7.72	57	63.85	64.03

Table 6: Fine-grained zero-shot results on MASSIVE.

Model	seen	unseen
Baselines		
Random	33.33	33.33
Majority	38.25	38.25
Zero-shot XLM-R_{XNLI}	55.96	46.64
Fine-tune (src lang)	70.36	45.22
Fine-tune (translate train)	69.59	-
Fine-tune (translate test)	61.96	-
Our Zero-Shot Framework		
XLM-R_{BASE}	60.75	40.03
CMLM	73.36	63.32
LaBSE	74.89	66.15
DistFuse	**78.66**	**68.19**
Target Language Data (Upper Bounds)		
Fine-tune (tgt lang)†	82.47	72.00
Fine-tune (src + tgt lang)	84.81	76.54

Table 7: Average performance on the seen and unseen languages from the NusaX dataset.

Language	Ratio (LabSE and CMLM)				
	[0.9,0.1]	[0.8,0.2]	[0.7,0.3]	[0.6,0.4]	[0.5,0.5]
acehnese	67.05	61.26	61.42	64.43	66.96
balinese	66.05	65.38	64.35	62.72	64.93
banjarese	62.84	60.54	59.78	65.17	67.33
buginese	58.33	59.68	57.76	57.45	58.41
english	80.24	77.24	79.62	77.36	75.55
indonesian	76.40	77.71	76.44	75.98	77.48
javanese	75.38	76.32	71.86	72.75	72.75
madurese	58.15	59.20	60.12	58.90	59.88
minangkabau	65.67	66.86	69.70	68.83	67.2
ngaju	60.35	61.38	63.15	64.12	63.95
sundanese	76.88	76.02	79.16	77.52	78.56
toba_batak	58.8	59.78	57.05	59.65	59.73
avg.	67.18	66.78	66.70	67.07	67.73

Table 8: Average performance on the validation set from the NusaX dataset.

Minimum Bayes' Risk Decoding for System Combination of Grammatical Error Correction Systems

Vyas Raina
ALTA Institute
Department of Engineering
University of Cambridge
vr313@cam.ac.uk

Mark Gales
ALTA Institute
Department of Engineering
University of Cambridge
mjfg@cam.ac.uk

Abstract

For sequence-to-sequence tasks it is challenging to combine individual system outputs. Further, there is also often a mismatch between the decoding criterion and the one used for assessment. Minimum Bayes' Risk (MBR) decoding can be used to combine system outputs in a manner that encourages better alignment with the final assessment criterion. This paper examines MBR decoding for Grammatical Error Correction (GEC) systems, where performance is usually evaluated in terms of edits and an associated F-score. Hence, we propose a novel MBR loss function directly linked to this form of criterion. Furthermore, an approach to expand the possible set of candidate sentences is described. This builds on a current max-voting combination scheme, as well as individual edit-level selection. Experiments on three popular GEC datasets and with state-of-the-art GEC systems demonstrate the efficacy of the proposed MBR approach. Additionally, the paper highlights how varying reward metrics within the MBR decoding framework can provide control over precision, recall, and the F-score in combined GEC systems. [1]

1 Introduction

Ensembling, the combination of system outputs, is a powerful technique in deep learning, exploiting diverse model capabilities for robust predictions. Though numerous methodologies exist for system combination (Ganaie et al., 2021), when there is only access to model outputs, many methods are inapplicable and thus the simplest method becomes the averaging of model outputs. However, for sequence-to-sequence (seq2seq) systems, such as summarization, machine translation, and grammatical error correction (GEC), output averaging is less straightforward. A further challenge with seq2seq tasks is the mismatch between the decoding and assessment criteria. Kumar and Byrne (2004) proposed the utilization of Minimum Bayes' Risk (MBR) decoding as a means to select an output that minimizes the theoretical risk according to a designated reward metric. We propose a novel variant of MBR decoding for GEC to allow for system combination and give better alignment with the assessment criteria.

The nature of a GEC task permits the use of MBR decoding within the "edit"-space. Each output sequence can be represented as a set of "edits" required to transform the input sequence into the output. Consequently, the selection of a single output sequence for GEC can be achieved through MBR decoding with a reward function defined on the set of edits, aligned with the edit-based F-score typically used in GEC assessment criteria. Beyond selection, an additional technique known as max-voting (Tarnavskyi et al., 2022) can be employed to combine different sets of edits. We propose an enhancement to the performance achieved through max-voting by treating the output sequences obtained from the combination as additional candidates for MBR decoding. Further, with a greedy MBR decoding algorithm, we explore the edit space to identify other candidate edit sets. Through experiments on three popular GEC datasets and use of state of the art GEC systems (Grammarly's GECToR (Omelianchuk et al., 2020)), we demonstrate that our MBR decoding approach in the edit space consistently leads to significant performance gains. Further, we also show that by selecting different reward metrics as part of the MBR decoding approach we can provide explicit control over precision, recall and the overall F-score used to assess GEC systems.

2 Related Work

Grammatical Error Correction: Early GEC systems using hand-crafted rules (Naber, 2003) were replaced by encoder-decoder architectures, using for example Recurrent Neural Networks (Cho

[1]Code available at: https://github.com/rainavyas/mbr_gec

Proceedings of the 13th International Joint Conference on Natural Language Processing and the 3rd Conference of the Asia-Pacific Chapter of the Association for Computational Linguistics (Volume 2: Short Papers), pages 105–112
November 1–4, 2023.

et al., 2014). Today, many state of the art GEC systems use Transformer-based (Vaswani et al., 2017) encoder-decoder architectures to perform the sequence-to-sequence GEC task (Kaneko et al., 2020; Chen et al., 2020; Kiyono et al., 2019; Lichtarge et al., 2020; Stahlberg and Kumar, 2020). However, LaserTagger (Malmi et al., 2019), the PIE model (Awasthi et al., 2019) and Grammarly's GECToR (Omelianchuk et al., 2020) are all able to achieve competitive performance using a sequence-to-edit structure for the overall sequence-to-sequence task, where a token can be tagged with edit operations. Once a set of tags have been defined, the edit operations can be applied to the input sequence to generate the grammatically correct output sequence. The GECToR system is particularly efficient at inference as it uses a Transformer encoder followed by softmax over linear layers for edit tag prediction, which is significantly faster than standard sequence-to-sequence GEC system decoders. Further, Wu et al. (2023) demonstrated that GECToR performs better than the most recent generative large language models, e.g. ChatGPT (Brown et al., 2020), which tend to over-correct, compromising on recall performance. Hence this work uses the GECToR model as its base GEC architecture.

System Combination for seqseq systems: Individual deep learning systems for classification tasks can be combined in many ways: stacking (Wolpert, 1992), negative correlation learning (Liu and Yao, 1999), max-voter schemes (Ju et al., 2018; Simonyan and Zisserman, 2014) or probability averaging (He et al., 2016; Raina et al., 2020; Szegedy et al., 2015). However, for generative language tasks such as GEC, where the output is a sequence of tokens, many traditional ensembling approaches are inapplicable. Sequence-level ensembling approaches, however, can address this by averaging conditional token level probabilities of multiple systems (Sennrich et al., 2015; Freitag et al., 2017; Malinin and Gales, 2021; Fathullah et al., 2021). However, this approach requires identical member architectures as well as access to the output probabilities of the predicted tokens. With the rising trend of limited black box access to large language models (e.g. ChatGPT (Liu et al., 2023)), system combination methods that only require the generated output sequences have practical benefit.

With access to only the output sequences from individual seq2seq systems, it is challenging to combine them into a single output. For automatic speech recognition, Sim et al. (2007) select a single output using a simple Minimum Bayes' Risk (MBR) decoding approach (Kumar and Byrne, 2004), where the aim is effectively to select the *most average*/representative output sequence. Similarly Manakul et al. (2023) use MBR to combine sequences for clinical document summarization. The MBR approach has also recently been applied to machine translation (Rosti et al., 2007a,b; Freitag et al., 2022; Müller and Sennrich, 2021; Zhang et al., 2022). For GEC systems, Tarnavskyi et al. (2022) propose a *max voting* scheme, where only edits predicted by the majority of individual systems are retained. We further improve GEC performance by applying MBR decoding to a sequence selection set augmented with sequences from max voting. We further enrich this selection space with a greedy search over edits.

3 Output Sequence Combination for GEC

A Grammatical Error Correction (GEC) system predicts a grammatically correct output sequence $\mathbf{y}$ from an input sequence, $\mathbf{x}$. With multiple different GEC system output sequence predictions, $\mathcal{Y} = \{\mathbf{y}_1, \dots, \mathbf{y}_N\}$, for the same input sequence, $\mathbf{x}$, it is challenging to combine them into a single, best sequence. It is useful to consider the *edit*-space, where a set of edits, $\mathbf{e}_n(\mathbf{x}, \mathbf{y}_n) = \{e_1, \dots, e_{|\mathbf{e}_n|}\}$ can be used to represent each predicted output sequence, $\mathbf{y}_n$ [2]. A single edit in the edit set can be defined fully by an input token in $\mathbf{x}$ and an edit operation to apply (insertion, deletion or substitution). This section describes how Minimum Bayes' Risk decoding can be used in the edit-space to combine the different output sequences in $\mathcal{Y}$.

3.1 MBR decoding for GEC

MBR decoding aims to select the most representative output sequence, $\mathbf{y}^* \in \mathcal{Y}$. For GEC, we aim to maximise a reward score $\mathcal{R}$ in the edit-space that encourages better alignment with the final assessment metric,

$$\mathbf{y}^* = \arg\max_{\mathbf{y} \in \mathcal{Y}} \left\{ \mathbb{E}_{p(\tilde{\mathbf{y}}|x)}[\mathcal{R}(\tilde{\mathbf{e}}(\mathbf{x}, \tilde{\mathbf{y}}), \mathbf{e}(\mathbf{x}, \mathbf{y}))] \right\}, \tag{1}$$

where the reward score, $\mathcal{R}(\tilde{\mathbf{e}}, \mathbf{e})$, views $\tilde{\mathbf{e}}$ as reference edits and $\mathbf{e}$ as the hypothesis/predicted edits.

[2]Given an input sequence $\mathbf{x}$ and an output sequence $\mathbf{y}$ it is simple to create an edit set, using tools such as ERRANT (Bryant et al., 2017).

In practice, it is difficult to meaningfully estimate the posterior distribution, $p(\tilde{\mathbf{y}}|x)$ for each output sequence. Hence, we consider only similarly performing systems' output sequences, $\mathcal{Y}^{(\mathrm{c})} \in \mathcal{Y}$ to calculate the expectation of the reward and so we approximate each of these sequences as equiprobable,

$$\mathbf{y}^* \approx \underset{\mathbf{y}\in\mathcal{Y}^{(\mathrm{s})}}{\arg\max} \left\{ \frac{1}{|\mathcal{Y}^{(\mathrm{c})}|} \sum_{\tilde{\mathbf{y}}\in\mathcal{Y}^{(\mathrm{c})}} \mathcal{R}(\tilde{\mathbf{e}}(\mathbf{x},\tilde{\mathbf{y}}), \mathbf{e}(\mathbf{x},\mathbf{y})) \right\}, \tag{2}$$

where $\mathcal{Y}^{(\mathrm{s})}$ represents the set of possible output sequences we want to select from.

3.2 MBR decoding with edit voting

Inspired by Tarnavskyi et al. (2022) the different edit sets, $\{\mathbf{e}_1, \ldots, \mathbf{e}_N\}$ associated with the different output sequences, can be combined to create a single edit set, $\mathbf{e}^{(m)}$ containing all the individual edits present in at least m of the edit sets (i.e. m *votes*). This new combined edit set represents a new combined output sequence, $\mathbf{y}^{(m)}$. The MBR decoding approach of Equation 1 can now be applied by simply including the combined sequence in the set of sequences to select from, such that $\mathbf{y}^{(m)} \in \mathcal{Y}^{(\mathrm{s})}$. Note that the voting scheme can generate a maximum of N different combined sequences, with $\mathbf{e}^{(1)}$ being the union of all edit sets and $\mathbf{e}^{(N)}$ the intersection. Hence the selection space of sequences $\mathcal{Y}^{(\mathrm{s})}$ can be made richer with an extra N sequences.

3.3 Greedy MBR decoding for edit selection

Instead of augmenting the selection set $\mathcal{Y}^{(\mathrm{s})}$ with only a few sequences, it is useful to consider all possible edit sets. However, it is computationally infeasible to consider every possible edit set. Hence, this work proposes a practical, greedy method to increase the richness of the selection set. The minimal edit set is arguably the intersection of all edit sets, $\mathbf{e}^{(N)}$. In contrast the set of possible edits is given by the union set, $\mathbf{e}^{(1)}$. Hence, we can insert individual edits one by one from the union set to the intersection set. Every new edit insertion into the existing edit set represents a new output sequence $\mathbf{y}$ (that can be added to $\mathcal{Y}^{(\mathrm{s})}$). However, we only retain the edit insertions that give a new output sequence that increases the MBR expected reward, $\frac{1}{|\mathcal{Y}^{(\mathrm{c})}|}\sum_{\tilde{\mathbf{y}}\in\mathcal{Y}^{(\mathrm{c})}} \mathcal{R}(\tilde{\mathbf{e}}(\mathbf{x},\tilde{\mathbf{y}}), \mathbf{e}(\mathbf{x},\mathbf{y}))$ from Equation 2. This way we can efficiently search a richer selection set, $\mathcal{Y}^{(\mathrm{s})}$ of output sequences to find the best combined output sequence $\mathbf{y}^*$.

3.4 MBR reward score

Equation 1 uses a reward score $\mathcal{R}(\tilde{\mathbf{e}}, \mathbf{e})$ to perform MBR decoding. Careful selection of the reward score allows for control over the desired metric to optimise. We can for example aim to combine systems in a manner that encourages better edit *recall*,

$$\mathcal{R}^{(\mathrm{rec})}(\tilde{\mathbf{e}}, \mathbf{e}) = \frac{|\tilde{\mathbf{e}} \cap \mathbf{e}|}{|\tilde{\mathbf{e}}|}. \tag{3}$$

Conversely, it may be desirable to have a system with high precision,

$$\mathcal{R}^{(\mathrm{prec})}(\tilde{\mathbf{e}}, \mathbf{e}) = \frac{|\tilde{\mathbf{e}} \cap \mathbf{e}|}{|\mathbf{e}|}. \tag{4}$$

However, it is usually desirable to have a GEC system with a good combination of precision and recall, as measured by a F-k score,

$$\mathcal{R}^{(\mathrm{f(k)})}(\tilde{\mathbf{e}}, \mathbf{e}) = \frac{(1+k^2)|\tilde{\mathbf{e}} \cap \mathbf{e}|}{|\tilde{\mathbf{e}}|k + |\mathbf{e}|}. \tag{5}$$

As the precision is more important than recall for GEC systems, this work aligns the reward metric with the F0.5 score. The Jaccard Similarity reward metric is also explored as an alternative in Appendix A.

4 Experiments

4.1 Experimental setup

We evaluate performance of the combined systems on three popular grammatical error correction corpora. **First Certificate in English (FCE)** corpus (Yannakoudakis et al., 2011) is a subset of Cambridge Learner Corpus (OpenCLC, 2019) made up of written examinations for general and business English of candidates from 86 different mother tongues, consisting of 2,720 test sentences. **Building Education Applications 2019 (BEA-19)** (Bryant et al., 2019) offers a test set of 4477 sentences, sourced from essays written by native and non-native English students. **Conference on Computational Natural Language Learning 2014 (CoNLL-14)** (Ng et al., 2014) test set consists of 1312 sentences sourced from 50 essays written by 25 non-native English speakers. Three different state of the art GECToR models are used as the individual systems to be combined [3]. Each system uses a different Transformer encoder (bert (b),

[3]GECToR model Weights: https://github.com/grammarly/gector#pretrained-models

roberta (r) or xlnet (x)). Table 1 gives the performance of these individual systems [4].

Model	conll	bea	fce
b	56.15 (61.75, 41.19)	65.41 (67.33, 58.71)	49.66 (54.47, 36.68)
r	56.82 (61.99, 42.59)	68.21 (70.21, 61.21)	49.86 (53.47, 39.28)
x	56.77 (61.74, 42.95)	68.00 (69.89, 61.36)	50.52 (53.49, 41.00)

Table 1: F0.5 and (precision, recall) performance for individual GECToR systems

4.2 Results

MBR decoding (Equation 2) is applied in the edit-space for the three individual GECToR systems' outputs (b,r,x). Here, as the systems have similar performance (equiprobable posterior assumption valid), we let the selection set and the set of sequences to calculate the expected reward be the same $\mathcal{Y}^{(s)} = \mathcal{Y}^{(c)} = \{b, r, x\}$. Table 2 compares the different reward functions, $\mathcal{R}$, when applying MBR decoding. Selection with precision (Equation 6) and F0.5 (Equation 5) oriented reward metrics give a significant increase in performance over the individual systems in Table 1. Although the recall reward (Equation 3) does not increase F0.5 performance, it does significantly increase recall performance. This demonstrates that a simple application of MBR decoding can be used to combine individual systems to improve performance and selection of the reward function gives specific control over precision and recall of the combined system.

Reward	conll	bea	fce
$\mathcal{R}^{(\text{rec})}$	55.13 (57.76, 46.66)	64.67 (64.59, 64.99)	48.74 (50.12, 43.90)
$\mathcal{R}^{(\text{prec})}$	**59.78** (69.38, 34.48)	**70.87** (75.93, 55.96)	**52.35** (60.13, 34.50)
$\mathcal{R}^{(\text{f05})}$	59.71 (66.42, 42.53)	69.95 (72.95, 60.07)	52.05 (56.61, 39.36)

Table 2: MBR with $\mathcal{Y}^{(c)} = \mathcal{Y}^{(s)} = \{b, r, x\}$.

Section 3.2 describes how MBR decoding can be applied to systems combined by a voting scheme in the edit space. Table 3 shows the performance of systems combined with voting, where an individual edit requires m votes (from b,r or x edit system predictions) to be included in the combined edit set, $\mathbf{e}^{(m)}$ to form the single combined sequence $\mathbf{y}^{(m)}$. Note here that $\mathbf{e}^{(1)}$ is the union set and $\mathbf{e}^{(3)}$ is the intersection and so these sequences encourage either a higher recall or precision respectively. Table 4 shows the impact of MBR decoding where all the separate voting sets $(\mathbf{y}^{(1)}, \mathbf{y}^{(2)}, \mathbf{y}^{(3)})$ are included in the selection set, $\mathcal{Y}^{(s)} = \{b, r, x, \mathbf{y}^{(1)}, \mathbf{y}^{(2)}, \mathbf{y}^{(3)}\}$. Note that we maintain the same set of sequences for the expected reward calculation, $\mathcal{Y}^{(s)} = \{b, r, x\}$ to ensure the equiprobable posterior assumption holds [5]. It is evident that a richer selection set allows for even greater improvements in model performance for precision and F0.5 reward MBR decoding.

System	conll	bea	fce
$\mathbf{y}^{(1)}$	47.13 (48.02, 43.89)	55.94 (55.03, 59.91)	41.76 (42.38, 39.43)
$\mathbf{y}^{(2)}$	60.58 (68.41, 41.54)	71.82 (75.86, 59.22)	52.73 (58.16, 38.38)
$\mathbf{y}^{(3)}$	59.60 (77.30, 31.10)	72.96 (84.32, 47.41)	52.50 (67.05, 28.01)

Table 3: Voting combination, $\mathbf{y}^{(m)}$ (m votes).

Reward	conll	bea	fce
$\mathcal{R}^{(\text{rec})}$	53.99 (55.99, 47.23)	63.81 (63.47, 65.25)	48.18 (49.29, 44.20)
$\mathcal{R}^{(\text{prec})}$	60.24 (76.59, 32.50)	**73.42** (83.40, 49.66)	**53.51** (66.74, 29.85)
$\mathcal{R}^{(\text{f05})}$	**60.43** (67.94, 41.90)	70.84 (74.48, 59.25)	52.71 (57.83, 38.92)

Table 4: MBR with $\mathcal{Y}^{(c)} = \{b, r, x\}$ and $\mathcal{Y}^{(s)} = \{b, r, x, \mathbf{y}^{(1)}, \mathbf{y}^{(2)}, \mathbf{y}^{(3)}\}$.

Finally, as described in Section 3.3, MBR decoding can be performed over a richer edit selection space by greedily adding individual edits to the intersection edit set, $\mathbf{e}^{(3)}$ from the union edit set, $\mathbf{e}^{(1)}$. Experiments revealed (Appendix B) that allowing for all edits to be included from the union set can significantly increase the risk of poor insertions, compromising performance. Hence, instead we only consider edits from $\mathbf{e}^{(2)}$ to be added to the intersection set $\mathbf{e}^{(3)}$. Table 5 demonstrates that MBR decoding over this richer set of sequences can give better performance (CoNLL) than MBR with voting, but does not always give the best performance (BEA and FCE have better performance in Table 4). This is perhaps because the expected reward over the individual systems (b,r,x) is not necessarily perfectly aligned with the final F0.5 score relative to the true reference edits used in evaluation and thus over-optimisation of the selection set for MBR decoding does not help performance for some datasets.

[4] GEC performance for CoNLL and FCE is measured using the ERRANT tool (Bryant et al., 2017). Note that CoNLL is often evaluated with a different scorer in other papers. BEA is evaluated using the online submission portal: `https://codalab.lisn.upsaclay.fr/competitions/4057`

[5] Experiments with an alternative set of sequences for $\mathcal{Y}^{(c)}$ are in Appendix C

Reward	conll	bea	fce
$\mathcal{R}^{(\text{rec})}$	$61.06\binom{69.50}{41.11}$	$72.20\binom{76.87}{58.08}$	$52.94\binom{58.87}{37.73}$
$\mathcal{R}^{(\text{prec})}$	$59.65\binom{76.58}{30.79}$	$\mathbf{72.76}\binom{84.18}{47.16}$	$52.62\binom{67.61}{27.89}$
$\mathcal{R}^{(\text{f05})}$	$\mathbf{61.08}\binom{69.71}{40.85}$	$72.34\binom{77.16}{57.19}$	$\mathbf{53.00}\binom{59.07}{37.57}$

Table 5: MBR with $\mathcal{Y}^{(\text{c})} = \{b, r, x\}$ and greedy search for $\mathcal{Y}^{(\text{s})}$.

5 Conclusions

The combination of sequence-to-sequence grammatical error correction (GEC) systems is challenging. There is also often a mismatch between the decoding criterion and assessment criterion used for GEC systems. This work demonstrates that a novel Minimum Bayes' Risk (MBR) decoding approach within the edit-space can give an effective system combination method that aligns better with the assessment criteria. We further showed that enhancing the selection space to encompass sequences formulated by max-voting over individual edits can further improve system performance. Moreover, the employment of a greedy search strategy, guided by an MBR reward function, can result in performance gains for the combined system. Crucially, the choice of a reward function in the MBR framework gives users the ability to optimize desired characteristics of the combined GEC system, such as precision, recall or the F-score.

6 Limitations

This work explored how MBR decoding can be used to combine individual GEC systems, as well as align the combined system's performance to the edit-based F-score used to assess GEC systems. Experiments were performed with Grammarly's GECToR based systems. It would be useful to extend these experiments to other state of the art GEC systems. Although these other systems are not as efficient as GECToR due to the use of an auto-regressive Transformer decoder (as opposed to GECToR's encoder only structure), it is still meaningful to understand how these systems react to MBR decoding used for system combination. This is particularly relevant as generative large language models are increasingly used for standard natural language tasks.

7 Ethics Statement

This work reports on an efficient method to combine individual GEC system outputs in a manner that better aligns with assessment and improve performance. There are no perceived ethical risks associated with this work.

8 Acknowledgements

This paper reports on research supported by Cambridge University Press & Assessment (CUP&A), a department of The Chancellor, Masters, and Scholars of the University of Cambridge.

References

Abhijeet Awasthi, Sunita Sarawagi, Rasna Goyal, Sabyasachi Ghosh, and Vihari Piratla. 2019. Parallel iterative edit models for local sequence transduction. *CoRR*, abs/1910.02893.

Tom B. Brown, Benjamin Mann, Nick Ryder, Melanie Subbiah, Jared Kaplan, Prafulla Dhariwal, Arvind Neelakantan, Pranav Shyam, Girish Sastry, Amanda Askell, Sandhini Agarwal, Ariel Herbert-Voss, Gretchen Krueger, Tom Henighan, Rewon Child, Aditya Ramesh, Daniel M. Ziegler, Jeffrey Wu, Clemens Winter, Christopher Hesse, Mark Chen, Eric Sigler, Mateusz Litwin, Scott Gray, Benjamin Chess, Jack Clark, Christopher Berner, Sam McCandlish, Alec Radford, Ilya Sutskever, and Dario Amodei. 2020. Language models are few-shot learners. *CoRR*, abs/2005.14165.

Christopher Bryant, Mariano Felice, Øistein E. Andersen, and Ted Briscoe. 2019. The BEA-2019 shared task on grammatical error correction. In *Proceedings of the Fourteenth Workshop on Innovative Use of NLP for Building Educational Applications*, pages 52–75, Florence, Italy. Association for Computational Linguistics.

Christopher Bryant, Mariano Felice, and Ted Briscoe. 2017. Automatic annotation and evaluation of error types for grammatical error correction. In *Proceedings of the 55th Annual Meeting of the Association for Computational Linguistics (Volume 1: Long Papers)*, pages 793–805, Vancouver, Canada. Association for Computational Linguistics.

Mengyun Chen, Tao Ge, Xingxing Zhang, Furu Wei, and Ming Zhou. 2020. Improving the efficiency of grammatical error correction with erroneous span detection and correction. *CoRR*, abs/2010.03260.

Kyunghyun Cho, Bart van Merrienboer, Çaglar Gülçehre, Fethi Bougares, Holger Schwenk, and Yoshua Bengio. 2014. Learning phrase representations using RNN encoder-decoder for statistical machine translation. *CoRR*, abs/1406.1078.

Yassir Fathullah, Mark J.F. Gales, and Andrey Malinin. 2021. Ensemble distillation approaches for grammatical error correction. In *ICASSP 2021 - 2021 IEEE International Conference on Acoustics, Speech and Signal Processing (ICASSP)*, pages 2745–2749.

Markus Freitag, Yaser Al-Onaizan, and Baskaran Sankaran. 2017. Ensemble distillation for neural machine translation. *arXiv preprint arXiv:1702.01802*.

Markus Freitag, David Grangier, Qijun Tan, and Bowen Liang. 2022. High quality rather than high model probability: Minimum Bayes risk decoding with neural metrics. *Transactions of the Association for Computational Linguistics*, 10:811–825.

Mudasir A. Ganaie, Minghui Hu, Mohammad Tanveer, and Ponnuthurai N. Suganthan. 2021. Ensemble deep learning: A review. *CoRR*, abs/2104.02395.

Kaiming He, Xiangyu Zhang, Shaoqing Ren, and Jian Sun. 2016. Deep residual learning for image recognition. In *Proceedings of the IEEE conference on computer vision and pattern recognition*, pages 770–778.

Cheng Ju, Aurélien Bibaut, and Mark van der Laan. 2018. The relative performance of ensemble methods with deep convolutional neural networks for image classification. *Journal of Applied Statistics*, 45(15):2800–2818.

Masahiro Kaneko, Masato Mita, Shun Kiyono, Jun Suzuki, and Kentaro Inui. 2020. Encoder-decoder models can benefit from pre-trained masked language models in grammatical error correction. *CoRR*, abs/2005.00987.

Shun Kiyono, Jun Suzuki, Masato Mita, Tomoya Mizumoto, and Kentaro Inui. 2019. An empirical study of incorporating pseudo data into grammatical error correction. *CoRR*, abs/1909.00502.

Shankar Kumar and William Byrne. 2004. Minimum Bayes-risk decoding for statistical machine translation. In *Proceedings of the Human Language Technology Conference of the North American Chapter of the Association for Computational Linguistics: HLT-NAACL 2004*, pages 169–176, Boston, Massachusetts, USA. Association for Computational Linguistics.

Jared Lichtarge, Chris Alberti, and Shankar Kumar. 2020. Data weighted training strategies for grammatical error correction. *CoRR*, abs/2008.02976.

Yiheng Liu, Tianle Han, Siyuan Ma, Jiayue Zhang, Yuanyuan Yang, Jiaming Tian, Hao He, Antong Li, Mengshen He, Zhengliang Liu, Zihao Wu, Dajiang Zhu, Xiang Li, Ning Qiang, Dingang Shen, Tianming Liu, and Bao Ge. 2023. Summary of chatgpt/gpt-4 research and perspective towards the future of large language models.

Yong Liu and Xin Yao. 1999. Ensemble learning via negative correlation. *Neural networks*, 12(10):1399–1404.

Andrey Malinin and Mark Gales. 2021. Uncertainty estimation in autoregressive structured prediction. In *International Conference on Learning Representations*.

Eric Malmi, Sebastian Krause, Sascha Rothe, Daniil Mirylenka, and Aliaksei Severyn. 2019. Encode, tag, realize: High-precision text editing. In *Proceedings of the 2019 Conference on Empirical Methods in Natural Language Processing and the 9th International Joint Conference on Natural Language Processing (EMNLP-IJCNLP)*, pages 5054–5065, Hong Kong, China. Association for Computational Linguistics.

Potsawee Manakul, Yassir Fathullah, Adian Liusie, Vyas Raina, Vatsal Raina, and Mark Gales. 2023. Cued at probsum 2023: Hierarchical ensemble of summarization models.

Mathias Müller and Rico Sennrich. 2021. Understanding the properties of minimum Bayes risk decoding in neural machine translation. In *Proceedings of the 59th Annual Meeting of the Association for Computational Linguistics and the 11th International Joint Conference on Natural Language Processing (Volume 1: Long Papers)*, pages 259–272, Online. Association for Computational Linguistics.

Daniel Naber. 2003. A rule-based style and grammar checker.

Hwee Tou Ng, Siew Mei Wu, Ted Briscoe, Christian Hadiwinoto, Raymond Hendy Susanto, and Christopher Bryant. 2014. The CoNLL-2014 shared task on grammatical error correction. In *Proceedings of the Eighteenth Conference on Computational Natural Language Learning: Shared Task*, pages 1–14, Baltimore, Maryland. Association for Computational Linguistics.

Kostiantyn Omelianchuk, Vitaliy Atrasevych, Artem N. Chernodub, and Oleksandr Skurzhanskyi. 2020. Gector - grammatical error correction: Tag, not rewrite. *CoRR*, abs/2005.12592.

OpenCLC. 2019. Open cambridge learner english corpus.

Vyas Raina, Mark J.F. Gales, and Kate M. Knill. 2020. Universal adversarial attacks on spoken language assessment systems. In *Interspeech 2020*. ISCA.

Antti-Veikko Rosti, Necip Fazil Ayan, Bing Xiang, Spyros Matsoukas, Richard Schwartz, and Bonnie Dorr. 2007a. Combining outputs from multiple machine translation systems. In *Human Language Technologies 2007: The Conference of the North American Chapter of the Association for Computational Linguistics; Proceedings of the Main Conference*, pages 228–235, Rochester, New York. Association for Computational Linguistics.

Antti-Veikko Rosti, Spyros Matsoukas, and Richard Schwartz. 2007b. Improved word-level system combination for machine translation. In *Proceedings of the 45th Annual Meeting of the Association of Computational Linguistics*, pages 312–319, Prague, Czech Republic. Association for Computational Linguistics.

Rico Sennrich, Barry Haddow, and Alexandra Birch. 2015. Improving neural machine translation models with monolingual data. *arXiv preprint arXiv:1511.06709*.

K. C. Sim, W. J. Byrne, M. J. F. Gales, H. Sahbi, and P. C. Woodland. 2007. Consensus network decoding for statistical machine translation system combination. In *2007 IEEE International Conference on Acoustics, Speech and Signal Processing - ICASSP '07*, volume 4, pages IV–105–IV–108.

Karen Simonyan and Andrew Zisserman. 2014. Very deep convolutional networks for large-scale image recognition. *arXiv preprint arXiv:1409.1556*.

Felix Stahlberg and Shankar Kumar. 2020. Seq2Edits: Sequence transduction using span-level edit operations. In *Proceedings of the 2020 Conference on Empirical Methods in Natural Language Processing (EMNLP)*, pages 5147–5159, Online. Association for Computational Linguistics.

Christian Szegedy, Wei Liu, Yangqing Jia, Pierre Sermanet, Scott Reed, Dragomir Anguelov, Dumitru Erhan, Vincent Vanhoucke, and Andrew Rabinovich. 2015. Going deeper with convolutions. In *Proceedings of the IEEE conference on computer vision and pattern recognition*, pages 1–9.

Maksym Tarnavskyi, Artem Chernodub, and Kostiantyn Omelianchuk. 2022. Ensembling and knowledge distilling of large sequence taggers for grammatical error correction. In *Proceedings of the 60th Annual Meeting of the Association for Computational Linguistics (Volume 1: Long Papers)*, pages 3842–3852, Dublin, Ireland. Association for Computational Linguistics.

Ashish Vaswani, Noam Shazeer, Niki Parmar, Jakob Uszkoreit, Llion Jones, Aidan N Gomez, Ł ukasz Kaiser, and Illia Polosukhin. 2017. Attention is all you need. In *Advances in Neural Information Processing Systems*, volume 30. Curran Associates, Inc.

David H Wolpert. 1992. Stacked generalization. *Neural networks*, 5(2):241–259.

Haoran Wu, Wenxuan Wang, Yuxuan Wan, Wenxiang Jiao, and Michael Lyu. 2023. Chatgpt or grammarly? evaluating chatgpt on grammatical error correction benchmark.

Helen Yannakoudakis, Ted Briscoe, and Ben Medlock. 2011. A new dataset and method for automatically grading ESOL texts. In *Proceedings of the 49th Annual Meeting of the Association for Computational Linguistics: Human Language Technologies*, pages 180–189, Portland, Oregon, USA. Association for Computational Linguistics.

Yidan Zhang, Yu Wan, Dayiheng Liu, Baosong Yang, and Zhenan He. 2022. Rmbr: A regularized minimum bayes risk reranking framework for machine translation.

A Jaccard Similarity as MBR Reward

Section 3.4 proposes three different reward functions, $\mathcal{R}$ to guide the MBR decoding process (Equation 1) to better align with desired assessment criteria. Here, we consider the Jaccard Similarity as an alternative reward function that can combine precision and recall properties,

$$\mathcal{R}^{(\text{jac})}(\tilde{\mathbf{e}}, \mathbf{e}) = \frac{|\tilde{\mathbf{e}} \cap \mathbf{e}|}{|\tilde{\mathbf{e}} \cup \mathbf{e}|}. \tag{6}$$

Table 6 gives the performance of systems combined with MBR decoding using the Jaccard reward function.

$\mathcal{Y}^{(\text{s})}$	conll	bea	fce
$\{b, r, x\}$	$59.22\binom{65.39}{43.01}$	$69.15\binom{71.55}{60.96}$	$51.56\binom{55.71}{39.73}$
$\{b, r, x, \mathbf{y}^{(1)}, \mathbf{y}^{(2)}, \mathbf{y}^{(3)}\}$	$59.21\binom{65.50}{42.76}$	$69.26\binom{71.87}{60.48}$	$51.63\binom{55.96}{39.45}$
Greedy	$60.94\binom{69.84}{40.37}$	$72.37\binom{77.29}{57.68}$	$52.92\binom{59.09}{37.33}$

Table 6: GEC system performance with Jaccard Similarity reward function for MBR decoding. In all settings, $\mathcal{Y}^{(\text{s})} = \mathcal{Y}^{(\text{c})} = \{b, r, x\}$

Comparing to results in the main experiments (Section 4.2), it can be seen that using the Jaccard similarity reward gives similar behaviour but slightly worse performance than the F0.5 reward function used for MBR decoding. This is perhaps expected because both metrics encourage good precision and recall, but the final GEC systems are assessed using the F0.5 score. Hence, the Jaccard similarity reward offers a worse approximation to the final assessment metric than an explicit F0.5 reward in MBR decoding.

B Greedy MBR Decoding Selection Space

Section 3.3 describes an approach where MBR decoding can be used to greedily search over an edit space between the intersection edit set, $\mathbf{e}^{(3)}$ and the union edit set, $\mathbf{e}^{(1)}$ to find a combined edit set that as per the expected reward in the MBR algorithm should give better performance. Results in the main paper in Table 5 search the edit space between the intersection set, $\mathbf{e}^{(3)}$ and $\mathbf{e}^{(2)}$. Table 7 shows that it is sensible to not continue searching for all edits in the union set, $\mathbf{e}^{(1)}$, as searching the entire space compromises performance. This is perhaps due to the increased noise added into the system by potentially including spurious edits from the union set.

Reward	conll	bea	fce
$\mathcal{R}^{(\text{rec})}$	$53.22\binom{56.48}{43.24}$	$63.82\binom{65.34}{58.38}$	$47.73\binom{50.77}{38.52}$
$\mathcal{R}^{(\text{prec})}$	$59.03\binom{76.58}{30.79}$	$72.58\binom{84.27}{46.67}$	$52.56\binom{67.71}{27.73}$
$\mathcal{R}^{(\text{f05})}$	$58.42\binom{67.33}{38.19}$	$69.66\binom{75.05}{54.11}$	$50.42\binom{57.33}{34.02}$

Table 7: Greedy MBR decoding performance with edit search from intersection edit set, $\mathbf{e}^{(3)}$ to the union edit set, $\mathbf{e}^{(1)}$. By considering all possible edits in the union set, we can reduce performance. Hence in the main paper we limit edits to be between $\mathbf{e}^{(2)}$ and $\mathbf{e}^{(3)}$.

C Alternative Expected Reward Set, $\mathcal{Y}^{(\text{c})}$

Equation 1 for MBR decoding can be simplified to equation 2, where we make the assumption that every sequence $\mathbf{y} \in \mathcal{Y}^{(\text{c})}$ used to calculate the expected reward is equiprobable (i.e. the posterior distribution is the same). We justify this assumption in the main paper by considering only similarly performing systems to form the set of sequences over which the expected reward is calculated: $\mathcal{Y}^{(\text{c})} = \{b, r, x\}$. It is interesting consider a situation where we violate/test this equiprobable posterior assumption by considering different possible sequence sets for $\mathcal{Y}^{(\text{c})}$ and observing the impact on performance after MBR decoding system combination. Table 8 reports the performance of MBR decoding with different output sequence sets, $\mathcal{Y}^{(\text{c})}$ used to calculate the expected reward. In comparison to the equivalent results in the main paper in Table 2, it is evident that a deviation from $\mathcal{Y}^{(\text{c})} = \{b, r, x\}$ does not compromises performance. This demonstrates that it is possible to diverge from the *similar performing system* constraint to validate the equiprobable posterior assumption to generate good combined systems using MBR decoding.

Reward	conll	bea	fce
$\mathcal{R}^{(\text{prec})}$	$59.83\binom{69.43}{38.52}$	$70.81\binom{75.81}{56.02}$	$52.40\binom{60.15}{34.57}$
$\mathcal{R}^{(\text{f05})}$	$59.96\binom{67.76}{41.07}$	$70.44\binom{74.21}{58.55}$	$52.09\binom{57.89}{37.19}$

Table 8: Impact of changing the set of sequences, $\mathcal{Y}^{(\text{c})}$ used to calculate the expected reward when using MBR decoding for system combination. We let $\mathcal{Y}^{(\text{c})} = \{b, r, x, \mathbf{y}^{(1)}, \mathbf{y}^{(2)}, \mathbf{y}^{(3)}\}$. In all settings we maintain the same selection set, $\mathcal{Y}^{(\text{s})} = \{b, r, x\}$.

Who Are All The Stochastic Parrots Imitating? They Should Tell Us!

Sagi Shaier[▽] **Lawrence E. Hunter**[†] **Katharina von der Wense**[▽◇♠]
[▽]University of Colorado Boulder
[†]University of Colorado Denver
[◇]Johannes Gutenberg University Mainz
[▽]{sagi.shaier, katharina.kann}@colorado.edu
[†]larry.hunter@cuanschutz.edu

Abstract

Both standalone language models (LMs) as well as LMs within downstream-task systems have been shown to generate statements which are factually untrue. This problem is especially severe for low-resource languages, where training data is scarce and of worse quality than for high-resource languages. In this opinion piece, we argue that LMs in their current state will never be fully trustworthy in critical settings and suggest a possible novel strategy to handle this issue: by building LMs such that can cite their sources – i.e., point a user to the parts of their training data that back up their outputs. We first discuss which current NLP tasks would or would not benefit from such models. We then highlight the expected benefits such models would bring, e.g., quick verifiability of statements. We end by outlining the individual tasks that would need to be solved on the way to developing LMs with the ability to cite. We hope to start a discussion about the field's current approach to building LMs, especially for low-resource languages, and the role of the training data in explaining model generations.

Figure 1: An actual conversation with ChatGPT in Hebrew on the effects of not drinking enough water. ChatGPT is unable to point the user to its sources and instead falls back to a general answer ("I am ChatGPT, an OpenAI model based on the GPT-3.5 deep learning model. I am powered by OpenAI's learning set, which has been raised with the help of machine learning techniques on Internet culture, including websites, books, articles, quotes, and more"). We argue that ChatGPT and similar models should be able to direct the user to the sources of their information, which will have multiple benefits, such as quick verifiability of model statements.

1 Introduction

Transformers (Vaswani et al., 2017) and related models have been improving rapidly, with applications in a surprisingly large number of domains, such as natural language generation (Zhang et al., 2019), machine translation (Wang et al., 2019), question answering (Akermi et al., 2020), and code generation (Svyatkovskiy et al., 2020), based on the ability to generate sensible outputs to prompts over a nearly limitless input domain.

Despite impressive performance on a wide array of benchmark tasks, these models are known to produce "AI-splaining," confident sounding but incorrect statements: "To the extent that a use case places importance on the truth of the outputs provided, it is not a good fit for GPT-3" (Dale, 2021); see also Church et al. (2022) and Marcus (2019).

This problem has proven to be especially true for models trained on low-resource languages (Guerreiro et al., 2023), where data may not only be scarce (Mager et al., 2018), but also not well curated with respect to correctness or quality, in comparison to higher-resource languages (Hedderich et al., 2021). Furthermore, model hallucination in such settings can result in toxic patterns that can be found in the training data (Guerreiro et al., 2023).

In accordance with the large LMs and low-resource languages theme track, we argue that while the performance and factuality of LMs has been improving, both in high-resource and low-resource settings, in their existing state, LMs will realistically never be fully trustworthy. Thus, in settings in which factuality is required, such as medicine, they are dangerous and unemployable.

[♠]Formerly: Katharina Kann

Proceedings of the 13th International Joint Conference on Natural Language Processing and the 3rd Conference of the Asia-Pacific Chapter of the Association for Computational Linguistics (Volume 2: Short Papers), pages 113–120
November 1–4, 2023.

This is further noted in Menick et al. (2022), who state that users cannot trust any claim a model makes without fact-checking.

Our proposal to address these concerns suggests both technical development and a simple regulatory framework: as we often ask students, journalists and scholars, **we should ask our models to name their sources and provide evidence for their assertions.** Currently, even popular LMs often fail at this, as seen on the ChatGPT (OpenAI, 2023) example in Figure 1. In the case of generative models, either the model itself or a post-hoc procedure could – and, under certain circumstances, *should be required to* – be designed to produce evidentiary justification for its output.

In this position paper, we overview which NLP tasks would benefit from such citation models, discuss the benefits they would bring, and present a roadmap to develop such models. Our goal is to motivate the field to start thinking about what is necessary to make current models truly useful in all sorts of – potentially critical – scenarios.

2 Background

Factuality and the Lack Thereof LMs store factual knowledge (Dong et al., 2022; De Cao et al., 2021; Elazar et al., 2021; Jiang et al., 2019) and previous work have shown that LMs can act as knowledge bases (Petroni et al., 2019; Sung et al., 2021). However, there is no guarantee that the retrieved knowledge is indeed factual, and unfortunately, often it is not. This can be seen in many areas, such as question answering (Xu et al., 2021), dialogue systems (Dziri et al., 2021; Shuster et al., 2021; Testoni and Bernardi, 2021), image captioning (Rohrbach et al., 2018), text summarization (Zhao et al., 2020b; Cao et al., 2022; Maynez et al., 2020) and translation (Raunak et al., 2021; Jeblick et al., 2022). This is especially true in low-resource settings (Guerreiro et al., 2023). In order for LMs to be fully utilized as such knowledge bases and in settings where factuality is crucial, the retrieved knowledge must first be factual. But, without knowing the source of such the model's knowledge, verifying its factuality is a challenge.

Citation Generation Although LMs, particularly those intended to produce scientific text, such as Meta's Galactica (Taylor et al., 2022), already produce text that looks as if it is a citation, frequently there is no document corresponding to the apparent citation or the cited document does not support the statement associated with it. Many existing approaches to citation recommendation offer productive avenues to explore for factuality testing, post-hoc generation of support, hybrid architectures, or creation of training data (Ali et al., 2022; Krasnova et al., 2023). There has also been work on citation generation, where the task is either: 1) given two documents, generate an explanation for the relation between them (Luu et al., 2020), or 2) generate a citation for an already existing text (Gu and Hahnloser, 2022; Xing et al., 2020; Wu et al., 2021; Fetahu et al., 2016). This is different from our suggestion to generate statements and citations simultaneously, and also not optimal: as LMs are being trained on massive datasets, evaluating whether each statement came from each of the potentially millions of article becomes impractical. Lastly, many existing systems that can in fact provide citations are based on search engines or retrieval models (Menick et al., 2022; Glaese et al., 2022), see also Perplexity AI♠, YouChat♣, or the ALCE benchmark (Gao et al., 2023). This is problematic because 1) it is far more time consuming than directly generating citations together with text; 2) access to the information sources needs to be provided at all times; 3) in contrast to our proposed approach, it does not increase model interpretability; and 4) for low-resource languages the quantity and quality of the data is often limited, and hence result in difficulties retrieving the relevant, factual source.

3 Citations and Their Pros and Cons

In this section, we will first discuss which NLP tasks – according to us – require LMs with an ability to cite their sources. We will then discuss the benefits and, subsequently, risks of such models.

3.1 Which Tasks Require Citations?

We propose to classify tasks via two questions: (1) Is the source of the generated text obvious? (2) Is the generated text an objective truth or a subjective statement? See Table 1 for examples.

If the answer to the first question is *yes*, no further citation is required. This is the case, e.g., for machine translation (Brants et al., 2007): the content of the generated text comes from the input sentence. The same holds true for summarization (See et al., 2017) and paraphrase generation (Zhou

♠https://www.perplexity.ai/

♣https://you.com/

and Bhat, 2021). However, this is only partially the case for text simplification (Sheang and Saggion, 2021): while most of the content comes from the original text, simpler versions of text sometimes contain additional explanations, which do require citations. In contrast, for many other tasks the input does not act as the source for text generation – instead, the output comes from information stored in the model parameters and, thus, originally from the training data. An ideal system would be able to cite the part of its training data responsible for any given output. This is the case for the popular NLP tasks of closed-book free-text question answering (Roberts et al., 2020), dialogue generation (Zhao et al., 2020a), or creative writing (Xu et al., 2020).

For tasks for which the answer to Question 1 is *no*, we then turn to the second aforementioned question and ask if the generated text without clear sources of information in the input contains what should be objective truths. This is typically true for closed-book free-text question answering, which, as a consequence, according to our rules does require citations. However, this is *sometimes* the case for other tasks too, such as the generation of additional explanations during text simplification or image captioning. Similarly, for dialogue generation, objective truths and subjective statements could be mixed within the same conversation. As a result, some generated statements for those tasks do require citations, while others are good without.

3.2 Benefits of Citations

Citations allow us to verify the factuality of generated text easily. In contrast, without knowing where the text came from we are often unable to verify that it is correct. Moreover, knowing what portion of the text is copied verbatim allows us to give credit to the author and prevent copyright violations. Citations also increase the explainability of the answer and allow users to learn more about interesting topics. Additionally, recent work in prompt engineering have shown that models providing justifications for their assertions (even when only partially correct) can improve the correctness of the outputs (Jung et al., 2022). Trustworthiness judgments among people often include a social aspect, so by doing a good job of identifying sources and influences has the potential to increase both the trust in AI systems and their trustworthiness. For example, human trustworthiness judgments about scientific claims are influenced by the interests of the authors (Gierth and Bromme, 2020).

3.3 Risks of Citations

Unfortunately, citations also come with risks. Just by having a citation next to a generated text, users are more likely to trust it (Thornley et al., 2015). However, it is likely that users will not examine each and every citation manually to verify that the text is indeed factual, or that the source is trustworthy (Simkin and Roychowdhury, 2002; Thornley et al., 2015). This will be exacerbated by the fact that it is incredibly unlikely that any automated system will ever produce 100% correct citations at all times, and may result in either users' diminishing trust and usage of such systems or a potential harm.

There is also the risk of decreased readability: backing up every statement with many citations, as the text may appear in multiple places, will reduce the readability of the text and may hinder users from reading or understanding it. Lastly, privacy concerns also arise from the training process of LMs. For example, state of the art LMs are often trained on a massive automatically extracted text (Radford et al., 2018). But, as manual examination of each text is not feasible for its size, there is a possibility that it may contain private user information, such as patient records. This may result in LMs cite information that should stay private.

3.4 Citations vs. Explainability

The goal to understand why a model generates any given output is shared with research on model explainability (Danilevsky et al., 2020). However, in contrast to the latter, we are not interested in the effect of certain input on the output. In addition, we do not necessarily require that the model describes its reasoning by providing citations – what we care about instead is that the citations back up the model's answer. This enables humans to verify the output – even if the cited source should not actually in the technical sense have been the reason for the model's output.

4 Road Map

4.1 The Big Picture

Meta-information Currently, the standard in the field is to train models on text, disjoint from its origin. Even though some models are trained on data that contain text with citations (e.g., Taylor et al. (2022)), the citations are only "attached" to statements taken from other sources, while any

Task	Q1	Q2	Citation?	Example
Creative writing	No	Sometimes	Sometimes	Penguins are known for their ability to survive in harsh Antarctic conditions [CITATION], but few people know that they also possess the power of telekinesis which they use to build intricate nests out of ice blocks.
Dialogue generation	No	Sometimes	Sometimes	Did you know that penguins can jump up to 6 feet out of water when leaping onto land or ice floes? [CITATION]. I think elephants can do the same.
Free-text QA	No	Yes	Yes	The current president is not a penguin [CITATION].
Image captioning	No	Sometimes	Sometimes	A group of penguins diving into the ocean to catch fresh fish for dinner, highlighting their impressive swimming abilities [CITATION], while one penguin emerges victorious with a giant fish twice its size.
Paraphrase generation	Yes	N/A	No	**Source text**: Penguins are social animals who live in large colonies. **Paraphrased sentence**: Penguins thrive in community living
Summarization	Yes	N/A	No	**Source text**: Emperor penguins are the largest species of penguin, standing up to 4 feet tall. They are skilled hunters, capable of catching fish and krill by diving hundreds of feet below the surface. **Summary**: Emperor penguins are notable for their size and hunting prowess, making them formidable predators in their environment.
Text simplification	Sometimes	Sometimes	Sometimes	**Source text**: Penguins have evolved unique adaptations that allow them to survive in environments as harsh as Antarctica, such as their countershaded dark and white plumage, which camouflages them from predators above and below the ice. **Simplified text**: Penguins live in Antarctica, which is year-round one of the coldest places on Earth [CITATION], and they look different than other birds so they don't get eaten.
Translation	Yes	N/A	No	**Source text**: Penguins are cool. **Translated text**: Pinguine sind cool.

Table 1: An overview of natural language generation tasks together with our opinion regarding if they require citations. Q1: *Obvious source?* Q2: *Objective truth?*

other text, even taken from the same article, does not have a citation attached to it. This results in LMs that can only sometimes, on a limited text, produce citations. In order to develop LMs that can cite their sources effectively, we need to give them the metadata which contain citation information.

Retrieval Say we trained a LM with the right data such that it has knowledge of which statement came from which article. How would we extract text with citations? One avenue for such knowledge extraction is to modify the pretraining, such that citation information is being generated together with every piece of generated text.

When To Cite? The above strategy would result in LMs that would always produce a citation. However, as mentioned in Section 3.1, not every task or statement requires a citation. For tasks that do require citations, we can just let the model always cite. For tasks that do not require citations, we can simply remove the citations. For tasks in between, where citation is sometimes required, we propose to utilize the existing subjectivity classification task (Wiebe et al., 1999).

4.2 Concrete Tasks to Master

Our goal is to lay out a roadmap for the community, which describes necessary steps for the development of models that can cite their sources. This is not trivial, as it requires improvements of models for existing tasks as well as the development of systems for novel challenges.

Simultaneous Citation and Text Generation As mentioned in Section 2, existing work mainly retrieve citations for already generated text, which becomes intractable as models are trained on ever more text and the number of possible source documents increases drastically. In contrast, we propose STANCE: the task of **S**imultaneous **T**ext **AN**d **C**itation g**E**neration. As an additional challenge, future work should also focus on MultiSTANCE: multihop citation generation, where the sources for a given text are spread across multiple texts. As the number of citations can be significant (though much smaller in the low-resource setting), we suggest to use topic modeling, as a potential avenue to reduce such large search space.

Subjectivity Classification As mentioned in Section 3.1, whether a task requires a citation partially depends on if the text is objective or subjective. This is not a novel task as the community has been working on subjectivity classification for quite some time (Wiebe et al., 1999; Wiebe and Riloff, 2005). However, to the best of our knowledge, models for this task have not been employed in the context of citations.

Citation-Text Correctness To ensure that the retrieval step (Section 4.1) is successful, we need to identify whether the statement appears in the source. For that, two existing tasks can be used: 1) identifying which part of the generated text refers to the citation (Wang et al., 2020). 2) Validate that the citation is appropriate for the selected text span (Karadzhov et al., 2017; Martín et al., 2021; Honovich et al., 2022; Mihaylova et al., 2018; Lee et al., 2020). Using such automatic methods instead of manually verifying citations will result in faster model development.

Source Trustworthiness We all know that Wikipedia is not a reliable source for citation. We propose CUE (**C**itation q**U**ality **E**valuation), the task of evaluating the quality of the source corresponding to a generated citation. We believe there are six main sub-tasks for CUE, which consist of classifying 1) the time of publication, 2) whether the source is credible, 3) how many times the source has been cited, 4) if the author is known, 5) if the source is unbiased, and 6) if the statement and citation are still relevant. For example, answering that the current US president is Barack Obama was *previously* factual, and may still show up in many source documents, but is not factual in 2023.

5 Conclusion

Language models (LMs) performance has been improving rapidly in a wide variety of areas. However, there is the crucial issue of their generated text often being nonfactual, especially for low-resource languages. We argue that, in order for LMs to be fully trustworthy, they must cite their sources – i.e., point users to the parts of their training data that back up their outputs. In this opinion piece, we discuss NLP tasks which would benefit from such citation models, highlight the benefits and risks such models would bring, and outline the individual tasks that would need to be solved on the way to develop such LMs.

Limitations

While developing the proposed language models that can cite their sources increase their utility, there is a risk that people would trust them more without actually verifying that the generated citations are actually correct. Such increase in trust would be especially problematic in time-critical scenarios where people cannot examine each citation manually. Ideally, our proposal will result in an increase of data cleaning, such that each citation is by default trustworthy. That being said, our approach does not solve copyright issues.

Ethics Statement

The main reason for this paper is to point out shortcomings of state-of-the-art language models, which can have significant social, health-related, and economic consequences. Future work should develop systems that can cite their sources in order to facilitate a verification of the factuality of generated statements.

Acknowledgments

We would like to thank the reviewers for taking the time to provide feedback on our work. Your insights have been valuable in helping us refine and enhance our manuscript. The authors acknowledge financial support from NIH grants OT2TR003422 and R01LM013400.

References

Imen Akermi, Johannes Heinecke, and Frédéric Herledan. 2020. Transformer based natural language generation for question-answering. In *Proceedings of the 13th International Conference on Natural Language Generation*, pages 349–359, Dublin, Ireland. Association for Computational Linguistics.

Zafar Ali, Guilin Qi, Khan Muhammad, Siddhartha Bhattacharyya, Irfan Ullah, and Waheed Abro. 2022. Citation recommendation employing heterogeneous bibliographic network embedding. *Neural Comput. Appl.*, 34(13):10229–10242.

Thorsten Brants, Ashok C. Popat, Peng Xu, Franz J. Och, and Jeffrey Dean. 2007. Large language models in machine translation. In *Proceedings of the 2007 Joint Conference on Empirical Methods in Natural Language Processing and Computational Natural Language Learning (EMNLP-CoNLL)*, pages

858–867, Prague, Czech Republic. Association for Computational Linguistics.

Meng Cao, Yue Dong, and Jackie Cheung. 2022. Hallucinated but factual! inspecting the factuality of hallucinations in abstractive summarization. In *Proceedings of the 60th Annual Meeting of the Association for Computational Linguistics (Volume 1: Long Papers)*, pages 3340–3354, Dublin, Ireland. Association for Computational Linguistics.

Kenneth Church, Valia Kordoni, Gary Marcus, Ernest Davis, Yanjun Ma, and Zeyu Chen. 2022. A gentle introduction to deep nets and opportunities for the future. In *Proceedings of the 60th Annual Meeting of the Association for Computational Linguistics: Tutorial Abstracts*, pages 1–6, Dublin, Ireland. Association for Computational Linguistics.

Robert Dale. 2021. Gpt-3: What's it good for? *Natural Language Engineering*, 27(1):113–118.

Marina Danilevsky, Kun Qian, Ranit Aharonov, Yannis Katsis, Ban Kawas, and Prithviraj Sen. 2020. A survey of the state of explainable AI for natural language processing. In *Proceedings of the 1st Conference of the Asia-Pacific Chapter of the Association for Computational Linguistics and the 10th International Joint Conference on Natural Language Processing*, pages 447–459, Suzhou, China. Association for Computational Linguistics.

Nicola De Cao, Wilker Aziz, and Ivan Titov. 2021. Editing factual knowledge in language models.

Qingxiu Dong, Damai Dai, Yifan Song, Jingjing Xu, Zhifang Sui, and Lei Li. 2022. Calibrating factual knowledge in pretrained language models.

Nouha Dziri, Andrea Madotto, Osmar Zaïane, and Avishek Joey Bose. 2021. Neural path hunter: Reducing hallucination in dialogue systems via path grounding. In *Proceedings of the 2021 Conference on Empirical Methods in Natural Language Processing*, pages 2197–2214, Online and Punta Cana, Dominican Republic. Association for Computational Linguistics.

Yanai Elazar, Nora Kassner, Shauli Ravfogel, Abhilasha Ravichander, Eduard Hovy, Hinrich Schütze, and Yoav Goldberg. 2021. Measuring and improving consistency in pretrained language models.

Besnik Fetahu, Katja Markert, Wolfgang Nejdl, and Avishek Anand. 2016. Finding news citations for wikipedia. In *Proceedings of the 25th ACM International on Conference on Information and Knowledge Management*. ACM.

Tianyu Gao, Howard Yen, Jiatong Yu, and Danqi Chen. 2023. Enabling large language models to generate text with citations.

L. Gierth and R. Bromme. 2020. Beware of vested interests: Epistemic vigilance improves reasoning about scientific evidence (for some people). *PLoS One*, 15(4):e0231387.

Amelia Glaese, Nat McAleese, Maja Trębacz, John Aslanides, Vlad Firoiu, Timo Ewalds, Maribeth Rauh, Laura Weidinger, Martin Chadwick, Phoebe Thacker, Lucy Campbell-Gillingham, Jonathan Uesato, Po-Sen Huang, Ramona Comanescu, Fan Yang, Abigail See, Sumanth Dathathri, Rory Greig, Charlie Chen, Doug Fritz, Jaume Sanchez Elias, Richard Green, Soňa Mokrá, Nicholas Fernando, Boxi Wu, Rachel Foley, Susannah Young, Iason Gabriel, William Isaac, John Mellor, Demis Hassabis, Koray Kavukcuoglu, Lisa Anne Hendricks, and Geoffrey Irving. 2022. Improving alignment of dialogue agents via targeted human judgements.

Nianlong Gu and Richard H. R. Hahnloser. 2022. Controllable citation text generation.

Nuno M. Guerreiro, Duarte Alves, Jonas Waldendorf, Barry Haddow, Alexandra Birch, Pierre Colombo, and André F. T. Martins. 2023. Hallucinations in large multilingual translation models.

Michael A. Hedderich, Lukas Lange, Heike Adel, Jannik Strötgen, and Dietrich Klakow. 2021. A survey on recent approaches for natural language processing in low-resource scenarios. In *Proceedings of the 2021 Conference of the North American Chapter of the Association for Computational Linguistics: Human Language Technologies*, pages 2545–2568, Online. Association for Computational Linguistics.

Or Honovich, Roee Aharoni, Jonathan Herzig, Hagai Taitelbaum, Doron Kukliansy, Vered Cohen, Thomas Scialom, Idan Szpektor, Avinatan Hassidim, and Yossi Matias. 2022. True: Re-evaluating factual consistency evaluation.

Katharina Jeblick, Balthasar Schachtner, Jakob Dexl, Andreas Mittermeier, Anna Theresa Stüber, Johanna Topalis, Tobias Weber, Philipp Wesp, Bastian Sabel, Jens Ricke, and Michael Ingrisch. 2022. Chatgpt makes medicine easy to swallow: An exploratory case study on simplified radiology reports.

Zhengbao Jiang, Frank F. Xu, Jun Araki, and Graham Neubig. 2019. How can we know what language models know?

Jaehun Jung, Lianhui Qin, Sean Welleck, Faeze Brahman, Chandra Bhagavatula, Ronan Le Bras, and Yejin Choi. 2022. Maieutic prompting: Logically consistent reasoning with recursive explanations.

Georgi Karadzhov, Preslav Nakov, Lluis Marquez, Alberto Barron-Cedeno, and Ivan Koychev. 2017. Fully automated fact checking using external sources.

F. V. Krasnova, I. S. Smaznevicha, and E. N. Baskakova. 2023. Text sampling strategies for predicting missing bibliographic links.

Nayeon Lee, Belinda Z. Li, Sinong Wang, Wen-tau Yih, Hao Ma, and Madian Khabsa. 2020. Language models as fact checkers?

Kelvin Luu, Rik Koncel-Kedziorski, Kyle Lo, Isabel Cachola, and Noah A Smith. 2020. Citation text generation. *arXiv preprint arXiv:2002.00317.*

Manuel Mager, Ximena Gutierrez-Vasques, Gerardo Sierra, and Ivan Meza-Ruiz. 2018. Challenges of language technologies for the indigenous languages of the Americas. In *Proceedings of the 27th International Conference on Computational Linguistics*, pages 55–69, Santa Fe, New Mexico, USA. Association for Computational Linguistics.

Gary Ernest Davis Marcus. 2019. *Rebooting AI: Building Artificial Intelligence we can Trust.*

Alejandro Martín, Javier Huertas-Tato, Álvaro Huertas-García, Guillermo Villar-Rodríguez, and David Camacho. 2021. Facter-check: Semi-automated fact-checking through semantic similarity and natural language inference.

Joshua Maynez, Shashi Narayan, Bernd Bohnet, and Ryan McDonald. 2020. On faithfulness and factuality in abstractive summarization. In *Proceedings of the 58th Annual Meeting of the Association for Computational Linguistics*, pages 1906–1919, Online. Association for Computational Linguistics.

Jacob Menick, Maja Trebacz, Vladimir Mikulik, John Aslanides, Francis Song, Martin Chadwick, Mia Glaese, Susannah Young, Lucy Campbell-Gillingham, Geoffrey Irving, and Nat McAleese. 2022. Teaching language models to support answers with verified quotes.

Tsvetomila Mihaylova, Preslav Nakov, Lluis Marquez, Alberto Barron-Cedeno, Mitra Mohtarami, Georgi Karadzhov, and James Glass. 2018. Fact checking in community forums.

OpenAI. 2023. Chatgpt: Optimizing language models for dialogue.

Fabio Petroni, Tim Rocktäschel, Patrick Lewis, Anton Bakhtin, Yuxiang Wu, Alexander H. Miller, and Sebastian Riedel. 2019. Language models as knowledge bases?

Alec Radford, Jeffrey Wu, Rewon Child, David Luan, Dario Amodei, and Ilya Sutskever. 2018. Language models are unsupervised multitask learners.

Vikas Raunak, Arul Menezes, and Marcin Junczys-Dowmunt. 2021. The curious case of hallucinations in neural machine translation.

Adam Roberts, Colin Raffel, and Noam Shazeer. 2020. How much knowledge can you pack into the parameters of a language model? In *Proceedings of the 2020 Conference on Empirical Methods in Natural Language Processing (EMNLP)*, pages 5418–5426, Online. Association for Computational Linguistics.

Anna Rohrbach, Lisa Anne Hendricks, Kaylee Burns, Trevor Darrell, and Kate Saenko. 2018. Object hallucination in image captioning. In *Proceedings of the 2018 Conference on Empirical Methods in Natural Language Processing*, pages 4035–4045, Brussels, Belgium. Association for Computational Linguistics.

Abigail See, Peter J. Liu, and Christopher D. Manning. 2017. Get to the point: Summarization with pointer-generator networks. In *Proceedings of the 55th Annual Meeting of the Association for Computational Linguistics (Volume 1: Long Papers)*, pages 1073–1083, Vancouver, Canada. Association for Computational Linguistics.

Kim Cheng Sheang and Horacio Saggion. 2021. Controllable sentence simplification with a unified text-to-text transfer transformer. In *Proceedings of the 14th International Conference on Natural Language Generation*, pages 341–352, Aberdeen, Scotland, UK. Association for Computational Linguistics.

Kurt Shuster, Spencer Poff, Moya Chen, Douwe Kiela, and Jason Weston. 2021. Retrieval augmentation reduces hallucination in conversation.

M. V. Simkin and V. P. Roychowdhury. 2002. Read before you cite!

Mujeen Sung, Jinhyuk Lee, Sean Yi, Minji Jeon, Sungdong Kim, and Jaewoo Kang. 2021. Can language models be biomedical knowledge bases?

Alexey Svyatkovskiy, Shao Kun Deng, Shengyu Fu, and Neel Sundaresan. 2020. Intellicode compose: Code generation using transformer.

Ross Taylor, Marcin Kardas, Guillem Cucurull, Thomas Scialom, Anthony Hartshorn, Elvis Saravia, Andrew Poulton, Viktor Kerkez, and Robert Stojnic. 2022. Galactica: A large language model for science.

Alberto Testoni and Raffaella Bernardi. 2021. "I've seen things you people wouldn't believe": Hallucinating entities in GuessWhat?! In *Proceedings of the 59th Annual Meeting of the Association for Computational Linguistics and the 11th International Joint Conference on Natural Language Processing: Student Research Workshop*, pages 101–111, Online. Association for Computational Linguistics.

Clare Thornley, Anthony Watkinson, David Nicholas, Rachel Volentine, Hamid R. Jamali, Eti Herman, Suzie Allard, Kenneth J. Levine, and Carol Tenopir. 2015. The role of trust and authority in the citation behaviour of researchers. *Inf. Res.*, 20.

Ashish Vaswani, Noam Shazeer, Niki Parmar, Jakob Uszkoreit, Llion Jones, Aidan N. Gomez, Lukasz Kaiser, and Illia Polosukhin. 2017. Attention is all you need.

Pancheng Wang, Shasha Li, Haifang Zhou, Jintao Tang, and Ting Wang. 2020. Toc-rwg: Explore the combination of topic model and citation information for automatic related work generation. *IEEE Access*, 8:13043–13055.

Qiang Wang, Bei Li, Tong Xiao, Jingbo Zhu, Changliang Li, Derek F. Wong, and Lidia S. Chao. 2019. Learning deep transformer models for machine translation. In *Proceedings of the 57th Annual Meeting of the Association for Computational Linguistics*, pages 1810–1822, Florence, Italy. Association for Computational Linguistics.

Janyce Wiebe and Ellen Riloff. 2005. Creating subjective and objective sentence classifiers from unannotated texts. In *Conference on Intelligent Text Processing and Computational Linguistics*.

Janyce M. Wiebe, Rebecca F. Bruce, and Thomas P. O'Hara. 1999. Development and use of a gold-standard data set for subjectivity classifications. In *Proceedings of the 37th Annual Meeting of the Association for Computational Linguistics*, pages 246–253, College Park, Maryland, USA. Association for Computational Linguistics.

Jia-Yan Wu, Alexander Te-Wei Shieh, Shih-Ju Hsu, and Yun-Nung Chen. 2021. Towards generating citation sentences for multiple references with intent control.

Xinyu Xing, Xiaosheng Fan, and Xiaojun Wan. 2020. Automatic generation of citation texts in scholarly papers: A pilot study. In *Proceedings of the 58th Annual Meeting of the Association for Computational Linguistics*, pages 6181–6190, Online. Association for Computational Linguistics.

Peng Xu, Davis Liang, Zhiheng Huang, and Bing Xiang. 2021. Attention-guided generative models for extractive question answering.

Peng Xu, Mostofa Patwary, Mohammad Shoeybi, Raul Puri, Pascale Fung, Anima Anandkumar, and Bryan Catanzaro. 2020. Megatron-cntrl: Controllable story generation with external knowledge using large-scale language models.

Haoyu Zhang, Jingjing Cai, Jianjun Xu, and Ji Wang. 2019. Pretraining-based natural language generation for text summarization. In *Proceedings of the 23rd Conference on Computational Natural Language Learning (CoNLL)*, pages 789–797, Hong Kong, China. Association for Computational Linguistics.

Xueliang Zhao, Wei Wu, Can Xu, Chongyang Tao, Dongyan Zhao, and Rui Yan. 2020a. Knowledge-grounded dialogue generation with pre-trained language models. In *Proceedings of the 2020 Conference on Empirical Methods in Natural Language Processing (EMNLP)*, pages 3377–3390, Online. Association for Computational Linguistics.

Zheng Zhao, Shay B. Cohen, and Bonnie Webber. 2020b. Reducing quantity hallucinations in abstractive summarization. In *Findings of the Association for Computational Linguistics: EMNLP 2020*, pages 2237–2249, Online. Association for Computational Linguistics.

Jianing Zhou and Suma Bhat. 2021. Paraphrase generation: A survey of the state of the art. In *Proceedings of the 2021 Conference on Empirical Methods in Natural Language Processing*, pages 5075–5086, Online and Punta Cana, Dominican Republic. Association for Computational Linguistics.

Incorporating Singletons and Mention-based Features in Coreference Resolution via Multi-task Learning for Better Generalization

Yilun Zhu[♠], **Siyao Peng**[♡], **Sameer Pradhan**[♣◇], and **Amir Zeldes**[♠]

[♠]Department of Linguistics, Georgetown University
[♡]Center for Information and Language Processing (CIS), LMU Munich
[♣]Linguistic Data Consortium, University of Pennsylvania
[◇]cemantix.org

{yz565, Amir.Zeldes}@georgetown.edu, siyaopeng@cis.lmu.de, pradhan@cemantix.org

Abstract

Previous attempts to incorporate a mention detection step into end-to-end neural coreference resolution for English have been hampered by the lack of singleton mention span data as well as other entity information. This paper presents a coreference model that learns singletons as well as features such as entity type and information status via a multi-task learning-based approach. This approach achieves new state-of-the-art scores on the OntoGUM benchmark (+2.7 points) and increases robustness on multiple out-of-domain datasets (+2.3 points on average), likely due to greater generalizability for mention detection and utilization of more data from singletons when compared to only coreferent mention pair matching.[1]

1 Introduction

Coreference is a linguistic phenomenon that occurs when two or more expressions in a text refer to the same entity (e.g. *the Vice President... She*). Conceptually, resolving coreference takes two steps: identifying all mention candidates from a text as opposed to non-referring expressions, and linking identified mentions into clusters. However, in a given document, some mentions are never referred back to: these are called singletons, i.e. mentions that, unlike non-referring expressions, could be referred back to in principle, but are not involved in any coreference relations in context. Singletons are important to coreference resolution since they represent true negatives in cluster linking (Kübler and Zhekova, 2011), but also to how humans understand discourse from a theoretical perspective (Grosz et al., 1995), since they also constitute mentioned entities (i.e. clusters of size 1).

However, due to the lack of singleton annotation in the most frequently used coreference dataset for English, i.e. OntoNotes V5.0 (Weischedel et al., 2011; Pradhan et al., 2013), previous attempts have either ignored singletons (Lee et al., 2017, 2018; Wu et al., 2020; Dobrovolskii, 2021) or incorporated pseudo-singletons into the model (Wu and Gardner, 2021; Toshniwal et al., 2021). The first approach is commonly used in contemporary end-to-end (e2e) systems which train directly on detecting coreferring mentions, but causes problems in that models cannot differentiate singleton spans from non-referring or random/meaningless spans, i.e. penalizing these two types equally. Though e2e has achieved significant progress on OntoNotes, it does not align with linguistic theories on how humans resolve the task. The second approach attempts to amend the model with pseudo-singletons by predicting non-coreferring mentions, but the accuracy gap between gold and generated singletons is unknown and ultimately leads to degradation.

Previous work has also shown that recent coreference models struggle with domain generalization (Moosavi and Strube, 2017; Zhu et al., 2021). To alleviate the problem, Moosavi and Strube (2018) proposed a novel algorithm to incorporate linguistic features and showed improvement in out-of-domain (OOD) data. Subramanian and Roth (2019) applied adversarial training to improve generalization. However, the first approach requires carefully designed linguistic features, and both papers evaluated generalization only on one single-genre dataset, limiting the validity of the results.

To tackle these challenges, we introduce a novel coreference model. Our contributions can be summarized as follows: First, we propose a multi-task learning (MTL) based neural coreference model with constrained mention detection, which jointly learns several mention-based tasks, including singleton detection, entity type recognition, and information status classification. Second, experiments demonstrate that the proposed model achieves new

[1]The code is publicly available at https://github.com/yilunzhu/coref-mtl.

Proceedings of the 13th International Joint Conference on Natural Language Processing and the 3rd Conference of the Asia-Pacific Chapter of the Association for Computational Linguistics (Volume 2: Short Papers), pages 121–130
November 1–4, 2023.

state-of-the-art performance on the OntoGUM test set. Third, we show that our model outperforms strong baselines on two OOD datasets, showing it generalizes more reliably to unseen data than plain e2e. We release all code and provide a system that detects and links all mentions, including singletons, and outputs predicted entity types.

2 Related Work

MTL for coreference Multitask learning (Caruana, 1997; Collobert and Weston, 2008) uses a single model with shared parameters trained to perform multiple tasks, with potential benefits arising from synergies between related objectives. Previous work has investigated the use of MTL for coreference by harnessing related pre-training tasks. Yu and Poesio (2020); Kobayashi et al. (2022) applied an MTL framework to a more specific bridging resolution problem, with standard coreference resolution as the additional task. Luan et al. (2018) used MTL with coreference resolution, entity recognition, and relation extraction for scientific knowledge graph construction. Lu and Ng (2021) used five MTL tasks for event coreference resolution.

Neural coreference resolution The e2e approach jointly learns mention detection and coreferent pair scoring (Lee et al., 2017), and achieved SOTA scores on the OntoNotes test set before several extensions were proposed. Lee et al. (2018); Kantor and Globerson (2019) improved span representations to improve pair matching. Joshi et al. (2020) added better pre-trained language models to gain additional score boosting. Wu et al. (2020) adapted a question-answering framework into the task and improved both span detection and coreference matching scores. Dobrovolskii (2021) also improved performance by initially matching coreference links via words instead of spans.

3 Methods

3.1 Model

Let N be the number of possible spans in a document D. The coreference task can be formulated as assigning an antecedent span y_i for each span i, where the set of possible antecedents for each span i contains a dummy antecedent ϵ and all preceding spans: $\mathcal{Y}(i) = \{\epsilon, 1, ..., i-1\}$.

$$s(i,j) = \begin{cases} 0, & j = \epsilon \\ s_m(i) + s_m(j) + s_c(i,j), & j \neq \epsilon \end{cases}$$

where $s_m(i)$ and $s_m(j)$ are the mention scores that determine how likely the selected text span is a mention candidate. Previous work utilizes a scoring function to measure how likely the span is a coreference markable. However, singletons in the training data are ignored and thus weaken the model's generalization capability. Therefore, our proposed model uses two scoring functions to represent the distributions of markables and mentions better. The mention scoring function uses two feed-forward networks fed by the representation of each span: one part is a markable score that calculates the score of the span being a coreferent markable in the document; the other is the mention candidate score that determines how likely a span is a mention candidate. The formula is represented as follows:

$$s_m(i) = \beta_1 \cdot s_{markable(i)} + \beta_2 \cdot s_{mention(i)}$$

$$s_{markable(i)} = w_{markble} \cdot \text{FFNN}(g_i)$$

$$s_{mention(i)} = w_{mention} \cdot \text{FFNN}(g_i)$$

where $\cdot$ denotes a dot product, FFNN denotes a feed-forward neural network, β_1 and β_2 denote model parameters that adjust the weights of markable scores and mention candidate scores, and g_i denotes the represented embeddings of the span (we use the same span representing method as in Lee et al. (2017)). The two scoring functions are computed via two standard feed-forward neural networks. The purpose of this design is to prevent random text spans being fed to the pair-matching step. Following the e2e approach (Lee et al., 2017, 2018; Joshi et al., 2020), we concatenate the boundary representations, the soft head vector and an additional feature vector ϕ containing speaker information, and feed the resulting vector into separate feed-forward neural networks to calculate markable scores and mention candidate scores.

In addition to the main pair-matching task, our model adds three mention-based tasks: a (possibly singleton) mention span detection task, entity type recognition, and information status classification (see below). For each task, the span vector is fed into a separate feed-forward network for classification. Each task is assigned a weight to calculate the total loss score:

$$\mathcal{L}_{total} = \sum_{c=1}^{C} \mathcal{W}_c \cdot \mathcal{L}_c$$

where $\mathcal{W}_c$ is the weight for task c. See Appendix A for an overview of the model architecture.

	Markble Detection			MUC			B^3			$CEAF_{\phi4}$			Avg. F1
	P	R	F1	P	R	F1	P	R	F1	P	R	F1	
In-domain - ONTOGUM													
Joshi et al. (2019)	**91.0**	71.9	80.3	**83.3**	69.7	75.9	70.8	59.2	64.5	70.5	45.8	55.5	65.5
MTL (sg)	90.2	75.0	**81.9**	82.7	72.8	77.4	70.4	63.1	66.5	71.5	49.2	58.3	67.6
MTL (sg+ent)	90.0	**75.1**	**81.9**	82.8	**72.9**	**77.6**	**71.2**	**63.6**	**67.2**	**71.9**	**50.2**	**59.1**	**68.2**
MTL (sg+ent+infs.)	90.0	75.0	81.8	82.1	72.3	76.9	70.0	62.3	65.9	70.0	48.6	57.3	66.9
Out-of-domain - ONTONOTES													
Joshi et al. (2019)	**83.9**	76.9	80.3	**77.6**	72.7	75.1	66.9	60.6	63.6	**64.3**	54.5	59.0	65.9
MTL (sg+ent)	82.2	**80.2**	**81.2**	77.0	**76.1**	**76.5**	**67.1**	**64.0**	**65.5**	63.6	**59.5**	**61.5**	**67.8**
Out-of-domain - WIKICOREF													
Joshi et al. (2019)	79.9	58.8	67.7	73.7	60.1	66.2	66.4	43.4	52.4	56.6	31.6	40.5	53.0
MTL (sg+ent)	**80.4**	**60.0**	**68.7**	**74.5**	**61.8**	**67.5**	**67.8**	**45.3**	**54.4**	**59.0**	**33.0**	**42.4**	**55.6**

Table 1: Comparison between Joshi et al. (2019) and our model on test sets of both in-domain (OntoGUM 8.0) and out-of-domain datasets (OntoNotes and WikiCoref). The overall F1 score is the average of F1s from three evaluation metrics MUC, B^3, and $CEAF_{\phi4}$. All models are trained on OntoGUM.

3.2 Task Selection

Since OntoNotes does not contain singletons, we choose a corpus for which singleton information is available but follows the same annotation scheme as OntoNotes. The OntoGUM corpus (Zhu et al., 2021) is an adapted version of the GUM corpus (Zeldes, 2017), a multi-layer corpus with a range of annotations at the word level (part-of-speech, morphology), phrase level (phrase trees, entity recognition, and linking), dependency level (Universal Dependencies syntax) and document-level (discourse parses and coreference). Although OntoGUM uses the same singleton-free coreference scheme as OntoNotes, information about singletons can be recovered from the original GUM corpus. We therefore select three annotations from GUM and investigate whether they are helpful for coreference resolution on OntoGUM: nested mention span detection, entity type, and information status.

Mention detection As outlined in Section 1, we integrate gold nested mentions, including singletons (sg), into our model to improve mention detection and coreference. The task aims to recognize meaningful referential text spans and makes more information available to the model than the plain e2e approach that only trains on coreferring mentions (~39% of mentions in GUM are singletons).

Entity type GUM assigns one of ten entity types (ent) to each mention – person, organization, etc. (see Figure 2 in Appendix D). Since a cluster usually has one entity type, this feature instructs the model regarding which mentions belong to the same semantic class.

Information status Information status (infs.) indicates how an entity was introduced into discourse, e.g. new, previously mentioned or inferrable from other mentions (Prince, 1981). Each mention is assigned one of six labels (see Appendix C). This task is expected to inform the model about the likelihood and how an entity was previously introduced.

4 Experiments

4.1 Datasets

OntoGUM (Zhu et al., 2021) is a coreference dataset following the same annotation scheme as OntoNotes. This paper adds other layers to the coreference annotation, such as mention spans (including singletons), aligned entity types, and information status, automatically extracted from the GUM corpus. We train the model with GUM v8.0, which includes 193 documents across 12 written and spoken genres with ~180K tokens.

We also evaluate our model on two OOD datasets of the same annotation scheme: OntoNotes and WikiCoref. OntoNotes includes richly annotated documents with layers including syntax, propositions, named entities, word senses, and coreference, but no singleton mentions or aligned (non-named) entity types (Pradhan et al., 2013). Its test set includes 348 documents with 170K tokens. WikiCoref (Ghaddar and Langlais, 2016) is a manually annotated corpus from English Wikipedia, containing 30 documents with ~60K tokens.

4.2 Baseline

Combining the e2e approach with a contextualized language model (LM) and span masking is one of the best models on OntoNotes. Following Joshi et al. (2020), we use large SpanBERT embeddings as the LM and the improved coarse-to-fine (Lee et al., 2018) SOTA model as our baseline model (see Appendix B for implementation details).

4.3 Task Weights

The task weights are a list of parameters that controls the relative importance of various tasks in our model, which are optimized via hyperparameter search on the OntoGUM dev set to achieve the best performance. In the optimal setting with 2 auxiliary tasks, the loss weight for the major task coreference relation identification is set to 0.4 and the weights for singleton detection and entity type recognition are set to 0.2 each. The weights are 0.15 for each auxiliary task when information status is added to training.

4.4 Results

In-domain Evaluation We train the model on OntoGUM and evaluate it in-domain. As shown in the first part of Table 1, our model with the best setting improves average F1 by 2.7 points and achieves new SOTA performance on the OntoGUM benchmark, indicating the benefit of the MTL tasks. We also note that recall scores of both mention detection and coreference matching show a significant increase by 3.2 and 4.0 points, respectively, which suggests that the MTL approach helps the model capture more non-trivial markable spans and coreference relations than the baseline model, with little or no precision cost. In addition, though information status contributes to the result as a sole auxiliary task (see Table 2), it is harmful when training with other tasks.

Out-of-domain Evaluation To test the robustness of our model, we evaluate on two OOD datasets sharing the same annotation scheme with OntoGUM. The second part of Table 1 shows that our best in-domain model with mention detection and entity type as auxiliary tasks outperforms the baseline model on both datasets by 2.3 points on average. For OntoNotes, though our model has slightly lower precision, the recall results in substantially better performance; for WikiCoref, our model performs better on both precision and recall. These results indicate that the knowledge gained from the multiple mention-based tasks can be transferred to unseen text types, and is likely a combination of more training data (since singletons include instances not considered by the baseline training) and the learning of features distinguishing non-mentions from mentions and ones corresponding to semantic types.

4.5 Ablation Study

To show the importance of each task in our model, we ablate each task in the architecture and report the average F1 on the OntoGUM development set. In Table 2, singleton scores and the mention detection task contribute 1.3 points to the final result, indicating that this feature is the most important one.

	Avg. F1	Δ
Base model	67.0	
w/ singleton detection (=sg)	68.3	+1.3
w/ sg + entity type (=et)	68.7	+0.4
w/ sg + et + information status	67.8	-0.9

Table 2: Comparison of various tasks included in the coreference model on the OntoGUM development data.

With the addition of the nested entity type recognition task, the model brings a smaller increase (0.4 points) to the final result. There could be several reasons for this: one is that the LM has already learned entity types latently, so giving this as an explicit feature is redundant; the other reason is that the baseline model rarely groups mentions with different entity types into clusters so that entity type features can only correct few errors.

When only integrating information status into the model, the result (avg. F1 67.6) outperforms the baseline model, showing the effectiveness of this type of information. However, when all three tasks are incorporated, the overall score (67.8) is lower than excluding information status classification (68.7), which shows that information status is redundant when other mention-based features are specified.

5 Error analysis

We conduct quantitative and qualitative error analyses to illustrate how our model differs from the baseline. Firstly we conduct a quantitative analysis following Lu and Ng (2020), who classify resolution errors into 13 classes. Following their approach, we merge coreference errors into 6 groups. Table 3 displays the distribution of errors observed in the OntoGUM development set. These errors are present in the baseline e2e model but correctly resolved by our proposed MTL model (e2e errors) or vice versa (mtl errors).

Error type	mtl errors		e2e errors	
Pronouns				
- 1st & 2nd person pronouns	6	3.6%	12	5.0%
- 3rd person pronouns	20	12.1%	68	28.3%
Definiteness				
- Definite nouns	63	38.2%	98	40.8%
- Indefinite nouns	13	7.9%	13	5.4%
Proper nouns	23	14.0%	19	7.9%
Others	40	24.2%	30	12.5%
Total	165	100.0%	240	100.0%

Table 3: Number and percentage of errors by class that are produced by e2e but avoided by the MTL model (e2e errors) and produced by the MTL model but resolved by the e2e model (mtl errors).

The majority of mtl errors involve definite nominals, revealing the challenge of resolving cherry-picked cases that must be memorized within a multi-genre context. However, our proposed model demonstrates its ability to correctly identify relations when multiple clusters are involved. Furthermore, nearly 16% of resolved errors are associated with pronouns, indicating that our model is more capable of accurately identifying coreference relationships within the context of third-person pronouns and demonstrates a slight improvement in handling pronouns in dialogue, particularly first and second-person pronouns.

We also observe that our proposed model reduces errors across nearly all types compared to the baseline model, particularly in the case of third-person pronouns. This result suggests that integrating entity type recognition and mention detection in the MTL framework enables accurate recognition of noun-pronoun relations, particularly for pronouns that do not provide explicit entity type information, e.g., *it*. Additionally, the MTL model demonstrates improved error avoidance with definite nouns. These findings highlight the enhanced performance of our proposed model in identifying coreference relations within the local context.

We also identify several errors that illustrate the impact of singleton detection and entity type recognition. Examples in Table 4 demonstrate how including singletons and mention-based features improves the retrieval of accurate mention spans and enhances coreference relationships. The first three examples highlight how entity-type recognition contributes to resolution by avoiding type mismatches. In example (1), the pressure from entity type recognition likely aids in identifying *Harrow* as a school (an ORGANIZATION). In example (2), the MTL model recognizes *it* as an EVENT, thereby correctly creating two distinct groups and

Entity type errors	
1	he did represent [the school]$_1$ during the very first Eton v [Harrow]$_1$ cricket match
2	Who cut [the grass]$_1$? Marlena did [it]$_2$. Marlena did [it]$_2$ a long time ago, but [it]$_1$ hasn't been watered. [It]$_1$'s dying.
3	I made [noises]$_1$ with my heels but [they]$_1$ were too loud so I stopped.
Singleton errors	
4	The main reason attributed for the pollution of Athens is because the city is enclosed by mountains in [a basin which does not let the smog leave]$_1$ ... have greatly contributed to better atmospheric conditions in [the basin]$_1$.
5	This means that if [the govt]$_1$ decided to print 1 quadrillion dollars in the span of a week ... we 're loaning [the US govt]$_1$ the very money it prints

Table 4: A qualitative analysis of OntoGUM dev errors that appear in the e2e model but are avoided by our MTL model. MTL predictions (gold) are represented by [brackets]$_x$. E2e predictions (errors) are highlighted in colored text and each color in an example denotes a coreference cluster.

avoiding coreference with *the grass* (a PLANT entity). Similarly, example (3) presents pressure to recognize that *they* is not an inanimate OBJECT, so it correctly prefers *noises* as the antecedent. Examples (4) and (5) illustrate how mention detection identifies missing mentions in the baseline model or improves boundary recognition. These representative examples provide valuable insights into the significance of incorporating singletons and auxiliary mention-based tasks into a coreference model.

6 Conclusion

This paper presents a neural coreference model that connects singletons and other mention-based features to coreference relation matching via an MTL architecture, which (1) outperforms a strong baseline and achieves new SOTA results on OntoGUM and (2) beats the baseline model on two unseen datasets. The results show the effect of singletons and mention features and indicate improvements in model robustness when transferring to unseen data rather than overfitting distributions in the training data. In addition, our resulting system can output all mentions (incl. singletons) with entity types out-of-the-box, which benefits a series of downstream applications such as Entity Linking, Dialogue Systems, Machine Translation, Summarization, and more, since our single model already outputs typed spans for all entities mentioned in a text (see Figure 2b in Appendix D for an illustration).

Limitations

In this work, we have experimented with training our model on OntoGUM. Due to the lack of singletons and other mention-based annotations, we do not train the model on the most frequently used and one of the largest coreference datasets. Thus the proposed model has not been tested on a large-scale dataset and compared with other coreference models on OntoNotes.

We evaluate the model on two English OOD datasets to investigate the model generalization. Several coreference datasets in other languages share the same annotation scheme as OntoGUM, such as Arabic (Pradhan et al., 2013), and Chinese (Pradhan et al., 2013). The proposed model needs to be evaluated on datasets in other languages and demonstrate the model generalization across languages. However, this would require singleton annotated data in those languages as well. With recent releases such as CorefUD (Nedoluzhko et al., 2022) promoting standardization of multilingual coreference annotations and singleton annotations, we are hopeful that such experiments will be possible in the near future.

References

Rich Caruana. 1997. Multitask learning. *Mach. Learn.*, 28(1):41–75.

Ronan Collobert and Jason Weston. 2008. A unified architecture for natural language processing: Deep neural networks with multitask learning. In *Proceedings of the 25th International Conference on Machine Learning*, ICML '08, pages 160—-167, New York, NY, USA. Association for Computing Machinery.

Vladimir Dobrovolskii. 2021. Word-level coreference resolution. In *Proceedings of the 2021 Conference on Empirical Methods in Natural Language Processing*, pages 7670–7675, Online and Punta Cana, Dominican Republic. Association for Computational Linguistics.

Abbas Ghaddar and Phillippe Langlais. 2016. Wiki-Coref: An English coreference-annotated corpus of Wikipedia articles. In *Proceedings of the Tenth International Conference on Language Resources and Evaluation (LREC'16)*, pages 136–142, Portorož, Slovenia. European Language Resources Association (ELRA).

Barbara J. Grosz, Aravind K. Joshi, and Scott Weinstein. 1995. Centering: A framework for modeling the local coherence of discourse. *Computational Linguistics*, 21(2):203–225.

Yufang Hou. 2020. Bridging anaphora resolution as question answering. In *Proceedings of the 58th Annual Meeting of the Association for Computational Linguistics*, pages 1428–1438, Online. Association for Computational Linguistics.

Mandar Joshi, Danqi Chen, Yinhan Liu, Daniel S. Weld, Luke Zettlemoyer, and Omer Levy. 2019. Span-BERT: Improving pre-training by representing and predicting spans. *CoRR*, abs/1907.10529.

Mandar Joshi, Danqi Chen, Yinhan Liu, Daniel S. Weld, Luke Zettlemoyer, and Omer Levy. 2020. Span-BERT: Improving pre-training by representing and predicting spans. *Transactions of the Association for Computational Linguistics*, 8:64–77.

Ben Kantor and Amir Globerson. 2019. Coreference resolution with entity equalization. In *Proceedings of the 57th Annual Meeting of the Association for Computational Linguistics*, pages 673–677, Florence, Italy. Association for Computational Linguistics.

Hideo Kobayashi, Yufang Hou, and Vincent Ng. 2022. Constrained multi-task learning for bridging resolution. In *Proceedings of the 60th Annual Meeting of the Association for Computational Linguistics (Volume 1: Long Papers)*, pages 759–770, Dublin, Ireland. Association for Computational Linguistics.

Sandra Kübler and Desislava Zhekova. 2011. Singletons and coreference resolution evaluation. In *Proceedings of the International Conference Recent Advances in Natural Language Processing 2011*, pages 261–267, Hissar, Bulgaria. Association for Computational Linguistics.

Kenton Lee, Luheng He, Mike Lewis, and Luke Zettlemoyer. 2017. End-to-end neural coreference resolution. In *Proceedings of the 2017 Conference on Empirical Methods in Natural Language Processing*, pages 188–197, Copenhagen, Denmark. Association for Computational Linguistics.

Kenton Lee, Luheng He, and Luke Zettlemoyer. 2018. Higher-order coreference resolution with coarse-to-fine inference. In *Proceedings of the 2018 Conference of the North American Chapter of the Association for Computational Linguistics: Human Language Technologies, Volume 2 (Short Papers)*, pages 687–692, New Orleans, Louisiana. Association for Computational Linguistics.

Jing Lu and Vincent Ng. 2020. Conundrums in entity coreference resolution: Making sense of the state of the art. In *Proceedings of the 2020 Conference on Empirical Methods in Natural Language Processing (EMNLP)*, pages 6620–6631, Online. Association for Computational Linguistics.

Jing Lu and Vincent Ng. 2021. Constrained multi-task learning for event coreference resolution. In *Proceedings of the 2021 Conference of the North American Chapter of the Association for Computational Linguistics: Human Language Technologies*, pages

4504–4514, Online. Association for Computational Linguistics.

Yi Luan, Luheng He, Mari Ostendorf, and Hannaneh Hajishirzi. 2018. Multi-task identification of entities, relations, and coreference for scientific knowledge graph construction. In *Proceedings of the 2018 Conference on Empirical Methods in Natural Language Processing*, pages 3219–3232, Brussels, Belgium. Association for Computational Linguistics.

Nafise Sadat Moosavi and Michael Strube. 2017. Lexical features in coreference resolution: To be used with caution. In *Proceedings of the 55th Annual Meeting of the Association for Computational Linguistics (Volume 2: Short Papers)*, pages 14–19, Vancouver, Canada. Association for Computational Linguistics.

Nafise Sadat Moosavi and Michael Strube. 2018. Using linguistic features to improve the generalization capability of neural coreference resolvers. In *Proceedings of the 2018 Conference on Empirical Methods in Natural Language Processing*, pages 193–203, Brussels, Belgium. Association for Computational Linguistics.

Anna Nedoluzhko, Michal Novák, Martin Popel, Zdeněk Žabokrtský, Amir Zeldes, and Daniel Zeman. 2022. CorefUD 1.0: Coreference meets Universal Dependencies. In *Proceedings of the Thirteenth Language Resources and Evaluation Conference*, pages 4859–4872, Marseille, France. European Language Resources Association.

Sameer Pradhan, Alessandro Moschitti, Nianwen Xue, Hwee Tou Ng, Anders Björkelund, Olga Uryupina, Yuchen Zhang, and Zhi Zhong. 2013. Towards robust linguistic analysis using OntoNotes. In *Proceedings of the Seventeenth Conference on Computational Natural Language Learning*, pages 143–152, Sofia, Bulgaria. Association for Computational Linguistics.

Ellen F. Prince. 1981. Toward a taxonomy of given-new information. In P. Cole, editor, *Syntax and semantics: Vol. 14. Radical Pragmatics*, pages 223–255. Academic Press, New York.

Ina Roesiger, Arndt Riester, and Jonas Kuhn. 2018. Bridging resolution: Task definition, corpus resources and rule-based experiments. In *Proceedings of the 27th International Conference on Computational Linguistics*, pages 3516–3528, Santa Fe, New Mexico, USA. Association for Computational Linguistics.

Sanjay Subramanian and Dan Roth. 2019. Improving generalization in coreference resolution via adversarial training. In *Proceedings of the Eighth Joint Conference on Lexical and Computational Semantics (*SEM 2019)*, pages 192–197, Minneapolis, Minnesota. Association for Computational Linguistics.

Shubham Toshniwal, Patrick Xia, Sam Wiseman, Karen Livescu, and Kevin Gimpel. 2021. On generalization in coreference resolution. In *Proceedings of the Fourth Workshop on Computational Models of Reference, Anaphora and Coreference*, pages 111–120, Punta Cana, Dominican Republic. Association for Computational Linguistics.

Ralph Weischedel, Eduard Hovy, Mitchell Marcus, Martha Palmer, Robert Belvin, Sameer Pradhan, Lance Ramshaw, and Nianwen Xue. 2011. OntoNotes: A large training corpus for enhanced processing. In Joseph Olive, Caitlin Christianson, and John McCary, editors, *Handbook of Natural Language Processing and Machine Translation: DARPA Global Autonomous Language Exploitation*. Springer.

Wei Wu, Fei Wang, Arianna Yuan, Fei Wu, and Jiwei Li. 2020. CorefQA: Coreference resolution as query-based span prediction. In *Proceedings of the 58th Annual Meeting of the Association for Computational Linguistics*, pages 6953–6963, Online. Association for Computational Linguistics.

Zhaofeng Wu and Matt Gardner. 2021. Understanding mention detector-linker interaction in neural coreference resolution. In *Proceedings of the Fourth Workshop on Computational Models of Reference, Anaphora and Coreference*, pages 150–157, Punta Cana, Dominican Republic. Association for Computational Linguistics.

Juntao Yu and Massimo Poesio. 2020. Multitask learning-based neural bridging reference resolution. In *Proceedings of the 28th International Conference on Computational Linguistics*, pages 3534–3546, Barcelona, Spain (Online). International Committee on Computational Linguistics.

Amir Zeldes. 2017. The GUM corpus: Creating multilayer resources in the classroom. *Language Resources and Evaluation*, 51(3):581–612.

Yilun Zhu, Sameer Pradhan, and Amir Zeldes. 2021. OntoGUM: Evaluating contextualized SOTA coreference resolution on 12 more genres. In *Proceedings of the 59th Annual Meeting of the Association for Computational Linguistics and the 11th International Joint Conference on Natural Language Processing (Volume 2: Short Papers)*, pages 461–467, Online. Association for Computational Linguistics.

A Model architecture oveview

Figure 1 shows the architecture of the model proposed in this paper.

B Implementation details

We use Pytorch and the pre-trained SpanBERT-large (Joshi et al., 2020) model from HuggingFace[2] for token representations. Experiments run on Nvidia RTX A6000 GPUs with 64GB RAM. Following previous work (Lee et al., 2018; Joshi

[2] https://huggingface.co/

et al., 2020), we use a batch size of 1 document for training and evaluation. The coreference task uses the same loss strategy as the baseline model (Joshi et al., 2020) and each auxiliary task uses Cross Entropy loss. We use AdamW to optimize coreference loss and Adam to optimize auxiliary loss. We train 14,500 steps with `task_learning_rate` of 0.0003 for baselines and our models.

C Information Status

There are six types of information status in the data:

- *new* (first, unmediated mention of an entity)
- *given:active* (subsequent mention after a recent previous mention)
- *given:inactive* (subsequent mention of a non-recently mentioned entity)
- *accessible:inferrable* (new entity whose existence could be inferred from other mentions, e.g. via bridging anaphora (Roesiger et al., 2018; Hou, 2020), as in *a house ... [the door]*)
- *accessible:commonground* (entities accessible to speakers in the situation, e.g. *pass [the salt]!*)
- *accessible:aggregate* (new entities referring back to multiple entities, i.e. split antecedents as in *Kim ... Yun ... [they]*).

When information status is included in the auxiliary tasks, our model is trained to predict the label for each mention.

D Sample data

Figure 2b shows the extent of annotations available to the MTL model for training, compared to the data restricted to coreferring pairs in Figure 2a, as used by the baseline e2e approach. Since OntoNotes-style data, such as OntoGUM, does not contain singletons, mention types or information status, only coreferring mentions and their spans can be used for learning by the baseline model. The information in the bottom panel, by contrast, is much richer and covers all referring expressions with information status and one of ten entity types: ABSTRACT, ANIMAL, EVENT, OBJECT, ORGANIZATION, PERSON, PLACE, PLANT, SUBSTANCE and TIME.

While each information type (coreference, mention boundaries, mention types, and information status) is not totally predictable from others, they overlap to some extent and exhibit different information densities: mention boundaries are available for many spans and are densely attested. Mention types are available for each mention, but some types are rare, e.g. abstract mentions marked by  in Figure 2 are the most common. Information status is mostly predictable from coreference, e.g. singletons and chain-initial mentions are *new*, and chain-medial or final mentions are given (*given:active* if recently mentioned, otherwise *given:inactive*). Accessible mentions are less trivial and comparatively rare (about 7.1% of mentions in GUM), indicating whether they are accessible in the common ground, their identity is inferrable from some other mention (*accessible:inferrable*), or by aggregating information from multiple mentions (*accessible:aggregate*). This information could help systems to learn whether a span is likely to have an antecedent.

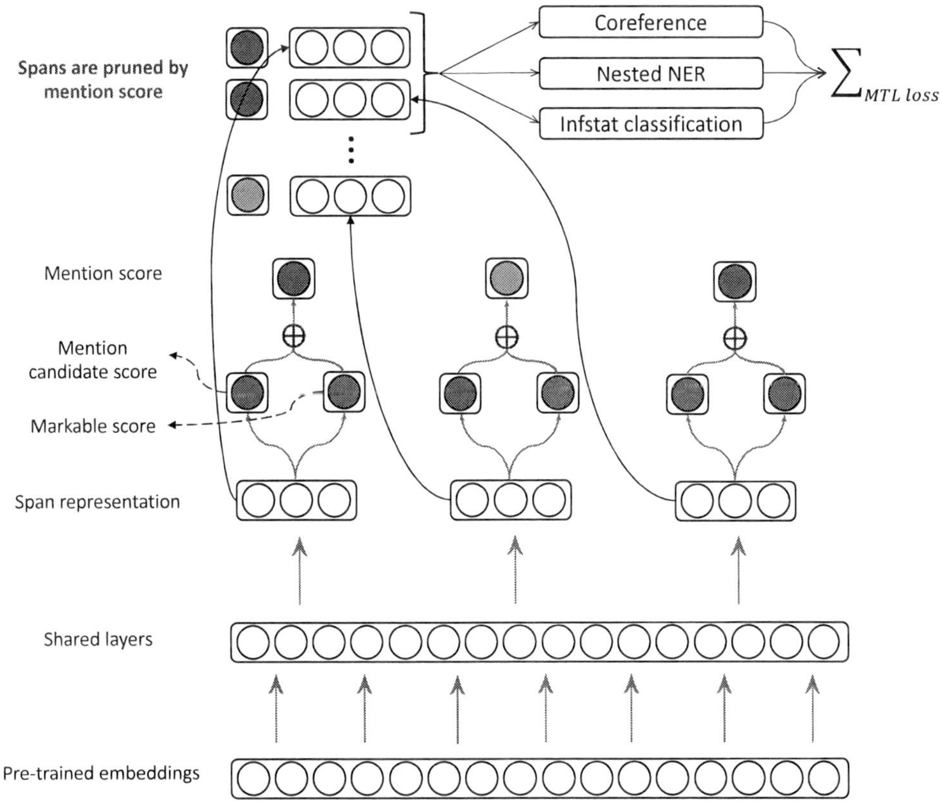

Figure 1: An overview of the proposed MTL model architecture. Only selected spans with high mention scores (in blue) are considered in the three auxiliary tasks.

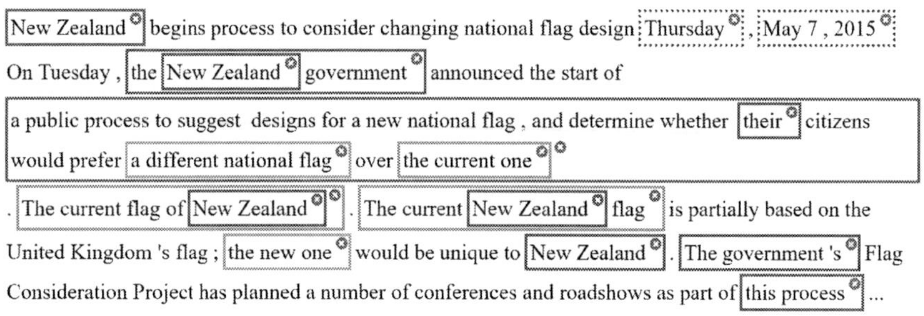

(a) Information available to the baseline e2e model.

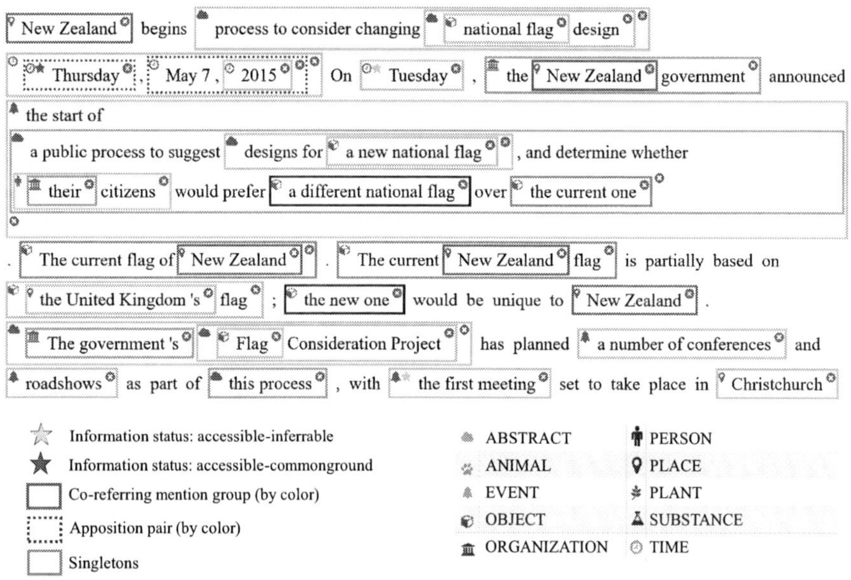

(b) Information available to the MTL model for the same document.

Figure 2: Training data from an OntoGUM article in the news genre.

All Labels Together: Low-shot Intent Detection with an Efficient Label Semantic Encoding Paradigm

Jiangshu Du
University of Illinois at Chicago
jdu25@uic.edu

Congying Xia
Salesforce Research
c.xia@salesforce.com

Wenpeng Yin
Penn State University
wenpeng@psu.edu

Tingting Liang
Hangzhou Dianzi University
liangtt@hdu.edu.cn

Philip Yu
University of Illinois at Chicago
psyu@uic.edu

Abstract

In intent detection tasks, leveraging meaningful semantic information from intent labels can be particularly beneficial for few-shot scenarios. However, existing few-shot intent detection methods either ignore the intent labels, (e.g. treating intents as indices) or do not fully utilize this information (e.g. only using part of the intent labels). In this work, we present an end-to-end `One-to-All` system that enables the comparison of an input utterance with all label candidates. The system can then fully utilize label semantics in this way. Experiments on three few-shot intent detection tasks demonstrate that `One-to-All` is especially effective when the training resource is extremely scarce, achieving state-of-the-art performance in 1-, 3- and 5-shot settings. Moreover, we present a novel pretraining strategy for our model that utilizes indirect supervision from paraphrasing, enabling zero-shot cross-domain generalization on intent detection tasks. Our code is at `https://github.com/jiangshdd/AllLablesTogether`.

1 Introduction

Few-shot intent detection aims to identify the intents of user utterances with only a few labeled examples. Recent works can be mainly summarized into three categories: 1) **Standard classifier-based approaches** (He et al., 2022a,b; Zhang et al., 2022, 2021), which leverage pretrained language models (PLMs) equipped with a standard classifier layer (e.g., MLP), treating intent labels as indices; 2) **Example-based approaches** (Zhang et al., 2020; Mehri and Eric, 2021; Vulić et al., 2021), which learn to compare the similarities between different examples and classify an input utterance based on the closest neighbor in the training data; 3) **Intent semantic aware approaches** (Qu et al., 2021; Xia et al., 2021; Du et al., 2022), which explicitly incorporate intent label words during training. However, both classifier-based and example-based methods disregard label semantic information, which is an important source of supervision in few-shot scenarios. Exiting intent semantic aware approaches also suffer from different drawbacks, such as relying on large-scale pretraining datasets and only partially using intent labels. More details on related work are discussed in Appendix A.

To solve these issues, we propose an end-to-end intent semantic aware model, `One-to-All`. It concatenates each utterance with the entire intent label set as the input and then encodes them simultaneously. In this way, the semantic information of all intents is fully utilized and integrated with utterances. The encoded embeddings of labels and utterances are subsequently used for contrastive learning. We define a new contrastive learning paradigm by comparing the representations of utterances and intents directly. This approach ensures utterances are moved closer to their gold intents while distancing them from any incorrect ones. Furthermore, we introduce a novel pretraining strategy for `One-to-All` that leverages indirect supervision from paraphrase identification datasets. Through this strategy, the model develops the ability to understand semantic similarities and distinctions among sentences, generalizing its comprehension to unseen intents in zero-shot intent detection tasks.

To demonstrate the effectiveness of our proposed model, we conduct experiments on three fine-grained intent detection tasks: BANKING77 (Casanueva et al., 2020), HWU64 (Liu et al., 2019a) and CLINC150 (Larson et al., 2019), under low-shot settings (0-, 1-, 3- and 5-shot). The results show that `One-to-All` is especially effective in extreme few-shot scenarios, with an average improvement of 4.62% in 1-shot and 2.60% in 3-shot settings over the state-of-the-art (SOTA) without any pretraining. Our model also achieves SOTA in 5-shot scenarios with pretraining on out-of-domain (OOD) data. Furthermore, `One-to-All` shows great cross-domain generalization capabilities in the zero-shot setting when further pretrained on

Proceedings of the 13th International Joint Conference on Natural Language Processing and the 3rd Conference of the Asia-Pacific Chapter of the Association for Computational Linguistics (Volume 2: Short Papers), pages 131–138
November 1–4, 2023.

paraphrasing identification datasets.

Our contributions can be summarized as follows. First, we proposed an end-to-end One-to-All system that enables the comparison of an input utterance with all label candidates via a newly defined contrastive learning paradigm. To our knowledge, this is the first work that can encode the entire label space while modeling the intent identification problem. Second, we go beyond few-shot intent detection and further achieve zero-shot cross-domain generalization with a novel pretraining stage of our model: pretraining on paraphrase identification datasets. This is the first work that effectively uses indirect supervision from paraphrasing to handle zero-shot intent identification tasks.

2 Methods

2.1 One-to-All Input Sequence Construction

Incorporating additional labels as contexts alongside utterances within an input sequence can help the model make a better decision (Du et al., 2022). One-to-All concatenates each utterance with the complete intent label set as the input and encodes them together. However, the limitation of the maximum input sequence length makes it impractical to include all labels in a single sequence, especially when the label space is large. Therefore, given an intent detection task with n intents, we take every k intents as a group and then all the intents will be divided into $m = \lceil n/k \rceil$ groups. To keep each group with a consistent number of elements, we introduce a special placeholder token *<plh>*. For the group whose number of intents (s) is less than k, we fill it with $(k - s)$ *<plh>*s to maintain consistency. Each utterance U is then duplicated m times and appended with the m groups of intents, respectively, yielding m input sequences, as shown in Figure 1(A). In this way, the model works on the entire intent space and incorporates multiple intents into a single sequence. In practice, we choose k by minimizing $n \bmod k$ to avoid introducing too many *<plh>*s. Each input sequence is then shuffled k times during training to perform data augmentation, which is beneficial for few-shot tasks.

2.2 Intent-Aware Contrastive Learning

To better exploit intent semantic information, we apply contrastive learning (CL) between utterances and intents. Previous works perform CL between input texts and their augmented views (Gao et al., 2021; Yan et al., 2021; Chen et al., 2020; Mou et al., 2022), or instances under different classes

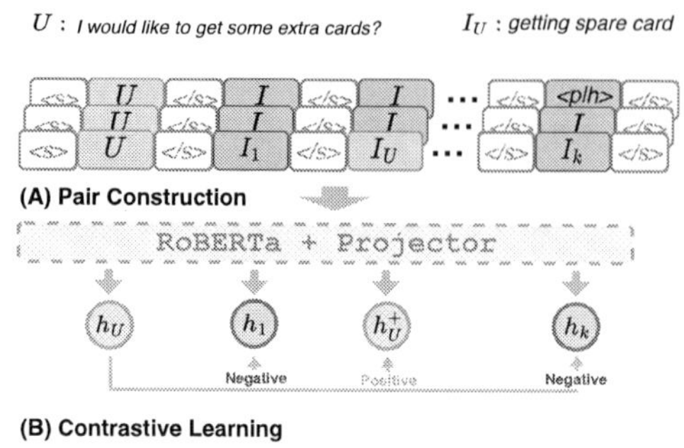

Figure 1: Overview of One-to-All. (A) shows the input sequence construction strategy. I_U indicates the gold intent of U. (B) shows positive and negative instances in contrastive learning.

(Zhang et al., 2021; Gunel et al., 2021; Lin et al., 2022), while we directly perform CL between input texts (utterances) and classes (intents) since intents usually contain useful semantic meanings. Therefore, the representations of intents can be regarded as different views of utterances or explicit cluster centroids. As shown in Figure 1 (B), we feed the input sequence constructed from Section 2.1 into RoBERTa and obtain a list of token-level representations. Then for the utterance U and all the intents $I_j, j \in \{1, ..., k\}$ in the input sequence, we average the representations of their corresponding tokens as their representations z_U and $z_j, j \in \{1, ..., k\}$. Finally, we use a shared MLP projector to project z_U and z_j into the same semantic space, yielding the final utterance representation h_U and intent representation h_j. We use h_U^+ to denote the representation of the gold intent I_U for U. Let $sim(u, v)$ denote the cosine similarity between u and v. The contrastive learning loss is then defined as follows:

$$l = -\frac{1}{N_b} \sum_{i=1}^{N_b} log \frac{e^{sim(\mathbf{h}_U^i, \mathbf{h}_U^{i+})/\tau}}{\sum_{j=1}^{k} e^{sim(\mathbf{h}_U^i, \mathbf{h}_j^i)/\tau}} \quad (1)$$

, where N_b is the batch size. h_*^i means the representation in the i-th input in a batch. τ is the temperature parameter. Through the contrastive loss, One-to-All pushes utterances closer to their gold intents and meanwhile drives them away from all the incorrect intents. For the input sequences that do not include gold intents, we simply set the numerator of Equation 1 to 1 so the model only pushes the utterance away from other intents.

By shuffling the order of concatenated intents within the sequence, a large number of training instances and distinct contrastive pairs can be generated. This is particularly beneficial for both few-shot and contrastive learning. Furthermore, a more robust model is yielded since we enforce the model to recognize the correct intent regardless of its location in the concatenated input sequence.

2.3 Zero-shot Intent Detection via Paraphrase Identification Pretraining

Paraphrase identification (Socher et al., 2011) is a task that aims at identifying if two sentences have the same meaning. Pretraining on the paraphrase detection identification dataset encourages models to capture the essence of utterances rather than relying solely on surface-level patterns. This can improve the ability of `One-to-All` to distinguish between similar intents that might have subtle differences in wording or phrasing. Therefore, we propose a novel pretraining stage to effectively use indirect supervision from paraphrasing for zero-shot intent detection task. Specifically, for each sentence, we regard its paraphrase as its gold label and select other t most similar sentences with the help of Sentence-BERT (Reimers and Gurevych, 2019) as the negative labels. For the target task with n intents, we set $t = n - 1$ so each sentence has totally n labels to compare as well. We set k, which is the number of intents in each group, the same as the target task to keep the pretraining and downstream tasks consistent.

Pretraining on out-of-domain (OOD) data can further improve the performance of `One-to-All`. Given an intent detection task, we treat other data which do not have domain overlapping with this task as the OOD data. During OOD pretraining, the intent space is a union of intents from all the OOD data. We follow the same sequence construction strategy and training process stated in Section 2.1 and Section 2.2.

3 Experiments

We conduct experiments on three intent detection tasks under both few-shot and zero-shot settings.

Datasets. Our model is evaluated on three fine-grained intent detection datasets: BANKING77 (Casanueva et al., 2020), HWU64 (Liu et al., 2019a), and CLINC150 (Larson et al., 2019). Each dataset contains one or multiple domains and a fine-grained intent space. Dataset statistics are shown in Appendix Table 2. We randomly sample 10% training data as the *dev set*, following Zhang et al. (2021) and Mehri et al. (2020). For each target task, we use the other two datasets excluding the similar domains and intents as its OOD pretraining data. For example, we take BANKING77 as the target task, which contains banking-related intents. To obtain its OOD pretraining data, we combine the data from HWU64 and CLINC150 but remove the "Banking" and "Credit Cards" domains. The statistics of the OOD data for each target task are shown in Appendix Table 3. We also sample 10% OOD data as the *dev set* for the OOD pretraining.

For paraphrase detection pretraining, we leverage the public Quora Question Pairs (QQP) dataset[1]. To incorporate more sentences in a single pair, we filter short sentence pairs from QQP by setting the max number of words and characters in a sentence as 10 and 40, respectively. The filtered QQP dataset contains 31,412 paraphrase pairs.

Baselines. We compare our method with six baselines in the three categories as we described in Section 1. Standard classifier-based baselines: 1) RoBERTa with a standard classifier. 2) CPFT (Zhang et al., 2021) performs self-supervised CL on multiple intent detection datasets and applies supervised CL on the target task. 3) RoBERTa-SPI (Zhang et al., 2022) introduces two regularizers to improve supervised pretraining via isotropization. For example-based approaches, we consider its prior SOTA model: 4) DNNC (Zhang et al., 2020), which identifies intents by finding the nearest neighbors of utterances in the training set and is pretrained on three natural language inference datasets. For intent semantic aware methods, we compare: 5) Context-TE and 6) Parallel-TE (Du et al., 2022). These approaches incorporate multiple intents into a single textual entailment sequence. Context-TE relies on indirect supervision from MNLI (Williams et al., 2018). Parallel-TE is more comparable to `One-to-All`, it also encodes utterances and intents simultaneously, but it is a pipeline model that only selects top-k intents for each utterance. Among all the baselines, CPFT and DNNC are the prior SOTA models for 5- and 10-shot settings. Our paper considers more challenging scenarios, specifically the 1- and 3-shot settings. The implementation of the baselines and our model are detailed in Appendix C.

Results. For few-shot experiments, we conduct three runs with distinct training data samples, following Du et al. (2022). Table 1 shows the average

[1]https://quoradata.quora.com/First-Quora-Dataset-Release-Question-Pairs

Model	BANKING77			HWU64			CLINC150		
	1-shot	3-shot	5-shot	1-shot	3-shot	5-shot	1-shot	3-shot	5-shot
RoBERTa	35.31 (2.22)	64.78 (0.76)	75.47 (1.69)	40.34 (2.66)	67.44 (1.37)	75.71 (1.26)	48.48 (1.03)	80.91 (2.10)	86.82 (1.40)
CPFT	40.71 (2.25)	71.57 (0.34)	79.73 (0.52)	50.61 (2.18)	72.91 (2.32)	79.82 (1.64)	58.58 (0.57)	83.12 (0.43)	90.60 (0.70)
RoBERTa-SPI	43.81 (2.01)	65.63 (0.66)	72.20 (1.45)	53.75 (2.13)	70.95 (1.14)	75.58 (1.24)	67.57 (0.99)	83.31 (1.78)	87.76 (1.08)
DNNC	30.23 (2.51)	72.21 (1.02)	79.94 (1.77)	29.77 (1.45)	75.25 (2.69)	79.31 (0.19)	30.17 (2.33)	87.07 (0.44)	90.44 (1.03)
Context-TE	64.22 (0.50)	73.27 (0.43)	77.07 (0.57)	64.39 (1.64)	73.45 (1.72)	78.16 (0.94)	74.71 (0.91)	84.56 (1.54)	87.61 (0.79)
Parallel-TE	64.34 (1.23)	72.20 (1.00)	76.23 (0.37)	61.96 (0.46)	74.10 (0.51)	78.10 (1.40)	74.54 (0.81)	83.66 (0.84)	86.61 (0.58)
One-to-All	**66.36** (0.46)	**76.13** (0.45)	79.75 (0.78)	**68.77** (1.94)	**78.16** (2.04)	**79.89** (0.30)	**77.63** (0.63)	**87.09** (1.44)	89.88 (0.81)
w/ OOD	**67.93** (0.28)	**76.92** (0.18)	**80.51** (0.88)	**73.17** (0.37)	**79.95** (0.68)	**82.50** (1.05)	**79.21** (0.43)	**88.01** (1.46)	**90.76** (0.63)

Table 1: Test accuracy (%) and standard deviation on three dataset under three few-shot scenarios. The first and second highest results are formatted in **bold** and underline, respectively.

accuracy and standard deviation on three datasets under 1-, 3-, and 5-shot settings. One-to-All outperforms all the baselines remarkably in 1- and 3-shot scenarios across three datasets without any pretraining. For example, One-to-All improves the state-of-the-art result for 1-shot on HWU64 by 6.81%. After pretraining on OOD data, the improvement percentage increases to 13.64%. For the 5-shot setting, One-to-All achieves comparable results without pretraining and outperforms all the baselines with pretraining on OOD. The example-based model DNNC performs extremely poorly on 1-shot tasks even though it achieves good performances in 5-shot, showing its limitation when training resources are extremely scarce.

For the zero-shot setting, we first did preliminary experiments evaluating all baselines and our model on the target tasks without extra pretraining. The results are reported in Appendix Table 4. Despite poor performance across all models, One-to-All remains the top-performing approach. Then we pretrain the model on OOD/QQP data without accessing any in-domain training data. The results are shown in Figure 2. The zero-shot performance of One-to-All exhibits significant improvement following pretraining on QQP data, indicating the effectiveness of our novel pretraining strategy. Comparing the zero-shot results with the few-shot results in Table 1, we can observe that the performance of One-to-All (OOD) under the zero-shot setting even outperforms some baselines (RoBERTa, CPFT, and DNNC) under the 1-shot setting. Thus, we compare our model, One-to-All, with the two strongest baselines, Context-TE and Parallel-TE, in the zero-shot setting. As shown in Figure 2, One-to-All (OOD) outperforms both Context-TE (OOD) and Parallel-TE (OOD) in most settings. The zero-shot performance of One-to-All is further boosted by pre-

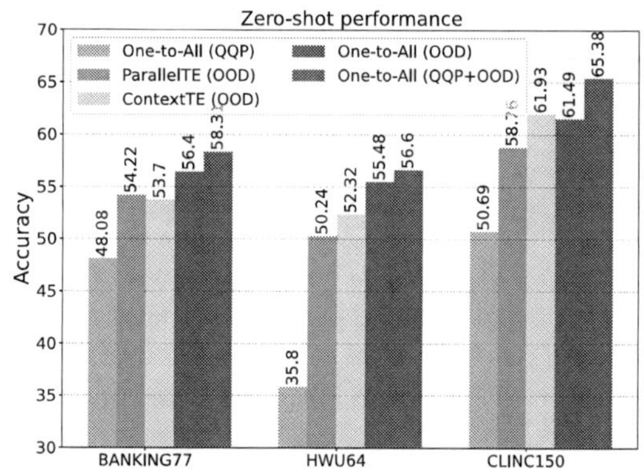

Figure 2: Zero-shot performance. OOD or QQP indicates that the model is pretrained on OOD or QQP data.

training on both OOD and QQP data, outperforming both Context-TE and Parallel-TE by a large margin. Once again, this finding highlights the effectiveness of utilizing indirect supervision from paraphrase identification datasets.

Analysis We investigate how our end-to-end design impacts our model performance by comparing it with Parallel-TE through a case study on BANKING77. We run One-to-All and Parallel-TE under the 3-shot setting three times. The top-k filtering step in Parallel-TE misses gold intents for 89 utterances in the *test set*, while One-to-All can correctly predict 34.7 of them on average, which brings a 1.1% improvement given the size of *test set* is 3080. This suggests that our end-to-end design effectively identifies partial intents that may have been overlooked by the pipeline system.

4 Conclusion

In this paper, we propose an end-to-end intent semantic aware intent detection model One-to-All to fully leverage intent semantics via contrastive learning. Experiments show that it is especially effective when training resource is scarce.

Limitations

Although we perform OOD pretraining on our model and gain performance improvement, the OOD data we use in our experiment is only from at most two datasets. There are many publicly available intent detection datasets from different domains, such as ATIS (Hemphill et al., 1990) and SNIPS (Coucke et al., 2018), can be used for the OOD pretraining. We believe pretraining on large-scale OOD datasets can further boost the performance of our model, and we leave it for our future work.

Acknowledgments

The authors appreciate the reviewers for their insightful comments and suggestions. This work is supported in part by NSF under grant III-2106758.

References

Pavel Burnyshev, Andrey Bout, Valentin Malykh, and Irina Piontkovskaya. 2021. InFoBERT: Zero-shot approach to natural language understanding using contextualized word embedding. In *Proceedings of RANLP*, pages 208–215.

Iñigo Casanueva, Tadas Temčinas, Daniela Gerz, Matthew Henderson, and Ivan Vulić. 2020. Efficient intent detection with dual sentence encoders. In *Proceedings of the 2nd Workshop on Natural Language Processing for Conversational AI*, pages 38–45.

Ting Chen, Simon Kornblith, Mohammad Norouzi, and Geoffrey Hinton. 2020. A simple framework for contrastive learning of visual representations. In *Proceedings of ICML*, volume 119, pages 1597–1607.

Alice Coucke, Alaa Saade, Adrien Ball, Théodore Bluche, Alexandre Caulier, David Leroy, Clément Doumouro, Thibault Gisselbrecht, Francesco Caltagirone, Thibaut Lavril, Maël Primet, and Joseph Dureau. 2018. Snips voice platform: an embedded spoken language understanding system for private-by-design voice interfaces. *ArXiv*, abs/1805.10190.

Jiangshu Du, Wenpeng Yin, Congying Xia, and Philip S. Yu. 2022. Learning to select from multiple options. *ArXiv*, abs/2212.00301.

Tianyu Gao, Xingcheng Yao, and Danqi Chen. 2021. SimCSE: Simple contrastive learning of sentence embeddings. In *Proceedings of EMNLP*, pages 6894–6910.

Beliz Gunel, Jingfei Du, Alexis Conneau, and Veselin Stoyanov. 2021. Supervised contrastive learning for pre-trained language model fine-tuning. In *Proceedings of ICLR*.

Wanwei He, Yinpei Dai, Binyuan Hui, Min Yang, Zheng Cao, Jianbo Dong, Fei Huang, Luo Si, and Yongbin Li. 2022a. SPACE-2: Tree-structured semi-supervised contrastive pre-training for task-oriented dialog understanding. In *Proceedings of COLING*, pages 553–569.

Wanwei He, Yinpei Dai, Min Yang, Jian Sun, Fei Huang, Luo Si, and Yongbin Li. 2022b. Unified dialog model pre-training for task-oriented dialog understanding and generation. In *Proceedings of SIGIR*, page 187–200.

Charles T. Hemphill, John J. Godfrey, and George R. Doddington. 1990. The ATIS spoken language systems pilot corpus. In *Speech and Natural Language: Proceedings of a Workshop Held at Hidden Valley, Pennsylvania, June 24-27,1990.*

Dmitry Lamanov, Pavel Burnyshev, Katya Artemova, Valentin Malykh, Andrey Bout, and Irina Piontkovskaya. 2022. Template-based approach to zero-shot intent recognition. In *Proceedings of INLG*, pages 15–28.

Stefan Larson, Anish Mahendran, Joseph J. Peper, Christopher Clarke, Andrew Lee, Parker Hill, Jonathan K. Kummerfeld, Kevin Leach, Michael A. Laurenzano, Lingjia Tang, and Jason Mars. 2019. An evaluation dataset for intent classification and out-of-scope prediction. In *Proceedings of EMNLP-IJCNLP*, pages 1311–1316.

Hongzhan Lin, Jing Ma, Liangliang Chen, Zhiwei Yang, Mingfei Cheng, and Chen Guang. 2022. Detect rumors in microblog posts for low-resource domains via adversarial contrastive learning. In *Findings of NAACL*, pages 2543–2556.

Xingkun Liu, Arash Eshghi, Pawel Swietojanski, and Verena Rieser. 2019a. Benchmarking natural language understanding services for building conversational agents. *ArXiv*, abs/1903.05566.

Yinhan Liu, Myle Ott, Naman Goyal, Jingfei Du, Mandar Joshi, Danqi Chen, Omer Levy, Mike Lewis, Luke Zettlemoyer, and Veselin Stoyanov. 2019b. Roberta: A robustly optimized bert pretraining approach. *ArXiv*, abs/1907.11692.

Shikib Mehri and Mihail Eric. 2021. Example-driven intent prediction with observers. In *Proceedings of NAACL-HLT*, pages 2979–2992.

Shikib Mehri, Mihail Eric, and Dilek Hakkani-Tür. 2020. Dialoglue: A natural language understanding benchmark for task-oriented dialogue. *CoRR*, abs/2009.13570.

Yutao Mou, Keqing He, Yanan Wu, Zhiyuan Zeng, Hong Xu, Huixing Jiang, Wei Wu, and Weiran Xu. 2022. Disentangled knowledge transfer for OOD intent discovery with unified contrastive learning. In *Proceedings of ACL (Short Papers)*, pages 46–53.

Aaron Mueller, Jason Krone, Salvatore Romeo, Saab Mansour, Elman Mansimov, Yi Zhang, and Dan Roth. 2022. Label semantic aware pre-training for few-shot text classification. In *Proceedings of ACL*, pages 8318–8334.

Jin Qu, Kazuma Hashimoto, Wenhao Liu, Caiming Xiong, and Yingbo Zhou. 2021. Few-shot intent classification by gauging entailment relationship between utterance and semantic label. In *Proceedings of the 3rd Workshop on Natural Language Processing for Conversational AI*.

Nils Reimers and Iryna Gurevych. 2019. Sentence-BERT: Sentence embeddings using Siamese BERT-networks. In *Proceedings of EMNLP-IJCNLP*, pages 3982–3992.

Richard Socher, Eric Huang, Jeffrey Pennin, Christopher D Manning, and Andrew Ng. 2011. Dynamic pooling and unfolding recursive autoencoders for paraphrase detection. In *Proceedings of NeurIPs*, pages 801–809.

Ivan Vulić, Pei-Hao Su, Samuel Coope, Daniela Gerz, Paweł Budzianowski, Iñigo Casanueva, Nikola Mrkšić, and Tsung-Hsien Wen. 2021. ConvFiT: Conversational fine-tuning of pretrained language models. In *Proceedings of EMNLP*, pages 1151–1168. Association for Computational Linguistics.

Adina Williams, Nikita Nangia, and Samuel Bowman. 2018. A broad-coverage challenge corpus for sentence understanding through inference. In *Proceedings of NAACL-HLT*, pages 1112–1122.

Chien-Sheng Wu, Steven C.H. Hoi, Richard Socher, and Caiming Xiong. 2020. TOD-BERT: Pre-trained natural language understanding for task-oriented dialogue. In *Proceedings of EMNLP*, pages 917–929.

Congying Xia, Wenpeng Yin, Yihao Feng, and Philip Yu. 2021. Incremental few-shot text classification with multi-round new classes: Formulation, dataset and system. In *Proceedings of NAACL-HLT*, pages 1351–1360.

Yuanmeng Yan, Rumei Li, Sirui Wang, Fuzheng Zhang, Wei Wu, and Weiran Xu. 2021. ConSERT: A contrastive framework for self-supervised sentence representation transfer. In *Proceedings of ACL*, pages 5065–5075.

Haode Zhang, Haowen Liang, Yuwei Zhang, Li-Ming Zhan, Xiao-Ming Wu, Xiaolei Lu, and Albert Lam. 2022. Fine-tuning pre-trained language models for few-shot intent detection: Supervised pre-training and isotropization. In *Proceedings of NAACL-HLT*, pages 532–542.

Jianguo Zhang, Trung Bui, Seunghyun Yoon, Xiang Chen, Zhiwei Liu, Congying Xia, Quan Hung Tran, Walter Chang, and Philip Yu. 2021. Few-shot intent detection via contrastive pre-training and fine-tuning. In *Proceedings of EMNLP*, pages 1906–1912.

Jianguo Zhang, Kazuma Hashimoto, Wenhao Liu, Chien-Sheng Wu, Yao Wan, Philip Yu, Richard Socher, and Caiming Xiong. 2020. Discriminative nearest neighbor few-shot intent detection by transferring natural language inference. In *Proceedings of EMNLP*, pages 5064–5082.

A Related Work

Recent research on low-shot intent detection can be broadly classified into three main categories: standard classifier-based, example-based, and intent semantic aware approaches.

Standard-classifier methods discard intent semantics and usually require an extra pretraining process on the extra corpus. For example, He et al. (2022a,b); Wu et al. (2020) pretrain models on large-scale dialog datasets. Zhang et al. (2021) pretrain a RoBERTa model on various intent datasets via self-supervised contrastive learning. Zhang et al. (2022) propose two regularizers to improve its supervised pretraining step via isotropization.

Example-based approaches aim to learn the similarities between various examples and classify an input utterance by identifying its closest neighbor in the training data. For instance, Zhang et al. (2020); Mehri and Eric (2021) determines the intent of an utterance by searching for its nearest neighbors among all training utterances. These approaches also ignore the semantic information of intents.

Existing intent semantic aware approaches also exhibit various drawbacks and limitations. For example, LSAP (Mueller et al., 2022) incorporates intent semantics into generative models via pretraining. More specifically, during the pretraining stage, LSAP takes partially masked utterance-intent pairs as the input and predicts the masked contents. However, this approach relies on large-scale pretraining data to obtain decent performance. Qu et al. (2021) and Xia et al. (2021) cast ID as textual entailment (TE), treating utterances and intents as premises and hypotheses, respectively. But these two models are only able to compare one single utterance with one single intent, which makes them unaware of other intent options. Du et al. (2022) learn to select the best intent for an utterance by providing the top-k intents for that utterance in one training example. Despite providing a one-to-many comparison, Du et al. (2022) are only able to view the top-k intents rather than the entire intent label set during training. Additionally, Du et al. (2022) propose a pipeline model. Their performance is constrained by the accuracy of the first stage of the pipeline, which is identifying the top-k intents. Moreover, Lamanov et al. (2022) propose a template-based approach for modeling intents and utterances as sentence pairs. Burnyshev et al. (2021) use a deep contextualized model to embed utterances and the natural language descriptions of user intents in zero-shot scenarios.

Different from all the literature we discussed above, we propose an end-to-end intent semantic aware system. By fully utilizing label semantics via contrastive learning, our model achieves SOTA performance even without pretraining on additional datasets.

B Dataset Statistics

Dataset	Domain	Utterance	Intent
BANKING77	1	13,083	77
HWU64	21	10,030	64
CLINC150	10	22,500	150

Table 2: Dataset statistics.

Target	Domain	Utterance	Intent
BANKING77	29	28,030	183
HWU64	11	35,453	225
CLINC150	21	9,854	63

Table 3: Statistics of the OOD pretraining data used for each target task.

C Implementation Details.

All the baselines and `One-to-All` adopt RoBERTa-base (Liu et al., 2019b) as the backbones for a fair comparison.

Baseline implementation. For the RoBERTa model, we implement it with the Hugging Face[2] library. For RoBERTa-SPI, DNNC, Context-TE, and Parallel-TE, we directly run their open-source code under our experiment settings. It is important to note that the original Context-TE and Parallel-TE models utilize RoBERTa-large as their base models. However, in our implementation, we replace it with RoBERTa-base to ensure a fair comparison. Regarding CPFT, we strive to replicate its methodology to the best of our ability, given the unavailability of its code and pretrained checkpoints to the public. The original paper trained CPFT on a fixed set of 5-shot data, while in our experiments,

[2]https://huggingface.co/

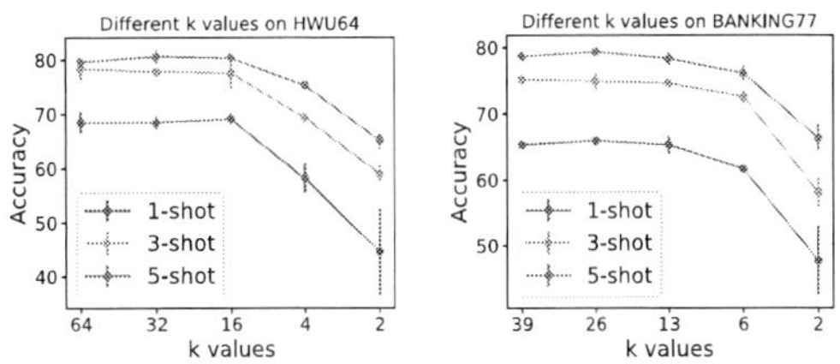

(a) HWU64 (b) BANKING77

Figure 3: Model performance with different k values on the *dev set* of HWU64 and BANKING77.

Model	BANKING	HWU	CLINC
RoBERTa	1.65	1.77	2.01
CPFT	1.91	2.03	2.78
RoBERTa-SPI	1.90	1.87	2.52
Context-TE	1.04	1.20	1.43
Parallel-TE	1.66	2.14	2.24
`One-to-All`	**6.04**	**13.05**	**5.84**

Table 4: Zero-shot performance (%) without pretraining on additional datasets. DNNC is not included since it requires at least one training example.

we conduct three runs with uniquely sampled few-shot training data, which mitigates the potential influence of data sampling bias.

`One-to-All` implementation. For few-shot tasks and OOD pretraining, we train the model for 10 and 3 epochs, respectively, and keep the best ones on the *dev set*. For paraphrase detection pretraining, we train the model for 3 epochs. All the training batch size is set to 8 and the learning rate is 2e-5. The output dimension of the MLP projector is set to 768 and the temperature parameter $\tau = 0.1$. We set k to 26, 32, 30 for BANKING77, HWU64, and CLINC150, respectively, according to the observations on their *dev sets*. Details are discussed in Appendix E.

D Zero-shot Preliminary Experiments

E Additional Analysis

We try to explore how the number of intents in each input sequence, k, influences the performance. We explore the influence of k by conducting experiments on the *dev set* of HWU64 and BANKING77 with different k values. As shown in Figure 3, the model performance stays similar when $k > 20$ but drops sharply when k is below 10. This is probably due to the reduction of contrastive instances in a single pair. Therefore, we set k to 26, 32, 30 for BANKING77, HWU64, and CLINC150, respectively, and it can bring two benefits: 1) it is more friendly for the paraphrase detection pretraining as it is the max number of the sentences that can be incorporated into a single pair; 2) it minimizes $n \bmod k$ as we discussed in Section 2.1.

Theia: Weakly Supervised Multimodal Event Extraction from Incomplete Data

Farhad Moghimifar[1] and **Fatemeh Shiri**[1] and **Van Nguyen**[2]
Yuan-Fang Li[1] and **Gholamreza Haffari**[1]
[1] Faculty of Information Technology, Monash University, Australia
[2] Information Sciences Division, Defence Science and Technology Group, Australia
{first.lastname}@monash.edu
van.nguyen5@defence.gov.au

Abstract

Event extraction from multimodal documents is an important yet under-explored problem. One challenge faced by this task is the scarcity of paired image-text datasets, making it difficult to fully exploit the strong representation power of multimodal language models. In this paper, we present Theia, an end-to-end multimodal event extraction framework that can be trained on incomplete data. Specifically, we couple a generation-based event extraction model with a customised image synthesizer that can generate images from text. Our model leverages capabilities of pre-trained vision-language models and can be trained on incomplete (i.e. text-only) data. Experimental results on existing multimodal datasets demonstrate the effectiveness of our approach for both synthesising missing data and extracting events over state-of-the-art approaches.

1 Introduction

Event extraction is an important task in natural language processing that aims to identify and extract structured information about events and their arguments from text. Despite the challenging nature of this task, being rooted in the ambiguity, complexity and diversity of natural language, recent years have seen significant improvements from end-to-end deep learning models (Wadden et al., 2019; Du and Cardie, 2020; Hsu et al., 2022) over the traditional rule-based approaches (Valenzuela-Escárcega et al., 2015; Bui et al., 2013).

There is a rapid increase of *multimodal* documents online, propelled by the high prevalence of camera-enabled devices. It has been shown that other modalities supplement the information that is available in text (Li et al., 2020). However, event extraction from multimodal information is an under-explored area, as existing methods were primarily developed for textual information.

Some recent works studied this question through the use of the visual modality (Li et al., 2022a, 2020). These approaches, however, suffer from two shortcomings. Firstly, existing models formulate event extraction as a classification problem, in which trigger words and entity recognition modules are used as features. This limits their performance in capturing high-level complex event structures. Secondly, these methods require a complete set of text-(corresponding)image pairs at the time of training, which limits their performance when models face *missing* data, where images are unavailable for all or a portion of the training data.

To overcome these shortcomings, we propose an end-to-end sequence-generation-based multimodal event extraction model. Our proposed approach incorporates an image synthesizer model to handle the missing images during training. The image synthesizer, conditioned on the given textual information, generates a visual representation that helps to train the encoder-decoder structure of our event extraction model, and customises the generated images by reducing the domain shift between the original domain of the pre-trained models and the target domain (Figure 1). Experiments on the task of multimodal event extraction confirm the strong superiority of our model, by a margin of 7%, over state-of-the-art models. Furthermore, empirical results using the images synthesise show the capability of our model to portray domain-dependant visual context.

2 Related Work

The task of event extraction has been widely studied (Ahn, 2006; Hogenboom et al., 2011), where initially rule-based classification approaches were developed to address this task (Bui et al., 2013; Ritter et al., 2012). With the advances in deep learning, models based on neural networks have also been developed for this task (Nguyen and Nguyen, 2019; Zhang et al., 2019). More recently, several studies leverage the strong representation and reasoning capabilities of pre-trained language models (Li et al.,

Proceedings of the 13th International Joint Conference on Natural Language Processing and the 3rd Conference of the Asia-Pacific Chapter of the Association for Computational Linguistics (Volume 2: Short Papers), pages 139–145
November 1–4, 2023.

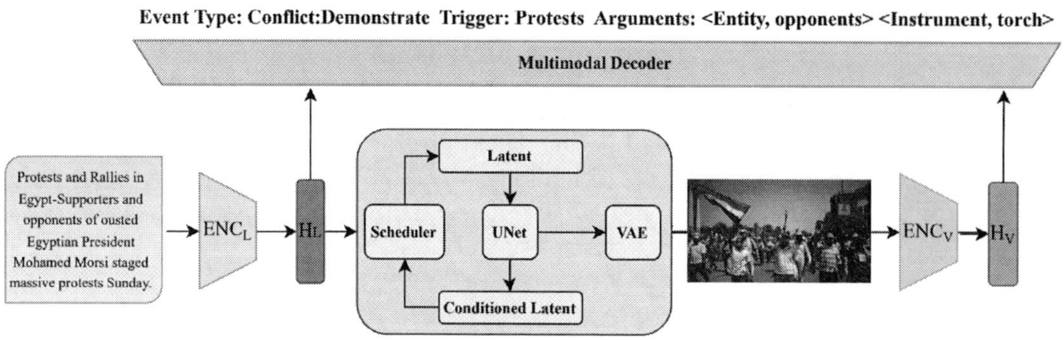

Figure 1: An overview of our proposed model. The textual encoder ($\mathbf{ENC}_L$) takes the text as input and feeds the encoded version to the image synthesizer, as well as the decoder. The visual encoder ($\mathbf{ENC}_V$) takes the synthesised image as input and feeds the encoded image into the multimodal transformer-based decoder, and the structured event information is generated as a sequence.

2021; Wu et al., 2022; Hsu et al., 2022).

While these studies achieve excellent performance on text-only benchmarks, they fail to account for other modalities. By proposing a new dataset and a multimodal event extraction model, Li et al. (2020); Zhang et al. (2017); Moghimifar et al. (2023) showed that including the visual context results in better extraction performance. Li et al. (2022a) proposed an approach based on pre-trained vision-language models (Radford et al., 2021) for addressing multimodal event extraction. However, these approaches cast event extraction as a classification problem, whereby their model is limited to a fixed schema. Furthermore, these models require a complete set of text-image pairs for training, which hinders their real-world practicality where it is highly likely that a part of the visual data is missing. Unlike these approaches, we propose a sequence generation model that is capable of synthesising the visual context to alleviate the problem of *missing* data.

3 Multimodal Event Extraction

Problem Formulation. Given a corpus of sequences of tokens $\mathbb{X} = \{x_1, \ldots, x_N\}$ of length N, where each $x_i = (w_i^1, w_i^2, \ldots)$ represents the i-th sentence of the corpus and w_i^m is a token from the vocabulary $\mathcal{W}$. In addition, there is the corresponding visual context $\mathbb{V} = \{v_1, \ldots, v_M\}$ of length M, where $M < N$, and for each $v \in \mathcal{V}$, it is paired with one sentence $x \in \mathcal{X}$. Our goal is to extract event mentions, including the event type $e \in \mathcal{E}$, and roles $r \in \mathcal{R}$ together with their arguments $a \in \mathcal{W}$.

Multimodal Event Generation. We formulate the task of multimodal event extraction as a sequence generation task, where our proposed model outputs a linearised representation of event mentions in a given sentence-image pair (x_i, v_i). Each event then is represented in the form of $y_i = \langle t_i, e_i, \langle a_i, r_i \rangle_1, \langle a_i, r_i \rangle_2, \ldots \rangle$, where $t_i \in W$ refers to a trigger word, $e_i \in \mathcal{E}$ indicates the event type, and $a_i \in W$ and $r_i \in \mathcal{R}$ represents an argument token and role, respectively. Thus, given an input pair (x, v), the goal of our proposed model is to generate sequence y of length T as follows:

$$p_{\theta_{\mathbf{SEQ}}}(y|x, v) = \prod_{t=1}^{T} p_{\theta_{\mathbf{SEQ}}}(y_t|y_{<t}, x, v) \quad (1)$$
$$= \prod_{t=1}^{T} \mathbf{DEC}_{\theta_{\mathbf{DEC}}}(y_t|y_{<t}, \mathbf{ENC}_{\theta_{\mathbf{ENC}}}(x, v)),$$

where $\mathbf{ENC}_{\theta_{\mathbf{ENC}}} = (\mathbf{ENC}_L, \mathbf{ENC}_V)$ and $\mathbf{DEC}_{\theta_{\mathbf{DEC}}}$ refers to an encoder and a decoder structure, respectively, and $\theta_{\mathbf{SEQ}} := \{\theta_{\mathbf{ENC}}, \theta_{\mathbf{DEC}}\}$ denotes the parameters of our sequence generation model.

Multimodal Architecture. The encoder $\mathbf{ENC}(\cdot)$ consists of a language encoder ($\mathbf{ENC}_L$) and a visual encoder ($\mathbf{ENC}_V$) to compute hidden representations of the textual ($\boldsymbol{H}_L$) and visual ($\boldsymbol{H}_v$) inputs separately. Hence, the hidden representation ($\boldsymbol{H}$) of the input (x, v) is formulated as:

$$\boldsymbol{H} = \mathbf{ENC}(x, v) = [\mathbf{ENC}_L(x); \mathbf{ENC}_V(v)] \quad (2)$$

The $\mathbf{DEC}(\cdot)$ is a multi-layer Transformer-based decoder, where each layer is a Transformer block.

At step t, the decoder generates the t-th token of sequence y_i and the hidden state $\boldsymbol{h}_t$ as follows:

$$y_t, \boldsymbol{h}_t = \mathbf{DEC}(y_{t-1}; \boldsymbol{H}_{y<t}, \boldsymbol{H}), \quad (3)$$

where $\boldsymbol{H}_{y<t} \in \mathbb{R}^{(t-1)\times d}$ denotes the past hidden state used for self-attention during decoding. Given the *complete* data (x, v, y), the **ENC-DEC** architecture can be trained by minimising the loss:

$$\mathcal{L}_{seq} = \mathbb{E}_{x,v,y}[-\log p(y|x, v; \theta_{seq})] \quad (4)$$

4 Training with Incomplete Data

During training, when the visual context of an input x_i is unavailable, we leverage an *image synthesizer* that produces visual representation z_i based on x_i. We then adapt the image synthesizer based on the complete and incomplete event extraction data.

Our proposed method is based on Denoising Diffusion Probabilistic Models (Ho et al., 2020). This generative model consists of a pre-trained autoencoder that maps images to a spatial latent code, a corresponding decoder that learns to map the latent representation back to the image, and a diffusion model that is conditioned on the textual input (x_i). Inspired by Ruiz et al. (2022), during training, we use the textual input of complete pairs of $(x^{\text{com}}, v^{\text{com}})$ to condition the model to regenerate v^{com}. Furthermore, we use the textual input of incomplete data points x^{inc} to synthesise visual context z. We then resort to the following reconstruction-based loss function to train the image synthesiser on the synthesised image z,

$$\begin{aligned}\mathcal{L}_{syn} = \mathbb{E}_{x^{\text{com}}, x^{\text{inc}}, v^{\text{com}}, z, \epsilon, \epsilon', t, t'} & \quad (5)\\ [\omega_t||\hat{V}_{\theta_{syn}}(\alpha_t v + \sigma_t \epsilon, x^{com}) - v^{com}||_2^2 + \\ \lambda_{syn}\omega_{t'}||\hat{V}_{\theta_{syn}}(\alpha_{t'} z + \sigma_{t'}\epsilon', x^{inc}) - z||_2^2],\end{aligned}$$

where $\hat{V}_{\theta_{syn}}$ is the image synthesizer function, $\epsilon \sim \mathcal{N}(0, I)$ is a noise term, and $\omega_t, \alpha_t, \sigma_t$ and $\omega_{t'}, \alpha_{t'}, \sigma_{t'}$ are the terms that control the noise schedule and sample quality for complete and incomplete data, respectively, where t (and t') $\sim \mathcal{U}([0, 1])$. λ_{syn} controls the trade-off between the images synthesizer's capability to regenerate the v^{com} conditioned on x^{com} and synthesising images conditioned on x^{inc}. The only trainable parameters of the image synthesier are those of the textual encoder, and we keep the other parameters frozen.

We train our models in an end-to-end manner, where the overall optimisation objective is defined as a weighted sum of the sequence generation loss and the image synthesizer loss:

$$\mathcal{L} = \mathcal{L}_{seq} + \lambda \mathcal{L}_{syn}, \quad (6)$$

where the hyperparameter λ controls the trade-off between extracting textual and visual semantic information for sequence generation and synthesising the visual features.

To train our model, we apply online hard EM (Neal and Hinton, 1999) by interleaving the following steps in an iterative manner:

- **E-step**: generate images z for data points x^{inc} using the current parameters of our proposed image synthesizer θ_{syn}.
- **M-step**: the model parameters (θ_{seq} and θ_{syn}) are the updated by minimising the loss Eq. 6.

5 Experiments

In this section, we report the performance of our model on the task of multimodal event extraction in comparison to the current state-of-the-art models.

5.1 Experimental Setup

Evaluation Metrics. Following previous work on multimodal event extraction (Li et al., 2020), we report the results of the macro-averaged F1 score (F1), precision (P) and recall (R). Since we have formulated this as a sequence generation task, we also report the BLEU score.

Baselines. We compare our model, Theia (VL), against Valhalla (Li et al., 2022b), RMMT (Wu et al., 2021), and Gated Fusion (Wu et al., 2021)[1]. Furthermore, we report the performance of GPT3.5 (Brown et al., 2020) and Flamingo (Alayrac et al., 2022), as two in-context learning approaches. In order to use visual information, we use BLIP-2 (Li et al., 2023) to extract *scene description* from images and then we feed them to the context of the model (GPT3.5/SC). In addition, we report the performance of our model in two ablation settings, firstly, when the visual context is fully disregarded in training (Theia (L)), and secondly, instead of the image synthesizer, we use an image retrieval model to fill in the missing data with the most relevant images from the full set of images in the dataset (Theia (R)).

Dataset. **M2E2** (Li et al., 2020) is a multimodal news event extraction dataset that expands upon ACE (Doddington et al., 2004). It consists of 6,167 sentences, with 1,297 event mentions and 1,965

[1]The results of Li et al. (2022a, 2020) are not reproducible, due to incomplete source code/data.

		Event			Argument				
Model	**BLEU**	**F1**	**P**	**R**	**F1**	**P**	**R**	Size	Method
Gated Fusion (Wu et al., 2021)	13.34	21.45	21.38	22.50	12.24	12.36	13.59	21.7M	SL
RMMT (Wu et al., 2021)	10.81	26.41	36.12	23.96	11.67	12.90	12.37	127.9M	SL
Valhalla (Li et al., 2022b)	15.23	19.19	17.53	24.62	10.83	10.51	15.10	49.1M	SL
OpenFlamingo (Awadalla et al., 2023)	-	7.7	13.49	14.17	5.42	7.68	8.27	9B	ICL
GPT3.5 (Brown et al., 2020)	-	19.56	17.78	31.31	12.11	10.77	**21.62**	-	ICL
GPT3.5/SC (Brown et al., 2020)	-	11.49	12.62	17.77	6.95	7.9	8.62	-	ICL
Theia (VL)	**18.48**	**52.48**	**51.84**	**53.05**	**16.44**	**16.31**	18.39	1.4B	SL
Theia (L)	17.83	46.75	47.31	48.03	15.21	15.70	17.47	1.4B	SL
Theia (R)	17.74	48.38	48.12	50.75	13.56	15.00	14.93	1.4B	SL

Table 1: Experimental results of multimodal event extraction and ablation studies, on M2E2 dataset. The column "Method" refers to the learning method, where ICL and SL indicate in-context and supervised learning.

argument roles. We split M2E2 into training, development, and test sets with a ratio of 60:20:20. We consider a *missing* data setting, where the training session has only 10 complete data points with text-image pairs, and the rest of the data lacks the visual modality. During inference, complete data points of text-image pairs are provided to the model.

Results. Table 1 summarises the performance of the models on M2E2, where at the training stage only 10 data points include both modalities. On the BLEU score, our model outperforms the second-best model by more than 3 absolute points. This indicates a higher quality of text generation, which results in better extraction of event information. This superiority is also backed up by the F1, precision and recall scores associated with both event and argument extractions. On F1 score, our model achieves a substantial 32% improvement on event trigger detection and a 5% improvement over the second-best model on argument extraction. The comparatively lower improvements of argument role extraction, when compared to event extraction, suggest the difficulty and complexity of argument representations. This is explained by the diversity of the mentions and the lower frequency of the mentions in the training data. Furthermore, we believe that this be caused by the degradation in the quality of longer generated sequences.

Compared to our full model, the poorer performance when the visual context is discarded (Theia (L)) suggests that using the visual context indeed improves the extraction of events. Moreover, the lower performance of Theia (R) indicates the positive effect of our image synthesizer in providing more context-related features.

To evaluate the effect of missing visual data, we reconfigure the training settings from 10 complete data points to 5, 50, 100, and the full set of

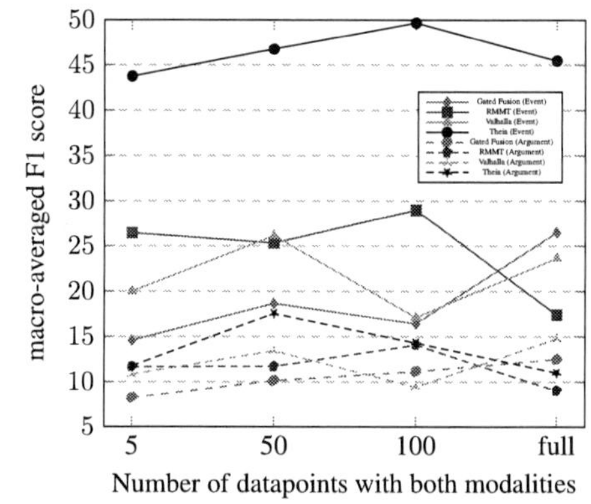

Figure 2: Performance of the models on M2E2, with different numbers of data point with both modalities during the training time.

data points, respectively. Figure 2 shows the results of this study. The x-axis shows the number of data points that, during training, include both textual and visual inputs, and the y-axis shows the F1 score. We see that on event trigger detection, our model outperforms all of the baselines in all settings. This observation suggests that the images generated by our image synthesizer model can capture more contextual information related to the textual input, hence resulting in improved performance. For argument extraction, our model performs the best in all settings except *full*, where Valhalla and Gated Fusion achieve better performance. The drop in performance of our model from 100 to full setting, suggests that the images associated with textual inputs (on full setting) carry less relevant information, and on the 100 setting when missing images are synthesised, the auxiliary images can provide better contextual information.

6 Conclusion

In this work, we address the task of *multimodal* event extraction, when the model faces *missing* vision modality in the training data. We propose an end-to-end sequence generation model, which leverages a customised image synthesizer model to provide visual context to the model. Empirical results show that our proposed approach effectively exploits the incomplete training data, and outperforms state-of-the-art techniques in this task.

7 Limitations

This paper discusses multimodal event extraction where textual input is represented at sentence level, therefore our model is limited by the length of the inputs and performs poorly on document-level event extraction. While our model showed a strong ability in addressing this task, real-world scenarios are more challenging due to distributional shift in data and noisy environments. While our model has proven to generate context-dependent images, its ability in generating facial features is limited, hence generated images of people are unrecognisable. In addition, the core part of our model, which is based on large-scale vision-language pre-trained models, can limit the deployment in situations with limited resources. Besides, all the reported results are by fixing a random seed and running all experiments once.

8 Ethics Statement

This project aimed at customising existing pre-trained image generation models (Stable Diffusion) towards the domain of news. While our image synthesizer might be biased toward specific attributes of the domain, it enables our model to extract better events from the text. Similar to existing generative models, the generated content might be used to mislead or manipulate. Therefore, our model inherits similar potential risks from this family of generative models.

References

David Ahn. 2006. The stages of event extraction. In *Proceedings of the Workshop on Annotating and Reasoning about Time and Events*, pages 1–8.

Jean-Baptiste Alayrac, Jeff Donahue, Pauline Luc, Antoine Miech, Iain Barr, Yana Hasson, Karel Lenc, Arthur Mensch, Katie Millican, Malcolm Reynolds, Roman Ring, Eliza Rutherford, Serkan Cabi, Tengda Han, Zhitao Gong, Sina Samangooei, Marianne Monteiro, Jacob Menick, Sebastian Borgeaud, Andy Brock, Aida Nematzadeh, Sahand Sharifzadeh, Mikolaj Binkowski, Ricardo Barreira, Oriol Vinyals, Andrew Zisserman, and Karen Simonyan. 2022. Flamingo: a visual language model for few-shot learning. *ArXiv*, abs/2204.14198.

Anas Awadalla, Irena Gao, Joshua Gardner, Jack Hessel, Yusuf Hanafy, Wanrong Zhu, Kalyani Marathe, Yonatan Bitton, Samir Gadre, Jenia Jitsev, Simon Kornblith, Pang Wei Koh, Gabriel Ilharco, Mitchell Wortsman, and Ludwig Schmidt. 2023. Openflamingo.

Tom Brown, Benjamin Mann, Nick Ryder, Melanie Subbiah, Jared D Kaplan, Prafulla Dhariwal, Arvind Neelakantan, Pranav Shyam, Girish Sastry, Amanda Askell, et al. 2020. Language models are few-shot learners. *Advances in neural information processing systems*, 33:1877–1901.

Quoc-Chinh Bui, David Campos, Erik van Mulligen, and Jan Kors. 2013. A fast rule-based approach for biomedical event extraction. In *proceedings of the BioNLP shared task 2013 workshop*, pages 104–108.

George R Doddington, Alexis Mitchell, Mark A Przybocki, Lance A Ramshaw, Stephanie M Strassel, and Ralph M Weischedel. 2004. The automatic content extraction (ace) program-tasks, data, and evaluation. In *Lrec*, volume 2, pages 837–840. Lisbon.

Xinya Du and Claire Cardie. 2020. Event extraction by answering (almost) natural questions. In *Proceedings of the 2020 Conference on Empirical Methods in Natural Language Processing (EMNLP)*, pages 671–683.

Jonathan Ho, Ajay Jain, and Pieter Abbeel. 2020. Denoising diffusion probabilistic models. *Advances in Neural Information Processing Systems*, 33:6840–6851.

Frederik Hogenboom, Flavius Frasincar, Uzay Kaymak, and Franciska De Jong. 2011. An overview of event extraction from text. *DeRiVE@ ISWC*, pages 48–57.

I-Hung Hsu, Kuan-Hao Huang, Elizabeth Boschee, Scott Miller, Prem Natarajan, Kai-Wei Chang, and Nanyun Peng. 2022. Degree: A data-efficient generation-based event extraction model. In *Proceedings of the 2022 Conference of the North American Chapter of the Association for Computational Linguistics: Human Language Technologies*, pages 1890–1908.

Diederik P Kingma and Jimmy Ba. 2015. Adam: A method for stochastic optimization. san diego. In *Third Annual International Conference on Learning Representations.*

Junnan Li, Dongxu Li, Silvio Savarese, and Steven Hoi. 2023. Blip-2: Bootstrapping language-image pretraining with frozen image encoders and large language models. *arXiv preprint arXiv:2301.12597.*

Manling Li, Ruochen Xu, Shuohang Wang, Luowei Zhou, Xudong Lin, Chenguang Zhu, Michael Zeng, Heng Ji, and Shih-Fu Chang. 2022a. Clip-event: Connecting text and images with event structures. In *Proceedings of the IEEE/CVF Conference on Computer Vision and Pattern Recognition*, pages 16420–16429.

Manling Li, Alireza Zareian, Qi Zeng, Spencer Whitehead, Di Lu, Heng Ji, and Shih-Fu Chang. 2020. Cross-media structured common space for multimedia event extraction. In *Proceedings of the 58th Annual Meeting of the Association for Computational Linguistics*, pages 2557–2568.

Sha Li, Heng Ji, and Jiawei Han. 2021. Document-level event argument extraction by conditional generation. In *Proceedings of the 2021 Conference of the North American Chapter of the Association for Computational Linguistics: Human Language Technologies*, pages 894–908.

Yi Li, Rameswar Panda, Yoon Kim, Chun-Fu Richard Chen, Rogerio S Feris, David Cox, and Nuno Vasconcelos. 2022b. Valhalla: Visual hallucination for machine translation. In *Proceedings of the IEEE/CVF Conference on Computer Vision and Pattern Recognition*, pages 5216–5226.

Farhad Moghimifar, Fatemeh Shiri, Reza Haffari, Yuan-Fang Li, and Van Nguyen. 2023. Few-shot domain-adaptative visually-fused event detection from text. In *2023 26th International Conference on Information Fusion (FUSION)*, pages 1–8. IEEE.

Radford Neal and Geoffrey Hinton. 1999. A view of the EM algorithm that justifies incremental, sparse, and other variants. In Michael I. Jordan, editor, *Learning in Graphical Models*, pages 355–368. MIT Press.

Trung Minh Nguyen and Thien Huu Nguyen. 2019. One for all: Neural joint modeling of entities and events. In *Proceedings of the AAAI conference on artificial intelligence*, volume 33, pages 6851–6858.

Alec Radford, Jong Wook Kim, Chris Hallacy, Aditya Ramesh, Gabriel Goh, Sandhini Agarwal, Girish Sastry, Amanda Askell, Pamela Mishkin, Jack Clark, et al. 2021. Learning transferable visual models from natural language supervision. In *International Conference on Machine Learning*, pages 8748–8763. PMLR.

Alan Ritter, Oren Etzioni, and Sam Clark. 2012. Open domain event extraction from twitter. In *Proceedings of the 18th ACM SIGKDD international conference on Knowledge discovery and data mining*, pages 1104–1112.

Robin Rombach, Andreas Blattmann, Dominik Lorenz, Patrick Esser, and Björn Ommer. 2022. High-resolution image synthesis with latent diffusion models. In *Proceedings of the IEEE/CVF Conference on Computer Vision and Pattern Recognition (CVPR)*, pages 10684–10695.

Nataniel Ruiz, Yuanzhen Li, Varun Jampani, Yael Pritch, Michael Rubinstein, and Kfir Aberman. 2022. Dreambooth: Fine tuning text-to-image diffusion models for subject-driven generation. *arXiv preprint arXiv:2208.12242*.

Marco A Valenzuela-Escárcega, Gus Hahn-Powell, Mihai Surdeanu, and Thomas Hicks. 2015. A domain-independent rule-based framework for event extraction. In *Proceedings of ACL-IJCNLP 2015 System Demonstrations*, pages 127–132.

David Wadden, Ulme Wennberg, Yi Luan, and Hannaneh Hajishirzi. 2019. Entity, relation, and event extraction with contextualized span representations. In *Proceedings of the 2019 Conference on Empirical Methods in Natural Language Processing and the 9th International Joint Conference on Natural Language Processing (EMNLP-IJCNLP)*, pages 5784–5789.

Tongtong Wu, Fatemeh Shiri, Jingqi Kang, Guilin Qi, Gholamreza Haffari, and Yuan-Fang Li. 2022. Kc-gee: Knowledge-based conditioning for generative event extraction.

Zhiyong Wu, Lingpeng Kong, Wei Bi, Xiang Li, and Ben Kao. 2021. Good for misconceived reasons: An empirical revisiting on the need for visual context in multimodal machine translation. In *Proceedings of the 59th Annual Meeting of the Association for Computational Linguistics and the 11th International Joint Conference on Natural Language Processing (Volume 1: Long Papers)*, pages 6153–6166.

Tongtao Zhang, Spencer Whitehead, Hanwang Zhang, Hongzhi Li, Joseph Ellis, Lifu Huang, Wei Liu, Heng Ji, and Shih-Fu Chang. 2017. Improving event extraction via multimodal integration. In *Proceedings of the 25th ACM international conference on Multimedia*, pages 270–278.

Yunyan Zhang, Guangluan Xu, Yang Wang, Xiao Liang, Lei Wang, and Tinglei Huang. 2019. Empower event detection with bi-directional neural language model. *Knowledge-Based Systems*, 167:87–97.

A Examples of Images by Theia

In this section, we present two samples of images generated by our model, Theia. We randomly selected two data points from the test set of M2E2. We then used the textual information to condition our image synthesizer into generating the visual representation of the text (Figure 3). As it can be seen, in the first example, *churches* is properly captured in the image generated by our model, Theia.

Figure 3: The images generated by our model for given textual inputs, compared to the original images from the news article, and the image generated by Stable Diffusion model (Rombach et al., 2022).

Similarly, in the second example, while stable diffusion fails to portray the *smoke*, our model represents this with fire/smoke, similar to the original image.

B Data Preparation

In order to develop our model, and run the experiments for all of the baselines as well, we convert the structured events into a sequence of tokens. To this end, a structured event represented in form of $y_i = \langle t_i, e_i, \langle a_i, r_i \rangle_1, \langle a_i, r_i \rangle_2, \dots \rangle$ (Section 3), is converted to the following span of tokens:
<TRIGGER> t_i </TRIGGER> <EVENT> e_i </EVENT> <ARG> a_i </ARG> <ROLE> r_i </ROLE>

where the tokens between <·> are special tokens added to the vocabulary set $\mathcal{W}$, and the embedding space of our encoder is then adjusted to the new length of vocab.

C Experimental Details

To train our model, we use CLIP ViT-L/14 (Radford et al., 2021) as a text and vision encoder. We also use the parameters of the pre-trained stable diffusion model (Rombach et al., 2022) to initialise the image synthesizer. This model is licensed with a CreativeML OpenRAIL++ license and free to use. We use an embedding size of 768, and a dropout of 0.3 over the textual encoder. We use Transformer-Base decoder in the sequence generator. Our model include more than 1.4B parameters, which belongs to both image synthesise and sequence generator. Optimisation is handled by Adam (Kingma and Ba, 2015) with a square root learning rate schedule and warm-up steps. We set the λ to 0.01 and use beam search with a beam size of 5 during inference. We ran our model on a machine with one NVIDIA A100 gpu. For the baselines, we follow the implementation details explained in their papers, and each model is trained with the same data preparation as our model. The best performing checkpoint on the development set then was used for testing. Since we kept the random seed constant throughout the experiments, we report the single-run results of each model. For running the experiments of GPT3.5, we prepare a prompt including task definition, definition of each event type and argument type and one example per event type, in addition to scene description, and ask the model to generate event information according to the instruction. We use model engine `gpt-3.5-turbo`. BLIP-2 [2] is used to extract description of the images, as a part of the prompt. The experiments related to OpenFlamingo [3] are conducted by using the open source implementation of Flamingo (Alayrac et al., 2022), where a prompt similar to prompt used in GPT3.5 experiments is used to instruct the model to generate information about events given a text and the corresponding image.

[2]https://github.com/salesforce/LAVIS/tree/main/projects/blip2
[3]https://github.com/mlfoundations/open_flamingo

Perplexity-Driven Case Encoding Needs Augmentation for CAPITALIZATION Robustness

Rohit Jain   Huda Khayrallah   Roman Grundkiewicz   Marcin Junczys-Dowmunt

{rjai,hkhayrallah,rogrundk,marcinjd}@microsoft.com

Abstract

Subword segmentation methods are the predominant solution to vocab sparsity in NMT. However, they cannot currently handle capitalization well. We re-encode case to allow the perplexity-driven SPM unigram language model algorithm to *learn* how to segment capitalization. Since naturally occurring data accurately describes the *prevalence* of capitalization but underestimates the *importance* humans ascribe to capitalization robustness, we propose data augmentation to fill this gap. We demonstrate that our proposed method improves translation quality on ALL CAPS, lower cased, and Title Case, while maintaining quality on standard test sets. In contrast to prior work, our proposed method has minimal impact on decoding speed. We release our code: github.com/marian-nmt/sentencepiece.

1 Introduction

Capitalization is supported by Latin script, and the Armenian, Cyrillic, Georgian and Greek alphabets. In addition to standard capitalization rules for a given language (e.g., sentence inital capitalization, German noun capitalization), variation also occurs, such as English *Title Casing*, *ALL CAPS FOR EMPHASIS*, or *all lower case in informal texts.*

For most NLP models, upper and lower case letters are represented with distinct code-points. In contrast, most people naturally connect upper and lower-cased letters as highly similar. Therefore, NLP models are expected to perform similarly on inputs that only differ in casing. However, that is often not the case, and NLP models are often unstable on non-standard casings.

Subword segmentation methods (e.g., BPE (Sennrich et al., 2016) and SPM (Kudo and Richardson, 2018)) handle the sparsity introduced by a variety of linguistic features by learning a segmentation of words into shorter sequences of characters. However, these do not currently handle the sparsity introduced by casing. For example, Table 1 shows that Transformer MT models trained with standard SentencePiece (SPM) segmentation drop >30 BLEU points when translating the ALL CAPS version. The target sequence length also increases dramatically, which leads to ≈3x slower translation. Prior work (Berard et al., 2019; Etchegoyhen and Gete, 2020) overcame this limitation by modifying the encoding or subword vocabulary in a way that breaks the encoding optimally of perplexity driven methods, improving quality at the cost of impractical sequence length/runtime.

	de→en		en→de	
wmttest22	BLEU↑	Time↓	BLEU↑	Time↓
Standard casing	48.5	4.1	46.3	4.4
ALL CAPS	17.4	12.6	10.4	12.9

Table 1: Standard training with no handling of casing produces poor quality on the ALL CAPS version of wmttest22 and increases translation time (seconds) dramatically, when compared to the unmodified version.

In this work, we re-encode capitalization to allow the subword segmentation model to learn how to best segment this linguistic feature. We propose a novel case encoding: we lowercase the entire text, then prefix previously cased words with markers (see Table 2). Since we prefix the words, and apply case encoding before perplexity-driven subword segmentation, that algorithm learns if a case marker should be split off. Naturally occurring data accurately describes the *prevalence* of capitalization; however, it underestimates the *importance* humans ascribe to capitalization robustness. We propose data augmentation to fill this gap.

In this work, we:

- increase translation quality on data with different casings (compared to standard SPM),
- without degrading quality for standard casing,
- and with minimal impact on decoding speed.

Proceedings of the 13th International Joint Conference on Natural Language Processing and the 3rd Conference of the Asia-Pacific Chapter of the Association for Computational Linguistics (Volume 2: Short Papers), pages 146–156
November 1–4, 2023. ©2023 Association for Computational Linguistics

raw text	This · IS · a · SHORT · PHRASE · ABOUT · a · PhD.
SPM	_This · _IS · _a · _S · HO · RT · _ · PH · RA · SE · _A · BO · UT · _a · _PhD · .
BPE (lowercased) + Berard et al.	_this · _is · _a · _short · _phrase · _about · _a · _phd . _this · <T> · _is · <U> · _a · _short · <U> · _phrase · <U> · _about · <U> · _a · _ph · <T> · d · <T> · .
Etchegoyhen and Gete + BPE	° · this · °° · is · a · °° · short · °° · phrase · °° · about · a · ° · ph ° · °° · d. _° · _this · _°° · _is · _a · _°° · _short · _°° · _phrase · _°° · _about · _a · _° · _ph · _° · _°° · _d · .
our case encoding + SPM (our method)	Tthis · Uis · a · Ashort · phrase · about · La · TphTd. Tthis_ · U · is_ · a_ · A · short_ · phrase · _ · about_ · L · a_ · Tph · Td · ._

Table 2: Examples of various case encodings. For readability, we show case markers in green and use '·' for spaces between tokens. Note that our method chooses to keep *Tthis* as one token—since *This* occurs capitalized often in the data—but the *U* marker is segmented off from *is*—since that rarely occurs in ALL CAPS.

2 Prior Work

Capitalization has been studied in NLP for nearly three decades (e.g., Gale et al., 1995; Mikheev, 1999, 2002).[1] Approaches vary from modeling case directly to ignoring it and increasing sparsity.

The most common method of handling capitalization, particularly in Statistical Machine Translation (SMT), was training a separate truecaser (Lita et al., 2003; Koehn et al., 2007).[2] Truecasers have fallen out of favor since they require additional pre- and postprocessing steps. For example, at WMT22 (Kocmi et al., 2022) only 3/25 system descriptions from the General MT Task mention the use of truecasing models.

Another common option in SMT was using factored translation (Koehn and Hoang, 2007) to encode capitalization as an additional linguistic feature. Levin et al. (2017) used factors in NMT (Sennrich and Haddow, 2016; García-Martínez et al., 2016) to encode case as additional factors on the embeddings. While factors allow the model to learn representations of capitalization, they require changes to model architecture which are complicated to deploy and not universally supported in modern NLP & NMT toolkits.[3] Our proposed method is model agnostic, and requires no changes to the translation model architecture. Niu et al. (2021) and Hieber et al. (2022) further explored the factorized approach in combination with data augmentation in NMT. However, Hieber et al. observe a 1.7-2.3 BLEU drop in quality between standard and ALL CAPS text; we observe a negligible drop of $\leq$0.1 BLEU (or $\leq$0.3 ChrF) in our experiments.

Berard et al. (2019) propose 'inline casing' for capitalization robustness. Inline casing lowercases all characters and then adds additional tokens to indicate capitalization. Berard et al. train and apply a Byte Pair Encoding subword model (BPE, Sennrich et al., 2016) on lower cased data, and then add back a space-separated case-marker token after each token that was cased. Etchegoyhen and Gete (2020) propose a variant where capitalization tokens are inserted as space-separated prefix tokens prior to learning the BPE segmentation. See Table 2 for examples of both case encodings.

Both methods can lead to considerably longer sequences, since they force additional tokens per cased tokens/words (respectively). This drastically impacts decoding speed, particularly for long sequences, as Transformer decoders are quadratic in output length.

Despite various options for case-handling, the current standard practice in NMT is using subword segmentation—e.g., SentencePiece (SPM; Kudo and Richardson, 2018)—without dedicated case processing. This often leads to the same sentence in different capitalizations encoded very differently, since case is not segmentable.

As noted in Kudo (2018, §3.4) SPM can be viewed as a compression method;[4] given a predefined vocab size, it will result in a (near) optimal sequence length for the training corpus. An interesting consequence of this is that a post-hoc manipulation will result in a longer sequence length. For example, adding a case marker after each to-

[1]Capitalization can convey semantic meaning, particularly for word sense disambiguation terminology: e.g., *Apple* the company vs *apple* the fruit (Mayhew et al., 2019; Gujral et al., 2016; Thompson et al., 2019; Alam et al., 2021).

[2]`github.com/moses-smt/mosesdecoder/blob/master/scripts/recaser/train-truecaser.perl`

[3]Fairseq (Ott et al., 2019), Hugging Face (Wolf et al., 2020), and NeMo (Kuchaiev et al., 2019) do not have factors. OpenNMT-py has source-side only (Klein et al., 2017). Marian (Junczys-Dowmunt et al., 2018), Nematus (Sennrich et al., 2017) and Sockeye (Hieber et al., 2022) have source & target.

[4]The same is true for BPE (Sennrich et al., 2016), which is a compression algorithm applied to segmentation.

ken after segmentation (Berard et al., 2019) will double the sequence length of an ALL CAPS sentence. This drastically increases decoding time, particularly for long sequences, as Transformer decoders are quadratic in output length. In contrast to Berard et al. and Etchegoyhen and Gete, our case marker is not initially space-separated from the word it marks, allowing SentencePiece (SPM) to learn where to segment for an optimal length. This results in shorter sequences and faster decoding.

3 Method

We introduce a case encoding method (§ 3.1) with data augmentation (§ 3.2) which allows the SPM algorithm to learn to segment case markings.

3.1 Case Encoding

Our encoding consists of the following steps, as demonstrated in Table 3.

1. **Character-level tagging**: pre-built case normalization tables map each cased character to a case tag + lower case character. P is used for punctuation, U is used for capitalization.
2. **Word-level tagging**: a state machine aggregates (1) into word-level case labels. T is used for word initial Capitalization, U is used for fully CAPITALIZED words.
3. **Span tagging**: A hand-tuned regex determines inter-word span labels: sequences of 3 or more words in ALL CAPS are marked with A; L denotes that the prior capitalization has ended.

After decoding, and removing the subword segmentation, these annotations are used to reconstruct the correctly cased text inside the SPM library.[5]

3.2 Data Augmentation

SPM maximizes the likelihood over its training data. While naturally occurring data accurately describes the *prevalence* of capitalization, it underestimates the *importance* humans ascribe to case handling (as evidenced by poor robustness of data-driven methods to such changes). We propose data augmentation to bridge the gap. We convert a small fraction of the (SPM and NMT model) training data to lowercase, ALL CAPS and (when applicable) English Title Case.[6] Lower casing and English Title Case are applied to the source only; ALL CAPS is applied to both the source and target, only if the source language script supports capitalization.

4 Experiments

4.1 Models

We train 12 layer Transformer big translation models using Marian NMT (Junczys-Dowmunt et al., 2018) and use a SentencePiece vocabulary size of 32k with the unigram model. See Appendix A.1 for full training details. For prior work, we follow their methods which use the BPE segmentation algorithm (Sennrich et al., 2016). Our experiments include:

1. No dedicated case encoding.
2. Berard et al.'s inline case encoding (§ 2) where markers are added *per subword*.
3. Etchegoyhen and Gete's inline case encoding (§ 2) where markers are added *per word*.
4. Our proposed case encoding method (§ 3.1).

We present experiments with data augmentation for the baseline and our case encoding for all language pairs. To ensure a thorough comparison we also add data augmentation to prior work—which did not propose augmenation—for en↔de. We use data augmentation 3% of the time for each type of augmentation. We considered 1% and 3% training data augmentation in pilot experiments. 3% worked well without quality degradation on standard test sets, so we use it throughout this work.

4.2 Implementation Details

We implement our inline casing directly in the SPM library, which has several advantages:

- Drop-in replacement for standard SPM: tools with support for SPM can take advantage of the built-in case encoding without additional pre/post-processing wrappers.
- Operates on raw text: no tokenization is needed, just like standard SPM.
- Processing speed: the normalization in SPM which we used for the character-level tagging (see Table 3) is highly optimized C++ code.

We leverage the case augmentation methods available within the Marian NMT Toolkit. A fixed

[5]We use `treat_white-space_as_suffix` in SPM to suffix space markers, so case markers are the only prefix.

[6]Case conventions in English titles vary, but typically all words except articles, prepositions, and conjunctions are capitalized. See `en.wikipedia.org/wiki/Title_case`.

0) raw text	This · IS · a · SHORT · PHRASE · ABOUT · a · PhD.
1) character-level tagging	Uthis · UiUs · a · UsUhUoUrUt · UpUhUrUaUsUe · UaUbUoUuUt · a · UphUdP.
2) word-level tagging	Tthis · Uis · a · Ushort · Uphrase · Uabout · a · TphTd.
3) span tagging	Tthis · Uis · a · Ashort · phrase · about · La · TphTd.
4) SPM	Tthis_ · U · is_ · a_ · A · short_ · phrase · _ · about_ · L · a_ · Tph · Td · ._

Table 3: Steps of our case encoding algorithm. We show case markers in green and use '·' for spaces.

	unmodified			ALL CAPS			lower			Title Case		
en → de	ChrF↑	TrgLen↓	Time (sec)↓	ChrF↑	TrgLen↓	Time (sec)↓	ChrF↑	TrgLen↓	Time (sec)↓	ChrF↑	TrgLen↓	Time (sec)↓
no case encoding	66.2	24.6	4.4 (base)	35.2	43.7	12.9 (+195%)	63.8	24.8	**4.4** (+2%)	63.3	24.8	**4.4** (+1%)
+ our data augment	66.3	24.6	**4.3** (-2%)	60.9	48.3	9.7 (+123%)	65.5	24.6	4.5 (+4%)	65.3	24.7	**4.4** (+1%)
Berard et al.	64.9	29.7	6.0 (+38%)	56.9	42.5	8.9 (+104%)	63.5	29.0	5.9 (+34%)	63.4	30.1	6.0 (+38%)
+ our data augment	65.1	29.4	5.2 (+20%)	66.6	44.1	8.4 (+93%)	64.5	29.1	5.1 (+16%)	64.5	29.5	5.5 (+26%)
Etchegoyhen and Gete	66.0	30.0	5.3 (+22%)	54.6	38.8	7.5 (+72%)	64.3	29.7	5.3 (+22%)	64.4	30.9	5.8 (+33%)
+ our data augment	66.4	30.1	5.4 (+25%)	**66.6**	40.3	7.5 (+72%)	**65.6**	30.0	5.3 (+21%)	65.5	30.5	5.7 (+31%)
our case encoding	**66.5**	25.3	4.5 (+4%)	35.2	26.7	**4.8** (+9%)	64.1	25.3	4.5 (+4%)	64.5	25.7	4.7 (+9%)
+ our data augment	66.3	25.4	4.6 (+5%)	66.0	26.9	**4.8** (+9%)	65.4	25.3	4.5 (+2%)	**66.5**	25.6	4.7 (+9%)

Table 4: Results for en→de. We outperform the no case encoding baseline on ChrF and decoding time, and are less than 10% longer than the baseline's encoding of unmodified text for the case variants.

fraction of the training data is transformed dynamically during the training for each batch, prior to applying SPM.[7]

4.3 Training Data

We use the WMT 2022 training data (Kocmi et al., 2022)[8]—including the potentially noisy ParaCrawl data (Bañón et al., 2020)—and use the sentence filtering pipeline released by Thompson and Post (2020a,b)[9] to reduce noise (Khayrallah and Koehn, 2018).

We train models for English↔German as an example of a high resource language pair (234M lines), plus English↔Japanese (26M lines) and English↔Russian (27M lines) to have a variety of scripts. See Appendix A.2 for data sources and filtering details.

4.4 Evaluation

We evaluate on `wmttest22` (Kocmi et al., 2022).

Robustness: We create additional synthetic robustness testsets by transforming `wmttest22` to lower case, ALL CAPS, or English Title Case. We apply ALL CAPS to both the source and target. For lowercase and English Title case the target side remains unmodified; ALL CAPS is introduced only if the source language support capitalization, and title-case only when English is the source text.

Metrics: Casing alters characters, hence we use ChrF (Popović, 2015) which correlates better with human judgment than BLEU (Kocmi et al., 2021). See Appendix B for BLEU (Papineni et al., 2002) and COMET (Rei et al., 2020) scores on the unmodified `wmttest22`.

Speed: We report speed as the average of 3 runs on a NVIDIA Zotac Trinity 4090 GPU.

5 Results

Table 4 shows results on the unmodified `wmttest22` and the robustness versions (ALL CAPS, lowercase, and English Title Case) for en→de. See Appendix B for de→en, en↔ru, and en↔ja. Our proposed method—case encoding + data augmentation—performs well across the board.

On unmodified data, our method performs as well as the no case encoding and no data augmentation baseline (±0.1 ChrF point); in other words, our method does not negatively impact the performance on texts with standard casing.

This is not true for prior work across all language pairs: quality on the unmodified `wmttest22` drops by up to 1.3 ChrF for Berard et al. (en-de) and up to 0.8 ChrF for Etchegoyhen and Gete (en-ja) when using those methods as originally proposed (i.e. without augmentation).

When evaluating in all language pairs and on all

[7] Offline data prepossessing is also an augmentation option. Another option is to use a data streaming approach supporting casing augmentation, such as Sotastream (Post et al., 2023).

[8] `statmt.org/wmt22/translation-task.html`

[9] `github.com/thompsonb/prism_bitext_filter`

casings our encoding is within 9% of runtime of standard SPM-trained model (no case encoding) for the unmodified test set. Our minimal increases in target sequence length mean that no matter the casing of the input, the runtime will be reasonable and stable.

In contrast, prior work significantly increases time even for the standard text, by up to 38% (en-de Berard et al.), which is impractical for a general MT model. The baseline is up to 4× slower on ALL CAPS (ru→en), while prior work is at least 49% slower across languages and up to 2.5× slower (de→en). Even when combining with our augmentation method, prior encodings are approximately 1.7× or 2.0× slower. `wmttest22` has an average of 16 words/sentence. Since Transformer decoders are quadratic in the output sequence length, this problem is even worse with longer sequences, e.g., for full document context in a document level MT system (Post and Junczys-Dowmunt, 2023) or a Large Language Model (Brown et al., 2020).

Data augmentation is crucial. Standard SPM with augmentation already matches or outperforms the quality of prior work without augmentation (at the cost of >2× slower translation of ALL CAPS data, as compared to runtime of standard SPM for unmodified data). Without our proposed augmentation method, both prior works perform poorly on ALL CAPS data. Adding our augmentation improves their quality, but runtimes remain impractical. We require augmentation for high quality but then have an advantageous combination of quality and speed.

6 Conclusion

Data-driven segmentation models are not aware of case and underestimate the importance of it; prior work addresses this in a way that breaks the encoding optimality of perplexity driven methods (resulting in much longer sequence lengths). We fix both by introducing a novel case encoding that allows the SPM algorithm to learn how to segment case markings, and introducing data augmentation. Our work increases translation quality on data with different casings (compared to standard SPM), without degrading quality for standard casing, and with minimal impact on decoding speed.

7 Limitations

While we attempt a thorough analysis, there are limitations to what we present.

We consider two different writing systems that use capitalization (Latin script, and the Cyrillic alphabet) and one that does not (Japanese) but this does not cover all writing systems. In particular, Armenian, Georgian and Greek alphabets use capitalization, but we do not demonstrate our method for them. We are limited in the total number of language pairs we can consider, and while we do not have a reason to believe this method will not extend to those alphabets, we leave that exploration to future work.

All our language pairs include English. Future work could investigate the results when translating between two morphological richer languages.

While we are able to encode mixed case words, we do not augment for them, nor do we test on them. This handles mixed case terms that occur naturally in text with reasonable frequency (e.g., PhD) but may not be ideal for some kinds of noisy text (e.g., sPoNgEbob MoCkINg texT[10]).

Finally, while we explore different data resource levels, our work focuses on relatively higher resource language pairs. In general, low resource pairs tend to benefit more from reduction in sparsity and data augmentation. Future work could explore this method in very low resource settings, where training data tends to be far noisier, and investigate how that noise interacts with the method.

8 Ethics Statement

This work focuses on case robustness within standard NMT models. On one hand, the ability to translate such data well can be an advantage to the person who needs/wants to understand text with non-standard casing. On the other hand, this may mean that some text that was intentionally made hard to translate through case-obfuscation is now easier to translate.

Acknowledgments

We thank Anthony Aue, Nikolay Bogoychev, Thamme Gowda, Rebecca Knowles, Matt Post and Brian Thompson for their helpful comments and feedback on the paper.

References

Md Mahfuz Ibn Alam, Ivana Kvapilíková, Antonios Anastasopoulos, Laurent Besacier, Georgiana Dinu,

[10] `teenvogue.com/story/mocking-spongebob-meme-social-media`

Marcello Federico, Matthias Gallé, Kweonwoo Jung, Philipp Koehn, and Vassilina Nikoulina. 2021. Findings of the WMT shared task on machine translation using terminologies. In *Proceedings of the Sixth Conference on Machine Translation*, pages 652–663, Online. Association for Computational Linguistics.

Marta Bañón, Pinzhen Chen, Barry Haddow, Kenneth Heafield, Hieu Hoang, Miquel Esplà-Gomis, Mikel L. Forcada, Amir Kamran, Faheem Kirefu, Philipp Koehn, Sergio Ortiz Rojas, Leopoldo Pla Sempere, Gema Ramírez-Sánchez, Elsa Sarrías, Marek Strelec, Brian Thompson, William Waites, Dion Wiggins, and Jaume Zaragoza. 2020. ParaCrawl: Web-scale acquisition of parallel corpora. In *Proceedings of the 58th Annual Meeting of the Association for Computational Linguistics*, pages 4555–4567, Online. Association for Computational Linguistics.

Alexandre Berard, Ioan Calapodescu, Vassilina Nikoulina, and Jerin Philip. 2020. Naver labs Europe's participation in the robustness, chat, and biomedical tasks at WMT 2020. In *Proceedings of the Fifth Conference on Machine Translation*, pages 462–472, Online. Association for Computational Linguistics.

Alexandre Berard, Ioan Calapodescu, and Claude Roux. 2019. Naver labs Europe's systems for the WMT19 machine translation robustness task. In *Proceedings of the Fourth Conference on Machine Translation (Volume 2: Shared Task Papers, Day 1)*, pages 526–532, Florence, Italy. Association for Computational Linguistics.

Tom B. Brown, Benjamin Mann, Nick Ryder, Melanie Subbiah, Jared Kaplan, Prafulla Dhariwal, Arvind Neelakantan, Pranav Shyam, Girish Sastry, Amanda Askell, Sandhini Agarwal, Ariel Herbert-Voss, Gretchen Krueger, Tom Henighan, Rewon Child, Aditya Ramesh, Daniel M. Ziegler, Jeffrey Wu, Clemens Winter, Christopher Hesse, Mark Chen, Eric Sigler, Mateusz Litwin, Scott Gray, Benjamin Chess, Jack Clark, Christopher Berner, Sam McCandlish, Alec Radford, Ilya Sutskever, and Dario Amodei. 2020. Language models are few-shot learners. *CoRR*, abs/2005.14165.

Mauro Cettolo, Christian Girardi, and Marcello Federico. 2012. WIT3: Web inventory of transcribed and translated talks. In *Proceedings of the 16th Annual conference of the European Association for Machine Translation*, pages 261–268, Trento, Italy. European Association for Machine Translation.

Alexis Conneau, Kartikay Khandelwal, Naman Goyal, Vishrav Chaudhary, Guillaume Wenzek, Francisco Guzmán, Edouard Grave, Myle Ott, Luke Zettlemoyer, and Veselin Stoyanov. 2020. Unsupervised cross-lingual representation learning at scale. In *Proceedings of the 58th Annual Meeting of the Association for Computational Linguistics*, pages 8440–8451, Online. Association for Computational Linguistics.

Shuoyang Ding, Adithya Renduchintala, and Kevin Duh. 2019. A call for prudent choice of subword merge operations in neural machine translation. In *Proceedings of Machine Translation Summit XVII: Research Track*, pages 204–213, Dublin, Ireland. European Association for Machine Translation.

Kevin Duh, Paul McNamee, Matt Post, and Brian Thompson. 2020. Benchmarking neural and statistical machine translation on low-resource African languages. In *Proceedings of the 12th Language Resources and Evaluation Conference*, pages 2667–2675, Marseille, France. European Language Resources Association.

Thierry Etchegoyhen and Harritxu Gete. 2020. To case or not to case: Evaluating casing methods for neural machine translation. In *Proceedings of the 12th Language Resources and Evaluation Conference*, pages 3752–3760, Marseille, France. European Language Resources Association.

William A Gale, Kenneth W Church, and David Yarowsky. 1995. Discrimination decisions for 100,000-dimensional spaces. *Annals of Operations Research*, 55(2):323–344.

Mercedes García-Martínez, Loïc Barrault, and Fethi Bougares. 2016. Factored neural machine translation architectures. In *Proceedings of the 13th International Conference on Spoken Language Translation*, Seattle, Washington D.C. International Workshop on Spoken Language Translation.

Biman Gujral, Huda Khayrallah, and Philipp Koehn. 2016. Translation of unknown words in low resource languages. In *Conferences of the Association for Machine Translation in the Americas: MT Researchers' Track*, pages 163–176, Austin, TX, USA. The Association for Machine Translation in the Americas.

Felix Hieber, Michael Denkowski, Tobias Domhan, Barbara Darques Barros, Celina Dong Ye, Xing Niu, Cuong Hoang, Ke Tran, Benjamin Hsu, Maria Nadejde, Surafel Lakew, Prashant Mathur, Anna Currey, and Marcello Federico. 2022. Sockeye 3: Fast neural machine translation with pytorch.

Marcin Junczys-Dowmunt, Roman Grundkiewicz, Tomasz Dwojak, Hieu Hoang, Kenneth Heafield, Tom Neckermann, Frank Seide, Ulrich Germann, Alham Fikri Aji, Nikolay Bogoychev, André F. T. Martins, and Alexandra Birch. 2018. Marian: Fast neural machine translation in C++. In *Proceedings of ACL 2018, System Demonstrations*, pages 116–121, Melbourne, Australia. Association for Computational Linguistics.

Huda Khayrallah and Philipp Koehn. 2018. On the impact of various types of noise on neural machine translation. In *Proceedings of the 2nd Workshop on Neural Machine Translation and Generation*, pages 74–83, Melbourne, Australia. Association for Computational Linguistics.

Guillaume Klein, Yoon Kim, Yuntian Deng, Jean Senellart, and Alexander Rush. 2017. OpenNMT: Open-source toolkit for neural machine translation. In *Proceedings of ACL 2017, System Demonstrations*, pages 67–72, Vancouver, Canada. Association for Computational Linguistics.

Tom Kocmi, Rachel Bawden, Ondřej Bojar, Anton Dvorkovich, Christian Federmann, Mark Fishel, Thamme Gowda, Yvette Graham, Roman Grundkiewicz, Barry Haddow, Rebecca Knowles, Philipp Koehn, Christof Monz, Makoto Morishita, Masaaki Nagata, Toshiaki Nakazawa, Michal Novák, Martin Popel, Maja Popović, and Mariya Shmatova. 2022. Findings of the 2022 conference on machine translation (wmt22). In *Proceedings of the Seventh Conference on Machine Translation*, pages 1–45, Abu Dhabi. Association for Computational Linguistics.

Tom Kocmi, Christian Federmann, Roman Grundkiewicz, Marcin Junczys-Dowmunt, Hitokazu Matsushita, and Arul Menezes. 2021. To ship or not to ship: An extensive evaluation of automatic metrics for machine translation. In *Proceedings of the Sixth Conference on Machine Translation*, pages 478–494, Online. Association for Computational Linguistics.

Philipp Koehn. 2005. Europarl: A parallel corpus for statistical machine translation. In *Proceedings of Machine Translation Summit X: Papers*, pages 79–86, Phuket, Thailand.

Philipp Koehn and Hieu Hoang. 2007. Factored translation models. In *Proceedings of the 2007 Joint Conference on Empirical Methods in Natural Language Processing and Computational Natural Language Learning (EMNLP-CoNLL)*, pages 868–876, Prague, Czech Republic. Association for Computational Linguistics.

Philipp Koehn, Hieu Hoang, Alexandra Birch, Chris Callison-Burch, Marcello Federico, Nicola Bertoldi, Brooke Cowan, Wade Shen, Christine Moran, Richard Zens, Chris Dyer, Ondřej Bojar, Alexandra Constantin, and Evan Herbst. 2007. Moses: Open source toolkit for statistical machine translation. In *Proceedings of the 45th Annual Meeting of the Association for Computational Linguistics Companion Volume Proceedings of the Demo and Poster Sessions*, pages 177–180, Prague, Czech Republic. Association for Computational Linguistics.

Oleksii Kuchaiev, Jason Li, Huyen Nguyen, Oleksii Hrinchuk, Ryan Leary, Boris Ginsburg, Samuel Kriman, Stanislav Beliaev, Vitaly Lavrukhin, Jack Cook, et al. 2019. Nemo: a toolkit for building ai applications using neural modules. *arXiv preprint arXiv:1909.09577*.

Taku Kudo. 2018. Subword regularization: Improving neural network translation models with multiple subword candidates. In *Proceedings of the 56th Annual Meeting of the Association for Computational Linguistics (Volume 1: Long Papers)*, pages 66–75, Melbourne, Australia. Association for Computational Linguistics.

Taku Kudo and John Richardson. 2018. SentencePiece: A simple and language independent subword tokenizer and detokenizer for neural text processing. In *Proceedings of the 2018 Conference on Empirical Methods in Natural Language Processing: System Demonstrations*, pages 66–71, Brussels, Belgium. Association for Computational Linguistics.

Pavel Levin, Nishikant Dhanuka, Talaat Khalil, Fedor Kovalev, and Maxim Khalilov. 2017. Toward a full-scale neural machine translation in production: the booking.com use case. *CoRR*, abs/1709.05820.

Lucian Vlad Lita, Abe Ittycheriah, Salim Roukos, and Nanda Kambhatla. 2003. tRuEcasIng. In *Proceedings of the 41st Annual Meeting of the Association for Computational Linguistics*, pages 152–159, Sapporo, Japan. Association for Computational Linguistics.

Stephen Mayhew, Tatiana Tsygankova, and Dan Roth. 2019. ner and pos when nothing is capitalized. In *Proceedings of the 2019 Conference on Empirical Methods in Natural Language Processing and the 9th International Joint Conference on Natural Language Processing (EMNLP-IJCNLP)*, pages 6256–6261, Hong Kong, China. Association for Computational Linguistics.

Andrei Mikheev. 1999. A knowledge-free method for capitalized word disambiguation. In *Proceedings of the 37th Annual Meeting of the Association for Computational Linguistics*, pages 159–166, College Park, Maryland, USA. Association for Computational Linguistics.

Andrei Mikheev. 2002. Periods, capitalized words, etc. *Computational Linguistics*, 28(3):289–318.

Graham Neubig. 2011. The Kyoto free translation task. http://www.phontron.com/kftt.

Xing Niu, Georgiana Dinu, Prashant Mathur, and Anna Currey. 2021. Faithful target attribute prediction in neural machine translation. *CoRR*, abs/2109.12105.

Myle Ott, Sergey Edunov, Alexei Baevski, Angela Fan, Sam Gross, Nathan Ng, David Grangier, and Michael Auli. 2019. fairseq: A fast, extensible toolkit for sequence modeling. In *Proceedings of the 2019 Conference of the North American Chapter of the Association for Computational Linguistics (Demonstrations)*, pages 48–53, Minneapolis, Minnesota. Association for Computational Linguistics.

Kishore Papineni, Salim Roukos, Todd Ward, and Wei-Jing Zhu. 2002. Bleu: a method for automatic evaluation of machine translation. In *Proceedings of the 40th Annual Meeting of the Association for Computational Linguistics*, pages 311–318, Philadelphia, Pennsylvania, USA. Association for Computational Linguistics.

Maja Popović. 2015. chrF: character n-gram F-score for automatic MT evaluation. In *Proceedings of the Tenth Workshop on Statistical Machine Translation*, pages 392–395, Lisbon, Portugal. Association for Computational Linguistics.

Matt Post. 2018. A call for clarity in reporting BLEU scores. In *Proceedings of the Third Conference on Machine Translation: Research Papers*, pages 186–191, Brussels, Belgium. Association for Computational Linguistics.

Matt Post, Thamme Gowda, Roman Grundkiewicz, Huda Khayrallah, Rohit Jain, and Marcin Junczys-Dowmunt. 2023. Sotastream: A streaming approach to machine translation training.

Matt Post and Marcin Junczys-Dowmunt. 2023. Escaping the sentence-level paradigm in machine translation.

Reid Pryzant, Youngjoo Chung, Dan Jurafsky, and Denny Britz. 2018. JESC: Japanese-English subtitle corpus. In *Proceedings of the Eleventh International Conference on Language Resources and Evaluation (LREC 2018)*, Miyazaki, Japan. European Language Resources Association (ELRA).

Ricardo Rei, Craig Stewart, Ana C Farinha, and Alon Lavie. 2020. COMET: A neural framework for MT evaluation. In *Proceedings of the 2020 Conference on Empirical Methods in Natural Language Processing (EMNLP)*, pages 2685–2702, Online. Association for Computational Linguistics.

Roberts Rozis and Raivis Skadiņš. 2017. Tilde MODEL - multilingual open data for EU languages. In *Proceedings of the 21st Nordic Conference on Computational Linguistics*, pages 263–265, Gothenburg, Sweden. Association for Computational Linguistics.

Elizabeth Salesky, Andrew Runge, Alex Coda, Jan Niehues, and Graham Neubig. 2018. Optimizing segmentation granularity for neural machine translation. *arXiv preprint arXiv:1810.08641*.

Holger Schwenk, Vishrav Chaudhary, Shuo Sun, Hongyu Gong, and Francisco Guzmán. 2021. WikiMatrix: Mining 135M parallel sentences in 1620 language pairs from Wikipedia. In *Proceedings of the 16th Conference of the European Chapter of the Association for Computational Linguistics: Main Volume*, pages 1351–1361, Online. Association for Computational Linguistics.

Rico Sennrich, Orhan Firat, Kyunghyun Cho, Alexandra Birch, Barry Haddow, Julian Hitschler, Marcin Junczys-Dowmunt, Samuel Läubli, Antonio Valerio Miceli Barone, Jozef Mokry, and Maria Nădejde. 2017. Nematus: a toolkit for neural machine translation. In *Proceedings of the Software Demonstrations of the 15th Conference of the European Chapter of the Association for Computational Linguistics*, pages 65–68, Valencia, Spain. Association for Computational Linguistics.

Rico Sennrich and Barry Haddow. 2016. Linguistic input features improve neural machine translation. In *Proceedings of the First Conference on Machine Translation: Volume 1, Research Papers*, pages 83–91, Berlin, Germany. Association for Computational Linguistics.

Rico Sennrich, Barry Haddow, and Alexandra Birch. 2016. Neural machine translation of rare words with subword units. In *Proceedings of the 54th Annual Meeting of the Association for Computational Linguistics (Volume 1: Long Papers)*, pages 1715–1725, Berlin, Germany. Association for Computational Linguistics.

Mariya Shmatova and Anton Dvorkovich. 2022. Sakhatyla dataset.

Brian Thompson, Rebecca Knowles, Xuan Zhang, Huda Khayrallah, Kevin Duh, and Philipp Koehn. 2019. HABLex: Human annotated bilingual lexicons for experiments in machine translation. In *Proceedings of the 2019 Conference on Empirical Methods in Natural Language Processing and the 9th International Joint Conference on Natural Language Processing (EMNLP-IJCNLP)*, pages 1382–1387, Hong Kong, China. Association for Computational Linguistics.

Brian Thompson and Matt Post. 2020a. Automatic machine translation evaluation in many languages via zero-shot paraphrasing. In *Proceedings of the 2020 Conference on Empirical Methods in Natural Language Processing (EMNLP)*, pages 90–121, Online. Association for Computational Linguistics.

Brian Thompson and Matt Post. 2020b. Paraphrase generation as zero-shot multilingual translation: Disentangling semantic similarity from lexical and syntactic diversity. In *Proceedings of the Fifth Conference on Machine Translation*, pages 561–570, Online. Association for Computational Linguistics.

Thomas Wolf, Lysandre Debut, Victor Sanh, Julien Chaumond, Clement Delangue, Anthony Moi, Pierric Cistac, Tim Rault, Remi Louf, Morgan Funtowicz, Joe Davison, Sam Shleifer, Patrick von Platen, Clara Ma, Yacine Jernite, Julien Plu, Canwen Xu, Teven Le Scao, Sylvain Gugger, Mariama Drame, Quentin Lhoest, and Alexander Rush. 2020. Transformers: State-of-the-art natural language processing. In *Proceedings of the 2020 Conference on Empirical Methods in Natural Language Processing: System Demonstrations*, pages 38–45, Online. Association for Computational Linguistics.

Michał Ziemski, Marcin Junczys-Dowmunt, and Bruno Pouliquen. 2016. The United Nations parallel corpus v1.0. In *Proceedings of the Tenth International Conference on Language Resources and Evaluation (LREC'16)*, pages 3530–3534, Portorož, Slovenia. European Language Resources Association (ELRA).

	raw	filtered	retained
de↔en	295,805,439	234,074,670	79%
en↔ja	33,875,119	26,218,426	77%
en↔ru	38,188,399	27,427,929	72%

Table 5: The number of lines of training data used for each language pair, before and after data filtering.

A Training setup

For easier replication of our experiments, we describe the training settings and datasets in details.

A.1 Training parameters

We train 6+6 layer Transformer big models with 8 heads using Marian NMT (Junczys-Dowmunt et al., 2018) and use a SentencePiece (Kudo and Richardson, 2018) vocabulary size of 32k and the unigram model.[11] Figure 1 shows the Marian training and decoding parameters. The model sizes are 209M parameters.

For prior work, we follow respective setups of Berard et al. (2019) and Etchegoyhen and Gete (2020), and use the BPE segmentation algorithm (Sennrich et al., 2016).

In experiments with data augmentation, we add the following parameters [12] for Marian training:

- `--all-caps-every N`
- `--all-lower-caps-every N`
- `--english-title-case-every N`

with $N = 33$.

A.2 Datasets

We train on data from the WMT 2022 General MT Task (Kocmi et al., 2022).[13] Table 6 presents the data sources used in training for each language pair. We filter the parallel data using the sentence filtering released by Thompson and Post (2020a).[14] Table 5 shows the total number of lines before and after data filtering.

B Full results

Tables 7–11 present full results in the same format as Table 4 on robustness `wmttest22` with unmodified, ALL CAPS, lower, and Title Case casing. Accuracy is computed against the reference.

Since COMET has not been well tested on differently-cased data, nor has the underlying model (XLM-RoBERTa-base; Conneau et al., 2020), in the main body of this paper we use it only to evaluate on data with original casing. In Table 12 we compare all systems on unmodified `wmttest22` using popular MT evaluation metrics.

We used SacreBLEU v2.0.0 (Post, 2018) with `case:mixed` when computing BLEU and ChrF scores. With COMET (Rei et al., 2020), we used the `wmt20-comet-da` model.

```
type: transformer
tied-embeddings-all: true
dim-emb: 1024
enc-depth: 6
dec-depth: 6
transformer-dim-ffn: 4096
transformer-depth-scaling: true
lemma-dim-emb: 0
transformer-decoder-autoreg: self-attention
transformer-ffn-activation: relu
transformer-heads: 8
transformer-postprocess-emb: d
transformer-postprocess: dan
transformer-dropout: 0.1
transformer-dropout-attention: 0
transformer-dropout-ffn: 0
cost-type: ce-sum
label-smoothing: 0.1
optimizer: adam
learn-rate: 0.0002
lr-warmup: 4000
lr-decay-inv-sqrt: 4000
mini-batch-round-up: true
optimizer-params:
  - 0.9
  - 0.999
  - 1e-08
  - 0.01
clip-norm: 0
dynamic-gradient-scaling:
  - 2
  - log
exponential-smoothing: 1e-3
mini-batch-fit: true
mini-batch-fit-step: 5
workspace: 13000
maxi-batch: 1000
mini-batch: 1000
mini-batch-words: 16000
max-length: 256
early-stopping: 10
valid-mini-batch: 32
beam-size: 4
normalize: 1
word-penalty: 0
```

Figure 1: Training and decoding parameters.

[11] Since prior work has shown that subword vocab size is important (Salesky et al., 2018; Ding et al., 2019; Duh et al., 2020) we performed a small sweep in initial experiments, and base our choice of 32k on that.

[12] Available in the `rjai/case_augmentations` branch of `marian-dev` repository

[13] `statmt.org/wmt22/translation-task.html`

[14] `github.com/thompsonb/prism_bitext_filter`

	de-en	ja-en	ru-en
Europarl v10 (Koehn, 2005)	✓		
ParaCrawl v9 (Bañón et al., 2020)	✓	✓	✓
Common Crawl (`statmt.org/wmt13/training-parallel-commoncrawl.tgz`)	✓		✓
News Commentary v16 (`data.statmt.org/news-commentary/v16`)	✓	✓	✓
Yandex Corpus (Shmatova and Dvorkovich, 2022)			✓
Wiki Titles v3 (`data.statmt.org/wikititles/v3`)	✓	✓	✓
UN Parallel Corpus V1.0 (Ziemski et al., 2016)			✓
Tilde MODEL corpus (Rozis and Skadiņš, 2017)	✓		✓
WikiMatrix (Schwenk et al., 2021)	✓	✓	✓
Japanese-English Subtitle Corpus (Pryzant et al., 2018)		✓	
The Kyoto Free Translation Task Corpus (Neubig, 2011)		✓	
TED Talks (Cettolo et al., 2012)		✓	

Table 6: The training data sources used for each language pair.

	unmodified			ALL CAPS			lower			Title Case		
en → ja	ChrF↑	TrgLen↓	Time↓	ChrF↑	TrgLen↓	Time↓	ChrF↑	TrgLen↓	Time↓	ChrF↑	TrgLen↓	Time↓
no case encoding	**32.0**	20.3	**3.8** (base)	20.9	24.4	10.3 (+171%)	28.3	20.4	4.1 (+9%)	29.5	20.4	4.1 (+9%)
+ our data augment	**32.0**	20.2	3.9 (+3%)	30.1	20.5	5.1 (+35%)	**31.5**	20.1	3.9 (+4%)	31.5	20.3	**3.9** (+3%)
Berard et al.	30.9	20.5	3.9 (+2%)	29.6	21.4	5.3 (+39%)	28.2	19.4	**3.7** (-1%)	29.6	20.8	4.5 (+19%)
Etchegoyhen and Gete	31.2	20.8	4.1 (+7%)	29.5	21.6	7.6 (+101%)	27.5	19.3	3.9 (+3%)	29.0	21.6	6.1 (+61%)
our case encoding	31.9	19.9	3.9 (+2%)	30.5	19.9	**3.9** (+3%)	28.5	20.2	4.5 (+19%)	30.1	20.1	4.5 (+18%)
+ our data augment	31.9	20.0	4.0 (+5%)	**31.9**	20.1	**3.9** (+2%)	31.4	19.9	3.9 (+2%)	**31.7**	20.1	4.0 (+4%)

Table 7: Results for en→ja. ChrF, target sequence length, and decoding time. Note, all results *with* data augmentation are our contribution; prior work did not use augmentation.

	unmodified			ALL CAPS			lower			Title Case		
en → ru	ChrF↑	TrgLen↓	Time↓	ChrF↑	TrgLen↓	Time↓	ChrF↑	TrgLen↓	Time↓	ChrF↑	TrgLen↓	Time↓
no case encoding	52.9	26.0	4.9 (base)	25.0	65.9	19.4 (+297%)	49.3	25.9	4.9 (+1%)	48.5	26.4	5.0 (+3%)
+ our data augment	52.9	26.0	**4.8** (-2%)	46.3	66.3	15.0 (+206%)	52.1	25.9	4.8 (-3%)	51.2	26.2	**5.0** (+1%)
Berard et al.	53.0	26.9	5.4 (+11%)	43.7	42.4	11.3 (+131%)	50.8	25.3	5.6 (+15%)	49.9	27.7	7.0 (+42%)
Etchegoyhen and Gete	**53.3**	26.7	**4.8** (-2%)	45.3	37.3	7.3 (+49%)	50.4	25.3	**4.7** (-4%)	50.2	27.7	5.3 (+9%)
our case encoding	53.2	27.2	5.2 (+6%)	37.6	27.1	**4.8** (-1%)	50.1	26.1	4.8 (-3%)	50.5	28.0	5.4 (+10%)
+ our data augment	53.0	27.3	4.9 (-1%)	**53.3**	27.0	4.9 (+0%)	**52.2**	27.1	4.9 (-0%)	**52.6**	27.5	5.2 (+5%)

Table 8: Results for en→ru: ChrF, target sequence length, and decoding time. Note, all results *with* data augmentation are our contribution; prior work did not use augmentation.

	unmodified			ALL CAPS			lower		
de → en	ChrF↑	TrgLen↓	Time↓	ChrF↑	TrgLen↓	Time↓	ChrF↑	TrgLen↓	Time↓
no case encoding	65.2	21.3	4.1 (base)	39.4	36.0	12.6 (+207%)	60.3	22.0	4.2 (+2%)
+ our data augment	65.2	21.4	**4.0** (-2%)	61.3	37.7	10.1 (+146%)	63.6	21.3	4.1 (+0%)
Berard et al.	64.3	23.1	4.4 (+7%)	62.0	37.4	8.6 (+110%)	59.9	21.2	4.8 (+17%)
+ our data augment	64.6	23.1	4.4 (+7%)	65.5	38.0	7.4 (+80%)	63.8	22.8	4.3 (+5%)
Etchegoyhen and Gete	65.1	23.2	4.5 (+10%)	61.9	35.6	10.2 (+149%)	60.1	21.2	**4.0** (-2%)
+ our data augment	65.1	23.2	4.5 (+10%)	65.4	36.1	7.1 (+73%)	63.8	23.0	4.4 (+7%)
our case encoding	65.2	21.9	4.1 (0%)	54.9	23.1	**4.2** (+2%)	61.2	21.9	4.2 (+2%)
+ our data augment	**65.3**	21.9	4.2 (+2%)	**65.7**	22.8	**4.2** (+2%)	**64.3**	21.8	4.1 (+0%)

Table 9: Results for de→en: ChrF, target sequence length, and decoding time. Note, all results *with* data augmentation are our contribution; prior work did not use augmentation.

ja → en	unmodified ChrF↑	TrgLen↓	Time↓
no case encoding	45.9	20.9	6.1 (base)
Berard et al.	43.4	25.9	7.8 (+28%)
Etchegoyhen and Gete	45.5	22.8	5.5 (-10%)
our case encoding	45.8	21.2	6.1 (+1%)

Table 10: Results for ja→en: ChrF, target sequence length, and decoding time. Note, all results *with* data augmentation are our contribution; prior work did not use augmentation.

	unmodified			ALL CAPS			lower		
ru → en	ChrF↑	TrgLen↓	Time↓	ChrF↑	TrgLen↓	Time↓	ChrF↑	TrgLen↓	Time↓
no case encoding	63.9	24.9	4.6 (base)	26.4	50.5	19.3 (+322%)	61.4	25.2	4.8 (+5%)
+ our data augment	63.6	24.9	4.8 (+4%)	56.4	52.3	12.0 (+161%)	62.9	25.0	4.7 (+3%)
Berard et al.	63.3	26.7	4.8 (+4%)	46.7	39.5	9.0 (+97%)	61.5	25.8	4.8 (+4%)
Etchegoyhen and Gete	63.6	26.9	5.0 (+8%)	46.6	36.7	8.5 (+86%)	61.4	26.0	4.9 (+6%)
our case encoding	63.9	25.5	4.8 (+6%)	32.2	26.1	6.0 (+30%)	61.9	25.1	4.8 (+4%)
+ our data augment	**64.0**	25.5	**4.5** (-1%)	**64.1**	26.2	**4.7** (+3%)	**63.3**	25.4	**4.6** (+1%)

Table 11: Results for ru→en: ChrF, target sequence length, and decoding time. Note, all results *with* data augmentation are our contribution; prior work did not use augmentation.

	en→de			en→ja			en→ru		
Method	BLEU	ChrF	COMET	BLEU	ChrF	COMET	BLEU	ChrF	COMET
no case encoding	46.3	66.2	54.3	22.8	**32.0**	**48.1**	26.7	52.9	43.8
+ our data augment	46.3	66.3	54.3	**22.9**	**32.0**	47.4	26.9	52.9	43.0
Berard et al.	44.1	64.9	50.0	21.8	30.9	42.9	26.4	53.0	41.7
Etchegoyhen and Gete	46.5	66.0	54.0	22.1	31.2	44.6	**27.2**	**53.3**	45.8
our case encoding	46.5	**66.5**	54.9	22.8	**31.9**	47.6	27.1	53.2	**46.9**
+ our data augment	**46.6**	66.3	**55.0**	22.7	31.9	47.5	27.1	53.0	45.1

	de→en			ja→en			ru→en		
Method	BLEU	ChrF	COMET	BLEU	ChrF	COMET	BLEU	ChrF	COMET
no case encoding	48.5	65.2	54.7	20.0	**46.0**	24.5	38.7	64.0	49.9
+ our data augment	48.6	65.2	54.1	—	—	—	38.2	63.5	49.4
Berard et al.	46.9	64.3	51.7	16.9	43.9	15.8	37.3	63.3	49.2
Etchegoyhen and Gete	48.4	65.1	53.9	19.5	45.5	23.1	37.9	63.6	49.5
our case encoding	48.4	65.2	**55.1**	**20.1**	**46.0**	**25.8**	38.7	**64.0**	**50.9**
+ our data augment	**48.7**	**65.3**	**55.1**	—	—	—	**39.0**	**64.0**	50.2

Table 12: Results out of (top table) and into (bottom table) English on the unmodified `wmttest22` testset. Since Japanese does not mark capitalization, there is no augmentation for ja→en.

Enhancing Open-Domain Table Question Answering via Syntax- and Structure-aware Dense Retrieval

Nengzheng Jin[1], **Dongfang Li**[1], **Junying Chen**[1], **Joanna Siebert**[1], **Qingcai Chen**[1,2*]
[1]Harbin Institute of Technology (Shenzhen), Shenzhen, China
[2]Peng Cheng Laboratory
{nengzhengjin,crazyofapple,junying.chen.cs,joannasiebert}@gmail.com
qingcai.chen@hit.edu.cn

Abstract

Open-domain table question answering aims to provide answers to a question by retrieving and extracting information from a large collection of tables. Existing studies of open-domain table QA either directly adopt text retrieval methods or consider the table structure only in the encoding layer for table retrieval, which may cause syntactical and structural information loss during table scoring. To address this issue, we propose a syntax- and structure-aware retrieval method for the open-domain table QA task. It provides syntactical representations for the question and uses the structural header and value representations for the tables to avoid the loss of fine-grained syntactical and structural information. Then, a syntactical-to-structural aggregator is used to obtain the matching score between the question and a candidate table by mimicking the human retrieval process. Experimental results show that our method achieves the state-of-the-art on the NQ-tables dataset and overwhelms strong baselines on a newly curated open-domain Text-to-SQL dataset[1].

1 Introduction

Open-domain table QA uncovers the necessity of table retrieval for practical applications. It slightly differs from most table QA tasks (e.g., table semantic parsing (Yin and Neubig, 2018; Wang et al., 2020) and end-to-end table QA (Müller et al., 2019; Eisenschlos et al., 2021)), which typically assume that the relevant tables of a question are provided at test time. This assumption can hardly hold when the user is asking questions through some open-domain natural language interface or querying large databases.

Hence, some recent studies (Herzig et al., 2021; Chen et al., 2022; Zhong et al., 2022) have started to explore open-domain table QA. Generally, these

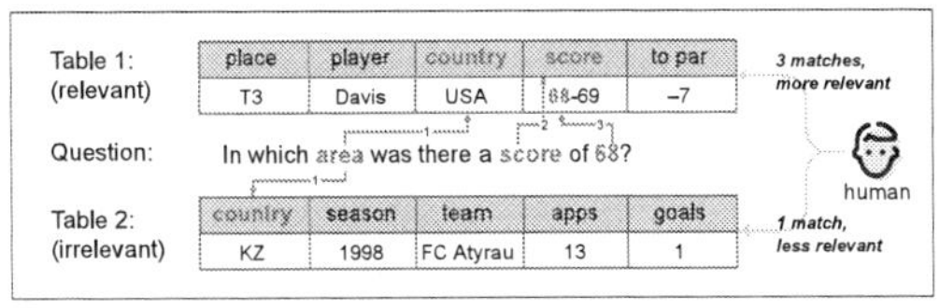

Figure 1: Illustration of fine-grained semantic matching when a human retrieves relevant tables for a question. If more fine-grained matches are found in a table, one will treat the table as more relevant.

methods are based on a two-stage framework, namely the retriever-reader (parser) framework. In such frameworks, the retriever is utilized to obtain relevant tables of the given question and the reader (parser) provides answers to the question directly or parses the question into an SQL query.

Since retrieval is the first key factor for open-domain table QA, recent works have investigated different approaches for table retrieval, which could be broadly classified into two categories. One is directly adopting text retrieval methods for table retrieval. Such methods typically linearize the tables into text and apply sparse text retrieval (e.g., BM25) (Li et al., 2021) or dense passage retrieval with a Bi-encoder model (Oguz et al., 2022; Chen et al., 2021; Huang et al., 2022). Another direction is to follow the framework of text retrieval models while also considering the unique characteristics of tables. For instance, DTR (Herzig et al., 2021) follows the Bi-encoder framework but incorporates row/column features into the table encoder, aiming to specify the cell location and enhance table understanding. UTP (Chen et al., 2023) introduces pre-training and cross-model contrastive regularization for better tabular understanding.

Although some of these methods (Herzig et al., 2021; Chen et al., 2023) have modeled the characteristics of tables, they still have two shortages. First, the learned tabular semantics may be compromised when all token embeddings are combined

*Corresponding author.

[1]The data and processing code are publicly available at https://github.com/nzjin/ODTQA.

Proceedings of the 13th International Joint Conference on Natural Language Processing and the 3rd Conference of the Asia-Pacific Chapter of the Association for Computational Linguistics (Volume 2: Short Papers), pages 157–165
November 1–4, 2023.

into a single table representation in the Bi-encoder retrieval framework (Gillick et al., 2018). Second, they neglect that table retrieval is a fine-grained semantic matching problem. As illustrated in Figure 1, humans would consciously match each meaningful phrase in the question to the table columns and rank the candidate tables by the matching degree.

Motivated by this, we propose a syntax- and structural-aware dense retrieval method to mimic this fine-grained matching process. We first apply syntax analysis to extract all possible meaningful phrases. Then, a corresponding syntactical representation is generated for each meaningful phrase based on the phrase token embeddings. To obtain fine-grained structural representations, we provide one representation for each table header. Further, we observe that the semantics of a table header and its value may be different; for example, a header may be "age" but the corresponding values are numbers. Therefore, we also provide one representation for the values of a column to retain the structural semantics better. Finally, the matching score between the question and a candidate table is obtained by performing syntactical-to-structural aggregation over the fine-grained representations, wherein the aggregation is analogous to the human behavior of counting matches.

2 Methodology

2.1 Overview

As shown in Figure 2, our proposed retrieval model comprises of 1) *Syntactical representation module* that generates fine-grained syntactical representations for the question; 2) *Structural representation module* that generates a limited number of structural representations for a table; 3) *Syntactical-to-structural aggregator* that produces the matching score between the question and a candidate table.

2.2 Syntactical Question Representation

Explicit syntactical representations. We utilize an explicit syntax parser from the Natural Language Toolkit (NLTK) (Bird et al., 2009) to extract the noun phrases in the question. To generate the question representations, we first feed the question tokens of length L into the encoder and treat the hidden states of the last layer as question token embeddings $\{\mathbf{h}_l\}_{l=1}^{L}$. Then, we apply a mean pooling function over the token embeddings that belong to a phrase, thus obtaining one representation $\mathbf{q}_i$ for the ith phrase in the question:

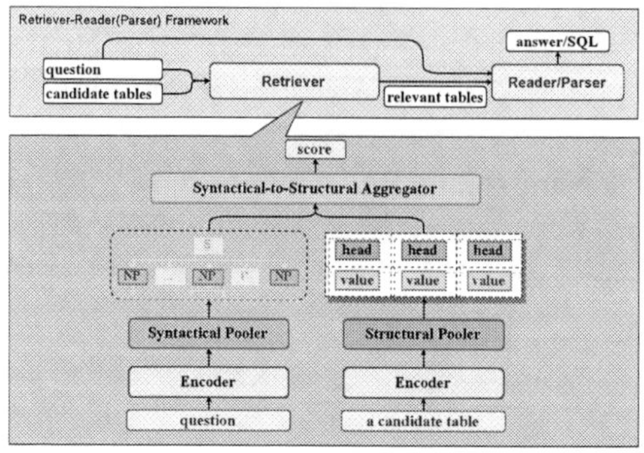

Figure 2: Illustration of the retriever-reader (parser) framework and our proposed retriever. Here, *head* and *value* denote the structural table representations. *NP* (noun phrase) denotes a syntactical question representation.

$$\mathbf{q}_i = \text{Pooling}(\mathbf{h}_{start_i}, ..., \mathbf{h}_{end_i}), \quad (1)$$

where $start_i$ and end_i denote the token span of the ith phrase. Applying the same operation for each phrase, we obtain a small group of fine-grained syntactical representations $\{\mathbf{q}_i\}_{i=1}^{n}$, where n is the number of the syntactical representations.

Implicit syntactical representations. Since explicit syntax parsing is associated with additional preprocessing time, we provide an implicit syntactical representation approach that does not require syntax parsing. It attempts to learn a static number of syntactical representations through an attentive learning mechanism based on the token embeddings $\{\mathbf{h}_l\}_{l=1}^{L}$. Specifically, we first define a set of randomly initialized learning embeddings $\{\mathbf{a}_i\}_{i=1}^{n}$. Then, we feed $\{\mathbf{a}_i\}_{i=1}^{n}$ and $\{\mathbf{h}_l\}_{l=1}^{L}$ into an attention layer to generate the final syntactical representations $\{\mathbf{q}_i\}_{i=1}^{n}$, where $\mathbf{q}_i$ is learned as in Eqn. 2 and Eqn. 3.

$$\mathbf{q}_i = \sum_l \mathbf{w}_l^i \mathbf{h}_l \quad (2)$$

$$(\mathbf{w}_1^i, .., \mathbf{w}_L^i) = \text{softmax}(\mathbf{a}_i \cdot \mathbf{h}_1, .., \mathbf{a}_i \cdot \mathbf{h}_L). \quad (3)$$

Here, $\mathbf{a}_i$ is used as a seed to learn an implicit syntactical representation $\mathbf{q}_i$ during training.

2.3 Structural Table Representation

For each candidate table, we linearize the table into a sequence by concatenating the columns, wherein a column sequence consists of the column name (also referred to as the header) and column values.

Then, we use the same encoder to encode the table sequence of length T. After obtaining table token embeddings $\{\mathbf{s}_l\}_{l=1}^{T}$, we apply a mean pooling function over the embeddings of each column name to generate a header representation $\mathbf{c}_j^{head}$. Additionally, we perform the same pooling function over the column value to generate a value representation $\mathbf{c}_j^{val}$. The pooling is only applied to the first column value rather than all values as it proved to be more effective and efficient in our preliminary experiments. After that, we obtain two representations for the jth column as follows:

$$\mathbf{c}_j^{head} = \text{Pooling}(\mathbf{s}_{start_j^{head}}, .., \mathbf{s}_{end_j^{head}}), \quad (4)$$

$$\mathbf{c}_j^{val} = \text{Pooling}(\mathbf{s}_{start_j^{val}}, .., \mathbf{s}_{end_j^{val}}). \quad (5)$$

Here, $start_j^{head/val}$ and $end_j^{head/val}$ represent the token span corresponding to the header (value) of the jth column.

2.4 Syntactical-to-Structural Aggregator

We obtain syntactical question representations $\{\mathbf{q}_i\}_{i=1}^{n}$ and structural table representations $\{\mathbf{c}_j\}_{j=1}^{2m}$ after representation generation, where $\{\mathbf{c}_j\}_{j=1}^{2m}$ includes $\{\mathbf{c}_j^{head}\}_{j=1}^{m}$ and $\{\mathbf{c}_j^{val}\}_{j=1}^{m}$, and m is the number of columns. Then, we perform a *maxsim* operation (Khattab and Zaharia, 2020; Luan et al., 2021a) over the syntactical and structural representations to retrieve tables. Specifically, we calculate the dot product similarity between each syntactical representation $\mathbf{q}_i$ and each structural representation $\mathbf{c}_j$ to obtain a fine-grained matching score w_{ij} as follows:

$$w_{ij} = \mathbf{q}_i \cdot \mathbf{c}_j \quad (6)$$

$$Score = \sum_{i}^{n} \max_{j \in [1,2m]} w_{ij}. \quad (7)$$

Subsequently, we select the fine-grained score of the most matched column for each syntactical representation and sum up all the greatest fine-grained scores as the final matching score between the question and a candidate table. This is analogous to the process of a human finding a match for each phrase and counting the number of matches when retrieving tables.

3 Experiments

3.1 Experimental Data and Settings

Datasets. We conducted experiments on two datasets: **NQ-TABLES** (Herzig et al., 2021), **WikiSQL** (Zhong et al., 2017). NQ-TABLES is an open-domain table QA database constructed from the Natural Question dataset (Kwiatkowski et al., 2019). In the original WikiSQL dataset, the relevant tables are given by humans. To simulate a realistic situation, we remove the table labeling of the questions and introduce table retrieval. Further details of the dataset modification can be seen in Appendix A. Concurrently with this work, (Kweon et al., 2023) also introduce an open-domain setting to the WikiSQL dataset but does not process those same-header database tables.

Model	R@1	R@10	R@50	EM
BM25	16.77	40.06	58.39	21.46
DTR-Schema	34.36	74.24	88.37	32.75
DTR	36.24	76.02	90.25	35.50
UTP	38.45	79.03	92.21	-
Ours(ex)	45.15	83.73	93.12	37.73
Ours(im)	**47.03**	**84.76**	**94.89**	**37.98**
With hard negatives training				
DTR	42.42	81.13	92.56	37.69
UTP	50.39	85.40	94.31	-
Tri-encoder	-	86.4	-	-
Ours(ex)	53.39	88.11	95.09	39.47
Ours(im)	**54.12**	**90.41**	**97.18**	**39.72**

Table 1: Experimental results on the NQ-TABLES dataset. R is short for recall. Here, ex/im denotes using explicit or implicit syntactical representations.

Settings. The uncased BERT-base (Devlin et al., 2019) is employed as the encoder. The number of implicit syntactical representations is set to 3 and Adam is utilized (Kingma and Ba, 2015) as the optimizer. To evaluate the performance of the retrievers, the recall@K and exact match accuracy (EM) of the final answers are utilized as the metrics. Since the focus of this work is to enhance open-domain table QA via improved retrievers, TAPAS (Herzig et al., 2020) and HydraNet (Lyu et al., 2020) are directly used as the reader (parser) on the NQ-TABLES and WikiSQL datasets, respectively.

3.2 Comparison Models

We compared the proposed retriever with the following baselines. 1) Sparse retrievers: **TF-IDF** and **BM25** (Robertson and Walker, 1994). 2) Dense retrievers using one representation, such as **Bi-encoder** (Gillick et al., 2018) with representation vectors from word2vec (w2v) and BERT, as well as **DTR** (Herzig et al., 2021) and **UTP** (Chen et al., 2023), which use a table-oriented pre-trained model as encoder. 3) Dense retrievers using multiple representations: **Tri-encoder** (Kostic et al.,

Model	R@1	R@5	R@20	EM
TF-IDF	8.93	22.86	44.05	7.24
BM25	28.19	44.71	61.22	26.18
Bi-encoder(w2v)	10.01	20.14	30.13	7.92
Bi-encoder(BERT)	48.89	73.15	86.64	41.26
MEBERT	49.05	73.30	87.34	41.32
PolyEncoder	49.33	73.61	87.78	41.63
Ours(ex)	**54.16**	**77.63**	89.81	**45.42**
Ours(im)	53.19	77.57	**90.02**	44.71

Table 2: Experimental results on the WikiSQL dataset.

2021), **PolyEncoder** (Humeau et al., 2020) and **MEBERT** (Luan et al., 2021a). We set the representation number of PolyEncoder and MEBERT to the average representation number used in our model.

3.3 Experimental Results and Analysis

Table 1 demonstrates the experimental results on the NQ-TABLES dataset. It shows that our proposed model outperforms the previous state-of-the-art model by a considerable margin with or without hard negative training (Gillick et al., 2019). Specifically, our model surpasses previous models by approximately 8 and 2 points in terms of recall@1 and EM accuracy. Furthermore, as Table 2 illustrates, our method consistently outperforms strong text retrievers on the WikiSQL dataset. This verifies the effectiveness of the proposed syntax- and structure-aware dense retrieval method.

The experimental results in Table 1 and 2 also indicate that the implicit syntactical question representations yield better performance compared to the explicit ones in most cases. The underlying reason may be that the attention layer in the implicit syntactical pooler can learn more delicate semantic information compared to simple pooling.

Ablation Study. To analyze the impact of different components of our proposed method, we conducted an ablation study in Table 3. 1) w/o $\mathcal{S}^1$ variant eliminates syntactical question representations and takes the embedding of the $[CLS]$ token in the question as the representation. The result of w/o $\mathcal{S}^1$ shows the importance of syntactical representations. Moreover, our method still outperforms text retrieval baselines in this case, which also verifies the effectiveness of structural table representations compared with multiple contextualized representations (Humeau et al., 2020; Luan et al., 2021b). 2) w/o $\mathcal{S}^2$ variant uses the embedding of the $[CLS]$ token in the table sequence as the table representation. The results of w/o $\mathcal{S}^2$, w/o $\mathcal{S}^2(head)$, and w/o $\mathcal{S}^2(value)$ indicate that structural header and value representations both contribute to better representations of a table. 3) w/o $\mathcal{S}^1 + \mathcal{S}^2$ variant leads to inferior performance but is slightly better than the w/o $\mathcal{S}^2$ variant, this suggests that the use of syntactical representations alone does not improve performance.

Model	R@1	R@5	R@20	EM
Ours(ex)	54.16	77.63	89.81	45.42
w/o $\mathcal{S}^1$	50.08	74.36	88.19	42.28
w/o $\mathcal{S}^2$ $(head)$	52.93	77.08	89.91	44.51
w/o $\mathcal{S}^2$ $(value)$	53.18	77.16	89.50	44.75
w/o $\mathcal{S}^2$	48.31	72.45	86.75	40.71
w/o $\mathcal{S}^1 + \mathcal{S}^2$	48.87	72.57	86.79	41.17

Table 3: Ablation sturdy on the WikiSQL dataset. $\mathcal{S}^1$ and $\mathcal{S}^2$ denote syntactical and structural representations.

Model	LAT.	Model	LAT.
TF-IDF	2.74	MEBERT	0.40
BM25	6.95	PolyEncoder	0.41
Bi-encoder(w2v)	0.32	Ours(ex)	$0.42 + 0.6^*$
Bi-encoder(BERT)	0.36	Ours(im)	0.47

Table 4: The retrieval latency (LAT.) per question (in milliseconds) on the WikiSQL dataset. $*$ denotes the latency of syntax parsing.

Latency Analysis. We compared the retrieval latency of the retrievers on the WikiSQL dataset. As Table 4 illustrates, our model has an acceptable latency increase compared to the baselines but makes considerable progress in retrieval performance.

4 Related Works

Open-domain table QA (ODTQA) is an extension of the closed-domain table QA task (Pasupat and Liang, 2015; Zhong et al., 2017; Yin et al., 2020; Chen et al., 2021). Traditional closed-domain table QA does not require table retrieval and can be addressed through two primary methodologies: employing end-to-end models or utilizing semantic parsing approaches. End-to-end models take both the questions and relevant tables as input, and then directly generate answers (Müller et al., 2019; Zhu et al., 2021; Nararatwong et al., 2022; Nan et al., 2022). Differently, semantic parsing approaches transform the question into a logical form (e.g., an SQL query), and then retrieve the answers by executing the logical form (Zhong et al., 2017; Yu et al., 2018; Wang et al., 2020; Zhu et al., 2021).

ODTQA is also closely related to open-domain

text-based QA (Kwiatkowski et al., 2019; Khashabi et al., 2021) and information retrieval (Luan et al., 2021a; Humeau et al., 2020; Tang et al., 2021). Compared to the text retrieval, the tabular characteristics need to be considered in ODTQA (Herzig et al., 2021; Chen et al., 2023; Kostic et al., 2021). Another task that ODTQA shares some degree of similarity with is keyword-based web table search (Zhang and Balog, 2018; Sun et al., 2019; Chen et al., 2020; Wang et al., 2021; Trabelsi et al., 2022). Compared with keyword-based web table search, table retrieval in open-domain table QA needs to process complex questions that may contain superfluous information rather than to process informative keyword queries. Hence, our work incorporates syntax analysis to extract useful syntactical representation, as well as uses simple yet effective structural representation and scoring mechanism for retrieval efficiency.

5 Conclusion

In this paper, we present a syntax- and structure-aware dense retrieval method for open-domain table QA. Specifically, our method mimics the human retrieval process by utilizing fine-grained syntactical and structural representations, as well as a syntactical-to-structural aggregator. Experimental results on two datasets demonstrate that our model surpasses the strong baselines while preserving a reasonable computation overhead.

References

Bird, Steven, Edward Loper, and Ewan Klein. 2009. *Natural Language Processing with Python*. O'Reilly Media Inc.

Nuo Chen, Linjun Shou, Ming Gong, Jian Pei, Chenyu You, Jianhui Chang, Daxin Jiang, and Jia Li. 2023. Bridge the gap between language models and tabular understanding. *CoRR*, abs/2302.09302.

Siqin Chen, Yubo Liu, Jiehui Wu, and Mengshu Hou. 2022. Retrieval augmented via execution guidance in open-domain table qa. *Proceedings of the 2022 5th International Conference on Algorithms, Computing and Artificial Intelligence*.

Wenhu Chen, Ming-Wei Chang, Eva Schlinger, William Yang Wang, and William W. Cohen. 2021. Open question answering over tables and text. In *9th International Conference on Learning Representations*, Virtual Event, Austria. OpenReview.net.

Zhiyu Chen, Mohamed Trabelsi, Jeff Heflin, Yinan Xu, and Brian D. Davison. 2020. Table search using a deep contextualized language model. In *Proceedings of the 43rd International ACM SIGIR conference on research and development in Information Retrieval, SIGIR 2020, Virtual Event, China, July 25-30, 2020*, pages 589–598. ACM.

Jacob Devlin, Ming-Wei Chang, Kenton Lee, and Kristina Toutanova. 2019. BERT: pre-training of deep bidirectional transformers for language understanding. In *Proceedings of the 2019 Conference of the North American Chapter of the Association for Computational Linguistics: Human Language Technologies, NAACL-HLT*, pages 4171–4186, Minneapolis, MN, USA. Association for Computational Linguistics.

Julian Eisenschlos, Maharshi Gor, Thomas Müller, and William W. Cohen. 2021. MATE: multi-view attention for table transformer efficiency. In *Proceedings of the 2021 Conference on Empirical Methods in Natural Language Processing, EMNLP 2021, Virtual Event / Punta Cana, Dominican Republic, 7-11 November, 2021*, pages 7606–7619. Association for Computational Linguistics.

Daniel Gillick, Sayali Kulkarni, Larry Lansing, Alessandro Presta, Jason Baldridge, Eugene Ie, and Diego García-Olano. 2019. Learning dense representations for entity retrieval. In *Proceedings of the 23rd Conference on Computational Natural Language Learning*, pages 528–537, Hong Kong, China. Association for Computational Linguistics.

Daniel Gillick, Alessandro Presta, and Gaurav Singh Tomar. 2018. End-to-end retrieval in continuous space. *CoRR*, abs/1811.08008.

Jonathan Herzig, Thomas Müller, Syrine Krichene, and Julian Eisenschlos. 2021. Open domain question answering over tables via dense retrieval. In *Proceedings of the 2021 Conference of the North American Chapter of the Association for Computational Linguistics: Human Language Technologies*, pages 512–519, Online. Association for Computational Linguistics.

Jonathan Herzig, Pawel Krzysztof Nowak, Thomas Müller, Francesco Piccinno, and Julian Martin Eisenschlos. 2020. Tapas: Weakly supervised table parsing via pre-training. In *Proceedings of the 58th Annual Meeting of the Association for Computational Linguistics*, pages 4320–4333, Online. Association for Computational Linguistics.

Junjie Huang, Wanjun Zhong, Qian Liu, Ming Gong, Daxin Jiang, and Nan Duan. 2022. Mixed-modality representation learning and pre-training for joint table-and-text retrieval in openqa. In *Findings of the Association for Computational Linguistics: EMNLP 2022*, pages 4117–4129, Abu Dhabi, United Arab Emirates. Association for Computational Linguistics.

Samuel Humeau, Kurt Shuster, Marie-Anne Lachaux, and Jason Weston. 2020. Poly-encoders: Architectures and pre-training strategies for fast and accurate multi-sentence scoring. In *8th International Conference on Learning Representations (ICLR)*, Addis Ababa, Ethiopia. OpenReview.net.

Daniel Khashabi, Amos Ng, Tushar Khot, Ashish Sabharwal, Hannaneh Hajishirzi, and Chris Callison-Burch. 2021. Gooaq: Open question answering with diverse answer types. In *Findings of the Association for Computational Linguistics: EMNLP 2021, Virtual Event / Punta Cana, Dominican Republic, 16-20 November, 2021*, pages 421–433. Association for Computational Linguistics.

Omar Khattab and Matei Zaharia. 2020. Colbert: Efficient and effective passage search via contextualized late interaction over BERT. In *Proceedings of the 43rd International ACM SIGIR conference on research and development in Information Retrieval*, pages 39–48, Virtual Event, China. ACM.

Diederik P. Kingma and Jimmy Ba. 2015. Adam: A method for stochastic optimization. In *3rd International Conference on Learning Representations (ICLR)*, San Diego, CA, USA.

Bogdan Kostic, Julian Risch, and Timo Möller. 2021. Multi-modal retrieval of tables and texts using tri-encoder models. *CoRR*, abs/2108.04049.

Sunjun Kweon, Yeonsu Kwon, Seonhee Cho, Yohan Jo, and Edward Choi. 2023. Open-wikitable: Dataset for open domain question answering with complex reasoning over table. *CoRR*, abs/2305.07288.

Tom Kwiatkowski, Jennimaria Palomaki, Olivia Redfield, Michael Collins, Ankur P. Parikh, Chris Alberti, Danielle Epstein, Illia Polosukhin, Jacob Devlin, Kenton Lee, Kristina Toutanova, Llion Jones, Matthew Kelcey, Ming-Wei Chang, Andrew M. Dai, Jakob Uszkoreit, Quoc Le, and Slav Petrov. 2019. Natural questions: a benchmark for question answering research. *Trans. Assoc. Comput. Linguistics*, 7:452–466.

Alexander Hanbo Li, Patrick Ng, Peng Xu, Henghui Zhu, Zhiguo Wang, and Bing Xiang. 2021. Dual reader-parser on hybrid textual and tabular evidence for open domain question answering. In *Proceedings of the 59th Annual Meeting of the Association for Computational Linguistics and the 11th International Joint Conference on Natural Language Processing (ACL/IJCNLP) (Volume 1: Long Papers)*, pages 4078–4088, Virtual Event. Association for Computational Linguistics.

Yi Luan, Jacob Eisenstein, Kristina Toutanova, and Michael Collins. 2021a. Sparse, dense, and attentional representations for text retrieval. *Trans. Assoc. Comput. Linguistics*, 9:329–345.

Yi Luan, Jacob Eisenstein, Kristina Toutanova, and Michael Collins. 2021b. Sparse, dense, and attentional representations for text retrieval. *Transactions of the Association for Computational Linguistics*, 9:329–345.

Qin Lyu, Kaushik Chakrabarti, Shobhit Hathi, Souvik Kundu, Jianwen Zhang, and Zheng Chen. 2020. Hybrid ranking network for text-to-sql. *CoRR*, abs/2008.04759.

Thomas Müller, Francesco Piccinno, Peter Shaw, Massimo Nicosia, and Yasemin Altun. 2019. Answering conversational questions on structured data without logical forms. In *Proceedings of the 2019 Conference on Empirical Methods in Natural Language Processing and the 9th International Joint Conference on Natural Language Processing, EMNLP-IJCNLP 2019, Hong Kong, China, November 3-7, 2019*, pages 5901–5909. Association for Computational Linguistics.

Linyong Nan, Chiachun Hsieh, Ziming Mao, Xi Victoria Lin, Neha Verma, Rui Zhang, Wojciech Kryściński, Hailey Schoelkopf, Riley Kong, Xiangru Tang, Mutethia Mutuma, Ben Rosand, Isabel Trindade, Renusree Bandaru, Jacob Cunningham, Caiming Xiong, Dragomir Radev, and Dragomir Radev. 2022. FeTaQA: Free-form table question answering. *Transactions of the Association for Computational Linguistics*, 10:35–49.

Rungsiman Nararatwong, Natthawut Kertkeidkachorn, and Ryutaro Ichise. 2022. Enhancing financial table and text question answering with tabular graph and numerical reasoning. In *Proceedings of the 2nd Conference of the Asia-Pacific Chapter of the Association for Computational Linguistics and the 12th International Joint Conference on Natural Language Processing, AACL/IJCNLP 2022 - Volume 1: Long Papers, Online Only, November 20-23, 2022*, pages 991–1000. Association for Computational Linguistics.

Barlas Oguz, Xilun Chen, Vladimir Karpukhin, Stan Peshterliev, Dmytro Okhonko, Michael Sejr Schlichtkrull, Sonal Gupta, Yashar Mehdad, and Scott Yih. 2022. Unik-qa: Unified representations of structured and unstructured knowledge for open-domain question answering. In *Findings of the Association for Computational Linguistics (NAACL)*, pages 1535–1546, Seattle, WA, United States. Association for Computational Linguistics.

Panupong Pasupat and Percy Liang. 2015. Compositional semantic parsing on semi-structured tables. In *Proceedings of the 53rd Annual Meeting of the Association for Computational Linguistics and the 7th International Joint Conference on Natural Language Processing of the Asian Federation of Natural Language Processing (Volume 1: Long Papers)*, pages 1470–1480, Beijing, China. The Association for Computer Linguistics.

Stephen E. Robertson and Steve Walker. 1994. Some simple effective approximations to the 2-poisson model for probabilistic weighted retrieval. In *Proceedings of the 17th Annual International ACM-SIGIR Conference on Research and Development in Information Retrieval.*, pages 232–241, Dublin, Ireland. ACM/Springer.

Yibo Sun, Zhao Yan, Duyu Tang, Nan Duan, and Bing Qin. 2019. Content-based table retrieval for web queries. *Neurocomputing*, 349:183–189.

Hongyin Tang, Xingwu Sun, Beihong Jin, Jingang Wang, Fuzheng Zhang, and Wei Wu. 2021. Improving document representations by generating pseudo query embeddings for dense retrieval. In *Proceedings of the 59th Annual Meeting of the Association for Computational Linguistics and the 11th International Joint Conference on Natural Language Processing (ACL/IJCNLP) (Volume 1: Long Papers)*, pages 5054–5064, Virtual Event. Association for Computational Linguistics.

Mohamed Trabelsi, Zhiyu Chen, Shuo Zhang, Brian D. Davison, and Jeff Heflin. 2022. Strubert: Structure-aware BERT for table search and matching. In *WWW '22: The ACM Web Conference 2022, Virtual Event, Lyon, France, April 25 - 29, 2022*, pages 442–451. ACM.

Bailin Wang, Richard Shin, Xiaodong Liu, Oleksandr Polozov, and Matthew Richardson. 2020. RAT-SQL: relation-aware schema encoding and linking for text-to-sql parsers. In *Proceedings of the 58th Annual Meeting of the Association for Computational Linguistics, ACL 2020, Online, July 5-10, 2020*, pages 7567–7578. Association for Computational Linguistics.

Fei Wang, Kexuan Sun, Muhao Chen, Jay Pujara, and Pedro A. Szekely. 2021. Retrieving complex tables with multi-granular graph representation learning. In *SIGIR '21: The 44th International ACM SIGIR Conference on Research and Development in Information Retrieval, Virtual Event, Canada, July 11-15, 2021*, pages 1472–1482. ACM.

Pengcheng Yin and Graham Neubig. 2018. TRANX: A transition-based neural abstract syntax parser for semantic parsing and code generation. In *Proceedings of the 2018 Conference on Empirical Methods in Natural Language Processing, EMNLP 2018: System Demonstrations, Brussels, Belgium, October 31 - November 4, 2018*, pages 7–12. Association for Computational Linguistics.

Pengcheng Yin, Graham Neubig, Wen-tau Yih, and Sebastian Riedel. 2020. Tabert: Pretraining for joint understanding of textual and tabular data. In *Proceedings of the 58th Annual Meeting of the Association for Computational Linguistics, ACL 2020, Online, July 5-10, 2020*, pages 8413–8426. Association for Computational Linguistics.

Tao Yu, Rui Zhang, Kai Yang, Michihiro Yasunaga, Dongxu Wang, Zifan Li, James Ma, Irene Li, Qingning Yao, Shanelle Roman, Zilin Zhang, and Dragomir R. Radev. 2018. Spider: A large-scale human-labeled dataset for complex and cross-domain semantic parsing and text-to-sql task. In *Proceedings of the 2018 Conference on Empirical Methods in Natural Language Processing*, pages 3911–3921, Brussels, Belgium. Association for Computational Linguistics.

Shuo Zhang and Krisztian Balog. 2018. Ad hoc table retrieval using semantic similarity. In *Proceedings of the 2018 World Wide Web Conference on World Wide Web, WWW 2018, Lyon, France, April 23-27, 2018*, pages 1553–1562. ACM.

Victor Zhong, Caiming Xiong, and Richard Socher. 2017. Seq2sql: Generating structured queries from natural language using reinforcement learning. *CoRR*, abs/1709.00103.

Wanjun Zhong, Junjie Huang, Qian Liu, Ming Zhou, Jiahai Wang, Jian Yin, and Nan Duan. 2022. Reasoning over hybrid chain for table-and-text open domain QA. *CoRR*, abs/2201.05880.

Fengbin Zhu, Wenqiang Lei, Youcheng Huang, Chao Wang, Shuo Zhang, Jiancheng Lv, Fuli Feng, and Tat-Seng Chua. 2021. TAT-QA: A question answering benchmark on a hybrid of tabular and textual content in finance. In *Proceedings of the 59th Annual Meeting of the Association for Computational Linguistics and the 11th International Joint Conference on Natural Language Processing, ACL/IJCNLP 2021, (Volume 1: Long Papers), Virtual Event, August 1-6, 2021*, pages 3277–3287. Association for Computational Linguistics.

A Dataset Modification

In the original WikiSQL dataset, tables relevant to each question are manually provided. To simulate a realistic situation, we removed the table labeling of the questions, introducing the task of table retrieval. Moreover, we merged the tables with the same headers into one distinct table, as it is implausible for an application database to accommodate two tables with identical headers. Furthermore, we created a mapping between the original tables and the distinct tables to enable using all samples for table retrieval and downstream tasks.

In consideration of the limited input length of a BERT-based encoder, we randomly sampled 5 rows of values for over-size tables, thereby obtaining smaller candidate tables during retrieval. If the resulting table sequence still exceeded the prescribed length limitation, we dynamically trimmed an equal number of values from each column until the specified limitation was met. The statistics of the processed WikiSQL dataset and the original NQ-TABLES dataset are reported in Table 5.

Dataset	Train	Dev	Test	# Tables
NQ-TABLES	9594	1068	966	169898
WikiSQL	56355	8421	15878	9898

Table 5: Statistics of NQ-TABLES and WikiSQL datasets.

B Experimental Setup

Our proposed retrieval model uses a training batch size of 144 and 128 on the NQ-TABLES dataset and WikiSQL dataset, respectively. The uncased BERT-base model is used as the encoder on two datasets. Following Tri-encoder (Kostic et al., 2021) and UTP (Chen et al., 2023), no down-projection is used for the final representations on the NQ-TABLES dataset. However, for a comprehensive evaluation, we also reported the performance of the proposed model with projection in Table 7. We trained the model for a maximum of 150 epochs on two datasets and adopted early stopping according to the recall numbers on the dev set. For efficiency, we only used the tables that appear in the dev set as the candidate pool for the early stopping, aligning with the method outlined in (Herzig et al., 2021).

We trained all models on 4 Nvidia Tesla A100 80GB GPUs. We tested each model on a single GPU. Detailed hyper-parameters for training the proposed retrieval model can be found in Table 6.

parameter	value
learning rate	2e-5
weight decay	0.01
warmup up ratio	0.05

Table 6: Hyper-parameters for training the proposed retrieval model.

Model	Size	Dim.	Bs.	R@1	R@10	R@50
DTR	large	256	256	36.24	76.02	90.25
Ours(ex)	base	256	144	41.29	82.06	91.86
Ours(im)	base	256	144	41.92	83.42	93.84

Table 7: Experimental results of the proposed method with down-projection on the NQ-TABLES dataset. Here, Size denotes the model size, Dim. denotes the dimensionality of each representation after down-projection, Bs. denotes the training batch size.

C Further Discussion

C.1 Impact of Different Pooling Functions on Performance

In the main experiments, we used the **mean pooling function** to retrieve explicit syntactical and structural representations. This function outputs the average of all input embeddings. Here, we explored the effect of two other pooling functions, namely the **max pooling function**, which selects the largest of the input embeddings as the output, and the **attentive pooling function**, which generates the output as a weighted sum of the input embeddings, with weights determined by a linear layer. As shown in Figure 8, the attentive pooling function achieves the best performance in most cases. This is likely due to the fact that the attentive pooling function is equipped with extra parameters to learn for pooling.

Model	R@1	R@5	R@20
Ours(mean pooling)	54.72	78.15	90.21
Ours(max pooling)	54.22	77.23	89.66
Ours(attentive pooling)	54.79	78.14	90.25

Table 8: Experimental results of the proposed method with different pooling functions on the WikiSQL dataset.

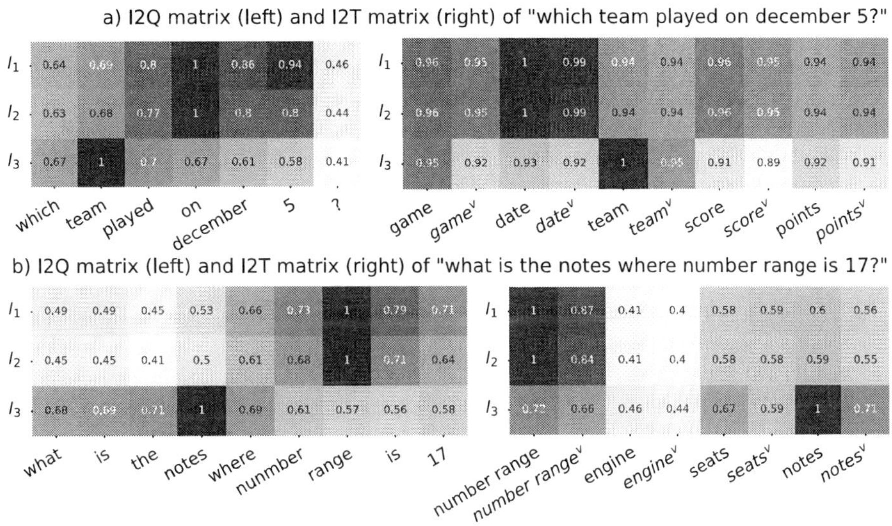

Figure 3: The coherence matrices of **I**mplicit syntactical representations ($\{I_j\}_{j=1}^3$) to **Q**uestion token embeddings (**I2Q**) and **T**able header/value representations (**I2T**). The matrices depict whether I_j learns syntactical information and matches the correct column. As shown in a), I_1 and I_2 learn information of "on December 5" and match the column "date" with the highest score. Here, $\mathbf{header^v}$ denotes value representations.

C.2 Coherence Matrices of Implicit Syntactical Representations

To investigate whether implicit syntactical representations effectively support fine-grained semantic matching akin to explicit representations, we visualized the normalized similarity matrix between implicit syntactical representations and question token embeddings (I2Q), as well as structural table representations (I2T) in Figure 3. The I2Q matrix indicates which tokens an implicit representation focuses on. Inspecting the I2Q matrix in Figure 3(a), it is clear that I_3 has the closest relationship with the phrase "*team*", while I_1 and I_2 both focus on the phrase "*on December 5*", as there are only two phrases in the question. We observe that different implicit representations usually focus on different syntactical phrases, which is similar to explicit representations. Then, carrying different syntactical information, I_j can perform neural fine-grained matching with structural header/value representations. As the I2T matrix in Figure 3(a) shows, I_3 matches the header "*team*" with the highest score, whereas I_1 and I_2 match the header and value of "*date*". Hence, the behavior of implicit representations is consistent with our design ideas.

The Language Model, Resources, and Computational Pipelines for the Under-Resourced Iranian Azerbaijani

Marzia Nouri[⋆†‡] **Mahsa Amani**[⋆†‡] **Reihaneh Zohrabi**[‡] **Ehsaneddin Asgari**[§]
[†]Language Processing and Digital Humanities Laboratory
[‡]Computer Engineering Department, Sharif University of Technology, IR
[§]AI Innovation Center, Data:Lab, Volkswagen AG, Munich, Germany
inquiries@language.ml

Abstract

Iranian Azerbaijani is a dialect of the Azerbaijani language spoken by more than 16% of the population in Iran (>14 million). Unfortunately, a lack of computational resources is one of the factors that puts this language and its rich culture at risk of extinction. This work aims to create fundamental natural language processing (NLP) resources and pipelines for the processing and analysis of Iranian Azerbaijani introducing standard datasets and starter models for various NLP tasks such as language modeling, text classification, part-of-speech (POS) tagging, and machine translation. The proposed resources have been curated and preprocessed to facilitate the development of NLP models for Iranian Azerbaijani and provide a strong baseline for further research and development. This study is an example of bridging the gap in NLP for low-resource languages and promoting the advancement of language technologies in underrepresented languages. To the best of our knowledge, for the first time, this paper presents major infrastructures for the processing and analysis of Iranian Azerbaijani, with the ultimate goal of improving communication and information access for millions of individuals. Furthermore, our translation model's online demo is accessible at https://azeri.parsi.ai/.

1 Introduction

While a few of the world's languages are blessed with a wealth of linguistic resources, most of the world's 7,000 languages are considered low-resource and face the danger of extinction (Cieri et al., 2016). Each of these low-resource languages is crucial in preserving humanity's shared heritage, benefiting all. Developing techniques for analyzing these languages is currently a major challenge in the field of NLP, especially in different regions (Zoph et al., 2016; Duthoo and Mesnard, 2018; Bansal et al., 2021; Han et al., 2022). Despite significant advancements in deep learning for NLP in high-resource languages, some low-resource languages lack even sufficient digitized raw texts (ImaniGooghari et al., 2021).

Azerbaijani, spoken in Iran, which we refer to as Iranian Azerbaijani in this paper, is a dialect of the Azerbaijani language spoken by a significant population in Iran written in Perso-Arabic script. This dialect, along with Azerbaijani spoken in Azerbaijan, which we denote as Azerbaijani, constitutes two distinct branches within the Azerbaijani language family. Azerbaijani with minor phonological, lexical, syntactic, and morphological variations uses the Latin script (Mokari and Werner, 2017; Rezaei et al., 2017). Despite the large number of speakers of Iranian Azerbaijani, the digitized resources are very limited placing this language among low-resource languages and putting this language and its associated culture at risk of extinction (Kuriyozov et al., 2020; Park et al., 2021).

Related Work

The field of low-resource language research encompasses two main streams: (i) resource building through collaborative effort (e.g. Unimorph (McCarthy et al., 2020a)) and (ii) parallel projection from high resource languages (Agić et al., 2016; Eger et al., 2018; Subburathinam et al., 2019; Xia et al., 2021), particularly from the related languages (Hedderich et al., 2021). Iranian Azerbaijani is a member of the Turkic language family, which also includes Turkish, Uzbek, Azerbaijani, Kazakh, and Uyghur (Mirzakhalov et al., 2021a).

Here we summarize the recent computational efforts on Turkic languages: **(i) High-resource Turkic NLP**: Turkish is a high-resource language among Turkic languages, with available datasets and models for various NLP tasks, such as stemming, segmentation, POS-tagging, parsing, and named entity recognition (Ehsani et al., 2012;

⋆ The first two authors contributed equally and their authorships were determined randomly.

Proceedings of the 13th International Joint Conference on Natural Language Processing and the 3rd Conference of the Asia-Pacific Chapter of the Association for Computational Linguistics (Volume 2: Short Papers), pages 166–174
November 1–4, 2023. ©2023 Association for Computational Linguistics

Safaya et al., 2022). Almost the entire NLP pipeline for Turkish exists in a toolkit, called TurkishDelightNLP (Alecakir et al., 2022). Text classification studies can also be observed for Turkish and Azerbaijani languages e.g., sentiment of social news articles in Azerbaijani (Mammadli et al., 2019), tweet topic classification (Yüksel et al., 2019) and sentiment analysis (Mutlu and Özgür, 2022) in Turkish. **(ii) Cross/multi-lingual models:** this track of research includes efforts on aligning monolingual embedding spaces of various Turkic languages, which are often affected by low-resource constraints (Kuriyozov et al., 2020). **(iii) Machine translation models:** machine translation have been developed for instances of Turkic languages (Gökırmak et al., 2019; Fatullayev et al., 2008)) as well as family-scale translations among Turkic languages (22 languages) (Mirzakhalov et al., 2021a,b). To the best of our knowledge, no prior work has developed a comprehensive NLP dataset or pipeline for Iranian Azerbaijani, which is a language spoken by more than 14 million individuals in Iran and written in the Perso-Arabic script. In addition, the translation scenario of Iranian Azerbaijani to Persian is significant in Iran as it can enhance communication among different generations and regions.

Contributions: our paper to the best of our knowledge, for the first time introduces: **(i)** comprehensive linguistic resources for Iranian Azerbaijani including raw texts of various genres, a POS-tagged corpus, text classification collection, and parallel corpora (in both Turkish and Persian) as well as **(ii)** important starter NLP models for Iranian Azerbaijani consisting of data cleanings, word embeddings, language modeling, post-tagging model, text classification models, and machine translation. Our primary focus has been to achieve a remarkable milestone by creating the first NLP pipeline and resource collection for a language spoken by at least 14 million people, while leveraging proven methodologies already established for other languages. In addition, through proposing the above-mentioned resources and models, we attempt **(iii)** to improve the language technology for the communication of millions of individuals and **(iv)** to contribute to preserving the Iranian Azerbaijani and its rich culture.

2 Materials and Methods

Workflow: the overview of our approach for Iranian Azerbaijani resource creation and model benchmarking is outlined in blocks of Figure 1: **(a) Azeri-standardization**: this part includes unifying the scripts of Azerbaijani and Iranian Azerbaijani to the Perso-Arabic script and a comprehensive preprocessing spanning removal of URLs, digits, text within parentheses, elimination of non-Azerbaijani characters, and discarding sentences shorter than 10 characters. We refer to the resulting cleaned and standardized text as Azeri-STD. **(b) Parallel dataset creation**: we create two parallel corpora for two different reasons: *Parallel to Turkish:* we use a parallel corpus between Azerbaijani and Turkish (the most high-resource Turkic language) for the purpose of annotation projection (Eger et al., 2018) and run Azeri-STD to generate the parallel corpus for the Iranian Azerbaijani, *Parallel to Persian:* we create this dataset for translation between Iranian Azerbaijani and Persian again using our Azeri-STD on collected data from different sources. **(c) Training of the starter models**: we develop and fine-tune starter models of different NLP tasks, including word embeddings, language modeling, text and token classification, and translation. **(d) Model evaluations**: we evaluate each task using appropriate metrics and evaluation datasets.

2.1 Datasets

Raw text dataset: Our monolingual data comes from two primary sources: transliterated text using a transformer-based solution (Zohrabi et al., 2023), and text originally written in the Perso-Arabic script. Table 2 provides information about our data (See Appendix A). The dataset includes $1.3M$ sentences spanning approximately $640K$ unique words.

Word analogy dataset: We propose a word analogy dataset for intrinsic evaluation of embedding spaces, inspired by previous literature such as (Gladkova et al., 2016). Our dataset includes 100 word analogies from four categories: inflectional morphology, derivational morphology, lexico-graphic, and encyclopedic semantics

Text classification dataset: For text classification, we use a collection of 400 articles from the Iranian Azerbaijani Wikipedia, divided into 4 categories: Literature, Sports, History, and Geography (100 articles per category). This dataset provides a diverse set of texts for training and evaluating text

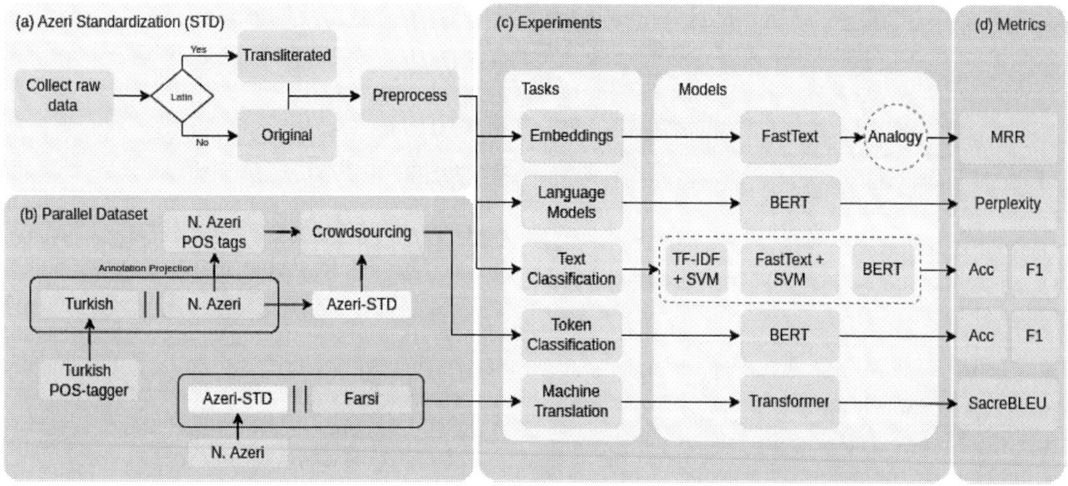

Figure 1: An overview of our pipeline for natural language processing of Iranian Azerbaijani, including data collection and preprocessing (block a), parallel corpus creation (block b), model development and fine-tuning (block c), and evaluation using various metrics (block d).

classification models. We use 80% for training and dev and 20% for test purpose.

Token classification dataset: We create a token classification dataset based on the POS-tagging of our parallel Turkish corpus. We use annotation projection techniques to align (Jalili Sabet et al., 2020) the Turkish POS-tags (Alecakir et al., 2022) with those of Azerbaijani. To ensure script consistency across the different dialects of Azerbaijani, the results are then transliterated to the Iranian Azerbaijani dialect. To improve the quality of the dataset, we leverage crowdsourcing to edit the tags. To summarize, we achieved a set of 200 tagged sentences. We use 90% for training and dev and 10% for test purpose. The agreement between the two annotators in the annotation task was evaluated using the kappa score, resulting in a value of 0.93, indicating substantial level of agreement. **Machine translation dataset:** we create a parallel dataset between Persian and Iranian Azerbaijani languages. This dataset comprises a total of 14,972 aligned sentence pairs. It is composed of three main sources (marked with (p) in Table 2 in Appendix A): 7851 pairs from the Bible (Mayer and Cysouw, 2014), 6175 pairs from the Quran [1], and 946 pairs from a compilation of short stories we carefully extracted from different web forums manually. We use 90% for training and dev and 10% for test purpose.

The only available bilingual data for Iranian Azerbaijani consists of the Quran, the Bible, and a few stories. Within the NLP community, religious texts are frequently employed as valuable resources for low-resource languages, primarily because of their inter-cultural nature, making them widely accessible across various languages (McCarthy et al., 2020b). The creation of high-quality aligned bibles in approximately 1000 languages has been a significant effort in this area (McCarthy et al., 2019).

To ensure data quality, our comprehensive preprocessing pipeline involved manual checks in some cases, successfully eliminating duplicates and noisy data from the dataset, resulting in a reduction in collection size from 2M to 1.3M sentences.

2.2 Models

Subword embedding: A proper word representation is critical for almost all NLP tasks. Since Azerbaijani languages are agglutinative, we use fastText embeddings that can properly use the subword information in the skip-gram architecture (Bojanowski et al., 2017). We evaluate this embedding extrinsically in the text classification task and intrinsically by measuring the Mean Reciprocal Rank (MRR) in the word analogy inference task.

Transformer language model: Transformer-based language-model embeddings proved to be state-of-the-art approaches on a variety of NLP tasks benefiting from proper modeling of contextual information of tokens (Devlin et al., 2019). Therefore, we train a BERT language model with a masked language modeling objective on our standardized raw text. We evaluate this model by measuring perplexity of the language model (Chen

[1] https://tanzil.net/download/

Task	Model	Evaluation Metric	Performance
Language model-based Embedding	FastText	MRR	0.46
Language Model	BERT	Perplexity	48.05
Text Classification	TF-IDF + SVM	Accuracy	0.79
	TF-IDF + SVM	F1-score	0.78
	FastText + SVM	Accuracy	0.86
	FastText + SVM	F1-score	0.86
	BERT	Accuracy	0.89
	BERT	F1-score	0.89
Token Classification	BERT POS-tagger	Accuracy	0.86
	BERT POS-tagger	Macro F1-score	0.67
Machine Translation	Text Translation azb2fa	SacreBLEU	10.34
	Text Translation fa2azb	SacreBLEU	8.07

Table 1: **Summary of performance results for various NLP tasks on Iranian Azerbaijani language.** The models and evaluation metrics are detailed for each task (azb: Iranian Azerbaijani, fa: Persian).

et al., 1998).
Text Classification: We include a text classification use case in our pipeline for Iranian Azerbaijani comparing three types of approaches: (i) an SVM model using TF-IDF embeddings, (ii) an SVM model using average fastText embeddings of a document, and (iii) supervised fine-tuning of our BERT model (Devlin et al., 2019). We evaluate the classification part by measuring accuracy and the F1 score on the test set.
Token Classification: For the example of token classification we use our POS-tagging dataset, that can benefit a range of NLP tasks. We fine-tune our BERT embedding model for the POS tagging. Since we have 11 categories, other than accuracy we evaluate the tagging on macro-F1 score as well.
Machine Translation: We train a low-resource transformer-based machine translation model between Iranian Azerbaijani and Persian. The model's computational efficiency makes it practical for use in situations where resources are limited (Kreutzer et al., 2019). We evaluate the quality of translation using the SacreBLEU (Post, 2018) on the test set.

3 Results

The objective of this research was to establish fundamental pipelines and resources for the Iranian Azerbaijani language. A collection of subword embedding (fastText), transformer language model (BERT), text classification, token classification (POS tagging), and machine translation models for Iranian Azerbaijani NLP is available at Hugging Face repository[2], with corresponding code found on GitHub[3].The obtained results are summarized in Table 1: **Embedding intrinsic evaluation:** Our fastText model obtained an MRR of 0.46 in word analogy intrinsic evaluation indicating that the model can guess the analogies on average in the second guess. **Language modeling perplexity:** We evaluated the model perplexity of our BERT language model, and achieved a perplexity score of 48.05. Given the constraints of a low-resource language, achieving a perplexity of 48.05 is quite commendable and suggests that despite the scarcity of training data, our model was able to produce relatively accurate predictions. **Text classification:** our fine-tuned BERT models performed better than the other two models on the text classification task. After the BERT model, the fastText-based baseline showed superior performance in comparison with the TF-IDF baseline (an extrinsic evaluation of the fastText embedding). We conducted a text classification comparison to showcase the impact of transliteration data for Iranian Azerbaijani in BERT masked language model pretraining. Our BERT model, trained on both transliterated and original Iranian Azerbaijani data, achieved an impressive macro-F1 of 0.89 in supervised text categorization.

[2]https://huggingface.co/language-ml-lab/iranian-azerbaijani-nlp
[3]https://github.com/language-ml/iranian-azerbaijani-nlp

In contrast, the BERT model trained solely on Iranian Azerbaijani data attained a significantly lower macro-F1 of 0.48. Moreover, training the model on transliterated data resulted in a mBert score of 0.85 macro-F1, further confirming the efficacy of utilizing transliterated data in transformer language models for downstream tasks. **Token classification:** The transformer-based tagger achieved a satisfactory performance with an accuracy of 0.86 and an F1-score of 0.67. This performance indicates that the fine-tuned BERT tagger is able to identify and classify language elements in the dataset with a moderate degree of accuracy and completeness. **Machine translation:** We assessed the model's performance using the SacreBLEU metric and obtained scores of 10.34 for Iranian Azerbaijani to Persian translation and 8.07 for Persian to Iranian Azerbaijani translation. Although these scores may not reach the level of high-resource settings, when compared to other low-resource languages and their respective scores, our model achieved a reasonable performance for a low-resource machine translation setting (Mirzakhalov et al., 2021a).

4 Conclusions

In this paper, to the best of our knowledge, for the first time, we introduced computational resources and pipelines for Iranian Azerbaijani language processing. Language technologies developed for this language can significantly contribute to the communications of >14M speakers of this endangered language. We introduced data sources and models on major NLP tasks including text cleaning, word embeddings, language modeling, text and token classifications, and machine translation. Our introduced embedding space, pos-tagger, and BERT language modeling can be used in a variety of other NLP tasks. Our translation model is the first technological effort toward closing the gap between generations that are not acquiring their grandparents' language. Our pipeline and prepared resources can play a key role in addressing the scarcity of computational resources for Iranian Azerbaijani and preserving the language and its culture.

5 Limitations

Our study has several limitations that must be acknowledged. A major limitation is the limited resources available for Iranian Azerbaijani, which resulted in a scarcity of data for our pipeline. This scarcity poses a significant challenge for training and evaluating our models and may impede their overall performance. Additionally, Azerbaijani is an agglutinative language, with postfixes added to words to indicate grammatical relationships and functions. However, the way postfixes are written and separated from words varies between Azerbaijani and Iranian Azerbaijani, In Iranian Azerbaijani, there are no clear rules for written language, leading to variations in the use of spaces and half-spaces between words and postfixes. The absence of standard and pre-defined rules also results in considerable noise in the data, making accurate analysis and understanding of the language difficult. We faced challenges in accurately tokenizing Azerbaijani because of these variations and decided to use spaces to tokenize words in our data, but this method sometimes resulted in incorrect segmentation. Furthermore, we used a significant portion of transliterated data from resources in Azerbaijani, which may be affected by phonological, lexical, syntactic, and morphological differences between the two dialects, and thus may impact the performance of our pipeline and limit the accuracy of our models.

6 Acknowledgment

We would like to extend our heartfelt gratitude to several individuals and groups whose invaluable contributions have significantly enriched our research. We are grateful to Aidin Sardarynia, Parviz Zare Shahmarasi, Ghasem Lazemi, Mohammad Ali Sadraei, and the authors of the "Borderless Azerbaijani Processing: Linguistic Resources and a Transformer-based Approach for Azerbaijani Transliteration" paper for their invaluable help.

References

Željko Agić, Anders Johannsen, Barbara Plank, Héctor Martínez Alonso, Natalie Schluter, and Anders Søgaard. 2016. Multilingual projection for parsing truly low-resource languages. *Transactions of the Association for Computational Linguistics*, 4:301–312.

Huseyin Alecakir, Necva Bölücü, and Burcu Can. 2022. TurkishDelightNLP: A neural Turkish NLP toolkit. In *Proceedings of the 2022 Conference of the North American Chapter of the Association for Computational Linguistics: Human Language Technologies: System Demonstrations*, pages 17–26, Hybrid: Seattle, Washington + Online. Association for Computational Linguistics.

Rachit Bansal, Himanshu Choudhary, Ravneet Punia, Niko Schenk, Émilie Pagé-Perron, and Jacob Dahl.

2021. How low is too low? a computational perspective on extremely low-resource languages. In *Proceedings of the 59th Annual Meeting of the Association for Computational Linguistics and the 11th International Joint Conference on Natural Language Processing: Student Research Workshop*, pages 44–59, Online. Association for Computational Linguistics.

Piotr Bojanowski, Edouard Grave, Armand Joulin, and Tomas Mikolov. 2017. Enriching word vectors with subword information. *Transactions of the Association for Computational Linguistics*, 5:135–146.

Stanley F Chen, Douglas Beeferman, and Roni Rosenfeld. 1998. Evaluation metrics for language models.

Christopher Cieri, Mike Maxwell, Stephanie Strassel, and Jennifer Tracey. 2016. Selection criteria for low resource language programs. In *Proceedings of the Tenth International Conference on Language Resources and Evaluation (LREC'16)*, pages 4543–4549.

Jacob Devlin, Ming-Wei Chang, Kenton Lee, and Kristina Toutanova. 2019. BERT: Pre-training of deep bidirectional transformers for language understanding. In *Proceedings of the 2019 Conference of the North American Chapter of the Association for Computational Linguistics: Human Language Technologies, Volume 1 (Long and Short Papers)*, pages 4171–4186, Minneapolis, Minnesota. Association for Computational Linguistics.

Elie Duthoo and Olivier Mesnard. 2018. CEA LIST: Processing low-resource languages for CoNLL 2018. In *Proceedings of the CoNLL 2018 Shared Task: Multilingual Parsing from Raw Text to Universal Dependencies*, pages 34–44, Brussels, Belgium. Association for Computational Linguistics.

Steffen Eger, Andreas Rücklé, and Iryna Gurevych. 2018. PD3: Better low-resource cross-lingual transfer by combining direct transfer and annotation projection. In *Proceedings of the 5th Workshop on Argument Mining*, pages 131–143, Brussels, Belgium. Association for Computational Linguistics.

Razieh Ehsani, Muzaffer Ege Alper, Gülşen Eryiğit, and Eşref Adali. 2012. Disambiguating main POS tags for Turkish. In *Proceedings of the 24th Conference on Computational Linguistics and Speech Processing (ROCLING 2012)*, pages 202–213, Chung-Li, Taiwan. The Association for Computational Linguistics and Chinese Language Processing (ACLCLP).

Rauf Fatullayev, Ali Abbasov, and Abulfat Fatullayev. 2008. Dilmanc is the 1st mt system for azerbaijani. *Proc. of SLTC-08, Stockholm, Sweden*, pages 63–64.

Anna Gladkova, Aleksandr Drozd, and Satoshi Matsuoka. 2016. Analogy-based detection of morphological and semantic relations with word embeddings: what works and what doesn't. In *Proceedings of the NAACL Student Research Workshop*, pages 8–15, San Diego, California. Association for Computational Linguistics.

Memduh Gökırmak, Francis Tyers, and Jonathan Washington. 2019. A free/open-source rule-based machine translation system for crimean tatar to turkish. In *Proceedings of the 2nd Workshop on Technologies for MT of Low Resource Languages*, pages 24–31, Dublin, Ireland. European Association for Machine Translation.

Xu Han, Yuqi Luo, Weize Chen, Zhiyuan Liu, Maosong Sun, Zhou Botong, Hao Fei, and Suncong Zheng. 2022. Cross-lingual contrastive learning for fine-grained entity typing for low-resource languages. In *Proceedings of the 60th Annual Meeting of the Association for Computational Linguistics (Volume 1: Long Papers)*, pages 2241–2250, Dublin, Ireland. Association for Computational Linguistics.

Michael A. Hedderich, Lukas Lange, Heike Adel, Jannik Strötgen, and Dietrich Klakow. 2021. A survey on recent approaches for natural language processing in low-resource scenarios. In *Proceedings of the 2021 Conference of the North American Chapter of the Association for Computational Linguistics: Human Language Technologies*, pages 2545–2568, Online. Association for Computational Linguistics.

Ayyoob ImaniGooghari, Masoud Jalili Sabet, Philipp Dufter, Michael Cysou, and Hinrich Schütze. 2021. ParCourE: A parallel corpus explorer for a massively multilingual corpus. In *Proceedings of the 59th Annual Meeting of the Association for Computational Linguistics and the 11th International Joint Conference on Natural Language Processing: System Demonstrations*, pages 63–72, Online. Association for Computational Linguistics.

Masoud Jalili Sabet, Philipp Dufter, François Yvon, and Hinrich Schütze. 2020. SimAlign: High quality word alignments without parallel training data using static and contextualized embeddings. In *Findings of the Association for Computational Linguistics: EMNLP 2020*, pages 1627–1643, Online. Association for Computational Linguistics.

Julia Kreutzer, Jasmijn Bastings, and Stefan Riezler. 2019. Joey NMT: A minimalist NMT toolkit for novices. In *Proceedings of the 2019 Conference on Empirical Methods in Natural Language Processing and the 9th International Joint Conference on Natural Language Processing (EMNLP-IJCNLP): System Demonstrations*, pages 109–114, Hong Kong, China. Association for Computational Linguistics.

Elmurod Kuriyozov, Yerai Doval, and Carlos Gómez-Rodríguez. 2020. Cross-lingual word embeddings for Turkic languages. In *Proceedings of the Twelfth Language Resources and Evaluation Conference*, pages 4054–4062, Marseille, France. European Language Resources Association.

Sevda Mammadli, Shamsaddin Huseynov, Huseyn Alkaramov, Ulviyya Jafarli, Umid Suleymanov, and Samir

Rustamov. 2019. Sentiment polarity detection in Azerbaijani social news articles. In *Proceedings of the International Conference on Recent Advances in Natural Language Processing (RANLP 2019)*, pages 703–710, Varna, Bulgaria. INCOMA Ltd.

Thomas Mayer and Michael Cysouw. 2014. Creating a massively parallel Bible corpus. In *Proceedings of the Ninth International Conference on Language Resources and Evaluation (LREC'14)*, pages 3158–3163, Reykjavik, Iceland. European Language Resources Association (ELRA).

Arya D. McCarthy, Christo Kirov, Matteo Grella, Amrit Nidhi, Patrick Xia, Kyle Gorman, Ekaterina Vylomova, Sabrina J. Mielke, Garrett Nicolai, Miikka Silfverberg, Timofey Arkhangelskiy, Nataly Krizhanovsky, Andrew Krizhanovsky, Elena Klyachko, Alexey Sorokin, John Mansfield, Valts Ernštreits, Yuval Pinter, Cassandra L. Jacobs, Ryan Cotterell, Mans Hulden, and David Yarowsky. 2020a. UniMorph 3.0: Universal Morphology. In *Proceedings of the Twelfth Language Resources and Evaluation Conference*, pages 3922–3931, Marseille, France. European Language Resources Association.

Arya D. McCarthy, Rachel Wicks, Dylan Lewis, Aaron Mueller, Winston Wu, Oliver Adams, Garrett Nicolai, Matt Post, and David Yarowsky. 2020b. The Johns Hopkins University Bible corpus: 1600+ tongues for typological exploration. In *Proceedings of the Twelfth Language Resources and Evaluation Conference*, pages 2884–2892, Marseille, France. European Language Resources Association.

Arya D. McCarthy, Winston Wu, Aaron Mueller, William Watson, and David Yarowsky. 2019. Modeling color terminology across thousands of languages. In *Proceedings of the 2019 Conference on Empirical Methods in Natural Language Processing and the 9th International Joint Conference on Natural Language Processing (EMNLP-IJCNLP)*, pages 2241–2250, Hong Kong, China. Association for Computational Linguistics.

Jamshidbek Mirzakhalov, Anoop Babu, Duygu Ataman, Sherzod Kariev, Francis Tyers, Otabek Abduraufov, Mammad Hajili, Sardana Ivanova, Abror Khaytbaev, Antonio Laverghetta Jr., Bekhzodbek Moydinboyev, Esra Onal, Shaxnoza Pulatova, Ahsan Wahab, Orhan Firat, and Sriram Chellappan. 2021a. A large-scale study of machine translation in Turkic languages. In *Proceedings of the 2021 Conference on Empirical Methods in Natural Language Processing*, pages 5876–5890, Online and Punta Cana, Dominican Republic. Association for Computational Linguistics.

Jamshidbek Mirzakhalov, Anoop Babu, Aigiz Kunafin, Ahsan Wahab, Bekhzodbek Moydinboyev, Sardana Ivanova, Mokhiyakhon Uzokova, Shaxnoza Pulatova, Duygu Ataman, Julia Kreutzer, Francis Tyers, Orhan Firat, John Licato, and Sriram Chellappan. 2021b. Evaluating multiway multilingual NMT in the Turkic languages. In *Proceedings of the Sixth Conference on Machine Translation*, pages 518–530, Online. Association for Computational Linguistics.

Payam Ghaffarvand Mokari and Stefan Werner. 2017. Azerbaijani. *Journal of the International Phonetic Association*, 47(2):207–212.

Mustafa Melih Mutlu and Arzucan Özgür. 2022. A dataset and BERT-based models for targeted sentiment analysis on Turkish texts. In *Proceedings of the 60th Annual Meeting of the Association for Computational Linguistics: Student Research Workshop*, pages 467–472, Dublin, Ireland. Association for Computational Linguistics.

Cheonbok Park, Yunwon Tae, TaeHee Kim, Soyoung Yang, Mohammad Azam Khan, Lucy Park, and Jaegul Choo. 2021. Unsupervised neural machine translation for low-resource domains via meta-learning. In *Proceedings of the 59th Annual Meeting of the Association for Computational Linguistics and the 11th International Joint Conference on Natural Language Processing (Volume 1: Long Papers)*, pages 2888–2901, Online. Association for Computational Linguistics.

Matt Post. 2018. A call for clarity in reporting BLEU scores. In *Proceedings of the Third Conference on Machine Translation: Research Papers*, pages 186–191, Brussels, Belgium. Association for Computational Linguistics.

Saeed Rezaei, Ashkan Latifi, and Arash Nematzadeh. 2017. Attitude towards azeri language in iran: a large-scale survey research. *Journal of Multilingual and Multicultural Development*, 38(10):931–941.

Ali Safaya, Emirhan Kurtuluş, Arda Goktogan, and Deniz Yuret. 2022. Mukayese: Turkish NLP strikes back. In *Findings of the Association for Computational Linguistics: ACL 2022*, pages 846–863, Dublin, Ireland. Association for Computational Linguistics.

Ananya Subburathinam, Di Lu, Heng Ji, Jonathan May, Shih-Fu Chang, Avirup Sil, and Clare Voss. 2019. Cross-lingual structure transfer for relation and event extraction. In *Proceedings of the 2019 Conference on Empirical Methods in Natural Language Processing and the 9th International Joint Conference on Natural Language Processing (EMNLP-IJCNLP)*, pages 313–325, Hong Kong, China. Association for Computational Linguistics.

Mengzhou Xia, Guoqing Zheng, Subhabrata Mukherjee, Milad Shokouhi, Graham Neubig, and Ahmed Hassan Awadallah. 2021. MetaXL: Meta representation transformation for low-resource cross-lingual learning. In *Proceedings of the 2021 Conference of the North American Chapter of the Association for Computational Linguistics: Human Language Technologies*, pages 499–511, Online. Association for Computational Linguistics.

Atıf Emre Yüksel, Yaşar Alim Türkmen, Arzucan Özgür, and Berna Altınel. 2019. Turkish tweet classification with transformer encoder. In *Proceedings of the International Conference on Recent Advances in Natural Language Processing (RANLP 2019)*, pages 1380–1387, Varna, Bulgaria. INCOMA Ltd.

Reihaneh Zohrabi, Mostafa Masumi, Omid Ghahroodi, Parham AbedAzad, Hamid Beigy, Mohammad Hossein Rohban, and Ehsaneddin Asgari. 2023. Borderless azerbaijani processing: Linguistic resources and a transformer-based approach for azerbaijani transliteration. In *Findings of the Association for Computational Linguistics: AACL-IJCNLP 2023*. Association for Computational Linguistics.

Barret Zoph, Deniz Yuret, Jonathan May, and Kevin Knight. 2016. Transfer learning for low-resource neural machine translation. In *Proceedings of the 2016 Conference on Empirical Methods in Natural Language Processing*, pages 1568–1575, Austin, Texas. Association for Computational Linguistics.

Appendix

A Data Collection

Our resources come from two sources: transliterated data from Azerbaijani and original data in Iranian Azerbaijani, We collected the original Iranian Azerbaijani data through various methods, including parsing Wikipedia dumps[4], gathering data from İshiq website[5], crawling Dashqapisi website archive[6], importing telegram channels[7], requesting content from Varliq quarterly journal[8], and manually extracting parallel sentences from translated short stories. For the Azerbaijani data, we collected news articles[9, 10], books[11], Quran[12] and Bible parallel corpora, and other textual resources from various sources including Github repositories[13]. Table 2 provides information about our data, including dataset name, transliteration status, number of sentences, unique words, and average words per sentence.

[4]https://azb.wikipedia.org/

[5]https://ishiq.net/

[6]https://dashqapi.blogsky.com/

[7]https://t.me/abcmedrese

[8]http://varliq.ir/

[9]https://wortschatz.uni-leipzig.de/en/download/Azerbaijani

[10]https://wortschatz.uni-leipzig.de/en/download/Azerbaijani

[11]https://github.com/raminrahimzada/az-corpus-nlp/blob/master/sentences/books_starting_with_a.txt

[12]https://tanzil.net/

[13]https://github.com/raminrahimzada/az-corpus-nlp/blob/master/sentences/others.zip

Name	Transliterated	#Sentences	#Words	#Avg. Words in Sent.
NewsCrawl	Yes	301403	210258	15.21
Books	Yes	116001	92891	6.08
Wikipedia	No	66449	88112	11.34
Ishiq	No	65321	146833	16.26
Bible (P)	Yes	42936	45693	13.36
New	Yes	19878	36875	15.68
DashQapisi	No	11071	27870	10.96
Quran (P)	Yes	8355	13176	11.3
Telegram	No	2263	10089	14.75
Varliq	No	816	5846	22.2
Stories (P)	No	676	2898	11.92
Others	Yes	699603	284642	5.98
Total	-	1323130	641861	9.55

Table 2: A summary of our collected datasets in Iranian Azerbaijani: (P) shows the parallel corpora.

B Azerbaijani vs. Iranian Azerbaijani

Azerbaijani, spoken in the Republic of Azerbaijan, commonly referred to as Azerbaijani, and Azerbaijani spoken in Iran, often denoted as Iranian Azerbaijani, are recognized as two distinct branches within the Azerbaijani language family. The usage patterns differ between the two branches, as Iranian Azerbaijani is primarily used as a spoken language, whereas Azerbaijani serves as an official, scientific, and literary language. Notably, the alphabets used by these branches exhibit dissimilarities. Azerbaijani has experienced multiple changes since 1928, whereas the Iranian branch continues to employ the Perso-Arabic alphabet. Vocabulary-wise, Azerbaijani in Iran incorporates loanwords from Persian, Arabic, and English, whereas the Azerbaijani branch includes loanwords from Russian, Arabic, Persian, and English. Furthermore, grammatical disparities exist between the two branches. The Iranian branch is primarily influenced by Persian in Iran, while the Azerbaijani branch draws influence from Russian in Azerbaijan. In summary, Azerbaijani and Iranian Azerbaijani are two distinct branches of the Azerbaijani language, differing in their usage patterns, alphabets, vocabulary, and grammatical features. These variations reflect the influence of Persian, Arabic, Russian, and English on the respective branches in their respective regions.

C POS Guideline

Introduction: This guideline provides instructions for annotating Part-of-Speech (POS) tags in the Azerbaijani language. The POS tags help identify the grammatical category of each word in a sentence. We have developed a comprehensive guideline featuring 11 tag categories. The tag categories include Noun, Punctuation, Verb,

Pronoun, Adverb, Conjunction, Number, Adjective, Postposition, Interjection, and Determiner. Examples for each category have been provided to assist in the annotation process.

Instructions: Each word should be tagged with one and only one POS tag from the provided categories. The function and the grammatical properties of the word while assigning the POS tag should be considered.

POS Tag Categories: a. Noun: Tags for common and proper nouns, including names of people, places, objects, etc. Example: "کیتاب" (book), "تهران" (Tehran).

b. Punctuation: Tags for punctuation marks. Example: ".", ",", "?".

c. Verb: Tags for verbs. Example: "یازدیم" (I wrote), "گئدیرم" (I am going).

d. Pronoun: Tags for words that replace nouns. Example: "من" (I), "سنین" (yours).

e. Adverb: Tags for words that modify verbs, adjectives, or other adverbs. Example: "یاواشجا" (quietly), "همیشه" (always).

f. Conjunction: Tags for words that connect words, phrases, or clauses. Example: "و" (and), "کي" (that).

g. Number: Tags for numeric values. Example: "ایکي" (two), "۱۰۰" (hundred).

h. Adjective: Tags for words that describe or modify nouns. Example: "گؤزل" (beautiful), "یاخشي" (good).

i. Postposition: Tags for words that come after nouns and show relationships. Example: "کیمي" (like), "اؤچؤن" (for).

j. Interjection: Tags for words that express strong emotions or surprise. Example: "!آي" (oh!), "!آه" (ah!).

k. Determiner: Tags for words that introduce or specify nouns. Example: "بو" (this), "هئچ" (any).

D Hyperparameters

The **BERT language model** was trained with hyperparameters set as follows: for pre-training, the number of epochs was 10, the batch size was 128, the learning rate was 5e-5, the vocabulary size was 10,000, and the maximum size of position embeddings was set to 64. For **text classification** tasks, the maximum sequence length was set to 64, the batch size was 32, and the number of epochs was 10. The learning rate for text classification was set to 275e-7. For **token classification** tasks, the maximum sequence length was set to 64, the learning rate was set to 2e-5, the batch size was 64, and the number of training epochs was 20.

E Error Analysis and Model Output Examples

Detailed examples for each task, along with model output samples, are available in the README section of our paper's GitHub repository.[14]

[14] `https://github.com/language-ml/iranian-azerbaijani-nlp`

Borderless Azerbaijani Processing: Linguistic Resources and a Transformer-based Approach for Azerbaijani Transliteration

Reihaneh Zohrabi⋆✦ **Mostafa Masumi**⋆✦ **Omid Ghahroodi**†✦ **Parham AbedAzad**†✦
Hamid Beigy✦ **Mohammad H. Rohban**✦ **Ehsaneddin Asgari**✳
Language Processing and Digital Humanities Laboratory
✦ Computer Engineering Department, Sharif University of Technology, IR
✳ AI Innovation Center, Data:Lab, Volkswagen AG, Munich, Germany
{zohrabi,m.masumi,omid.ghahroodi98,parhamabedazad,beigy,rohban}@sharif.edu and asgari@berkeley.edu

Abstract

Recent advancements in neural language models have revolutionized natural language understanding. However, many languages still face the risk of being left behind without the benefits of such advancements, potentially leading to their extinction. One such language is Azerbaijani in Iran, which suffers from limited digital resources and a lack of alignment between spoken and written forms. In contrast, Azerbaijani in the Republic of Azerbaijan has seen more resources and is not considered as low-resource as its Iranian counterpart. In this context, our research focuses on the computational progress made in Iranian Azerbaijani language. We propose a transliteration model that leverages an Azerbaijani parallel dataset, effectively bridging the gap between the Latin and Persian scripts. By enabling seamless communication between these two scripts, our model facilitates cultural exchange and serves as a valuable tool for transfer learning. The effectiveness of our approach surpasses traditional rule-based methods, as evidenced by the significant improvements in performance metrics. We observe a minimum 15% increase in BLEU scores and a reduction of at least 1/3 in edit distance. Furthermore, our model's online demo is accessible at https://azeri.parsi.ai/.

1 Introduction

The Azerbaijani language belongs to the Turkish language family and is spoken in two distinct dialects, primarily in the Republic of Azerbaijan and the Azerbaijani regions of Iran. While these dialects exhibit minor variations, they share a considerable linguistic commonality, making it feasible to transition from one dialect to the other by adapting existing letters and phonetic elements. This linguistic compatibility enables seamless communication between the two dialects, facilitating the utilization of their shared linguistic resources.

Azerbaijani is the official language of the Republic of Azerbaijan. However, according to statistics from the Population and Housing Census conducted by the Statistical Center of Iran[1] in 2015, the population of East and West Azerbaijan, Ardabil, and Zanjan provinces in Iran was approximately 9.5 million. Iranian Azerbaijani, spoken in these regions, is recognized as an ethnic spoken language without an established official writing system, rendering it a low-resource language.

Unlike Iranian Azerbaijani, the Azerbaijani language has recieved substantial attention within the field of natural language processing. For instance, Suleymanov et al. (2019) employs machine learning techniques, including decision trees, support vector machines, and Naive Bayes, to categorize Azerbaijani texts for various applications, such as news classification, sentiment analysis, and recommender systems. Moreover, Akhundova (2021) introduces models that incorporate both rule-based and machine learning approaches for Azerbaijani named entity recognition. Additionally, while Azerbaijani benefits from a repository[2] dedicated to collecting data and computing resources, which greatly simplifies computational tasks related to the language, no similar resources or initiatives had existed for Iranian Azerbaijani until the recent pioneering work (Marzia et al., 2023). This innovative research effort represents the initial and significant step toward establishing essential NLP resources for Iranian Azerbaijani, encompassing the development of standard datasets and starter models for various NLP tasks. It plays a pivotal role in preserving the language and culture of Iranian Azerbaijani.

In this research, we have developed a transliteration model bridging the Iranian and Azerbaijani variants, facilitating the processing of Iranian multilingual texts. We refer to the Iranian variant of

⋆, † Equal contribution

[1] https://www.amar.org.ir/

[2] https://github.com/alexeyev/awesome-Azerbaijani-nlp

Proceedings of the 13th International Joint Conference on Natural Language Processing and the 3rd Conference of the Asia-Pacific Chapter of the Association for Computational Linguistics (Volume 2: Short Papers), pages 175–183
November 1–4, 2023.

Azerbaijani spoken in Iran and the Azerbaijani variant spoken in Azerbaijan. Due to the scarcity of linguistic resources and prior computational work for the Iranian variant, challenges arise when processing this language. There is a lack of pre-processing tools and pre-trained language models, even within extensive multilingual resources like Facebook's FastText (Bojanowski et al., 2017). For the Azerbaijani variant, there are existing works (Huseynov et al., 2021) that have utilized word2vec (Mikolov et al., 2013) and Glove (Pennington et al., 2014) for vocabulary representation. Furthermore, the existence of different scripts for the Iranian variant has led to data source multiplicity, necessitating script unification through pre-processing. "Suzelrin Vahid Yazilishi: Calligraphy Style and Orthographic Culture of Azerbaijani Turkish (Consistent Spelling of Words)" describes the currently approved Iranian variant of the Azerbaijani script (Perso-Arabic script).

Our primary contributions include:

I. The creation of a parallel dataset encompassing both Iranian and Azerbaijani variants of Azerbaijani.

II. A thorough analysis of existing transliteration tools for Iranian Azerbaijani.

III. The development of a transliteration model, applied in (Marzia et al., 2023), to enhance resources for Iranian Azerbaijani.

We facilitate access to our dataset and code on GitHub and Hugging Face via the provided links [3],[4].

2 Related Works

Considering the significance of transliteration between the two variants of the Azerbaijani language, various efforts have been made to address this challenge, exemplified by tools like **AzConvert**[5] and the **Azalpha plugin**. However, these prior approaches rely on predefined rules and exhibit limitations in terms of accuracy, adherence to standard scripts, and contextual awareness. The rule-based methodologies employed can become overly intricate due to the inherent ambiguities across languages, with one such challenge being homographs. In languages like Azerbaijani, homographs can introduce errors in rule-based transliteration. Furthermore, the lack of adherence to standard scripts in numerous existing Iranian Azerbaijani sources renders rule-based methods unsuitable for handling such content.

There are other works for transliteration between different languages, such as **polyglot**[6] (Chen and Skiena, 2016), a natural language processing tool with various applications, including transliteration between different languages. This tool can support transliteration between 69 different languages, including Azerbaijani and Persian, but there is no such tool for Iranian Azerbaijani. Other studies focus on transliteration between closely related languages, which we categorize into three groups:

2.1 Rule-based methods:

In these methods, transliteration is accomplished through the application of pre-defined rules. Bhalla et al. (2013) employs a rule-based model for syllabification and statistical techniques, specifically for translating English into Punjabi. Similarly, Ahmadi (2019) adopts a rule-based approach for converting the two primary written systems of the Surani Kurdish language (Middle Kurdish) into each other. This is achieved by identifying characters in words, resolving potential ambiguities, and mapping them to the target text. Moreover, Oh and Choi (2002) utilizes pronunciation and content rules for the transliteration process, specifically from English to Korean.

2.2 PGM methods:

These methods typically employ probabilistic modeling techniques, aiming to maximize the probability of parallel word pairs between source and target languages. For instance, in the work of Pingali et al. (2008), a sophisticated statistical transliteration approach is introduced. Remarkably, this technique stands out for its language-independence, making it applicable to a wide range of language pairs. In the initial phase, it leverages hidden Markov model alignment, a powerful tool for capturing linguistic patterns and associations. Subsequently, in the next phase, the approach employs conditional random fields, further enhancing its transliteration capabilities. This multi-phase approach not only contributes to the robustness of the transliteration model but also allows for adaptability across various language

[3] https://github.com/language-ml/Borderless-Azerbaijani-Processing

[4] https://huggingface.co/datasets/language-ml-lab/parallel_azeri_dataset

[5] https://github.com/mousamk/azconvert

[6] https://github.com/aboSamoor/polyglot

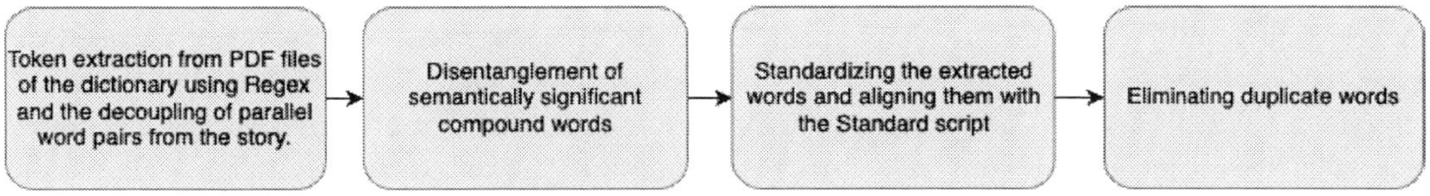

Figure 1: Overview of Preprocessing Steps Applied to the Dataset

contexts, making it a valuable resource in the field of cross-lingual text processing and machine translation research.

2.3 Neural network methods:

These methods include models based on LSTM and transformers. (Shao and Nivre, 2016) is an example of using neural networks for transliteration between English and Chinese. In this paper, the network architecture includes a convolutional layer to extract character-level information and a recurrent layer to process the text. Mahdi Mahsuli and Safabakhsh (2017) uses the encoder-decoder approach with the attention mechanism for transliteration from English to Persian, where instead of randomly initializing the weights of the encoder network, they use the vector representation of the words of the source language as the initial value for the weights. In general, sequence-to-sequence models with an attention mechanism use a recurrent neural network encoder to learn input text representations and a recurrent neural network decoder to generate output sequences from hidden representations created by the encoder. The attention mechanism (Bahdanau et al., 2014) allows the decoder to focus on different input parts for each time step in the output sequence. It can be seen as similar to the alignment mechanism used in traditional statistical translation models. Rosca and Breuel (2016) also uses this type of model with LSTM and GRU.

3 Materials and Methods

3.1 Data collection and preprocessing

Training of the transliteration model necessitates parallel datasets in both the source and target languages. However, due to the unavailability of such a dataset for processing purposes, we collaborated with the Azerbaijani Turkish Language Department of the University of Tabriz (Faculty of Persian and Foreign Languages). Through their cooperation, we were able to gather sources containing parallel texts in both Latin and Persian scripts. Our primary contribution lies in generating resources for this low-resource language.

Latin	Iranian	Example
ü	ۆ	Gün-گۆن
u	و	vurdu-ووردو
o	ؤ	yol-یؤل
ö	ؤ	Göz-گؤز
I	ى̆	baxdı-باخدى̆
I	ی	bir-بیر
e	ئ	dedi-دئدی

Table 1: Potentially misused vowel characters of Iranian Azerbaijani.

These sources encompass a portion of the Azerbaijani epic 'Koroğlu' written in both languages and utilizing the standard Azerbaijani script. Additionally, for out-of-domain evaluation, we obtained the Azerbaijani folklore tale 'Qurqud Dədə' written in both scripts, with the assistance of the aforementioned group.Additionally, we obtained the 'Azerbaycan sözlüğü' (Esmayil Jafarli, 2013) dictionary, which comprises 120,000 original words, Azerbaijani translations, place names, and the names of renowned individuals and poets, compiled in three PDF volumes.

After collecting the data above, we performed a series of word extraction and pre-processing operations to ensure that the words closely align with the standard script. The pre-processing procedures applied to the data typically adhered to the subsequent steps illustrated in Figure 1.

In the data normalization stage, we carefully assessed specific conditions to ensure the accurate substitution of Iranian Azerbaijani vowel characters with their corresponding Latin counterparts. It is important to note that the Iranian Azerbaijani language has multiple vowel characters that resemble the character "و" (such as "ؤ", "ۆ" and "ؤ"). However, in numerous existing sources, these vowels are often represented by the initial form, leading to inaccuracies in the written Iranian

Azerbaijani words. Therefore, we implemented pre-processing techniques to precisely replace the vowels based on their Latin forms, thereby enhancing the accuracy of the word representations. The table 1 shows vowel characters of the Iranian Azerbaijani language that must be observed in the standard script and may be used incorrectly.

We have summarized the information from the final dataset in Table 2, showcasing the count of parallel word pairs available in both languages. Additionally, you can find sample examples from this dataset in Appendix 1.1. In Iranian variant, the average token length is 7.34 characters, while in Azerbaijan variant, it is 7.73 characters. These word pairs serve as valuable resources for training our transliteration model. It's important to emphasize that the limited availability of linguistic resources for this language significantly hinders the applicability of data augmentation techniques.

	all tokens	after pre-processing
Dictionary	120000	72000
Koroğlu	700	500
Total	120700	72500

Table 2: Summary of the number of Parallel Word Pairs in the Final Azerbaijani Dataset.

To train the transliteration model, the data was divided into 5 clusters based on character patterns (using n-grams with lengths of 2 to 6). Clustering helped create distinct training and validation sets by reducing similarity between sub-words. Mean and standard deviation analysis assessed model overfitting and stability.

3.2 Model

The Transformer model, known for its powerful architecture in natural language processing tasks, including transliteration, has shown exceptional performance in capturing long-range dependencies. This makes it particularly suitable for transliteration tasks involving languages like Iranian and Azerbaijan variants of the Azerbaijani language. It employs a self-attention mechanism that allows the model to focus on different parts of the input sequence, capturing contextual relationships crucial for accurate transliteration.

The Transformer model consists of an encoder-decoder architecture. The encoder generates a representation capturing relevant information from the source language sequence, while the decoder uses this representation to generate the transliterated output sequence. By utilizing positional encodings, multiple stacked layers, and large-scale parallel data during training, the Transformer model effectively learns the mappings between input and output sequences.

Given its ability to handle sequence-to-sequence tasks and capture long-range dependencies, the Transformer model has become a prominent choice for transliteration tasks across various languages. In our research on two variants of Azerbaijani transliteration, we employ the Transformer model as the primary framework. Our model operates at the character level, where each character serves as an individual token. Token embeddings are initialized with random values to capture a wide range of linguistic nuances.

To assess the performance of the trained model, we measure the BLEU score (Papineni et al., 2002) and Levenshtein distance. During training, cross-validation is employed, with one cluster serving as the test set and the others as training and validation data. A ten percent subset is allocated for validation. The optimal hyperparameters for training are determined based on this setup, with further details provided in the appendix 1.2. We calculated the mean length in a collection of prefixes, suffixes, and morphemes in Iranian Azerbaijani to be near 3. We thus opted to calculate the BLEU score using an n-gram level of 3.

4 Results

The comparison results presented in Table 3 highlight the significant performance improvements achieved by the Transformer model compared to the Azconvert rule-based and polyglot statistical methods. Remarkably, the trained transliteration model attained an impressive BLEU score of 0.94 for both directions, despite the limited resources and calligraphy-related challenges. Furthermore, to provide a comprehensive evaluation and comparison with our Transformer-based approach, we introduced an LSTM-based model, which achieved BLEU scores of 0.91 and 0.92 for Persian-to-Latin and Latin-to-Persian conversions, respectively. In contrast, the Azconvert and polyglot models struggled to surpass a BLEU score of 0.79 in any transliteration direction.

Furthermore, the superiority of the transformer model extends to the minimum edit distance met-

Method	Persian to Latin			Latin to Persian		
	Min. Edit Dist. d	Avg. Len.	BLEU	Min. Edit Dist	Avg. Len.	BLEU
Transformer	**0.31 ± 0.1**	8	**0.94 ± 2.6**	**0.33 ± 0.06**	7	**0.94 ± 1.7**
polyglot	3.56	8	0.45	3.03	7	0.53
Azconvert	1.12	8	0.79	1.33	7	0.74
LSTM	0.47	8	0.91	0.43	7	0.92

Table 3: Comparison of Transliteration Methods: Persian to Latin and Latin to Persian Scripts. The table presents the minimum edit distance, average word length, and BLEU score for each method. Performance of the Transformer method was evaluated using five folds in a cross-validation setup, and the mean and standard deviation are reported.

Method	Persian to Latin			Latin to Persian		
	Min. Edit Dist. d	Avg. Len.	BLEU	Min. Edit Dist	Avg. Len.	BLEU
Transformer	**0.17**	5.2	**0.96**	**0.32**	5.3	**0.91**
polyglot	2.34	5.2	0.21	2.09	5.3	0.51
Azconvert	0.64	5.2	0.83	0.96	5.3	0.71
ChatGPT	1.49	5.2	0.66	1.28	5.3	0.65

Table 4: Out-of-Domain Comparison of Transliteration Methods: Persian to Latin and Latin to Persian Scripts. The table presents the minimum edit distance, average word length, and BLEU score for each method on the out-domain data.

ric. The model's character-level output exhibits a high level of accuracy, requiring minimal edits compared to the existing models. Additionally, the low standard deviation of the BLEU score indicates the model's stability during training, even when faced with variations in subword patterns across different cross-validation folds. The consistently high BLEU scores across all categories, coupled with excellent subword discrimination, indicate that the model effectively avoids overfitting on the training data. A detailed analysis of the trained models and their corresponding outputs is presented in the appendix 1.3 for further examination and understanding.

For out-of-domain evaluation, we employed the 'Qurqud Dədə' dataset and also utilized ChatGPT's predictions to gain additional perspectives. The evaluation results revealed that there was no significant drop in the BLEU score. In fact, for Persian-to-Latin conversion, the BLEU score increased by 2 points, while for Latin-to-Persian conversion, it decreased by just 3 points. These findings indicate that the model's performance remains robust. Detailed results can be found in Table 4.

5 Conclusion

The rapid growth of language technologies emphasizes the importance of linguistic resources and computational tasks for endangered languages like Azerbaijani in Iran. It connects theologians with Azerbaijani speakers worldwide, benefiting both Azerbaijani communities.

In this research, we undertook the collection and pre-processing of Azerbaijani data, enabling the creation of a parallel dataset for Azerbaijani in both Latin and Persian scripts. Through this effort, we trained a two-way transliteration model capable of converting between Latin and Persian scripts. Despite the inherent challenges, we achieved remarkable accuracy. This work represents a significant milestone in the advancement of Azerbaijani language technologies, and we look forward to further research in related domains to enhance the development of this language.

6 Limitations

It is crucial to recognize that this study's limitations are primarily rooted in two key factors: resource constraints and the scarcity of digitized materials available for the Iranian Azerbaijani language. These constraints have inevitably led to limitations in the depth of our training dataset.

The most conspicuous limitation is evident when we delve into certain word contexts, especially those involving infrequent words and senses. In such cases, the data available for training the model remains sparse. Consequently, effectively addressing infrequent ambiguities becomes a challenging

task.
The scarcity of data has a direct impact on the model's ability to accurately identify the spellings of ambiguous words, particularly those that were not encountered during its training phase. When faced with such unseen words, the model may struggle to provide precise predictions, as its exposure to such linguistic nuances is inherently limited.

7 Acknowledgment

We wish to express our deep appreciation to numerous individuals and organizations whose exceptional contributions have greatly enriched our research. In particular, we extend our heartfelt thanks to Mohammad Ali Sadraei for his invaluable assistance.

References

Sina Ahmadi. 2019. A rule-based kurdish text transliteration system. *ACM Trans. Asian Low-Resour. Lang. Inf. Process.*, 18(2).

Natavan Akhundova. 2021. Named entity recognition for the azerbaijani language. In *2021 IEEE 15th International Conference on Application of Information and Communication Technologies (AICT)*, pages 1–7.

Dzmitry Bahdanau, Kyunghyun Cho, and Yoshua Bengio. 2014. Neural machine translation by jointly learning to align and translate. *arXiv preprint arXiv:1409.0473*.

Deepti Bhalla, Nisheeth Joshi, and Iti Mathur. 2013. Rule based transliteration scheme for english to punjabi. *arXiv preprint arXiv:1307.4300*.

Piotr Bojanowski, Edouard Grave, Armand Joulin, and Tomas Mikolov. 2017. Enriching word vectors with subword information. *Transactions of the Association for Computational Linguistics*, 5:135–146.

Yanqing Chen and Steven Skiena. 2016. False-friend detection and entity matching via unsupervised transliteration. *arXiv preprint arXiv:1611.06722*.

Esmayil Jafarli. 2013. *Azerbaijani Türkçe Sözlüğü (Azerbaijani Sözlüğü) - Turkish Dictionary*. Ehrar Publications in cooperation with Sumer Publishing, Tabriz.

Faculty of Persian and Foreign Languages. Faculty of Persian and Foreign Languages. https://literature.tabrizu.ac.ir/en.

Kamran Huseynov, Umid Suleymanov, Samir Rustamov, and Javid Huseynov. 2021. Training and evaluation of word embedding models for azerbaijani language. In *Digital Interaction and Machine Intelligence*, pages 37–48, Cham. Springer International Publishing.

Mohammad Mahdi Mahsuli and Reza Safabakhsh. 2017. English to persian transliteration using attention-based approach in deep learning. In *2017 Iranian Conference on Electrical Engineering (ICEE)*, pages 174–178.

Nouri Marzia, Amani Mahsa, Zohrabi Reihaneh, and Ehsaneddin Asgari. 2023. The language model, resources, and computational pipelines for the under-resourced iranian azerbaijani. In *Findings of the Association for Computational Linguistics: AACL-IJCNLP 2023*. Association for Computational Linguistics.

Tomas Mikolov, Kai Chen, Greg Corrado, and Jeffrey Dean. 2013. Efficient estimation of word representations in vector space. *arXiv preprint arXiv:1301.3781*.

Jong-Hoon Oh and Key-Sun Choi. 2002. An English-Korean transliteration model using pronunciation and contextual rules. In *COLING 2002: The 19th International Conference on Computational Linguistics*.

Kishore Papineni, Salim Roukos, Todd Ward, and Wei-Jing Zhu. 2002. Bleu: a method for automatic evaluation of machine translation. In *Proceedings of the 40th Annual Meeting of the Association for Computational Linguistics*, pages 311–318, Philadelphia, Pennsylvania, USA. Association for Computational Linguistics.

Jeffrey Pennington, Richard Socher, and Christopher Manning. 2014. GloVe: Global vectors for word representation. In *Proceedings of the 2014 Conference on Empirical Methods in Natural Language Processing (EMNLP)*, pages 1532–1543, Doha, Qatar. Association for Computational Linguistics.

Prasad Pingali, Surya Ganesh, Sreeharsha Yella, and Vasudeva Varma. 2008. Statistical transliteration for cross language information retrieval using HMM alignment model and CRF. In *Proceedings of the 2nd workshop on Cross Lingual Information Access (CLIA) Addressing the Information Need of Multilingual Societies*.

Mihaela Rosca and Thomas Breuel. 2016. Sequence-to-sequence neural network models for transliteration. *arXiv preprint arXiv:1610.09565*.

Yan Shao and Joakim Nivre. 2016. Applying neural networks to English-Chinese named entity transliteration. In *Proceedings of the Sixth Named Entity Workshop*, pages 73–77, Berlin, Germany. Association for Computational Linguistics.

Umid Suleymanov, Behnam Kiani Kalejahi, Elkhan Amrahov, and Rashid Badirkhanli. 2019. Text classification for azerbaijani language using machine learning and embedding. *CoRR*, abs/1912.13362.

A Appendix

1.1 Examples of Parallel Azerbaijani Dataset

Table 5 presents several examples from the prepared dataset, illustrating parallel word pairs in both variants of the Azerbaijani language.

Latin	Iranian
eşitmək	ائشیتمک
özgə	اؤزگه
tökülüşmək	تؤکۆلۆشمک
Parildamaq	پاریلداماق

Table 5: Examples of parallel word pairs in Azerbaijani language.

Parameter	Value
Batch size	128
Number of attention heads	8
Feed-forward dimension	512
Number of encoder layers	4
Number of decoder layers	4
Loss	Cross-entropy
Optimizer	Adam
Learning rate	1e-4

Table 6: Transformer hyperparameters.

Parameter	Value
Insertion cost	0.5
Deletion cost	1
Substitution cost	2

Table 7: Edit distance hyperparameters.

1.2 Hyperparameters

The model training process is optimized with the following set of hyperparameters provided in table 6. Also, table 7 provides the test parameters used to calculate the minimum edit distance.

1.3 Model Output Analysis and Review

The table 8 showcases examples of transliteration model outputs for words between the Latin and Iranian scripts. The correct spellings of the words are presented in the first two columns, while the corresponding model outputs are displayed in the subsequent columns. Analyzing these outputs allows us to identify the strengths and weaknesses of each Azerbaijani transliterator.

The Polyglot model: Since there is no direct mapping between the Latin and the Iranian scripts, we have employed a linguistic bridge in this model. Consequently, the model does not generate special Azerbaijani vowels. Substituting unfamiliar vowels with Persian counterparts often results in unfamiliar words. Even for common words shared between Azerbaijani and Persian, like the word "ترفیع" in table 8, the model's

Latin Script	Iranian Script	Direction	Azconvert	polyglot	Our approach
oğlan	اوْغلان	Persian to Latin	uğlan	aoqholan	oğlan
		Latin to Persian	اوغلان	وگلان	اوْغلان
tərfi	ترفیع	Persian to Latin	tərfi	trfiya	tərfi
		Latin to Persian	ترفی	تارفی	ترفیع
düşünürəm	دۆشۆنۆرم	Persian to Latin	düşünürm	doşonorm	düşünürm
		Latin to Persian	دوشونوره م	دوشونورام	دۆشۆنۆرم
baxdı	باخدیٚ	Persian to Latin	baxdi	bachdi	baxdı
		Latin to Persian	باخ دی	بخدی	باخدیٚ
gördü	گؤردۆ	Persian to Latin	gördü	qordo	gördü
		Latin to Persian	گؤردو	گوردو	گؤردو
uzun	اوزون	Persian to Latin	uzun	aozon	uzun
		Latin to Persian	اوزون	وزون	اوزون
üzün	اۆزۆن	Persian to Latin	üzün	aozon	üzün
		Latin to Persian	اوزون	وزون	اۆزۆن
dedi	دئدی	Persian to Latin	dedi	dedi	dedi
		Latin to Persian	دئدی	دادی	دئدی
ayrılıq	آیرٚلٚق	Persian to Latin	ayrılıq	ayriliq	ayrılıq
		Latin to Persian	آیری لیق	ایرلیگ	آیرٚلٚق

Table 8: Sample Outputs of Transliteration Models for transliterating Azerbaijani Words between two variants.

performance was unsatisfactory. Furthermore, this model operates at a slower speed compared to other models.

The Azconvert model: This model does not have some Iranian Azerbaijani vowels such as "ۆ" and "ؽ" which can be seen in table 8 for the words "دۆشۆنۆرم", "باخدؽ" and "گؤردۆ". One of the advantages of this rule-based model is that it uses more appropriate writing for better readability; for example, for the word "آیرتلؽق", separating the sub-words "آیری" (separate) and "لیق" (infinitive noun suffix) helps for its readability. This method does the same for this word.

The Transformer model: The transformer model can produce a variety of consonant and vowel patterns due to various learning data from the dictionary. Therefore, the trained model is very consistent with the standard script and can recognize words that are similar in appearance. However, sometimes it does not correctly recognize the spelling of ambiguous words that it did not see in the training, such as "اسیل" in the second line of table 9, which should be "اصیل".

It is important to highlight that the trained model can also be utilized for the transliteration of entire sentences since there is a one-to-one correspondence between words in both languages. Examples of sentence transliterations are illustrated in tables 9 and 10.

Latin	Persian
türkün dili tək sevgili istəkli dil olmaz	تۆرکۆن دیلی تک سئوگیلی ایستکلی دیل اؤلماز
özgə dili qatsan bu əsil dil əsil olmaz	اؤزگه دیلی قاتسان بو اسیل دیل اسیل اؤلماز
hər kəsin fikir və söz azadliği vardir	هرِ کسین فکرِ وه سؤز آزادلیغیِ واردیر
necə görsənir	نئجه گؤرسهنیر
mən onu dünən göndərdim	من اونو دۆنن گؤندردیم

Table 9: Sample Outputs of Azerbaijani Sentences transliterated from Latin to Persian Script.

Persian	Latin
سئوگیلیم عشق اؤلماسا دۆنیا بۆتۆن افسانه دیر	sevgilim əşəq olmasa dünya bütün əfsanə dir
گؤر خبرلر وار یا یوخ	gör xəbərlər var ya yox
دۆز دئییرسن	duz deyirsən
چوخ گؤزلدیر	çox gözəldir

Table 10: Sample Outputs of Azerbaijani Sentences transliterated from Persian to Latin Script.

Are Machine Reading Comprehension Systems Robust to Context Paraphrasing?

Yulong Wu[1], **Viktor Schlegel**[1,2] **and Riza Batista-Navarro**[1]
[1] Department of Computer Science, University of Manchester, United Kingdom
[2] ASUS Intelligent Cloud Services (AICS), Singapore
{yulong.wu, riza.batista}@manchester.ac.uk
viktor_schlegel@asus.com

Abstract

Investigating the behaviour of Machine Reading Comprehension (MRC) models under various types of test-time perturbations can shed light on the enhancement of their robustness and generalisation capability, despite the superhuman performance they have achieved on existing benchmark datasets. In this paper, we study the robustness of contemporary MRC systems to context paraphrasing, i.e., whether these models are still able to correctly answer the questions once the reading passages have been paraphrased. To this end, we systematically design a pipeline to semi-automatically generate perturbed MRC instances which ultimately lead to the creation of a paraphrased test set. We conduct experiments on this dataset with six state-of-the-art neural MRC models and we find that even the minimum performance drop of all these models exceeds 41%, whereas human performance remains high. Retraining models with augmented perturbed examples results in improved robustness, though the performance remains lower than on the original dataset. These results demonstrate that the existing high-performing MRC systems are still far away from real language understanding[1].

Question: In what year did Harvard President Joseph Willard die?
Original Context: [...] When the Hollis Professor of Divinity David Tappan died in 1803 and the president of Harvard Joseph Willard died a year later, in 1804, a struggle broke out over their replacements. [...] **Prediction:** 1804
Paraphrased Context: [...] When the Hollis professor of divinity David Tappan died in 1803, the President of Harvard Joseph Willard died a year later, a battle broke out in 1804 for their successors. [...] **Prediction:** 1803 **Prediction by a human:** 1804

Figure 1: An instance where the RoBERTa-large model (Liu et al., 2019) can get the answer correct over the original reading passage, but is misled when presented with a whole context paraphrased version.

1 Introduction

Machine reading comprehension (MRC), the task of automatically reading a passage of text and answering related questions, serves as an important testbed for evaluating various Natural Language Understanding (NLU) capabilities of computer systems (Chen, 2018). While neural MRC systems approach or even surpass human performance on benchmark datasets (Devlin et al., 2019; Lan et al., 2020; He et al., 2021), it remains uncertain whether they can indeed solve the MRC task (Schlegel et al., 2020; Wu et al., 2021b; Sugawara et al., 2022; Shinoda et al., 2023; Schlegel et al., 2023). In particular, recent studies have shown that instead of performing consistently well, contemporary models are brittle under various test-time perturbations (Ribeiro et al., 2020; Si et al., 2021; Wu et al., 2021a; Schlegel et al., 2021; Yan et al., 2022). This raises the question of the suitability of existing gold standard datasets to establish a model's robustness and the need to improve the reliability of these MRC systems (Wang et al., 2022).

Paraphrase understanding plays a role in measuring the robustness and generalisation ability of MRC models. Intuitively, a trustworthy MRC system should demonstrate robust generalisation on paraphrased contexts and/or questions, i.e., those that convey the same semantic meaning using different surface forms. Previous studies have attempted to paraphrase the questions (Gan and Ng, 2019) and strategically modify portions of the reading passage, e.g., paraphrase only the answer sentence using the back-translation (Lai et al., 2021) or generate paraphrases that exclude the top five im-

[1]Our code and data are available at https://github.com/Yulong-W/context-paraphrasing.

Proceedings of the 13th International Joint Conference on Natural Language Processing and the 3rd Conference of the Asia-Pacific Chapter of the Association for Computational Linguistics (Volume 2: Short Papers), pages 184–196
November 1–4, 2023.

portant words in the context (Wu et al., 2021a). By assessing model performance on the paraphrased test sets, they concluded that MRC models might be vulnerable to paraphrasing-oriented attacks.

The reading comprehension task assesses a model's real understanding of a given context, i.e., a *passage*. Though the findings in the work of Lai et al. (2021) and Wu et al. (2021a) provide insights into the weaknesses of MRC datasets to benchmark partial-context paraphrasing understanding, their designed strategic paraphrasing approach may hinder the generated perturbed examples from accurately simulating real-world text disruptions, which can pervade any part of a passage, not just specific words or answer sentences. Furthermore, it is not clear whether the modifications introduced as part of the perturbations changed the meaning of the original context. Therefore, to precisely reveal the capability of existing gold standard datasets to benchmark paraphrase understanding, we argue that it is crucial to examine the robustness of MRC systems to paraphrasing the whole context as well.

In this paper, our aim is to evaluate how well current reading comprehension systems generalise to a modified benchmark in which all contexts were paraphrased while preserving the same meaning and thus keeping the same gold standard answer. Different from prior robustness assessment research (Gan and Ng, 2019; Wu et al., 2021a; Yan et al., 2022), we design a pipeline to generate and identify perturbations of MRC examples that demonstrate the lack of robustness of a strong MRC system RoBERTa-large (Liu et al., 2019) to context paraphrasing (see Figure 1 for an example). In doing so, we also underscore the limitation of a large language model to handle the paraphrased contexts. This proposed evaluation framework leads to the construction of a paraphrased test set drawn from the original Stanford Question Answering Dataset v1.1 (SQuAD 1.1) benchmark (Rajpurkar et al., 2016). Results of our experiments show that the performance of five other MRC models except the RoBERTa-large on our created dataset is substantially lower, indicating the transferability of such adversarial attack against MRC models and the insufficiency of the SQuAD 1.1 to benchmark context paraphrasing understanding. Utilising a straightforward training data augmentation approach, we also show the possibility to enhance the robustness of these models in dealing with context paraphrasing. These suggest that there is a need to create gold standard datasets in which context paraphrasing challenges are sufficiently represented.

2 Experiment Setup

MRC Dataset. In this paper, we investigated an extractive English MRC dataset SQuAD 1.1 (Rajpurkar et al., 2016) (License: CC-BY 4.0) due to its simplicity and the fact that it is the dataset on which current MRC models have already achieved superhuman performance, hence allowing us to focus on analysing the robustness of models to context paraphrasing. The statistics for the dataset are reported in Appendix A.

Models. We chose the following models for the task of machine translation and reading comprehension, respectively.

Machine translation: We used the neural translation models provided by OPUS-MT (Tiedemann and Thottingal, 2020) which are based on the popular Marian-Neural Machine Translation framework (Junczys-Dowmunt et al., 2018) pre-trained on the OPUS (Tiedemann, 2012) multilingual corpus.

Reading comprehension: We selected the RoBERTa-large model (Liu et al., 2019) to generate the paraphrased test set mainly due to its impressive performance (93.1% F1) on the original development set of SQuAD 1.1 (Rajpurkar et al., 2016). The process of generating the challenge set also entails the utilisation of a Generative Pretrained Transformer (GPT) (Brown et al., 2020) series model, specifically GPT-3.5-turbo, through the OpenAI ChatGPT API. In the final evaluation stage, we used multiple strong MRC models including BERT (Devlin et al., 2019), DistilBERT (Sanh et al., 2019), ALBERT (Lan et al., 2020), SpanBERT (Joshi et al., 2020) and DeBERTa (He et al., 2021), to comprehensively demonstrate the challenge posed by our created dataset. We fine-tuned these pre-trained language models on the training set of SQuAD 1.1 and evaluated them on each of the original and perturbed test sets by making use of HuggingFace's *Transformers* library (Wolf et al., 2020). Model details and the hyperparameters used in model fine-tuning are shown in Appendix B.

3 Context Paraphrasing-Oriented Challenge Set Generation

In this section, we describe our methodology for generating a semantics-preserving context-paraphrased dataset. Four steps are involved in the perturbation pipeline, which are detailed below.

Language	Performance (EM/F1)	
	Original	Paraphrased
Sino-Tibetan		
Chinese	91.07/94.38	80.60/86.05$_{-8.83}$
Indo-European		
Hindi	92.50/95.29	70.89/76.11$_{-20.13}$
Spanish	89.80/93.99	87.75/92.51$_{-1.57}$
French	90.26/94.24	87.20/92.02$_{-2.36}$
Russian	90.69/94.38	85.29/90.27$_{-4.35}$
German	89.95/94.22	87.51/92.29$_{-2.05}$
Italian	90.07/94.13	86.85/91.99$_{-2.27}$
Dutch	89.43/93.98	86.98/92.08$_{-2.02}$
Swedish	89.70/94.04	87.26/92.16$_{-2.0}$
Austronesian		
Indonesian	91.07/94.53	84.39/89.54$_{-5.28}$
Austro-Asiatic		
Vietnamese	91.73/95.06	77.14/82.89$_{-12.8}$
Uralic		
Finnish	91.20/94.62	85.15/90.22$_{-4.65}$

Table 1: The performance (%) of the RoBERTa-large (Liu et al., 2019) on the original and paraphrased test sets generated using 12 pivot languages across five language families. Values in smaller font are changes in F1 (%) relative to the original performance of the model.

3.1 Automatic Context Paraphrasing

We explored paraphrasing the reading passages in the development set of an MRC dataset using a back-translation approach, by which each sentence in the context is translated from a source language (English) to a pivot language and then back to the source language. We identified twelve languages across five language families as the pivot language, informed by their number of speakers (Eberhard et al., 2022) and the performance of their associated pre-trained neural translation models (Tiedemann and Thottingal, 2020). After obtaining the paraphrases, we kept only those with at least one question where all annotated answers can still be found in the paraphrased context. The original contexts of those paraphrases were then extracted from the development set, to keep it aligned with the modified test set and the performance comparable.

3.2 Preliminary Evaluation

As presented in Section 3.1, we generated perturbed test subsets (one for each of the 12 pivot languages) in which contexts were paraphrased using back-translation, and their corresponding original versions. Then, we examined the performance of a strong MRC model, RoBERTa-large (Liu et al., 2019), on these datasets, as demonstrated in Table 1. It can be seen from Table 1 that paraphrasing the contexts using different pivot languages caused various degrees of degradation in terms of the performance of the RoBERTa-large model. Nonetheless, we cannot simply conclude that this indicates the vulnerability of MRC models to the context paraphrasing attack as it is unclear whether these context paragraphs were indeed *paraphrased*, i.e., remain semantically equivalent while lexical/syntactic features were changed. Therefore, we manually verified the validity of the perturbed MRC instances in the next step.

3.3 Human Evaluation

With the aim of studying the lack of robustness of MRC models to context paraphrasing, from each generated perturbed test set, we identified MRC examples on which the RoBERTa-large model (Liu et al., 2019) predicts a wrong answer span whereas it provides the correct answer given the original passage. Afterwards, we randomly sampled 10% examples from each filtered perturbed test set; this resulted in a total of 247 candidate examples, based on which human performance was assessed. A candidate perturbed MRC example has the ability to demonstrate the vulnerability of a model to context paraphrasing, if the model makes a wrong prediction on the paraphrased context paragraph, but a human can answer the question correctly. We refer to such candidates as *suitable* examples. Out of 247 examples, we identified 53 as suitable. The identification process is detailed in Appendix C. In addition, Figure 2 measures the languages contribution of suitable examples within the annotated dataset, from which it is evident that employing Finnish for back-translation/paraphrasing yields the most suitable examples.

3.4 Paraphrased Test Set Generation

While human evaluation enables us to identify suitable MRC instances precisely, it requires significant human annotation effort. Hence, we explored the viability of two different approaches to auto-

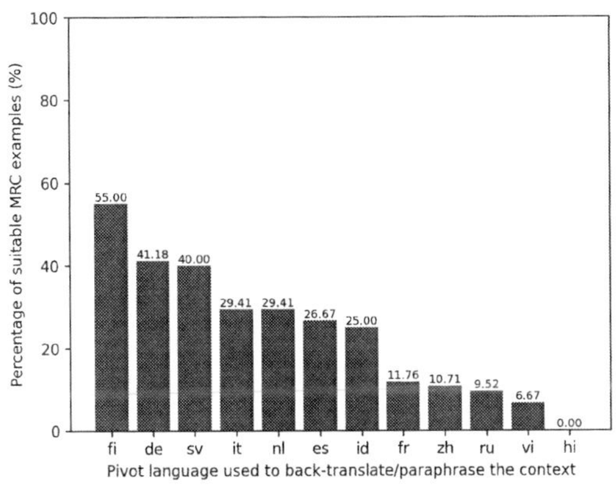

Figure 2: Percentage of suitable MRC examples within the candidate instances generated by using each pivot language, respectively.

matically determine whether a perturbed MRC example is suitable: one based on Machine Learning (ML) techniques and the other employing the GPT-3.5-turbo model. The process and outcomes derived from experimenting with these two methods are detailed in Appendix D and Appendix E. The best-performing model, GPT-3.5-turbo under zero-shot scenario (0.69 precision in predicting suitable example), was then applied on the filtered perturbed instances generated using Finnish, Spanish, Vietnamese, Italian and Swedish, 182 of which were classified as suitable (from 150 original contexts). For multiple paraphrased contexts that correspond to the same original passage, we only kept the perturbed one with the most questions preserved, or in case of a tie, the one with the lowest average question–context lexical overlap (Shinoda et al., 2021). Our final paraphrased test set contains 150 contexts and 158 questions in total. For the purposes of comparison, we also created an *Original* version of the test set keeping only the original passages and questions corresponding to those that were included in the *Paraphrased* version.

4 Results and Discussion

4.1 Evaluation

We assessed the performance of six state-of-the-art MRC models on the newly created challenge set, as shown in Table 2. The table shows that all the evaluated neural language models demonstrated poor generalisation to our generated test set. RoBERTa-large suffered the largest performance drop of 85.07%—this is within our expectation since its errors were used to identify suitable examples. For the other five model architectures, the relative changes were smaller than that of RoBERTa-large, but still very noticeable with over 41% performance decrease. This demonstrates the poor capability of these reading comprehension systems to properly deal with the paraphrased contexts. Apart from RoBERTa and ALBERT, the performance of other four MRC models remained consistent across both original and paraphrased test set, with DeBERTa achieving the highest EM and F1 score, followed by SpanBERT, BERT and DistilBERT. While the performance of ALBERT on the original dataset was slightly lower than that of DeBERTa, it notably outperformed the latter on the paraphrased test set, attaining the highest performance score (54.16 F1). We also found that the consistency in original model performance rankings might not apply to their robustness to context paraphrasing, with the BERT-large model demonstrating the greatest F1 decrease (50.2%) and the ALBERT-xxlarge-v1 exhibiting the smallest performance decline (41.54%).

Model	Original (EM/F1)	Paraphrased (EM/F1)
RoBERTa-large	100/100	0/14.93$_{-85.07}$
DistilBERT-base	66.46/73.5	27.22/39.05$_{-46.87}$
BERT-large	75.32/81.7	32.91/40.69$_{-50.2}$
SpanBERT-large	77.85/84.72	32.91/42.62$_{-49.69}$
ALBERT-xxlarge-v1	88.61/92.64	44.3/54.16$_{-41.54}$
DeBERTa-large	89.24/93.58	41.14/49.74$_{-46.85}$

Table 2: The performance (%) of the fine-tuned MRC models on the original and the paraphrased test set.

4.2 Error Analysis

To explore the source of model inaccuracies in paraphrased contexts, we manually checked 50 perturbed examples on which the examined MRC models failed and identified three potential sources of model errors. We observed that the paraphrasing of keywords in the sentence that is required to answer the question, along with some other lexical changes, might lead models to provide an incorrect answer (see Figure 9 in Appendix F). Moreover, another source of errors might be the change in the answer sentence structure (see Figure 10 in Appendix F as an example). Paraphrasing other contextual sentences may also inadvertently lead to the generation of incorrect responses by MRC models, particularly when such paraphrases result in keyword overlap with the question. However, unraveling the sources of these errors in the midst of full-context paraphrasing perturbation remains a complex problem that requires further investigation. Overall, our findings suggest that these high-performing systems might mostly rely on certain words matching between the question and the context to generate the answer, rather than truly understanding the passage. However, we also observed in a small proportion of examples that a mismatch between the answer provided by a model and the gold standard answer, does not necessarily mean that the model's answer is erroneous: in some cases, the semantic meaning of the paraphrased context has changed or the model's answer is arguably correct. This indicates that this work might be underestimating the robustness of the investigated models.

4.3 Robustness Improvement

An intuitive strategy to enhance the models' robustness to context paraphrasing involves exposing them to suitable examples. To this end, we selected 2694 MRC contexts (comprising 12723 questions) from the original SQuAD 1.1 training set (Rajpurkar et al., 2016) and paraphrased them using Finnish, a language that has been demonstrated to be the most effective for generating suitable MRC examples. We then curated the perturbed examples where the answer span still contained within the corresponding paraphrased context, yielding 2459 paraphrased contexts across a total of 8075 questions. The investigated models were then re-trained on the SQuAD 1.1 training set, augmented with these perturbed instances. Table 3 shows their performance on both the original and the paraphrased test sets, before and after re-training.

Model	**Performance (EM/F1)**	
	Before	After
DistilBERT (base)	66.46/73.5	65.19/73.58
	27.22/39.05	24.68/36.18
BERT (large)	75.32/81.7	81.65/85.77
	32.91/40.69	34.18/43.58
SpanBERT (large)	77.85/84.72	83.54/88.96
	32.91/42.62	38.61/48.29
ALBERT (xxlarge-v1)	88.61/92.64	88.61/93.52
	44.3/54.16	46.84/55.78
DeBERTa (large)	89.24/93.58	90.51/94.81
	41.14/49.74	43.04/51.77

Table 3: The performance (%) of MRC systems on the original and the paraphrased test set, before and after re-training. Performance figures displayed in white cells correspond to results obtained on the original test set, whereas the results shown in the shaded areas represent the performance on the generated challenge set.

From Table 3, we can see that on the original test set, apart from the DistilBERT-base, which experienced a slight performance decline in terms of the EM metric, all retrained models demonstrated higher performance than the one trained on the original training set of SQuAD 1.1, though the augmented contexts-paraphrased set contains noises, i.e., those are not suitable examples. These findings showcase the potential for enhancing performance on the original dataset by training models with context-paraphrased MRC examples. On the paraphrased challenge set, for all models expect the DistilBERT-base, re-training with the additional perturbed examples improved the performance and thus their robustness to context paraphrasing. However, for the DistilBERT-base model, exposing it to the paraphrased examples even resulted in a moderate performance drop (7.35% F1), further compromising its robustness in handling context paraphrasing. This might due to the unsuitable examples included in the augmented training set, but also demonstrate the challenging nature of the whole context paraphrasing perturbation on the DistilBERT-base (Sanh et al., 2019).

5 Conclusion

In this paper, we reveal the weaknesses of contemporary reading comprehension systems to context paraphrasing. With the proposed perturbation framework, we generated a paraphrased challenge set, to which six high-performing MRC models generalise poorly. We also demonstrate that a training data augmentation approach can enhance the robustness of the majority of models when exposed to the paraphrased contexts. This informs us that to equip models with context paraphrasing understanding ability, there is a need to create benchmarks in which this reasoning challenge is precisely represented. Future work will include the design of better techniques to remove the noise existing in the challenge set and the optimise of the perturbation pipeline so that it can be generalisable to more challenging datasets.

Limitations

In this work, our annotated gold dataset might contain potentially debatable instances of suitable MRC examples. To address this concern, there is a pressing need for the establishment of theoretical foundations which clearly define *human answerable* under the context-paraphrasing oriented perturbations and other types of perturbations. Building upon this, research efforts are needed to evaluate and enhance the precision of automatic approaches for identifying suitable examples, enabling precise assessment of models robustness against test-time perturbations. Further, there is potential to design better document-level paraphrasing methods and expand this study to include other sophisticated MRC datasets and diverse NLU tasks.

Ethics Statement

The SQuAD 1.1 benchmark and models utilized in this paper are all publicly available. During the phase of human annotation, explicit instructions regarding the annotation task were provided to all annotators, and they were informed about the intended use of their annotations. Only their responses to the questions were collected, and no sensitive information was gathered. Consequently, we do not anticipate any ethical concerns arising from our work.

Acknowledgements

The authors express the gratitude to the anonymous reviewers from the ACL Rolling Review April and June 2023 for their invaluable suggestions. We would also like to thank Michael White and Jing Wang in annotating the perturbed MRC examples. Part of the experiments were conducted with the support of the Computational Shared Facility at The University of Manchester, for which the authors are grateful. This work was supported by the University of Manchester Department of Computer Science Kilburn Scholarship.

References

Tom Brown, Benjamin Mann, Nick Ryder, Melanie Subbiah, Jared D Kaplan, Prafulla Dhariwal, Arvind Neelakantan, Pranav Shyam, Girish Sastry, Amanda Askell, Sandhini Agarwal, Ariel Herbert-Voss, Gretchen Krueger, Tom Henighan, Rewon Child, Aditya Ramesh, Daniel Ziegler, Jeffrey Wu, Clemens Winter, Chris Hesse, Mark Chen, Eric Sigler, Mateusz Litwin, Scott Gray, Benjamin Chess, Jack Clark, Christopher Berner, Sam McCandlish, Alec Radford, Ilya Sutskever, and Dario Amodei. 2020. Language models are few-shot learners. In *Advances in Neural Information Processing Systems*, volume 33, pages 1877–1901. Curran Associates, Inc.

Danqi Chen. 2018. *Neural Reading Comprehension and Beyond*. Ph.D. thesis, Stanford University.

Jacob Cohen. 1960. A coefficient of agreement for nominal scales. *Educational and Psychological Measurement*, 20(1):37–46.

Scott A. Crossley, Kristopher Kyle, and Mihai Dascalu. 2019. The Tool for the Automatic Analysis of Cohesion 2.0: Integrating semantic similarity and text overlap. *Behavior Research Methods*, 51(1):14–27.

Jacob Devlin, Ming-Wei Chang, Kenton Lee, and Kristina Toutanova. 2019. BERT: Pre-training of deep bidirectional transformers for language understanding. In *Proceedings of the 2019 Conference of the North American Chapter of the Association for Computational Linguistics: Human Language Technologies, Volume 1 (Long and Short Papers)*, pages 4171–4186, Minneapolis, Minnesota. Association for Computational Linguistics.

Eberhard, David M., Gary F. Simons, and Charles D. Fennig (eds.). 2022. Ethnologue: Languages of the World. Available at https://www.ethnologue.com.

Wee Chung Gan and Hwee Tou Ng. 2019. Improving the robustness of question answering systems to question paraphrasing. In *Proceedings of the 57th Annual Meeting of the Association for Computational Linguistics*, pages 6065–6075, Florence, Italy. Association for Computational Linguistics.

Pengcheng He, Xiaodong Liu, Jianfeng Gao, and Weizhu Chen. 2021. {DEBERTA}: {DECODING}-{enhanced} {bert} {with} {disentangled} {attention}. In *International Conference on Learning Representations*.

Mandar Joshi, Danqi Chen, Yinhan Liu, Daniel S. Weld, Luke Zettlemoyer, and Omer Levy. 2020. SpanBERT: Improving pre-training by representing and predicting spans. *Transactions of the Association for Computational Linguistics*, 8:64–77.

Marcin Junczys-Dowmunt, Roman Grundkiewicz, Tomasz Dwojak, Hieu Hoang, Kenneth Heafield, Tom Neckermann, Frank Seide, Ulrich Germann, Alham Fikri Aji, Nikolay Bogoychev, André F. T. Martins, and Alexandra Birch. 2018. Marian: Fast neural machine translation in C++. In *Proceedings of ACL 2018, System Demonstrations*, pages 116–121, Melbourne, Australia. Association for Computational Linguistics.

Yuxuan Lai, Chen Zhang, Yansong Feng, Quzhe Huang, and Dongyan Zhao. 2021. Why machine reading comprehension models learn shortcuts? In *Findings of the Association for Computational Linguistics: ACL-IJCNLP 2021*, pages 989–1002, Online. Association for Computational Linguistics.

Zhenzhong Lan, Mingda Chen, Sebastian Goodman, Kevin Gimpel, Piyush Sharma, and Radu Soricut. 2020. Albert: A lite bert for self-supervised learning of language representations. In *International Conference on Learning Representations*.

Yinhan Liu, Myle Ott, Naman Goyal, Jingfei Du, Mandar Joshi, Danqi Chen, Omer Levy, Mike Lewis, Luke Zettlemoyer, and Veselin Stoyanov. 2019. Roberta: A robustly optimized BERT pretraining approach. *CoRR*, abs/1907.11692.

Pranav Rajpurkar, Jian Zhang, Konstantin Lopyrev, and Percy Liang. 2016. SQuAD: 100,000+ questions for machine comprehension of text. In *Proceedings of the 2016 Conference on Empirical Methods in Natural Language Processing*, pages 2383–2392, Austin, Texas. Association for Computational Linguistics.

Marco Tulio Ribeiro, Tongshuang Wu, Carlos Guestrin, and Sameer Singh. 2020. Beyond accuracy: Behavioral testing of NLP models with CheckList. In *Proceedings of the 58th Annual Meeting of the Association for Computational Linguistics*, pages 4902–4912, Online. Association for Computational Linguistics.

Victor Sanh, Lysandre Debut, Julien Chaumond, and Thomas Wolf. 2019. DistilBERT, a distilled version of BERT: smaller, faster, cheaper and lighter. In *5th Workshop on Energy Efficient Machine Learning and Cognitive Computing @ NeurIPS 2019*.

Viktor Schlegel, Goran Nenadic, and Riza Batista-Navarro. 2021. Semantics altering modifications for evaluating comprehension in machine reading. *Proceedings of the AAAI Conference on Artificial Intelligence*, 35(15):13762–13770.

Viktor Schlegel, Goran Nenadic, and Riza Batista-Navarro. 2023. A survey of methods for revealing and overcoming weaknesses of data-driven natural language understanding. *Natural Language Engineering*, 29(1):1–31.

Viktor Schlegel, Marco Valentino, Andre Freitas, Goran Nenadic, and Riza Batista-Navarro. 2020. A framework for evaluation of machine reading comprehension gold standards. In *Proceedings of the Twelfth Language Resources and Evaluation Conference*, pages 5359–5369, Marseille, France. European Language Resources Association.

Kazutoshi Shinoda, Saku Sugawara, and Akiko Aizawa. 2021. Can question generation debias question answering models? a case study on question–context lexical overlap. In *Proceedings of the 3rd Workshop on Machine Reading for Question Answering*, pages 63–72, Punta Cana, Dominican Republic. Association for Computational Linguistics.

Kazutoshi Shinoda, Saku Sugawara, and Akiko Aizawa. 2023. Which shortcut solution do question answering models prefer to learn? *Proceedings of the AAAI Conference on Artificial Intelligence*.

Chenglei Si, Ziqing Yang, Yiming Cui, Wentao Ma, Ting Liu, and Shijin Wang. 2021. Benchmarking robustness of machine reading comprehension models. In *Findings of the Association for Computational Linguistics: ACL-IJCNLP 2021*, pages 634–644, Online. Association for Computational Linguistics.

Saku Sugawara, Nikita Nangia, Alex Warstadt, and Samuel Bowman. 2022. What makes reading comprehension questions difficult? In *Proceedings of the 60th Annual Meeting of the Association for Computational Linguistics (Volume 1: Long Papers)*, pages 6951–6971, Dublin, Ireland. Association for Computational Linguistics.

Jörg Tiedemann. 2012. Parallel data, tools and interfaces in OPUS. In *Proceedings of the Eighth International Conference on Language Resources and Evaluation (LREC'12)*, pages 2214–2218, Istanbul, Turkey. European Language Resources Association (ELRA).

Jörg Tiedemann and Santhosh Thottingal. 2020. OPUS-MT – building open translation services for the world. In *Proceedings of the 22nd Annual Conference of the European Association for Machine Translation*, pages 479–480, Lisboa, Portugal. European Association for Machine Translation.

Xuezhi Wang, Haohan Wang, and Diyi Yang. 2022. Measure and improve robustness in NLP models: A survey. In *Proceedings of the 2022 Conference of the North American Chapter of the Association for Computational Linguistics: Human Language Technologies*, pages 4569–4586, Seattle, United States. Association for Computational Linguistics.

Jason Wei, Xuezhi Wang, Dale Schuurmans, Maarten Bosma, brian ichter, Fei Xia, Ed Chi, Quoc V Le, and Denny Zhou. 2022. Chain-of-thought prompting elicits reasoning in large language models. In *Advances in Neural Information Processing Systems*, volume 35, pages 24824–24837. Curran Associates, Inc.

Thomas Wolf, Lysandre Debut, Victor Sanh, Julien Chaumond, Clement Delangue, Anthony Moi, Pierric Cistac, Tim Rault, Remi Louf, Morgan Funtowicz, Joe Davison, Sam Shleifer, Patrick von Platen, Clara Ma, Yacine Jernite, Julien Plu, Canwen Xu, Teven Le Scao, Sylvain Gugger, Mariama Drame, Quentin Lhoest, and Alexander Rush. 2020. Transformers: State-of-the-art natural language processing. In *Proceedings of the 2020 Conference on Empirical Methods in Natural Language Processing: System Demonstrations*, pages 38–45, Online. Association for Computational Linguistics.

Winston Wu, Dustin Arendt, and Svitlana Volkova. 2021a. Evaluating neural model robustness for machine comprehension. In *Proceedings of the 16th*

Conference of the European Chapter of the Association for Computational Linguistics: Main Volume, pages 2470–2481, Online. Association for Computational Linguistics.

Yulong Wu, Viktor Schlegel, and Riza Batista-Navarro. 2021b. Is the understanding of explicit discourse relations required in machine reading comprehension? In *Proceedings of the 16th Conference of the European Chapter of the Association for Computational Linguistics: Main Volume*, pages 3565–3579, Online. Association for Computational Linguistics.

Jun Yan, Yang Xiao, Sagnik Mukherjee, Bill Yuchen Lin, Robin Jia, and Xiang Ren. 2022. On the robustness of reading comprehension models to entity renaming. In *Proceedings of the 2022 Conference of the North American Chapter of the Association for Computational Linguistics: Human Language Technologies*, pages 508–520, Seattle, United States. Association for Computational Linguistics.

Wenxuan Zhou, Sheng Zhang, Hoifung Poon, and Muhao Chen. 2023. Context-faithful prompting for large language models.

A Dataset Statistics

Table 4 presents the number of contexts and questions contained within the SQuAD 1.1 training and development set, respectively.

	Training	Development
Context	18,896	2,067
Question	87,599	10,570

Table 4: Number of contexts and questions in the SQuAD 1.1 training and development sets (Rajpurkar et al., 2016).

B Hyperparameters of the Neural Reading Comprehension Models

Table 5 shows the hyperparameters used to fine-tune the pre-trained MRC models in this work. We utilised 2 16GB Nvidia v100 GPUs to fine-tune and evaluate each model.

$\text{Model}_{parameters(M)}$	d	b	lr	ep
$\text{RoBERTa-large}_{(355)}$	384	8	3e-5	2.0
$\text{DistilBERT-base}_{(65)}$	384	8	3e-5	3.0
$\text{BERT-large}_{(340)}$	384	8	3e-5	2.0
$\text{SpanBERT-large}_{(340)}$	512	4	2e-5	4.0
$\text{ALBERT-xxlarge-v1}_{(223)}$	384	4	3e-5	2.0
$\text{DeBERTa-large}_{(350)}$	384	4	3e-6	3.0

Table 5: The hyperparameters used to fine-tune each pre-trained MRC model (with its number of parameters). d is the size of the token sequence fed into the model, b is the training batch size, lr is the learning rate, and ep is the number of training epochs. We used stride = 128 for documents longer than d tokens.

C Human Annotation

This Appendix details the process of manually identifying the perturbed MRC examples that are suitable for context paraphrasing oriented robustness assessment. A total of three human annotators were involved in this task, including the first author of this paper. Prior to starting the annotation task, we asked all annotators to check a few examples and report the average time they spent for annotating each example. Based on this, we paid the annotators for their work by offering them coupons with a value of 20 pence for each example they annotate.

For the randomly sampled 247 candidate instances, we first asked two annotators to answer each question based on the corresponding paraphrased context, respectively. The annotators were required to select the shortest continuous span in the paraphrased context that answered the question only if they are confident that the paraphrased context still makes it possible to answer the associated question and were allowed to leave the answer as blank if the question is not answerable anymore. Full text of instruction given to the annotators can be seen in Figure 3. Afterwards, for each example, we measured the correctness of the answer span provided by each annotator through comparing it with the ground truth answers, respectively , and labelled the example as suitable or unsuitable based on the criteria described in Section 3.3. To conduct a precise analysis, we manually checked all examples with the answer span given by the annotator(s) does not exact match any of the ground truth answers and decided the correctness of the answer by taking into account the corresponding context and the question as well. Figure 4 demonstrates one such example. We then measured the inter-annotator agreement by computing the Cohen's kappa coefficient (Cohen, 1960), which is around 0.48. This might indicate that there exists moderate discrepancies between the two annotators concerning the answerability of the questions predicated on the contexts that have been paraphrased. Finally, we presented the examples on which the two annotators share a disagreement to the third annotator and provided them the label that agreed by the majority of annotators. This yielded a total of 66 suitable examples. From the identified 66 examples, we further manually eliminated 13 wherein the prediction of the RoBERTa-large (Liu et al., 2019) could be reasonably deemed accurate, thus rendering them unsuitable for the robustness assessment (see Figure 5 as an example). Our final annotated dataset contains 53 (out of 247) suitable examples. In an effort to curtail potential bias, all annotators were solely provided with the paraphrased context and the corresponding question for their examination.

Thanks for contributing to this project! Your task is to read each given context and answer a question about it. We will compare the answer you provide with the ground truth answers to determine the human answerability of the question, and then screen out the examples that are suitable for the robustness assessment of reading comprehension systems. When you are answering the questions:
(1) If you meet a question that you truly think you can answer it based on the given context, then select the shortest continuous span in the context as the answer.
(2) If you meet a question that is completely unanswerable, leave the answer as blank.

Figure 3: Instructions for the annotation task.

Context: [...] The production of major food staples such as corn is subject to sharp weather-related fluctuations. [...]

Paraphrased Context: [...] The production of staple foods, such as maize, is affected by severe weather-related fluctuations. [...]

Question: What can cause fluctuations in the production of corn?

Ground Truth Answers:
weather-related fluctuations, weather-related, weather
Prediction Under Context Paraphrasing:
Human Annotator 1:
severe weather
Human Annotator 2:
severe weather-related

Figure 4: An instance requiring human effort for the validation of answer accuracy. Both answer spans provided by the two annotators are considered correct, despite yielding an EM score of 0.

Context: Kenya [...], officially the Republic of Kenya, is a country in Africa and a founding member of the East African Community (EAC). Its capital and largest city is Nairobi. Kenya's territory lies on the equator and overlies the East African Rift covering a diverse and expansive terrain that extends roughly from Lake Victoria to Lake Turkana (formerly called Lake Rudolf) and further south-east to the Indian Ocean. [...]

Paraphrased Context: Kenya (Kenya: "Kenya") is a country in Africa and one of the founding members of the East African Community (EAC). The capital and largest city is Nairobi. The area of Kenya lies on the equator and survives the East African Rift which covers a diverse and vast area that stretches roughly from Lake Victoria to Lake Turkana (formerly Lake Rudolf) and further south-eastern to the Indian Ocean. [...]

Question: Where is Kenya located?

Ground Truth Answers:
Africa, in Africa
RoBERTa-large's Prediction Under Context Paraphrasing: on the equator

Figure 5: A perturbed example that is not suitable for the robustness assessment since the answer span offered by the RoBERTa-large model (Liu et al., 2019) is reasonably accurate, albeit not an exact match for any of the ground truth answers.

D Automated Identification of Suitable MRC Instances

To circumvent the substantial effort required for manual annotation, we attempted to automatically classify whether a perturbed reading comprehension example is qualified to demonstrate the lack of robustness of MRC models to context paraphrasing. In the following, we elaborate on the two approaches undertaken and present the empirical results derived from these experiments.

ML-based Approach: We trained and evaluated multiple classifiers on our 247 annotated examples with 129 input features that were calculated by TAACO (Crossley et al., 2019), a tool that measures various linguistic features of the passage such as lexical density and adjacent sentence overlap. The designed classification pipeline involves data standardisation, features selection and random oversampling. Hyperparameter tuning was carried out to determine the optimal configuration. The obtained best-performing model, Random Forest (with 40 selected features), only achieved 0.39 precision in predicting suitable example, which implies that those extracted features might not sufficient to represent this challenging task. Therefore, we shifted our attention to the GPT series models, given their exceptional efficacy in transforming many tasks into generative tasks.

GPT Series Models: Compared to traditional ML methods, GPT series models offer the advantage of not requiring the construction of linguistic features, thereby simplifying the approach to automatically classify suitable MRC examples. Drawing upon the human annotation process described in Appendix C, we first manually constructed the zero-shot prompt encompassing the paraphrased context, question, ground truth answers, the answer span given by the RoBERTa-large (Liu et al., 2019), and tasked the model to generate binary output (0 or 1) to indicate whether an example is suitable for robustness assessment, adhering to a predefined set of decision rules. We also experimented with the few-shot prompt by adding three randomly selected in-context exemplars of input-label pairs (demonstrations) (Brown et al., 2020) in the zero-shot prompt. Under both zero-shot and few-shot scenarios, we further investigated the use of the Chain-of-Thought (CoT) (Wei et al., 2022) by adding "let's think step by step" and CoT demonstrations in the corresponding prompt, respectively. The templates for the four prompting strategies are shown in Appendix G. In order to mitigate the influence of prior dialogues, each request was sent individually to produce the corresponding response. When processing the responses, especially under the zero-shot CoT and few-shot CoT scenarios, we only consider an example as suitable if its response includes a solid explanation and judgement. Labels generated by the model under the four distinct test configurations were subsequently compared with the gold labels annotated by human evaluators, respectively. The results are shown in Table 6.

Prompting Method	Precision
Zero-shot	0.41
Zero-shot CoT	0.23
Few-shot	0.26
Few-shot CoT	0.28

Table 6: Precision of the GPT-3.5-turbo model in predicting suitable example using four different prompting methods.

It can be seen from Table 6 that on the precision of predicting suitable MRC example, prompting under the zero-shot scenario provides the best result, which is 0.41. Surprisingly, the incorporation of demonstrations and the adoption of the CoT prompting considerably attenuate model performance, a finding that deviates from existing literature asserting enhancements in performance across many NLU tasks with the inclusion of in-context demonstrations (Brown et al., 2020) and the CoT method (Wei et al., 2022). The observed unsatisfactory performance could potentially be attributed to two factors: (1) The ambiguity inherent to the task of automated identification of suitable MRC example, as viewed from the dataset annotation perspective. As indicated in Appendix C, a moderate level of disagreement was even observed between two human annotators in determining whether a question is indeed answerable based on the paraphrased context, with an inter-annotator agreement score of 0.48. This suggests that our annotated set of 247 examples might contain contentious cases, thereby rendering the task notably challenging for the model. (2) From the model's perspective, we investigated potential reasons for performance degradation following the adoption of in-context examples and CoT by manually scrutinizing some responses under these testing conditions. Our findings reveal that despite guidance from demonstrations and CoT, the model frequently produces reasoning that contradicts the predicted label or even generates hallucinations. For instance, under the zero-shot CoT scenario, model produces response like "*This example is suitable for robustness assessment. The ground truth answers (GTAs) and RoBERTa's answer A are different, indicating that there is potential for the model to make mistakes. Therefore, it is important to test the model's robustness by presenting it with similar but slightly different contexts and questions to ensure that it can generalize well and provide accurate answers.*", which even not relevant to the task. While we acknowledge that there exists scope to improve the prompts used in this work, it remains evident that the GPT-3.5-turbo model, despite its significant accomplishments in some NLU tasks, still falls short of attaining human-level language comprehension.

Though the performance of the obtained best model, i.e., GPT-3.5-turbo under the zero-shot scenario, is not satisfactory, we attempted to measure its precision in predicting suitable example from the candidate perturbed instances generated by using each pivot language, respectively, as shown in Table 7. From Table 7, we can see that in classifying perturbed examples paraphrased using Finnish, the model exhibits flawless performance, achieving a precision score of 1.0. In contrast, for other languages, such as Russian, Chinese and Indonesian, the precision score is notably low or even zero. Therefore, to generate our paraphrased challenge set, we restricted model's application to filtered perturbed examples produced using Finnish, Spanish, Vietnamese, Italian and Swedish (with precision greater than 0.5), which yielded a final precision score of 0.69, while excluding instances generated using other languages.

Pivot Language(s)	Precision
Finnish	1.0
Spanish	0.8
Vietnamese	0.67
Italian, Swedish	0.5
German	0.33
Dutch, Russian	0.25
Chinese	0.16
Hindi, Indonesian, French	0

Table 7: Precision of the GPT-3.5-turbo in predicting suitable example from the candidate perturbed instances generated using each of the 12 pivot languages.

E Analysis of Disparities in Adversarial Examples Perception: GPT-3.5-turbo vs. Human

The zero-shot prompt, as designed in Appendix D, directly solicits a binary response from the GPT-3.5-turbo model concerning the suitability of a perturbed MRC example for robustness assessment. To validate the stability of the obtained performance (0.41 precision) and also examine the divergence in the perception of whole context-paraphrased adversarial examples between the GPT-3.5-turbo model and human observers, we conducted further experiments by directly asking the model to extract the shortest continuous span as the answer given the paraphrased context and the question. We utilised the prompting method based on both instruction and opinion (Zhou et al., 2023) to improve the faithfulness of the model to paraphrased context when formulating responses, thereby precluding the use of its parametric knowledge to a great extent. Additionally, an "I do not know" option was allowed to encourage the model to abstain from providing the answer if the paraphrased context does not make it possible to answer the question anymore. Figure 6 demonstrates the used prompt template.

> Instruction: read the given information and answer the corresponding question. The output should only be the shortest continuous span from the context and should not include any explanation. Output "I do not know" if the context makes it impossible to answer the corresponding question.
> Bob said, "context"
> Q: question in Bob's opinion based on the given text?

Figure 6: An instruction-opinion based prompt template (Zhou et al., 2023).

Afterwards, we determined the accuracy of each response generated by the GPT-3.5-turbo model and assigned a binary label (1 or 0) to signify its appropriateness for robustness assessment. We then compared the obtained results with the gold standard labels of the annotated dataset version containing 66 suitable examples (see Appendix C), as our provided prompt does not require the model to consider the correctness of the prediction made by the RoBERTa-large (Liu et al., 2019). Experimental results revealed that the GPT-3.5-turbo model maintained a consistent 0.41 precision score in predicting suitable MRC example, thereby suggesting its stability on this task to some extent. Figure 7 and Figure 8 demonstrate a failure case of the GPT-3.5-turbo model on the suitable example classification, respectively. In Figure 7, the model is still able to extract the correct answer span "John Sutcliffe" from the paraphrased context, though both human annotators deem that the question is not answerable. On the contrary, as can be seen from Figure 8, while human annotators can get the answer correct, the model abstains from answering the question and thus generates "I do not know" as the answer. These findings suggest the existence of a significant gap between the GPT-3.5-turbo model and human performance in discerning whole context paraphrasing oriented textual attacks and the GPT-3.5-turbo is still substantially distant from achieving human-level NLU capability.

Context: [...] The game was called by ESPN Deportes' Monday Night Football commentary crew of Alvaro Martin and Raul Allegre, and sideline reporter John Sutcliffe. [...]
Paraphrased Context: [...] The game was called by ESPN Deportes' Monday Night Football comment crew Alvaro Martin and Raul Allegre, and side EPOR John Sutcliffe. [...]
Question: Who was the ESPN Deportes sideline commentator for Super Bowl 50?
Prediction Under Context Paraphrasing: **Human Annotators:** Unanswerable **GPT-3.5-turbo:** John Sutcliffe

Figure 7: Demonstration of a failure case of the GPT-3.5-turbo model in predicting suitable example. While both human annotators deem that the question is not answerable over the paraphrased context, the model still provides the correct answer span.

Context: Sudbury model democratic schools claim that popularly based authority can maintain order more effectively than dictatorial authority for governments and schools alike. They also claim that in these schools the preservation of public order is easier and more efficient than anywhere else. [...]
Paraphrased Context: Model schools in Sudbury argue that popular authority can maintain order more effectively than dictatorial authority for governments and schools. They also claim that, in these schools, the preservation of public order is easier and more effective than anywhere else. [...]
Question: In addition to schools, where else is popularly based authority effective?
Prediction Under Context Paraphrasing: **Human Annotators:** governments **GPT-3.5-turbo:** I do not know

Figure 8: Illustration of the robustness deficiency of the GPT-3.5-turbo model to whole context paraphrasing. The model was unable to generate the correct answer span, despite both human annotators supplying the accurate response.

F Suitable Examples Demonstration

We present two perturbed examples from the constructed challenge set on which the MRC models demonstrated unsatisfactory generalisation, as shown in Figure 9 and Figure 10, respectively.

Paragraph: The game's media day, which was typically held on the Tuesday afternoon prior to the game, was moved to the Monday evening and re-branded as Super Bowl Opening Night. [...]
Paraphrased Paragraph: The video day of the game, which was usually held on Tuesday afternoon before playing games, was moved to Monday night and was reset as Super Bowl Opening Night. [...]
Question: What day of the week was Media Day held on for Super Bowl 50?
Original Prediction: Monday **Prediction Under Adversary:** Tuesday

Figure 9: A perturbed example primarily involves lexical changes, ultimately leading the model to provide the wrong answer.

Paragraph: A method to lessen the magnitude of this heating and cooling was invented in 1804 by British engineer Arthur Woolf, who patented his Woolf high-pressure compound engine in 1805. [...]
Paraphrased Paragraph: British engineer Arthur Woolf, who patented Woolf's high pressure engine in 1805, invented in 1804 a method to reduce the volume of this heating and cooling. [...]
Question: What nationality was Arthur Woolf?
Original Prediction: British **Prediction Under Adversary:** engineer

Figure 10: Illustration of the brittleness of MRC systems when dealing with a syntactic form changed context.

G Templates for Various Prompting Strategies

Figure 11 illustrates the diverse templates employed to prompt the GPT-3.5-turbo model to classify the suitable perturbed MRC example.

Instructions: Given an example which contains a context, question, ground truth answers (GTAs) and RoBERTa's answer A, decide whether it is suitable for robustness assessment by choosing one of the following options: '0': A is reasonably correct or A is wrong and you cannot correctly answer the question purely relying on the context as well. '1': A is wrong but you can correctly answer the question purely relying on the context.
zero-shot: [Instructions] Generate either '0' or '1', do not include the explanation. Context: [context] Question: [question] GTAs: [GTAs] A: A
zero-shot CoT: [Instructions] Context: [context] Question: [question] GTAs: [GTAs] A: A Let's think step by step and then generate the response ([0] or [1]):
few-shot: [Instructions] Generate either '0' or '1', do not include the explanation. Example: Context: Model schools in Sudbury argue that popular authority can maintain order more effectively than dictatorial authority for governments and schools. [. . .] Question: In addition to schools, where else is popularly based authority effective? GTAs: ['governments'] A: governments and schools. They also claim that, in these schools, the preservation of public order is easier and more effective than anywhere else. Response: 1 Example: Context: [context] Question: [question] GTAs: [GTAs] A: A
few-shot CoT: [Instructions] Example: Context: Model schools in Sudbury argue that popular authority can maintain order more effectively than dictatorial authority for governments and schools. [. . .] Question: In addition to schools, where else is popularly based authority effective? GTAs: ['governments'] A: governments and schools. They also claim that, in these schools, the preservation of public order is easier and more effective than anywhere else. Response: Firstly, compare RoBERTa's answer A with GTAs. Since *governments and schools. They also claim that, in these schools, the preservation of public order is easier and more effective than anywhere else.* is wrong, then there is a need to thoroughly check the context and question. Since the context provides sufficient information to enable us to get the answer correct, the response is 1. Example: Context: [context] Question: [question] GTAs: [GTAs] A: A

Figure 11: Prompt templates provided to the GPT-3.5-turbo model. Due to space limitations, we only show one in-context input-label pair in the few-shot and few-shot CoT template.

It's not only What You Say, It's also Who It's Said to: Counterfactual Analysis of Interactive Behavior in the Courtroom

Biaoyan Fang[†] **Trevor Cohn**[†*] **Timothy Baldwin**[†,♠] **Lea Frermann**[†]
[†]The University of Melbourne, Australia
[♠]MBZUAI

{biaoyan,tcohn,tbaldwin,lfrermann}@unimelb.edu.au

Abstract

To what extent do personal attributes affect the way we are spoken to? Answering this question requires the precise reproduction of a conversational context except for one personal attribute of interest, amounting to a classical, yet infeasible, causal inference problem. We present a method based on counterfactual analysis by manipulating speaker attributes in observational data. We propose a case study of Advocate responses to Justices in debates in the Supreme Court of the United States. Specifically, we measure changes in politeness and coordination of Advocates when responding to (a) real Justices and (b) counterfactually-manipulated Justices, with responses generated with GPT2. We first validate our method, showing that GPT2-generated outputs capture coordination and politeness. Our results confirm a known impact of the attribute *gender*, and suggest a weaker effect of *seniority* on coordination.[1]

[ADVRES] [...] This is an obstacle preemption case masquerading as a field preemption case. [...] and the Nuclear Regulatory Commission have repeatedly reaffirmed that states have the ability to regulate mining up to and including by banning it altogether [...] [BADER-GINSBURG]
~~[KAVANAUGH]~~ ~~Yeah~~. So the mining and milling occur together, correct? In other words [...] you don't have mining without milling; you don't have milling without mining
[ADVRES] [...] there's a way – the in situ leaching process, they literally occur at the same time.

Figure 1: An example instance from our dataset. We measure politeness and coordination in the true or generated [ADVRES] response (bottom) to a question from a Justice (middle) in context (top). Counterfactuals replace the **true** Justice identity tag (male) with a **different** one (female).

1 Introduction

Does the way we speak to others depend on the personal attributes of the addressee? Speakers employ different strategies when replying to persons of different social status (Niederhoffer and Pennebaker, 2002; Taylor and Thomas, 2008; Danescu-Niculescu-Mizil et al., 2012, 2013; Mizukami et al., 2016). Well-known strategies are linguistic accommodation, e.g., in adjusting in style to a more senior conversation partner (Kulesza et al., 2014; Danescu-Niculescu-Mizil et al., 2012; Noble and Fernández, 2015; Xu et al., 2018), and politeness, where speakers vary the level of formality and word choice (Danescu-Niculescu-Mizil et al., 2013; Fu et al., 2020; Li et al., 2020). A better understanding of the factors that cause such strategies is not only of interest to social scientists, but could also render dialogue systems more natural.

To directly address this question would require a dataset of paired situations which are identical except for one speaker's personal attribute of interest. This would allow us to measure the causal effect of the attribute value (treatment) on language style (outcome) (Pearl, 2009; Imbens and Rubin, 2015).

Since this is not achievable, we present a counterfactual methodology based on manipulation of observational data and the power of pre-trained language models. Specifically, we require a dataset of observed conversations involving persons for which: (a) personal attribute values are known; (b) sufficient conversational data is available to fine-tune LMs; and (c) these conversations occur in a relatively controlled context. Here, we use conversations between Advocates and Justices in arguments from the US Supreme Court (SCOTUS) and investigate differences in politeness (Danescu-Niculescu-Mizil et al., 2013) and coordination (Danescu-Niculescu-Mizil et al., 2012) of Advocate responses to questions asked by Justices with different personal and professional attributes (Figure 1).

To validate our approach, we first show that pre-trained language models reliably capture politeness and coordination (Section 3). We do so

*Now at Google DeepMind.

[1]Dataset and code are made available at https://github.com/biaoyanf/SCOTUS-counterfactual.

Proceedings of the 13th International Joint Conference on Natural Language Processing and the 3rd Conference of the Asia-Pacific Chapter of the Association for Computational Linguistics (Volume 2: Short Papers), pages 197–207
November 1–4, 2023.

by comparing the politeness and coordination levels of real Advocate answers in the SCOTUS data against answers generated by a large pre-trained language model (GPT2; Radford et al. (2019)) when prompted with the same context (Figure 1, blue).

We consider three binary Justice attributes — gender, nominating party, and seniority — and compare politeness and coordination in GPT2 generated responses in factual vs. counterfactually-manipulated situations where the inquiring Justices' attribute value is flipped (Section 4; Figure 1, red → blue). We ask *would an Advocate's response change in politeness (coordination) had the question been asked by a Justice from a different social group?*

We show that LMs are sensitive to social cues, beyond the inherent biases in LMs and data sets (Section 6), prompting further research on fairness and bias from a sociolinguistic perspective.

2 Methodology

Data We use a subset of a published set of SCOTUS arguments[2] (Chang et al., 2020), covering transcripts from 1955 to 2019, comprising 4.5K cases, 35 Justices, and >1M utterances. We randomly selected one case per year to include in the dev and test sets, respectively, and used the remainder to fine-tune GPT2. We removed Justices with <80 turns from the test set.[3]

The published SCOTUS data includes the speaker identity (name) and function (e.g., Justice or Advocate) for each turn. We retain the full Justice name and map the Advocates to the side they stand for, i.e. petitioner (`[ADVPET]`) or respondent (`[ADVRES]`).[4] From this, we construct our final dataset, where each instance consists of 400 words of preceding context, followed by a Justice turn directly followed by an Advocate's response. Figure 1 shows an example context. The statistics of our dataset are listed in Table 1 and Appendix A provides additional details on the data set.

Demographic and Personal Attributes We study the impact of three binary attributes of a Justice on the politeness and coordination levels of the Advocates' response to their questions: gender (m, f); seniority (Chief Justice or not); and the party which nominated the Justice (Democrat, Republican).

	Train	Dev	Test
Number of Instances	402,230	6,366	6,129
Number of Cases	4,445	65	65
Number of Justices	35	35	20
Total #Turns	981,492	15,653	14,901
Avg. #token/Turn	48.38	45.33	48.11
Avg. #token/Justice Turn	29.93	29.64	29.49
Avg. #token/Advoc. Turn	64.93	60.05	63.56

Table 1: Statistics of our SCOTUS dataset, where individual instances are comprised of 400-token preceding context + Justice Turn + Advocate Turn.

Coordination and Politeness Prior work has proposed measures of coordination (Danescu-Niculescu-Mizil et al., 2012) and politeness (Danescu-Niculescu-Mizil et al., 2013), which have been used to study the connection between linguistic choices and personal attributes. We consider those measures to analyze the behavior of Advocates in the courtroom. Particularity, we directly use the coordination indicator from ConvoKit,[5] which quantifies the coordination of a respondent adv to a speaker jst wrt. a linguistic marker[6] lm by calculating how much the fact that jst used lm increases the probability of adv using lm in a direct response. We average across markers, and instead of considering individual jst, we measure coordination to groups of jst who share an attribute value a (e.g., all male or female Justices), obtaining coordination measure $\hat{y_c}^{jst=a}$.

We similarly measure politeness as the probability of observing a politeness marker[7] pm in an utterance by adv in response to jst, normalized by the prior probability of adv using pm; again, we average over values pm and all jst that share an attribute value, obtaining a politeness measure $\hat{y_p}^{jst=a}$.

Method We used GPT2 to generate responses given factual (Figure 1, red) and counterfactual (Figure 1, blue) contexts. We fine-tuned GPT2 on the SCOTUS training set for 50 epochs to incorporate a notion of typical Advocates' response

[2] https://convokit.cornell.edu/documentation/supreme.html

[3] See Appendix A for data construction details.

[4] Note that while the distinction is not strictly necessary for the experiments, it is intuitive that social alignment is impacted by the position of the conversation partner. See Appendix C for a detailed analysis of advocates' attributes.

[5] https://convokit.cornell.edu/

[6] E.g., auxiliaries, conjunctions, or quantifiers; cf., Danescu-Niculescu-Mizil et al. (2012) for full list.

[7] E.g, greetings, apologies or hedges; cf. Danescu-Niculescu-Mizil et al. (2013) for the full list.

behavior, and selected the best model based on dev set perplexity. We generated Advocate responses with GPT2 given a Justice question with preceding context. Each turn includes a speaker tag (see [TAGs] in Figure 1). We chose GPT2 because, unlike its successors GPT3 and ChatGPT, it can be fine-tuned to a target domain.

Factuals We first present factual SCOTUS contexts cxt (Figure 1, top and middle context) with true speaker tags (Figure 1, red) as prompts to GPT2 and have it generate a factual response. We obtain a final coordination (or, equivalently, politeness) score, by averaging over all generated responses to questions by Justices with attribute a:

$$y^{jst=a}|\{cxt\}^a, jst=a, \quad (1)$$

where scores y can pertain to coordination or politeness, and we omit subscripts to avoid clutter. In Section 3 we verify that GPT2 scores $y^{jst=a}$ mirror the true values $\hat{y}^{jst=a}$ across attribute values, for both coordination and politeness.

Counterfactual Speakers We next manipulate *only* a Justices' attribute of interest while keeping the rest of the context fixed, to examine its effect on the Advocate's response. We do so by changing the speaker tag (Figure 1, red $\rightarrow$ blue). For instance, to test the effect of gender on politeness (or, equivalently, coordination), we take all contexts involving male Justices $\{cxt\}^m$ and replace the male Justice's indicator (e.g., [KAVANAUGH]) with a female Justice's name (e.g., [BADER-GINSBURG]). We do this exhaustively for all male-female combinations and average over counterfactually generated responses towards female Justice tags to obtain a 'generic female' $\hat{f}$ politeness (coordination) score $y^{jst=\hat{f}|m}$ under male context $\{cxt\}^m$. Equivalently, we obtain a 'generic male' $\hat{m}$ politeness (coordination) score $y^{jst=\hat{m}|m}$ under male context $\{cxt\}^m$ by substituting male indicators with other male tags:

$$\begin{aligned} &y^{jst=\hat{f}|m}|\{cxt\}^m, do(jst=m\rightarrow\hat{f}),\\ &y^{jst=\hat{m}|m}|\{cxt\}^m, do(jst=m\rightarrow\hat{m}), \end{aligned} \quad (2)$$

where we denote the counterfactual manipulation with the *do* operator from the causal inference literature (Pearl, 2009). In sum, we fix the context (e.g., $\{cxt\}^m$) but manipulate properties of the Justices (e.g., $\hat{m}$ vs. $\hat{f}$) and measure the difference between politeness (or, equivalently, coordination) scores to test the effect of attribute values in speakers.[8]

Preference	Factual (Exp 1) Rel	Factual (Exp 1) Info	Factual (Exp 1) Cons	C'factual (Exp 2) Rel	C'factual (Exp 2) Info	C'factual (Exp 2) Cons
None	**0.88**	**0.53**	**0.71**	**0.77**	**0.43**	**0.52**
Real	0.04	0.37	0.14	0.07	0.23	0.16
Generated	0.08	0.10	0.14	0.16	0.34	0.32

Table 2: Human preferences of Relevance (Rel), Informativeness (Info) and Consistency (Cons).

Counterfactual Contexts Alternatively, to understand the effect of context spoken by groups with different values, we hold the properties of the Justices constant, and change the conditioning contexts. E.g., we fix the gender of the asking Justice, e.g., to a 'generic male' $\hat{m}$ by exhaustively inserting male Justice names as described above, and generate responses when (i) contextualized with male Justices' contexts $\{cxt\}^m$, or (ii) female Justices' contexts $\{cxt\}^f$, and compare their differences:

$$\begin{aligned} &y^{jst=\hat{m}|m}|\{cxt\}^m, do(jst=m\rightarrow\hat{m}),\\ &y^{jst=\hat{m}|f}|\{cxt\}^f, do(jst-f\rightarrow\hat{m}). \end{aligned} \quad (3)$$

In sum, we fix the properties of the Justices (e.g., $\hat{m}$) but manipulate the context from different justices (e.g., $\{cxt\}^m$ vs. $\{cxt\}^f$) and measure the difference between politeness (coordination) scores to test the effect of spoken context.

In Section 4 we apply both counterfactual comparisons (Equations (2) and (3)) across our three binary attributes, and politeness and coordination measures.

3 Experiment 1: Factual generation

First, we validated that generated Advocate responses to Justice questions resemble true responses in both content and coordination/politeness. We compared scores as estimated from the SCOTUS data against those generated by GPT2 when prompted with factual contexts (Equation (1)).

Content validity We observed a decrease in dev perplexity (116.22 to 2.75) after fine-tuning GPT-2. Additionally, we manually evaluated the generated responses in terms of their informativeness, relevance, and consistency (Finch and Choi, 2020). We hired two English native-speaker social scientists not involved in the project and presented them

[8]Analogously we obtain $y^{jst=\hat{m}|f}$ and $y^{jst=\hat{f}|f}$ by manipulating Justice groups in female contexts $\{cxt\}^f$.

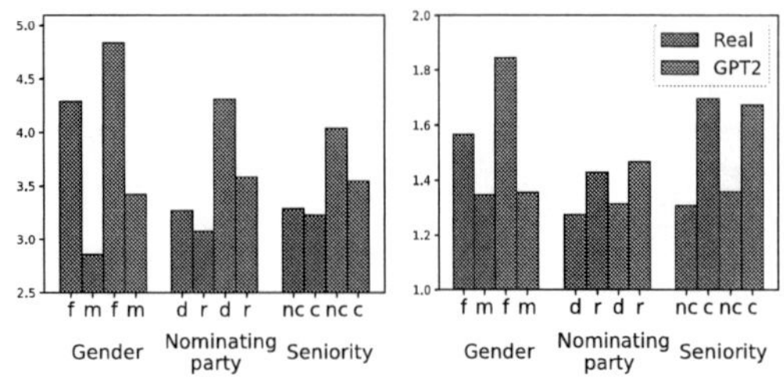

(a) Coordination. (b) Politeness.

Figure 2: Coordination and politeness scores in Advocates' responses to factual Justices. Gender: (m=Male, f=Female); Nominating party: (d=Democrat, r=Republican); Seniority (c=Chief jst, nc=Non-Chief). The coordination and politeness scores are scaled by 100 and 10 for clarity, respectively, and the same scaling applies to the following Figures.

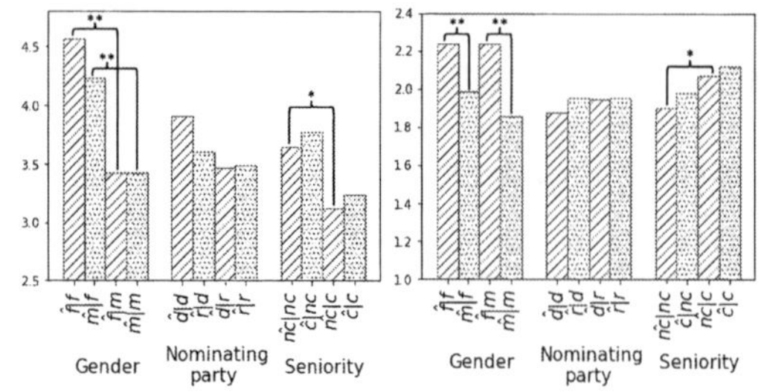

(a) Coordination. (b) Politeness.

Figure 3: Coordination and politeness scores in Advocate responses to counterfactually-manipulated Justices. x-labels as in Figure 2. Colors indicate attribute-specific contexts. Shading indicates Justice attribute value. Pairwise significant differences according to Welch's t-test at $p<0.1$ (*) and $p<0.05$ (**).

with the same prompt as GPT2 and the real and generated answers, and asked to indicate for each category which answer is preferred or whether both are equal. Table 2 (left) shows that overwhelmingly both answers were rated as equal. For cases where one answer was preferred, we verified that the distribution did not differ significantly from random (Binomial test, $p>0.05$, n=46).

Coordination and Politeness Do GPT2 responses reflect the differences in coordination and politeness in responses observed in the original SCOTUS data? Figure 2 shows that predicted coordination scores (green bars) consistently align with true scores (purple bars) in terms of direction and magnitude; the same holds for politeness in Figure 2b. Gender produces the largest difference in coordination (Figure 2a left), echoing the finding of Danescu-Niculescu-Mizil et al. (2012) that gender impacts speaker coordination in legal discourse. Gender and seniority incur politeness differences.[9]

4 Experiment 2: Counterfactual Generation

Having demonstrated that GPT2-generated responses reflect content and group-specific social signaling (Section 3), we now apply the counterfactual framework (Equations (2) and (3)). First, we ensured the content validity of *counterfactually* generated utterances via human evaluation as in Section 3. Table 2 (right) confirms that annotators did not prefer real responses over generated ones (or vice versa) for the vast majority of instances.[10]

We first ask to what extent social cues in an Advocate response vary wrt. a manipulated attribute of the asking party (Justice). This corresponds to Equation (2) and comparison of *lined vs. dotted bars of the same color* in Figure 3a (coordination) and Figure 3b (politeness). We find a significant difference (Welch's t-test, $p<0.05$) in politeness in response to Justice gender: Advocates are significantly more polite to real and counterfactual female Justices given the same context. This holds in both directions (a significant increase when manipulating 'generic male' $\hat{m} \to \hat{f}$ (red) and decrease when turning 'generic female' $\hat{f} \to \hat{m}$ (blue)).

Next, we investigate the impact of context on social signals in a response, by keeping properties of Justices fixed, but embedding them in different contexts originating either from Justices with binary attribute label a or $\neg a$ (Equation (3)). We inspect the results by *comparing the blue vs. red bars of the same shade (both lined or both dotted)* in Figure 3. We find a significant difference in coordination, when embedding female Justices in female vs. male contexts (left block Figure 3a blue lined vs. red lined) and male Justices in female vs. male contexts (same block, blue dotted vs. red dotted). With marginal significance ($p<0.1$, n=16), we observe a decrease in coordination and increase in politeness when embedding non-Chief Justices in non-Chief vs. Chief contexts (blue vs. red lines in the right blocks in Figures 3a and 3b).

[9] Appendix C presents further evidence for this, over 7 personal attributes across Advocates and Justices.

[10] Example pairs of real and generated responses are in Appendix D. Preferences are again not significantly different from random (Binomial, $p>0.05$).

5 Discussion

Does the way we speak depend on the personal attributes of our interlocutor? We addressed this question with a new methodology involving counterfactual manipulation and high-quality response generation from a powerful language model. Our method isolates social cues in responses to questions from groups of people with different social or demographic attributes in otherwise controlled contexts. We presented a case study on Advocate responses to Justices in SCOTUS arguments, where we manipulated the Justices' attributes of gender, seniority, and nominating political party.

We found that (1) the Justice's gender has a significant impact on Advocate *politeness*: Advocates are more polite toward female Justices; (2) Advocate *coordination* changes significantly in response to the *context* invoked by male vs. female Justices. We also found weak evidence that Advocate coordination and politeness change in response to the *context* invoked by Chief vs. non-Chief Justices.

Our method extends a line of work of leveraging LMs for causal inference with observational text data (Keith et al., 2020; Veitch et al., 2020; Pryzant et al., 2021; Feder et al., 2022), which has predominantly studied the causal effects of different linguistic properties (treatment) on some non-textual outcome, whereas we manipulate speaker attributes (treatment) and study their effect on language as an outcome. We address the problem of confounding (variables that affect both treatment and outcome) by: (a) tight control of contexts as legal court arguments; and (b) verification that our method of GPT2 fine-tuning and attribute-conditioned generation is both faithful in content to the original, and captures real-world differences in expression pertaining to our attributes of interest.

Our proposed counterfactual framework can be further applied to other conversations such as online discussions (Danescu-Niculescu-Mizil et al., 2012), interviews (Fu et al., 2016) and congressional records (Gentzkow et al., 2018), to investigate the effect of attribute groups in various scenarios; and to other sociolinguistic phenomena, such as persuasion (Dimitrov et al., 2021) in order to explore additional perspectives on the social dynamics in conversations.

While current debiasing research (Wang et al., 2020; Kaneko and Bollegala, 2021; Guo et al., 2022) is focused on the semantic level (i.e. unwarranted associations between attributes and content), our study shows that LMs also capture subtle sociolinguistic biases (i.e. coordination and politeness). We hope our counterfactual framework spurs future work on evaluating fairness and bias from a sociolinguistic perspective.

6 Ethical Discussion

6.1 Potential Bias

We conduct our counterfactual analysis using LMs, which have been proven to be biased (Nadeem et al., 2021; Delobelle et al., 2022). The generated results might contain inherited bias from the pre-trained language models. This could introduce confounds in the generated responses: (1) LMs might be a prior more likely to (not) generate selective politeness/coordination markers due to exposure in the training data.[11] (2) Historical biases — as LMs were predominantly trained on contemporary language leading to a temporal confound where predictions on earlier data points might be noisier than those for more recent SCOTUS discussions. We acknowledge that this could further bring undetected harm in analyzing Advocate court behaviors, especially in the counterfactual setting.

Our analysis is based on groups of speakers who share an attribute value, and makes no claims about the content/professional level, nor on individuals. Although our framework could generate intermediate results for individual Justices and, in theory, could derive personal conclusions in court, we strongly caution against this.

6.2 Human annotations

To test the content validity of GPT2, we recruited two native-speakers with social science backgrounds not involved in this project through the authors' contacts. We did not record any personal information (e.g. demographics). Authors were debriefed in full after completion of the task, and paid an hourly rate of USD$38, which far exceeds the local minimum pay rate.

7 Limitations

For modeling speaker behavior, we consider social cues based on coordination and politeness. Other dimensions, such as sentiment (Feldman, 2013), persuasion (Dimitrov et al., 2021), or rate of interruption (Epstein et al., 2010), could be further ex-

[11]We investigate coordination scores under breakdown markers in Appendix E, with Advocates towards male vs. female Justices as an example.

plored to better understand social dynamics in the courtroom. It would also be interesting to explore the interactions among the proposed sociolinguistic perspectives. Also, we focus on the responses from Advocates toward Justices. A study from the other direction could complement this work, and aid in better understanding the dynamics of legal oral arguments. What's more, another type of speaker, e.g. amici curiae ("friends of the court") has been shown to have influences on legal judgments (Sim et al., 2015) and is also worthy of investigation.

All experiments were based on GPT2 (Radford et al., 2019). There is room for exploration of pretrained language models, such as GPT3 (Floridi and Chiriatti, 2020), ChatGPT, BART (Lewis et al., 2020), or T5 (Raffel et al., 2022). In natural language generation, current work (Wu et al., 2020; Hu and Li, 2021) has introduced casual models to generate counterfactual text, and this could further aid the analysis of the impacts of different social factors.

Our study is based on a subset of SCOTUS cases.[12] While they have similar statistics to full cases, they do not reflect the full conversation history of the US Supreme Court or represent the current state of the court. Also, all claims in this paper are bound to this specific use case. They are not generalizable to other SCOTUS parties, legal systems, social strategies, etc. Additionally, although, in preliminary experiments, we applied a temporal train/test split (holding out the final year, I.e. 2019, as test data) and verified that the general pattern of results (i.e. perplexity) is identical in both the random and the temporal split, temporal effects on SCOTUS cases, especially from a sociolinguistic perspective, would be worthy for further investigation.

[12]We extract a subset form the Covokit dataset (Chang et al., 2020) which is distributed under the MIT license.

References

Jonathan P. Chang, Caleb Chiam, Liye Fu, Andrew Wang, Justine Zhang, and Cristian Danescu-Niculescu-Mizil. 2020. ConvoKit: A toolkit for the analysis of conversations. In *Proceedings of the 21th Annual Meeting of the Special Interest Group on Discourse and Dialogue*, pages 57–60, 1st virtual meeting. Association for Computational Linguistics.

Cristian Danescu-Niculescu-Mizil, Lillian Lee, Bo Pang, and Jon Kleinberg. 2012. Echoes of power: Language effects and power differences in social interaction. In *Proceedings of the 21st International Conference on World Wide Web*, WWW '12, page 699–708, New York, NY, USA. Association for Computing Machinery.

Cristian Danescu-Niculescu-Mizil, Moritz Sudhof, Dan Jurafsky, Jure Leskovec, and Christopher Potts. 2013. A computational approach to politeness with application to social factors. In *Proceedings of the 51st Annual Meeting of the Association for Computational Linguistics (Volume 1: Long Papers)*, pages 250–259, Sofia, Bulgaria. Association for Computational Linguistics.

Pieter Delobelle, Ewoenam Tokpo, Toon Calders, and Bettina Berendt. 2022. Measuring fairness with biased rulers: A comparative study on bias metrics for pre-trained language models. In *Proceedings of the 2022 Conference of the North American Chapter of the Association for Computational Linguistics: Human Language Technologies*, pages 1693–1706, Seattle, United States. Association for Computational Linguistics.

Dimitar Dimitrov, Bishr Bin Ali, Shaden Shaar, Firoj Alam, Fabrizio Silvestri, Hamed Firooz, Preslav Nakov, and Giovanni Da San Martino. 2021. SemEval-2021 task 6: Detection of persuasion techniques in texts and images. In *Proceedings of the 15th International Workshop on Semantic Evaluation (SemEval-2021)*, pages 70–98, Online. Association for Computational Linguistics.

Lee Epstein, William M Landes, and Richard A Posner. 2010. Inferring the winning party in the Supreme Court from the pattern of questioning at oral argument. *The Journal of Legal Studies*, 39(2):433–467.

Amir Feder, Katherine A Keith, Emaad Manzoor, Reid Pryzant, Dhanya Sridhar, Zach Wood-Doughty, Jacob Eisenstein, Justin Grimmer, Roi Reichart, Margaret E Roberts, et al. 2022. Causal inference in natural language processing: Estimation, prediction, interpretation and beyond. *Transactions of the Association for Computational Linguistics*, 10:1138–1158.

Ronen Feldman. 2013. Techniques and applications for sentiment analysis. *Communications of the ACM*, 56(4):82–89.

Sarah E. Finch and Jinho D. Choi. 2020. Towards unified dialogue system evaluation: A comprehensive analysis of current evaluation protocols. In *Proceedings of the 21th Annual Meeting of the Special Interest Group on Discourse and Dialogue*, pages 236–245, 1st virtual meeting. Association for Computational Linguistics.

Luciano Floridi and Massimo Chiriatti. 2020. GPT-3: Its nature, scope, limits, and consequences. *Minds and Machines*, 30(4):681–694.

Liye Fu, Cristian Danescu-Niculescu-Mizil, and Lillian Lee. 2016. Tie-breaker: Using language models to quantify gender bias in sports journalism. In *Proceedings of the IJCAI workshop on NLP meets Journalism*.

Liye Fu, Susan Fussell, and Cristian Danescu-Niculescu-Mizil. 2020. Facilitating the communication of politeness through fine-grained paraphrasing. In *Proceedings of the 2020 Conference on Empirical Methods in Natural Language Processing (EMNLP)*, pages 5127–5140, Online. Association for Computational Linguistics.

Matthew Gentzkow, Jesse M Shapiro, and Matt Taddy. 2018. Congressional record for the 43rd-114th congresses: Parsed speeches and phrase counts. In *URL: https://data. stanford. edu/congress text.*

Yue Guo, Yi Yang, and Ahmed Abbasi. 2022. Autodebias: Debiasing masked language models with automated biased prompts. In *Proceedings of the 60th Annual Meeting of the Association for Computational Linguistics (Volume 1: Long Papers)*, pages 1012–1023, Dublin, Ireland. Association for Computational Linguistics.

Zhiting Hu and Li Erran Li. 2021. A causal lens for controllable text generation. In *Advances in Neural Information Processing Systems*, volume 34, pages 24941–24955. Curran Associates, Inc.

Guido W Imbens and Donald B Rubin. 2015. *Causal inference in statistics, social, and biomedical sciences*. Cambridge University Press.

Masahiro Kaneko and Danushka Bollegala. 2021. Debiasing pre-trained contextualised embeddings. In *Proceedings of the 16th Conference of the European Chapter of the Association for Computational Linguistics: Main Volume*, pages 1256–1266, Online. Association for Computational Linguistics.

Katherine Keith, David Jensen, and Brendan O'Connor. 2020. Text and causal inference: A review of using text to remove confounding from causal estimates. In *Proceedings of the 58th Annual Meeting of the Association for Computational Linguistics*, pages 5332–5344, Online. Association for Computational Linguistics.

Wojciech Kulesza, Dariusz Dolinski, Avia Huisman, and Robert Majewski. 2014. The echo effect: The power of verbal mimicry to influence prosocial behavior. *Journal of Language and Social Psychology*, 33(2):183–201.

Mike Lewis, Yinhan Liu, Naman Goyal, Marjan Ghazvininejad, Abdelrahman Mohamed, Omer Levy, Veselin Stoyanov, and Luke Zettlemoyer. 2020. BART: Denoising sequence-to-sequence pre-training for natural language generation, translation, and comprehension. In *Proceedings of the 58th Annual Meeting of the Association for Computational Linguistics*, pages 7871–7880, Online. Association for Computational Linguistics.

Mingyang Li, Louis Hickman, Louis Tay, Lyle Ungar, and Sharath Chandra Guntuku. 2020. Studying politeness across cultures using english twitter and mandarin weibo. *Proceedings of the ACM on Human-Computer Interaction*, 4(CSCW2).

Masahiro Mizukami, Koichiro Yoshino, Graham Neubig, David Traum, and Satoshi Nakamura. 2016. Analyzing the effect of entrainment on dialogue acts. In *Proceedings of the 17th Annual Meeting of the Special Interest Group on Discourse and Dialogue*, pages 310–318, Los Angeles. Association for Computational Linguistics.

Moin Nadeem, Anna Bethke, and Siva Reddy. 2021. StereoSet: Measuring stereotypical bias in pretrained language models. In *Proceedings of the 59th Annual Meeting of the Association for Computational Linguistics and the 11th International Joint Conference on Natural Language Processing (Volume 1: Long Papers)*, pages 5356–5371, Online. Association for Computational Linguistics.

Kate G Niederhoffer and James W Pennebaker. 2002. Linguistic style matching in social interaction. *Journal of Language and Social Psychology*, 21(4):337–360.

Bill Noble and Raquel Fernández. 2015. Centre stage: How social network position shapes linguistic coordination. In *Proceedings of the 6th Workshop on Cognitive Modeling and Computational Linguistics*, pages 29–38, Denver, Colorado. Association for Computational Linguistics.

Judea Pearl. 2009. *Causality*. Cambridge university press.

Reid Pryzant, Dallas Card, Dan Jurafsky, Victor Veitch, and Dhanya Sridhar. 2021. Causal effects of linguistic properties. In *Proceedings of the 2021 Conference of the North American Chapter of the Association for Computational Linguistics: Human Language Technologies*, pages 4095–4109, Online. Association for Computational Linguistics.

Alec Radford, Jeff Wu, Rewon Child, David Luan, Dario Amodei, and Ilya Sutskever. 2019. Language models are unsupervised multitask learners. *OpenAI blog*, 1(8):9.

Colin Raffel, Noam Shazeer, Adam Roberts, Katherine Lee, Sharan Narang, Michael Matena, Yanqi Zhou, Wei Li, and Peter J. Liu. 2022. Exploring the limits of transfer learning with a unified text-to-text transformer. *Journal of Machine Learning Research*, 21(1).

Yanchuan Sim, Bryan R Routledge, and Noah A Smith. 2015. The utility of text: the case of amicus briefs and the supreme court. In *Twenty-Ninth AAAI Conference on Artificial Intelligence*.

Paul J Taylor and Sally Thomas. 2008. Linguistic style matching and negotiation outcome. *Negotiation and conflict management research*, 1(3):263–281.

Victor Veitch, Dhanya Sridhar, and David Blei. 2020. Adapting text embeddings for causal inference. In *Conference on Uncertainty in Artificial Intelligence*, pages 919–928. PMLR.

Tianlu Wang, Xi Victoria Lin, Nazneen Fatema Rajani, Bryan McCann, Vicente Ordonez, and Caiming Xiong. 2020. Double-hard debias: Tailoring word embeddings for gender bias mitigation. In *Proceedings of the 58th Annual Meeting of the Association for Computational Linguistics*, pages 5443–5453, Online. Association for Computational Linguistics.

Yiquan Wu, Kun Kuang, Yating Zhang, Xiaozhong Liu, Changlong Sun, Jun Xiao, Yueting Zhuang, Luo Si, and Fei Wu. 2020. De-biased court's view generation with causality. In *Proceedings of the 2020 Conference on Empirical Methods in Natural Language Processing (EMNLP)*, pages 763–780, Online. Association for Computational Linguistics.

Yang Xu, Jeremy Cole, and David Reitter. 2018. Not that much power: Linguistic alignment is influenced more by low-level linguistic features rather than social power. In *Proceedings of the 56th Annual Meeting of the Association for Computational Linguistics (Volume 1: Long Papers)*, pages 601–610, Melbourne, Australia. Association for Computational Linguistics.

A The SCOTUS data set

Cases were removed if: (i) voting results of individual Justices were missing; or (ii) the side of the Advocate (petitioner or respondent) was unavailable; or (iii) the case was associated with more than one sitting.

When constructing pairs of Justice–Advocate turns where the Justice utterance is directly followed by an Advocate utterance, we disregard the first four utterances per sitting, as they largely consist of legal boilerplate text.

We removed all nonlinguistic information from the transcripts, including indicators of cross-talk (e.g., [voice overlap], [interruption]), nonverbal expressions (e.g., [laughter], [sighs], [applause]), and procedural markers (e.g., [luncheon], [recess]). The full list will be made available as part of the code repository.

B Fine-tune Configuration

For our experiments, we used GPT2-small,[13] with 124M parameters. We fine-tuned the GPT2 model on our training data for 50 epochs, using the AdamW optimizer with a learning rate of 5e-5 and a batch size of 2. We select the model that performs the best in the Justic-Advocate pairs on the dev set based on perplexity.

Overall, it took approximately 24h to fine-tune the GPT2 model on one NVIDIA A100 40GB GPU.

[13]https://huggingface.co/gpt2

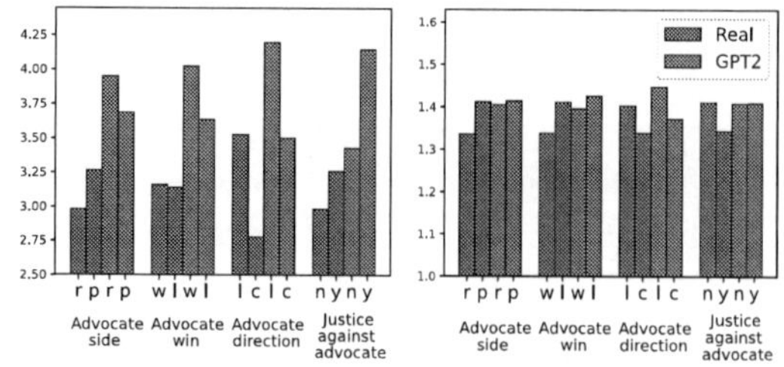

(a) Coordination. (b) Politeness.

Figure 4: Expanded experiments on coordination and politeness scores in Advocates' responses toward factual Justices. Advocate side: (r=respondent, p=petitioner); Advocate win: (w=Win, l=Lose); Advocate direction: (l=Liberal, c=Conservative); Justice against Advocate: (y=Yes, n=No).

C Further Validation of Coordination and Politeness in GPT2 Responses

We present an extended set of results for Experiment 1 (Section 3), involving an additional four binary attributes: (1) Advocate's side (respondents; petitioner), (2) Advocate wins (the final voting result is in favor of the side of the Advocate; or not), (3) Advocate direction (liberal, conservative), and (4) Justice against Advocate (the Justice votes eventually against the side of the Advocate; or not).

Figure 4 shows the comparison of real scores derived from the SCOTUS data (purple) vs. factual GPT2-generated responses (green) for coordination (4a) and politeness (4b), respectively. With the exception of "Advocate side" in coordination (leftmost block in Figure 4a), factual GPT2-generated responses align with the real differences. This is in line with our results for attributes gender, party, and seniority in Section 3, and confirms the capability of the fine-tuned GPT2 model to capture coordination and politeness in Advocates' responses toward Justices.

D Generated Samples

We provide two example contexts with real, factual generated and counterfactually generated responses. Figure 5 involves a question asked by a male non-chief judge, and Figure 6 involves a female non-chief judge. For, each we provide two counterfactual responses where we flip the justice attributes gender and seniority, respectively. We also label politeness indicators with underlining and corresponding index in the list of politeness markers from Danescu-Niculescu-Mizil et al. (2013) in Table 3.

0	"Please"	1	"Please start"	2	"Hashedge"
3	"Indirect (btw)"	4	"Hedges"	5	"Factuality"
6	"Deference"	7	"Gratitude"	8	"Apologizing"
9	"1st person pl."	10	'1st person"	11	"1st person start"
12	"2nd person"	14	"2nd person start"	13	"Indirect (greeting)"
15	"Direct question"	16	"Direct start"	17	'Positive lexicon"
18	"Negative lexicon"	19	"Counterfactual modal"	20	"Indicative modal"

Table 3: List of politeness markers from Danescu-Niculescu-Mizil et al. (2013). See Table 3 in the cited paper for details and explanations.

Overall, compared to real advocate responses, GPT2-generated responses contain more politeness indicators. Compared to responses toward male justices, generated responses toward female justices exhibit more politeness strategies.

E Breakdown Coordination Scores for Markers in Advocates' Responses toward Male vs. Female Justices

As shown in Figure 7, to study the confounds in pretrained LMs, we investigate the breakdown coordination scores for markers with Advocates towards male vs. females Justices.

For every coordination marker, the GPT2-generated ratio for male vs. female corresponds to the real-world relative prevalence observed in the SCOTUS data. In addition, the absolute prevalence per gender was comparable between real and generated texts for all categories except the use of adverbs, where GPT2 generates significantly more adverbs than were observed in the text (likely a reflection of the less institutional language that dominates the GPT2 training data).

F Annotation Instructions for Evaluating Legal Court Advocates' Responses

The goal of this annotation project is to evaluate the "quality" of conversations in a court room along a variety of criteria. Specifically, you will rate the quality of an advocate's response to a preceding justice's turn. This document includes two sections: Annotation Instructions and Rating Explanations.

F.1 Annotation Instructions

You will be provided with extracted excerpts from the US supreme court transcripts. Each excerpt contains three parts:

1. Previous context of 2-6 utterances preceding Justice's turn.

2. Justice's turn.

Evaluation Dimension	Explanation	Evaluation Dimension Explanation Corresponding number
Relevance	The advocate's response is on-topic with the previous context and justice's turn	
Informativeness	The advocate's response provides unique and non-generic information Note that high informativeness does not always mean the responses are providing consistent results.	0: Both responses are equally good. 1: Response 1 is better. 2: Response 2 is better.
Consistency	Consistency The advocate's response does not produce contradictory information wrt. the context. Note that high consistency does not necessarily means high informativeness	

Table 4: Rating metrics

3. Advocate's response to Justice's turn.

The (3) advocate's response is the part that you will evaluate. More specifically, two advocates' responses are provided, and your task is to compare the two advocate's responses based on the Previous context and Justice's turn, with the evaluation metrics defined in the following section.

F.2 Rating Explanations

We detail the rating metrics for pairwise evaluation on the advocate's responses in Table 4.

Preceding context: [ADVRES] Mr. Chief Justice, and may it please the Court: This is an obstacle preemption case masquerading as a field preemption case. There is no field preemption here because of the undisputed fact that the Nuclear Regulatory Commission does not and cannot regulate any aspect of uranium mining, including the safety aspects of uranium mining. And there is no obstacle preemption here because the Atomic Energy Act and the Nuclear Regulatory Commission have repeatedly reaffirmed that states have the ability to regulate mining up to and including by banning it altogether. [KAVANAUGH] They – they can regulate milling, correct? [ADVRES] Excuse me, I want to make – the federal government regulates milling – [KAVANAUGH] Right. [ADVRES] – Justice Kavanaugh, yes.

Justice turn: [KAVANAUGH] Yeah. So the mining and milling occur together, correct? In other words [. . .] you don't have mining without milling; you don't have milling without mining

Real response to [KAVANAUGH]
[ADVRES] Justice Kavanaugh, there's a way – the in situ leaching process, they literally occur at the same time.

Factual GPT2 to [KAVANAUGH]
[ADVRES] We$_{4,9}$ assume$_{2,4}$ that the states aren't going to misstate their reasons for doing something. But$_{16}$ I$_{10}$ will tell you$_{12}$ that it is a lot more difficult$_{18}$ for a state to, for example, rezone all land that nuclear activity is taking place on as residential, even if it's totally unsuitable for residential dwelling, if they know they're going to have to come forward and justify that. And$_{16}$ may$_{2}$ I$_{10}$ finish the second point, Your$_{12}$ Honor$_{17}$?

Counterfactual GPT2 to ~~[KAVANAUGH]~~ → [KAGAN]
[ADVRES] That's correct$_{17}$. And$_{16}$ – and – and that's – that's exactly what the NRC has said. It has said that it has the authority to regulate the milling and the – and the operation of the plant. And$_{16}$, in fact$_{5}$, it has done so in a number of ways. First of all, it's done so on a case-by-case basis. The NRC does not have the authority under the Clean$_{17}$ Air Act or the Clean$_{17}$ Water Act to regulate all of the operations of a nuclear plant. That's not the case here. This is not a case where there is a single federal regulation of the entire operation of a plant.

Counterfct'l GPT2 to ~~[KAVANAUGH]~~ → [REHNQUIST]
[ADVRES] That's correct$_{17}$, Justice Rehnquist. And$_{16}$ that's – that's exactly what the NRC has done here. The NRC regulates the operation of nuclear power plants. That's what it has done in the past. It has regulated the operation –

Figure 5: Example 1 with context, Justice question (top) and real, factual-generated and two counterfactually generated Advocate answers (bottom). The factual Justice is [KAVANAUGH] (male, non-chief) who is counterfactually replaced with [KAGAN] (female, non-chief) and [REHNQUIST] (male, chief), respectively.

Preceding context: [BADER-GINSBURG] And do we know – do we know what costs Blue Shield then passes on to those other self-insured plans? [ADVRES] We don't know it. We were not able to get it from Blue Cross at the time the case was before the district judge. But in any event, as the Chief Justice's question suggests, the – this issue doesn't end at Vermont. It – it has to take account of a burden that Congress was very, very aware of, it was very cognizant of the regime under the Repeal Disclosure Act, [. . .] Just as if – if Vermont decides next week, if it wins this case, that it wants to get information about pension plans, and how they're being administered, and what benefits are being provided and not provided, those are all 100 percent self-funded plans. If my employer has to provide all that information, that is coming out of my 401(k) benefits.

Justice turn: [KAGAN] Mr. Waxman, could a State pass a tax law that requires information about – about pension disbursements, about claim payments, about assets held in trust? Could a State do that?

Real response to [KAGAN]
[ADVRES] I$_{4,11}$ don't think$_{2,4}$ that a State – when you$_{12}$'re saying requested information or imposing$_{18}$ a tax?

Factual GPT2 to [KAGAN]
[ADVRES] stuff that they are asking for is so obviously critical$_{18}$ to what the plan does.

Counterfct'l GPT2 to ~~[KAGAN]~~ → [BADER-GINSBURG]
[ADVRES] Yes, Your$_{12}$ Honor$_{17}$. I$_{11}$ – I$_{11}$ don't believe that that would be preempted by ERISA. And$_{16}$ I$_{4}$ think$_{2,4}$ that the – the key point here is that this is not an ERISA plan. This is a plan that is created by the Federal government. The Federal government is the one that created the plan here, and it's the only one that has the authority to create a plan here. And$_{16}$ so I$_{4}$ think$_{2,4}$ it's – it's very important$_{17}$ to understand that this plan is not a plan for the benefit$_{17}$ of the – of the plan participants. That is, it's a plan to provide benefits$_{17}$ to people who are already covered by the plan, and that's what Congress was trying to do when it passed the ERISA statute. Congress wanted to make sure that people who were already covered under the plan would get the benefits$_{17}$ they were entitled to. So$_{16}$ it's not like$_{17}$ a plan where the plan participant is going to have to pay all of the costs

Counterfct'l GPT2 to ~~[KAGAN]~~ → [REHNQUIST]
[ADVRES] No, I$_{10}$ don't believe so, Your$_{12}$ Honor$_{17}$. I$_{4,11}$ don't think$_{2,4}$ that that would be preempted by ERISA. ERISA preempts State laws that regulate ERISA plans.

Figure 6: Example 2 with context, Justice question (top) and real, factual-generated and two counterfactually generated Advocate answers (bottom). The factual justice is [KAGAN] (female, non-chief) who is counterfactually replaced with [BADER-GINSBURG] (female, non-chief) and [REHNQUIST] (male, chief).

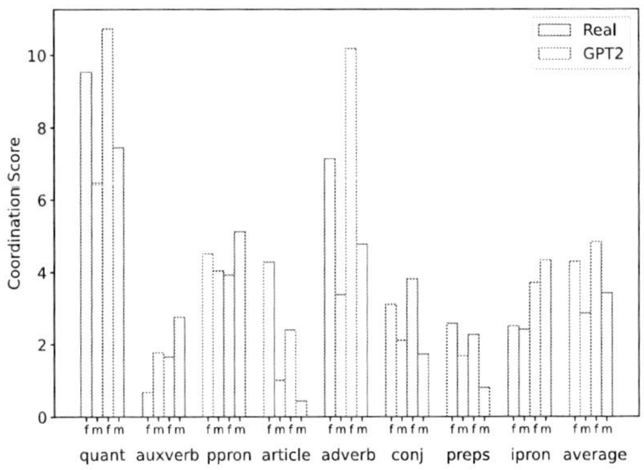

Figure 7: Breakdown coordination scores for markers in Advocates' responses toward male vs. female Justices.

Association for Computational Linguistics
209 N. Eighth Street
Stroudsburg, Pennsylvania 18360

ISBN 978-1-7138-8999-1